For almost five decades, Pakistan has encountered frequent, unresolved political crises. They are woven into its concepts of political community, and have underscored uneasy relationships between state institutions and civil society. Pakistan's politics has also been characterised by incomplete constitution-making, a process that has placed the burden of constitutional interpretation and political change on state instruments ranging from the bureaucracy to the military to the judiciary. The superior courts in particular have played unusually important roles in determining the country's fate, often superseding legislatures and executives alike. In a penetrating and comprehensive study of the ways in which the superior judiciary has mediated relationships between state and society, Paula Newberg demonstrates how the courts have influenced the structure of the state, and their evolving jurisprudence has fashioned Pakistan's constitutions and uncertain constitutionalism. By examining judicial decisions, including those that determined the fate of governments, she explores the ways that the courts have affected fundamental rights, the practice of politics, and Pakistan's democratic prospects.

*Cambridge South Asian Studies*

# Judging the state

*Cambridge South Asian Studies*



*A list of the books in the series will be found at the end of the volume*

# Judging the state

## *Courts and constitutional politics in Pakistan*

Paula R. Newberg
*Carnegie Endowment for International Peace*

CAMBRIDGE
UNIVERSITY PRESS

Published in South Asia by

Foundation Books
2/19 Ansari Road
New Delhi-110 002



First South Asian Edition 1995



ISBN 81-85618-67-4

This edition of "Paula R. Newberg: Judging the State-Courts and Constitutional Politics in Pakistan", is published by arrangement with Cambridge University Press, The Edinburgh Building, Shaftesbury Road, Cambridge CB2 2RU, U.K.

*Acknowledgement:*

Cover Illustration from "Aijazuddin: Lahore-Illustrated views of the 19th Century" published by Vanguard, Lahore.

Published by Manas Saikia for Foundation Books and printed by Mohan Makhijani at Rekha Printers Pvt Ltd, A-102/1 Okhla Industrial Area, Phase-II, New Delhi-110 020.

The beginning of a thing is a mirror of its end.

Asadullah Khan Ghalib

Yet in revolt there is hope at least.

Momin Khan Momin

# Contents

# Contents

# Preface

While exploring Pakistani politics in this last decade I have incurred countless debts to colleagues, associates, interlocutors and friends. With their counsel I have learned to decipher Pakistan's society and polity and to begin to understand the ways its histories frame its future. As a prelude to my private thanks, I hope they recognize in this rendering of constitutional politics their energies as much as my own.

Many people helped me to locate and understand source materials, to learn to interpret their absences when they were inaccessible and to navigate the labyrinths of judicial procedure, including a score of attorneys at the high courts across Pakistan and Bangladesh. I am particularly obliged to retired Justices Fakhruddin Ebrahim, Anwar ul Haq, Aftab Hussain, Dilawar Mahmood, Dorab Patel and K.M.A. Samdani in Pakistan, and K.M. Subhan and Kemaluddin Hossain in Bangladesh, all of whom patiently described the vagaries as well as the constancies of judicial and constitutional history. A host of politicians, party organizers, diplomats and bureaucrats of every political stripe have given me countless hours of their time for this and many other endeavors. My colleagues among Pakistan's journalists and untiring civil rights activists have long piloted me through their country's argumentative national politics. Additionally, friends and readers on several continents provided provocative comments on portions of this manuscript.

I owe debts of long standing to Mubashir Hasan, who tirelessly helped me pursue people and papers in order to reconstruct the environments in which law and politics have evolved, and to Eqbal Ahmad, who first introduced me to the complexities that comprise Pakistan. And to the Gilani, Lari, Lodhi, Mumtaz, Rahman and Rashid families, and the several Ahmad-Omar-Hoodbhoy households, my thanks for many years of bed, board, forbearance and amused indulgence.

# Preface

While organizing [illegible] positions [illegible] I have travelled [illegible] countries [illegible]

Many people's [illegible]

[illegible] and Bangladesh [illegible]

[illegible]

# Introduction

In Georg Buechner's drama recreating the conflicts of Jacobin France, a deputy of the National Convention describes a constitution as "a transparent garment clinging to the body politic."[1] His comment encapsulates the dialectic that is always present in constructing a constitution, for constitutions reflect at once the imperfections and the aspirations of a political community. Tensions between the ideal and the real – making a political community out of diverse parts, creating something new while retaining the identities of the old – highlight the obstacles and opportunities that states and citizens encounter as they configure their political means and ends. Similar problems confront old states and new, those seeking to redefine their ideological foundations within accustomed territorial borders, and those establishing legal entities in equally new physical circumstances.

The process of constituting a new state – literally, writing its constitution – involves both political and juridical tasks. In the first instance, writing a constitution provides a legal frame for the state, a method of organizing authority and adjudicating conflicts about power. It also speaks to the political pasts and futures of those who comprise it – establishing the sources, character and conditions of collective identity and sovereignty. These activities are mutually reinforcing: citizenship must be meaningful to individuals in political society and effective in the state structure. When collective memory and expectations do not support the ways power is distributed and used, relations between state and civil society can undercut the constitution and the institutions it creates, and erode the concept and practice of constitutionalism.

These conflicts are sometimes played out on the political stage in elections and constitutional draftings; sometimes they are inscribed in wider conflicts in society, in public actions against the state and occasionally, in civil wars. At other times, the state absorbs these tensions in

[1] Georg Buechner, *Danton's Death*, translated by Victor Price (Oxford: Oxford University Press, 1971), p. 7.

itself, reworking political arrangements within its own establishments while grasping tightly the framework that endows these institutions with their authority. Such choices and actions are as apparent today in constitutional struggles in Central Europe and the former Soviet Union as they are in third world states that have moved from colonial status to independence, and from authoritarianism toward democracy.

All of these problems are dramatically illustrated in Pakistan, where incomplete constitution-making has placed the burdens of constitutional interpretation on state instruments ranging from the bureaucracy to the military to the judiciary. The country has survived several wars, all of which have challenged variously the distribution of power in the state and the meanings that its citizens ascribe to it. Its civil war in 1971, which resulted in partition and the formation of Bangladesh, was the culmination of political conflicts that had raged since Pakistan's founding, and that linger in Pakistan today.

Pakistan's history has been defined by uneasy relationships between state institutions and civil society. In its executive-dominated state, the superior courts in particular have played unusually important parts in determining the country's political fate. When constitutions have not accomplished their tasks – when they have not adequately constituted the state in terms meaningful to its citizens – judges and lawyers have reconstituted the state anew. Courts engage in rituals of recreation: they interpret the constitution of the day, and read political history and constitutional language to establish new understandings of political community. Judicial proceedings thus embrace an autonomy only partly written into the constitutions that create them and lend to their judgments a crucial importance in the development of the state.

This study explores relationships between state and civil society through the medium of the superior judiciary. It shows how, over the course of almost five decades, the courts have influenced the development of its constitutions and the structure of the state. By examining judicial decisions, particularly at times of political crisis, it isolates discussions about concepts of constitutional rule between the judiciary and other institutions, and looks at the way tensions within the judiciary, and between courts and other state institutions, have affected the ways that political society sees itself. And finally, it explores the consequences of these debates for the formal organization of political power.

Pakistan's political history, like many of its neighbors, is one of frequent crisis and incomplete resolution. These crises are woven into the texture of its history, its concepts of itself and its sense of political possibility. The country has fought foreign wars over its physical and constitutional boundaries and domestic wars over conflicting concepts of citizenship, equality and representation; the disruptions and discontents of civil society have often skirted the edges of state violence, and have given continued cause for citizens to reexamine their relationships to the state in which they live. Its history and future alike are intricately linked to its overlapping ideological moorings, its economic and social conditions, and the instrumental goals of the state. For almost five decades, conflicts over the role of religion in society, democracy in the polity and the transformative capacities of state institutions in the economy have been the underpinnings for a politics of unique opportunity and often, profound division and dismay.

This history poses problems of definition and interpretation that are embodied in the variegated traditions with which its constitutions describe the state. Many attempts to write and execute constitutions have defined the successes and failures of the federal state and its politicians, the nature of fundamental rights and the scope of dissent. Like other post-colonial states, Pakistan's constitutional law has developed partly from colonial legacy and partly from reaction to it; the two processes have been intertwined to produce a state of mixed political and legal parentage.

Early constitutional experiments combined two related and problematic efforts at self-definition. First, they attempted to provide a written constitution that would use the language of British constitutionalism to define sovereignty and yet separate the new state from the Empire. This was surely an imperfect enterprise, for sovereignty – overlaid with conflicting notions of territoriality, nationality, ethnicity, franchise and state authority – was paired with an executive-dominated state already created by imperial instruments of governance. The justices who ruled in 1954 in *Tamizuddin Khan's case*, the country's first major constitutional trial, initially tried to sort out these differences but ended by trying to combine them in the doctrine of necessity, presumptively defining public order as the paramount task of political rule. Not long thereafter, some of the same justices ruled in 1958 in *Dosso's case* to justify a military *coup d'état*, imposing a renewed centralism on the state through the doctrine of revolutionary legality. This doctrine, in turn, provided a legal basis for undemocratic rule for many years; only the end of the Bangladesh war provided the possibility in 1972 for a new judicial examination of this form of legality, in *Asma Jilani's case*. The vice-regal state, combined with an increasingly strong military and bureaucracy, surpassed colonialism only gradually and incompletely; the state, armed with legal support from the courts, developed in ways that still affect the polity today.

The first attempts to write a constitution also established a form of political dialogue that colors constitutionalism five decades later. The first drafters tried to describe a state comprised primarily of Muslims but not necessarily or fully defined by Islam. A variety of philosophies was marshaled by political constituencies who eschewed compromise, setting an uncompromising tone for political debate and hardening the choices available to politicians and institutions like the judiciary. Moreover, the respective terms of identity and discourse that characterized each side – which offer vastly different notions of the individual's place in politics – undercut the process of constituting the state and making its sovereignty concrete. Nonetheless, deceivingly similar vocabularies of constitutionalism permeate these political philosophies. The search for appropriate and acceptable ways to understand citizenship and its corollary rights – and political power and its corollary duties – has been both furthered and frustrated by these inherited languages. Neither elections nor parliaments nor courts – secular or religious – have successfully untangled the many layers of meaning and expectation that were cast so early on in political society.

A pattern of strong executive power was thus enshrined in constitutional instruments to sidestep political schism, although the concentration of power inevitably created additional conflicts. Ultimately, as we shall see, this habit became self-defeating for heads of state, heads of government, constitutions and citizens alike. Administering the state became an endeavor separate from resolving problems of political identity, and thus pushed problems of identity to the edges of the political agenda. Ideological issues were either set aside or manipulated – always present and contentious, frequently used to represent or disguise the pursuit of power, but rarely at the critical center of state authority. The end of stability has been used consistently to justify the means of maneuvering constitutions to suit the executive-oriented – and too often, praetorian – state.

That the same ends have been firmly inscribed in judicial judgments that were nevertheless intended to clarify and occasionally challenge the terms of power is a theme that characterizes much of Pakistan's history, and that reappears throughout this study. It surfaces not only in the ways that courts have defined and justified the mechanics of power in Pakistan, but also in the special contours of judicial independence. Courts everywhere live in a delicate balance between upholding and challenging the distribution of power, but courts in authoritarian states carry extra burdens. If constitutions and executives allow them to function, they must in some way heed them. Courts can limit some executive power, but executives possess the power to legitimate the capacity to judge; in turn, the polity must, however distantly in some instances, legitimize them both. When this equation has been broken in Pakistan, only the blunt force of military rule and martial law has kept the polity within bounds.

Thus, limits on judicial independence have always influenced the force of judicial judgments, and they in turn have determined the strategic calculations that underscore judicial doctrine. In this sense, by occasionally accepting – politically and jurisprudentially – the fact that they function on the basis of privilege as much as right, courts have both reflected and determined the ways that power works.

These conundrums, and the institutional bargains they represent, deeply influence politics. From the country's first decade, Pakistan's judges have tried to match their constitutional ideals and legal language to the exigencies of current politics. Their judgments have often supported the government of the day, presumably to retain a degree of future institutional autonomy. This was their chosen path through the 1950s when there was no constitution; during the martial law period of the 1960s, when the constitution was a moving target; and under the mixed constitutional rule of Zulfikar Ali Bhutto in the 1970s, when hopes for democracy outweighed its reality. To remain open for business, courts accepted limits on their practice that were not always consonant with the conceptual foundations of their rulings – a disjunction that operates today. At the same time, when superior courts have felt emboldened by stronger constitutional instruments – as they did under the amended 1962 Constitution – or have chafed under political strictures that allowed them little constitutional ground – as they did under the early martial law of General Zia ul Haq – they have challenged the state on behalf of civil society. In both of these cases, however, they provoked the executive sufficiently to have their powers checked.

If the stature of the courts has almost inevitably waxed during democracy and waned under autocracy, periods of transition – certainly the most prevalent in recent Pakistani history – have provided the judiciary's most profound challenges. The superior courts have often been handmaidens of political change, and always guardians of legal transition. It is small wonder that by 1993 – after eight years of virtually perpetual transition from strict military rule toward civilian government under an internally contradictory constitution – almost every major political issue in the country found its way to the courts. During 1993 alone, the superior courts ruled on issues ranging from the disposition of territories contested as part of the Kashmir dispute to the right of former military officers to comment on past political activities to the constitutional division of powers and ultimately, the effect of past judicial judgments. The responsibilities imposed on the courts by the weaknesses of other institutions, and the additional obligations that their judgments (and their consequences) dictate, pose serious questions about the constitutional basis of the state and the abilities and proprieties of courts to navigate its complexities.

Relativism and related sensitivities to real and imagined political pressures have thus been constant factors in Pakistan's law as much as in politics. At times, judges and courts have by their undue prudence contributed to the uncertainty of Pakistan's experiments with democracy. At other times, their continued functioning has provided a tentative model of an open institution when others are absent or inadequate. As such, the judiciary's attempts to grapple with conflicts intrinsic to the process of building a state provide lessons, both inside and outside Pakistan, about the ways that courts try to speak to the state on behalf of society, and the ways that law tries to offer a meaningful context for politics.

The story of Pakistan's politics has been told in many ways for many different purposes. Each narrative chooses new victors and victims, internal and external. This book, however, takes as its starting point Pakistan's unique conjuncture of politics and jurisprudence, and particularly, the distinctive role that the superior judiciary and its judgments have played during the past forty-five years. It is therefore a story with neither heroes nor villains, although some will seem to emerge. Rather, it chronicles the ways the state has been viewed by one of its own institutions, and the intricate ways that sitting in judgment has affected courts and constitutions, and state and society.

The judicial role has never been appraised consistently in Pakistan. Indeed, when I visited the country to review its human rights record during the 1980s, politicians and lawyers would describe in detail the evolution of Pakistan's political travails by reciting the history of constitutional experiments and the role of the courts in various constitutional frameworks. Each recounting would begin by explaining that Pakistan's courts were the country's only independent institutions, and would end by castigating the courts for ensuring a persistently inequitable state burdened with frequently unpopular governments. The tensions between assumptions and conclusions, however – surely influenced by the times – were rarely explored.

My initial concern that something was missing in the myths of judicial independence and blame was confirmed by the contrary manner in which former judges themselves viewed the courts. They had come to see the judicial task as intensely political and the compromises struck between courts and state as open equally to praise and criticism. Supreme Court Justice Fakruddin Ebrahim, for example, has occasionally emphasized the successful efforts of superior courts to represent civil society during times of political strain, and his assessment is correct; but Baluchistan High Court Chief Justice Mir Khuda Bakhsh Marri has documented lamentable miscarriages of justice by both civil and military courts, under both civilian and military rule. Responding to criticism that the courts should have done more to forestall repression, Supreme Court Justice Dorab Patel has asked pointedly, referring to past judgments, "how do you expect five men alone, unsupported by anyone, to declare martial law illegal?" Lahore High Court Justice K.M.A. Samdani, perhaps most critical of past behavior, finds judicial decisions wanting, lamenting that

> most of the confusion that has arisen in the country as a result of which the institution of democracy has suffered almost irreparably, stemmed from the fact that by and large the judiciary in Pakistan tried, in times of crises, to avoid confrontation with the executive and went out of its way to take the path of least resistance. It upheld the de facto situation rather than declare the de jure position.

And former Peshawar High Court Justice Qazi Muhammad Jamil reflects a continuing debate between the political and judicial branches of government when he notes that by fighting their political battles in court, politicians and government alike have prevented the judiciary from becoming truly independent.[2]

These evaluations – neither fully consonant nor completely contradictory – reflect the unseemly weight that has been placed on the courts for the entire period since independence. In the absence of workable constitutions, participatory politics and representative governments, the superior courts have stubbornly persevered in their appointed tasks – when their judgments were unlikely to be heeded as often as when they were likely to be castigated for having issued them. Their persistence has created a breach between the fact of judging and the judgments themselves, a gap between process and substance that parallels so much else in Pakistan's politics. The difference between keeping the courts open for business on the one hand, and tailoring their decisions for expedience or, at times, simple survival on the other, has led to these divergent assessments of success and failure. Superior court judgments have, indeed, sometimes helped to cement the overweening power of the state, or at the least, not judicially prevented usurpers from keeping their power. However, open courts have helped to retain the possibilities of open politics and the possibility that citizens will have yet another day in court.

The contours of this political landscape thus offer opportunities to question the judiciary's institutional reach, and, more generally, the

[2] Fakruddin Ebrahim, interview with Zafar Abbas, *Herald*, May 1990, pp. 157–62; Dorab Patel, interview in *Newsline*, February 1993; K.M.A. Samdani, untitled, unpublished manuscript, p. 1; Mir Khuda Bakhsh Marri, *A Judge May Speak* (Lahore: Ferozsons (Pvt.) Ltd., 1990); Qazi Jamil, interview with Syed Haider Ali Shah, *Frontier Post*, 1 January 1990, p. 11. See also Dorab Patel, interview with Wahab Siddiqui, *Mag*, 22–28 March 1984 and 31 January–6 February 1985.

attributes of a jurisprudence of crisis and the political prerequisites for justice in a conflicted state. Pakistan's superior courts provide intriguing vehicles with which to discover the ties that bind state and citizen. The superior judiciary is important precisely for the analysis it brings to bear on critical constitutional issues. Unlike the subordinate courts, which rule on the daily problems of living within the legal confines of the state, the superior courts take as their starting point the critical issues that define society and state, and thus provide the context for choice and judgment. The courts teach us that the content of their developing jurisprudence, as well as the role of legal exposition and decision, provide keys to understanding political change.

Taken together, these judgments demonstrate the influence of judicial precedent in politics. The doctrines of necessity and revolutionary legality used to judge crucial executive actions have not only determined a long course of events, but also have provided incremental blueprints for constitutional design and policy – a useful reminder in a world coping with similar problems elsewhere today. The state has used these judgments to imbue executive action with colors of constitutionalism even when its actions were anticonstitutional, offering a veneer of legitimacy through the medium of legality. But the superior judiciary has kept alive political ideals that have often been attacked or allowed to erode by the same state that its judgments sustain. The judiciary's pursuit of these ideals has helped to create a constituency for ideas of citizen rights and state obligations within a state that sometimes seems impervious to sustained rights claims, and, more broadly, meaningful politics. Its quest calls into question the distance between the ideal and the real, and the depth of the prudence and realism that have guided judgment; it also provokes us to ask serious questions about the final impact of their accomplishments.

The quality of this political debate is often more elusive than its legal language conveys. Ultimately, courts cannot take decisions about ideology and power or constitute the state as the polity should. As Thomas Paine cautioned in *The Rights of Man*, a country's constitution is "not the act of its government, but of the people constituting a government." The dilemmas of this difference continue to face Pakistan today.

# 1 Structuring the state

> The constables took Ustad Mangu to the police station. On the way and at the police station, he kept yelling, "The new constitution . . . the new constitution." But no one understood what he was referring to. "What are you shouting about . . . what new laws and rights are you shouting about . . . the laws are the same old ones . . ." And Ustad Mangu was locked up in a cell.
>
> Sadaat Hasan Manto, "New Constitution."

> A Constitution is not the cause but a consequence of personal and political freedom.
>
> Justice Muhammad Munir.

In the forty-five years since its independence, Pakistan has struggled with constitutions, governments and the structure of the state. It has swung between the poles of dictatorship and democracy, and between civilian and military rule. Although it was established with a parliamentary system of government, the military has seized power four times since 1947, ruling directly and indirectly for more than half the life of the country. Intervening periods of elected, civilian government have responded to popular fears of renewed military rule by accommodating the army to prevent its reemergence in politics. Each permutation of power has therefore embodied deep popular concerns and ambivalences about government, its patrons and its beneficiaries.

Many of the same problems of ideology, sovereignty and voice that were present at independence still trouble Pakistan and Pakistanis today. The country has fought wars over its boundaries and domestic battles over conflicting ideas of citizenship, equality and representation. Its history and future are linked to its competing ideological moorings, its economic and social conditions and the instrumental goals of the state. For more than four decades, discord about the role of religion in society, about democracy in the polity and about the transformative capacities of state institutions in the economy have formed a politics of unusual opportunity and, often, profound division and dismay.

From the beginning, the desires of Pakistan's founders faltered on the state's incapacity to rise above many of its colonial inheritances and its inability to match its government with the democratic rhetoric and constitutional principles that characterized the independence movement. This legacy continues. Pakistan's history has been defined equally by the state's efforts to assert authority over a frequently divided polity, and citizen attempts to wrest control from those in power – patterns of frequent crisis and incomplete resolution that have become woven into its political fabric. The result has been unstable political institutions and a praetorian state often deeply at odds with its society.

Viewed in broad schematic outline, its politics reflects unresolved tensions between two competing models of government. The vice-regal tradition of colonial India was embedded in plans for Pakistan's own governance. It was absorbed by the state's founders, who used it to establish the outline for its constitutions and agendas for its post-colonial rulers, who in turn perpetuated the tradition in the new state. By contrast, the liberal, representative tradition characterized the rhetoric of political opposition in India and the anti-colonial activities that helped to establish its successor states; it has permeated the language and program of anti-government politics in Pakistan. Both traditions were inherited unevenly. Together, however, they anchor the real and the ideal in Pakistan – the state that has existed and does exist, and the one that was expected at independence and that has lived in the minds of political reformers. Conflicts between vice-regal and liberal views have been expressed consistently, if not entirely accurately, as contests between executive and parliamentary power, and between central authority and local self-rule. These dissonant conceptions of sovereignty and federalism have established a broad arena for political opposition. The vast conceptual and practical divide between these concepts of politics and power has repeatedly called into question the legitimacy of particular governments and the sources of legitimacy for the state.

Political institutions have been drawn into these conflicts. In response to perceptions of regional uncertainty, the military was endowed early with far greater powers and resources than civilian parliaments have been able to accommodate. By buttressing executive rule the army helped to keep parliaments at bay; by absorbing a huge share of the national exchequer, the military influenced the distribution of resources, the nature of domestic political debate and the flexibility of executive rule. Executives holding the trump card of central power, with the backing of the civil bureaucracy, have continually undermined parliaments, despite popular resistance to abuses of executive authority. Political parties, however, have played only limited parts in establishing the terms of political debate, and have thus often constrained the role of representative bodies rather than support them. Many parties have reflected only the ambitions of their founders and most have had few electoral followers; those with populist mandates and programs have alternately been abolished, banned or restricted by executives to lessen their mobilizing effects. Public opinion has been considered peripheral and often oppositional rather than necessary to legitimate the state.

As parties to the basic political disputes that have plagued the country since its inception, neither executives nor parliaments nor political parties have been able to mediate conflicts about the distribution of formal powers or the quality of political participation. In consequence, those who hold power have been at odds with the society on whose behalf they are to govern. Civil society has more frequently been the state's opponent than its legitimator. As a corollary, civil rights have been violated in order to silence dissent and reasserted by civil society in order to establish an uneasy balance with the state.

Only the superior judiciary has been able to mediate such discord, and then only incompletely. Building on popular perceptions that colonial courts were impartial and independent arbiters – although they were in fact as much instruments of colonial will as any other government agency – Pakistan's judiciary has consistently been treated as an institution apart from the tainted tussles of politics. The courts have tried to bridge the breach created by institutional incompatibilities and have provided a forum for society to articulate its demands. They have therefore acquired a place of primacy in society and politics quite apart from their modest constitutional profile and government efforts to restrict their purview. By stepping into the vacuum too often created by conflicts that might render the state ungovernable, the superior judiciary has occupied a place of unique political opportunity. Through their proceedings and judgments, the courts have profoundly influenced the ways that state institutions accommodate each other and the ways that state and society attempt to resolve their differences; in the process, they have helped to outline the limits of acceptable political behavior. Political legitimacy is a difficult concept to parse in the Pakistani political context: the courts are a crucial vehicle, and their jurisprudence a critical language through which to try to understand it.

The judiciary's role has been complex and its record mixed. Perhaps most important, the superior courts have literally judged the state, ruling on constitutional issues directly affecting national sovereignty, political participation and government organization. They have decided conflicts between heads of state and government resulting in the dissolution of legislatures (1954, 1988, 1990, 1993), the validation of *coups d'état* (1958, 1977), efforts to restructure transitions between civil and military governance (1972, 1986–88), and continuing attempts to define substantively and procedurally the meaning of politics, of constitutional governance and occasionally, of democracy. With the state in almost continuous transition, Pakistan's courts become, *sui generis*, both the subjects and objects of political change.

The courts have been at once the state's conduits, commentators and critics. As institutions of the state they derive their authority from the governance instruments that organize them – constitutions when they are available, executive or military promulgated rules when they are not. When representative legislative bodies have been absent and executive authority arbitrary, the courts have remained accountable to seemingly objective rules. Additionally, the courts have heard all who bring their cases to judgment, enabling equity rather than privilege. To take full advantage of the judiciary, both state and civil society have invested the concept and language of law with tremendous importance, even when the rule of law has been barely respected.

As commentators and critics, the courts have helped to provide alternative interpretations of politics and history when those in power have written authoritarian scripts for the state. Although free expression has often been limited, the superior courts have been allowed to witness relatively open exchanges of political views and interpretations of political events. Even when judicial power and jurisdiction have been explicitly restricted, courtrooms have been used by those in power, those seeking power and those searching to redress grievances against the state to articulate their interests and demands. The judiciary has played two counterbalancing roles: although it has functioned at the behest of authority and has been used to further the interests of the state against its citizens, it has also provided a forum for political exchange. The prospect for institutional manipulation by those holding power is countenanced by possibilities for achieving success by those who do not.

Civil courts have lived in the space between strong executives and weak parliaments and parties. Their arena is primarily rhetorical, their power surely derivative; without the possibility of coercing obedience to their judgments, their decisions are always tentative. In Pakistan, paradoxically, this quality has also strengthened their deliberations, for in the absence of coercion they can be respected in their own right. Citizens participate in their proceedings precisely because they can choose to do so. At the same time, they indirectly invest the state – the judiciary's patron – with a legitimacy that they might otherwise reserve. By allowing courts to operate, even if under stricture, the state has been the ultimate beneficiary of judicial largesse.

The courts have struck bargains with the state to be accessible to the polity. Judges have supported the government of the day and accepted limits on their jurisdiction, and extensions of executive rule inconsistent with the conceptual foundations of their rulings in order to judge at all. These strategies have endowed judicial actions with a political consequentialism that itself has restricted judicial autonomy. They have limited the ability to give force to constitutional government, to give meaning to the concept of judicial independence and finally, to judge the state.

The judiciary and the executive thus engage in a dialogue that parallels one between jurisprudence and politics. The content is specifically constitutional, involving questions of state structure and institutions. It is a debate somewhat removed from the vernacular of mass politics, but not from executive policy; the venue of the courtroom has therefore protected the structure of elite politics. The processes of politics – far less orderly, far closer to the needs and desires of the citizenry – form the backdrop for judicial deliberations, the literal picture that judgments try to frame but not redraw explicitly. Courts have underscored the separation between elite and mass politics, and their different notions of representation, even while they have struggled to give voice to civil society. The tension between these institutional postures has affected the judiciary's concept of itself and its perceptions of its powers.

Just as the founding principles of parliamentary politics were ill-matched to the praetorian state that developed in the first decade of independence, so judges have often found their arsenal of constitutional ideals and legal language ill-suited to the exigencies of post-colonial politics. Even before a constitution was drafted for the new state, judges treated the idea of a constitution as a handbook of rules for politics, and consistently used colonial constitutional instruments this way. Constitutionalism in Pakistan, however, has been as much about the uses of power as about the way that constitutional documents articulate rules. The judiciary's relationship to written constitutions, civil law and military regulations has been part of a process of give and take among those holding power rather than strictly a process of enforcing rules. This political and legal relativism has reinterpreted the relationship between judicial autonomy and political liberty, and has determined the content of constitutions and the languages of power that courts employ.

The uneven pairing of the formal organization of authority and the exercise of power reflects these conceptual contradictions and has earmarked the stresses and strains of Pakistan's politics. The roots of these institutional problems, and related problems of personal and social self-definition, lie in the country's pre- and post-independence history. The colonial experiences of its founders determined who would create the new state, who would benefit from it, who would become its citizens, and how its laws would organize its structure. Post-colonial relationships between government and citizens quickly restricted the scope of popular politics and redefined the limits of power to give breadth to vice-regal government in the independent state. The variegated concepts of constitutionalism that have emerged from this mix have helped to give Pakistani politics its distinctive blend of populism and autocracy.

## Antecedents

Pakistan was born of crises of law and politics, and many of them have been repeated since its birth. Anti-colonialism was built on the foundations of British colonial laws, instruments of control and administration designed to master the vast territory of the Indian subcontinent and channel its human and natural resources for British gain. If one set of laws failed to keep a balance between economic profit, social stability and military advantage, another was drafted to take its place, a constant if only partially successful effort to transform the order of Indian society to suit the order of English control. Indian reactions to British power were often fashioned in response to these legal instruments; political protests took their cue from laws that grew in scope and depth as the task of governing India grew in complexity.

Complementing the evolving administrative state was a process of partial enfranchisement and cooptation. To monopolize power meant to monopolize resources; in turn, the state could provide payment for political loyalty. Feudal fealty was assumed to mesh with colonial patronage so that transfers of capital, land and trade would create the basis for political support. This process so succeeded in parts of the subcontinent – including the western Punjab, which became part of Pakistan after partition – that an entire class of political influentials across northern India participated vigorously in the colonial state. They became increasingly entrenched in its system of rewards and with their feudal compatriots and religious leaders in other provinces, often dominated local politics. But they remained alienated from peasant society and gradually separated their political interests from the urban, commercial classes as well. As the independence movement gained strength, personal economic interests determined in some measure the loyalties of Muslim leaders: although some supported the Congress Party, many large agriculturalists in the Muslim majority provinces supported the British until the independence movement was well under way; the commercial elite and middle classes in Muslim minority provinces ultimately joined with Mohammed Ali Jinnah to lead the Muslim League and form the Pakistani state.

These political and legal divides helped to define some of the parameters of anti-colonialism, and, as we shall observe, also presaged problems for those who championed the Pakistan movement. Their content covered the entire spectrum of political life – citizenship and representation, the reach of executive power, the bounds of territoriality, and perhaps most crucially, the nature of political sovereignty – all problems that resurfaced after independence. British laws created legal definitions of community membership and political rights, the feudal state built on older and more comprehensive concepts of obligation, and the administrative-patronage state tried to mesh the two in a new concatenation of economic and strategic advantage. Imperialism survived the tensions that these conflicting notions of society fostered, primarily by employing a vast array of administrative controls. But colonially imposed social and economic relations bred political contradictions; in time, these tensions became the seeds of an anti-colonial struggle that brought independence through partition.

The anti-colonial struggle was characterized by rituals of British constitutional thrusts and Indian political parries – the former to secure control, the latter to try to wrest a measure of autonomy from colonial overlords. Conflicts between colonial administration and local politics were symptoms of vastly dissimilar concepts of sovereignty and rule. The colonial state gave an administrative language to its political preferences. It described the central executive as an impartial executor rather than the political presence he was known to be, resting his powers on colonial administration and his authority on the edifice of British law. The state's epistemology embodied its ontology. Its administrative imperatives formed the background against which conflicts between Governors-General and legislatures were played, and colored the language of India's diverse resistance movements.

These efforts to formalize relationships between colonizer and colonized also determined political relations among the colonized. Instruments of governance – the colonizer's constitutions – bound together concepts of political representation and communal identity. Communal representation was established as a legal principle by 1909, after the partition of Bengal renewed Indian awareness of imperial power, and gave the British new ways to mold Indian public opinion. This made political identity coterminous with religious group membership; demands and grievances would then be articulated from within these social groups rather than across classes or ethnic lines. The British treated the mechanism of separate communal electorates as a means to rectify imbalances of income, voice and opportunity. In fact, separate electorates underscored differences in treatment among religious groups and separated them from one another politically; these divisions recurred in Indian attempts to secure independence, and have been repeated in similar constitutional experiments in Pakistan.

The same laws gave priority to provinces as agents both for administration and political change. Provincial legislatures were given occasional chances to organize political demands but true power was, of course, vested in the central, executive-dominated, colonial government. Because legislatures were creatures of the colonial state and their members were often beneficiaries of colonial largesse, the state was their first client. Yet, limits on provincial powers chafed at the ambitions of newly empowered politicians, and fueled provincial legislatures with the grievances of absent authority and the dismay of the communal groups they were to represent. To the extent that provincial legislatures could successfully represent communal demands, their local legitimacy was partially sanctioned; to the extent that they failed, communal groups, especially political parties, sought to speak and act outside organized channels. Law's weakness generated protests against it.

Colonial concepts of rights were conceived abstractly and inconsistently. There was a difference between protecting the rights of individual Muslims and providing rights for the Muslim community, writ broadly: the first might have been an impetus for individual political participation, but the second offered a confused sense of group identity connected to colonial politics. To bind communal identity with provincial politics was to militate against an Indian national identity, all the while underscoring conflicts between central power and provincial protest. Political parties, including both the Congress Party and the All-India Muslim League, suffered from this legacy of divided platform and voice.

With time, the British reconceived their concepts of control, less to accommodate Indian protests against its exercise than to create a flexible state structure that might respond to local challenges to colonial power. The constitutional reforms of 1919 were a first step in the direction of creating a governance structure that included Indians as active partners in the state and even more, in developing a plan to transfer powers from the center to the provinces. The attendant concepts of devolution and dyarchy – and the kinds of power they symbolized – became entrenched in colonial India and remained so in Pakistan. At the same time, the use of force was an ever-present accompaniment to these activities.

Indeed, the anti-colonial struggle was partially scripted by the colonialists themselves. The language of liberalism earnestly inscribed in British parliamentary preparations for the 1935 Government of India Act – a document designed to face the practicalities if not the emotional basis of self-rule – assumed notions of the common weal that were not shared by Indian parties. Even though concepts of democracy and the common good were affirmed in communal and provincial terms, the goal of the Act was to sustain imperial power rather than encourage real self-government. For its part, the Muslim League tried – ultimately ineffectually – to overcome these weaknesses: on the one hand, it tried to cement its constituencies in Muslim majority areas with energetic support for provincial powers; on the other hand, it sustained proposals for reserved communal seats in provincial bodies in Muslim minority areas. The League parted company with the British because their competing concepts of participation and sovereignty found little common ground; similar differences of perception later split the Congress Party and the Muslim League and finally, India and Pakistan.

By the time the Government of India Act was passed in 1935, tensions between colonizer and colonized had taken the form of a dialectic between British constitutional experiments and Indian reactions to them. The 1935 Act therefore submerged widely divergent notions of governance. It was a document of partial self-rule for India, a constitutional outline that appropriated the language and institutions of the liberal state but that emphasized British parliamentary control, in part by the pervasive possibility, and use, of emergency powers. Local, communal and provincial politics could not conform to the requirements of this kind of state. The Act's weaknesses in recognizing and responding to developing political demands – or seeing them wrongly – underscored the incompleteness of self-rule rather than paths toward self-determination, exacerbating, in the words of a Congress Party spokesman, the "inherent . . . seeds of a civil War."[1] They contributed to the march of independence, but also to partition.

By the time of its March 1940 meeting in Lahore, therefore, the Muslim League's continuing demands for provincial sovereignty and weak central government were in direct opposition to the 1935 Act. Its Lahore (Pakistan) Resolution called for explicit safeguards for the Muslim minority and commitments for the sovereignty of areas of Muslim majority. It thus tried to unite Muslim politicians by proposing protections for individual and community. Using the vehicle of provincial autonomy, the League pursued ascendance in the independence movement while establishing an agenda for negotiations with the British.

[1] K.T. Shah, *Provincial Autonomy (Under the Government of India Act, 1935)* (Bombay: Vora & Co., Ltd., 1937), p. 50.

Nonetheless, the text of the Resolution was misleadingly general, particularly for a document that would soon be seen as an organizing plan for a new state. It referred simply to future "independent states" whose "constituent units shall be autonomous and sovereign" – words whose meaning is still uncertain in Pakistan today, despite their invocation as an anthem of Pakistani patriotism. The immediate political message, however, was clear. The Lahore Resolution reflected the League's growing anti-colonialism and its dismay with the Congress Party, which refused to share power after elections in 1937 – a dual reaction to perceived political inequities toward Muslims and the repressive potential of vice-regal government. The Resolution thus became a call for an independent state.

Colonial constitutional experiments thus provided the carriage and content for the Pakistani state. The 1935 Act influenced protest against colonial rule and even more, helped to structure the post-colonial state in Pakistan; the 1940 Resolution gave the anti-colonial struggle a formal goal and a language with which to pursue it. Despite the Resolution's political sweep, Pakistan's constitutions have generally followed the model of the 1935 Act; the 1947 Indian Independence Act, an enabling document for independence, was built on its vice-regal foundations. For nine years of intermittent constitution-drafting, the two imperial acts functioned with modifications as Pakistan's Provisional Constitution Act. The 1940 Resolution came to symbolize the conscience of the state's domestic opponents, and remains a rallying cry for provincialists opposed to centralized versions of the federation in Pakistan today.

When independence arrived, the constitutional poles of 1935 and 1940 exacerbated the uncertainties of Pakistani political life. The constituent Assembly elected indirectly in 1946 under the 1935 Act – responsible to communities identified by the British as deserving representation in 1935, but by 1947 existing in wholly new territorial and political environments – was entrusted with framing a constitution for the new state. The Assembly was forced to confront the accumulated contradictions of independence and partition in critical constitutional areas that provided widely divergent foundations for rights.

First, the Pakistani state was an amalgam of territories structured and governed differently and rarely with relation to the others. The literal distance between their furthest points – Bengal to Baluchistan, Kashmir to Karachi – was embellished by the figurative distance between their histories and expectations. Provincial autonomy held vastly different meanings to local political, tribal and princely leaders; the meaning of accession to the new state is still contested among some of their political descendants today. In addition, feudal relationships between leaders and followers were not only unchanged after partition, but were assured by the manner of political representation. As long as the landed gentry were spokesmen for province and nation, economic change would be limited in reach and kind. Land reform barely reached Pakistan, and each attempt to foster changes in distribution and taxation has been met with unceasing protest from those who hold political power. Without a more equitable distribution of resources, the material basis of representation was unlikely to change.

Thus, the Lahore Resolution proposed a manner of governance it was unable to mandate, and the administrative structure of the 1935 Act helped to mute its assertion. Even more problematic, by providing considerable political sway to the landed provincial elite, the Resolution heralded the alliance between Muslims from the majority and minority provinces. When the Muslim League joined hands with the landlords in their provincial assemblies, it also joined in their version of communal politics. The early victims of this anti-colonial alliance were federalism, secularism and liberalism: from this point, both the Pakistan movement and Muslim politics generally were unclear about who would be a citizen, who would represent whom, and to what ends. Contemporary Pakistan's continuing difficulties to reach concord on issues of representation and democracy are derived in some measure from this early decision to view provincial, economic and political rights through the lens of provincial and feudal interests.

Second, the problematic nexus between indeterminate provincial autonomy and strong centralized rule was underscored by the pre-eminence of the executive, both central and provincial, under the 1935 Act. In the anti-colonial lexicon, provincial power meant the prospect of legislative authority counterposed to the central, executive-dominated colonial state. The center was now no longer colonist, but the first Governors-General held an unusually wide array of powers that weakened the rest of government. From the start, Pakistan's Constituent Assembly struggled to assert its preeminence as a legislature and its predominance as a constitutive body, two difficult tasks it only partly achieved. This pattern of conflict between the executive and the legislature established a model of government that undercuts the concepts of equal representation and opportunity today. Pakistan's early courts would struggle mightily to reconcile the idealism of the country's political rhetoric with the realism determined by these power struggles; their inability to oversee such resolution can be seen in today's judgments as well.

Third, the equation between communal identity and political representation in colonial India was translated into one between communal identity and citizenship in Pakistan. Critically, the question of Islam was left to debate until after independence. Whether one argues that a concept of Islamic community was embedded in the League's nationalist activities, or that its use of such solidarities helped to forward the pace of independence, the constitutional issue was inconclusive at best. The discourse of Islamic law need not conflict at every turn with the language of secular liberalism, but in Pakistan each philosophy was marshaled by political constituencies who eschewed compromise. The resolution of profound philosophical differences was left to a series of diffuse assemblies and strong executives who never polled their constituents. Instead, the original outline of a secular state was rapidly sacrificed to the articulations of the religious right, but contentiously and incompletely. The possibilities of an Islamic state – including crucial issues of individual sovereignty and moral agency, of rights and obligations for both citizens and state, of the sources and character of law and constitution – posed serious questions that remain open today. The absence of consensus or even partial agreement about the terms of dispute, even today, is partly attributable to the confusions about responsibility and accountability written into the beginnings of the state.

Finally, the Muslim League that took the helm at independence was a weak party at best. Unlike India's Congress Party, it was populist neither in membership nor ideology. It had usefully spawned a separatist independence movement, but seemed incapable of translating its democratic postures into a political movement to support the new state. The ruling party identified itself with the state and damaged prospects for vibrant party-based debate. With the early deaths of Governor-General Mohammed Ali Jinnah and Prime Minister Liaqat Ali Khan – both representatives from Muslim minority provinces, rather than members of the dominant feudal elite – the party and the state easily fell prey to the growing powers of the bureaucracy, the landlords and the military. These groups in turn solidified their common interests into a formidable alliance that defined, and still defines, the structure of the state.

The definitions of citizenship and representation were therefore more confused after independence than before. Not only was the status of non-Muslims uncertain, but the collective role of those without land – the mohajirs who migrated from India with Jinnah – was determined as much by circumstance as design. Although many helped to establish Pakistan's commercial and institutional foundations, the prior equivalence between territory and nationality – the latter a term without constitutional or legal status in Pakistan – left this "fifth nationality" a place apart from the feudal, territorial base that defined politics for the rest of the country. Decades later, these divisions are in some ways as deep – perhaps deeper – than they were at partition.

All these problems of concept and process translated into conflicts about how to define the sovereignty of the state and concomitantly, how to locate the sources of that sovereignty within the state. Sovereignty implies power and authority, but the legitimacy of the state's spokesmen and the repository of their powers were persistently questioned. New minorities were created with the Muslim state and new tensions arose between territorial nationalities and refugees, urban and rural interests, those with resources and those without, and among sectarian groups. The sources of sovereignty reposed alternately in territory, a concept that could be given constitutional interpretation, and in previously formed communal, ethnic and tribal groups, concepts less accessible to constitutional meaning. Their spokesmen represented political parties whose origins, loyalties, interests and ideologies often predated the state: provincial assemblies with roots quite apart from the state; sectarian organizations that sometimes did not even recognize the state; and finally, legislative assemblies that grew increasingly to represent only themselves.

These overlapping sources of sovereignty, used interchangeably without priority, were drawn closely to public doubts about the state-building enterprise and its legitimacy. They also helped the civil and military establishments to justify their frequent incursions into politics. In the sequence of regimes that followed independence, the vice-regal model provided a constitutional structure for military rule and martial law; its resilience even during periods of parliamentary rule gave it a permanent presence in the state. Feudal interests merged with the vice-regal state and limited – by occasional logic and frequent dictate – the voices of traditional liberalism. The contours of political discourse – from executive pronouncement to popular resistance to military incursions into the domains of civil society – became increasingly difficult to revise. The stage was thus set for the developing national security state and for Pakistan's politics of crisis.

## Precedents

The sweep of Pakistan's political history has become a familiar tale to those who watch politics in the Indian subcontinent. Tensions between the inherited vice-regal state and its unevenly distributed economic endowments, between liberal ideals and incompatible constitutional principles, and between imposed Islamic precepts and military dominance have provided a canvas for frequent changes in governments and constitutions. From the sporadic parliamentarianism of the state's founders to the opportunistic populism of the People's Party to the conservative Islamic Jamoori Ittehad, civilian government has spanned a wide range of ideologies that belie the similarities of their constitutional and political profiles. Similarly, the army-led states of Generals Mohammed Ayub Khan, Agha Mohammed Yahya Khan, and Mohammed Zia ul Haq all governed with similar instruments of martial law, and all tried to mix military rule with a civil praetorianism whose contradictions undercut civil society.

With each regime has come a new constitution, a new iteration of the place of constitutional law in politics, and a slightly revised role for the superior courts. The legal rendering of the vice-regal state has been accompanied at intervals by calls for greater and more equal political representation; together, these impulses have determined a sadly predictable sequence of constitutional instruments that have invited abrogation as much as adherence. When the British parliament suggested prior to partition that constitutional success was dependent "far more upon the manner and spirit in which it is worked than upon its formal provisions," it did not take account of political preconditions that have rendered this wisdom inadequate and misguided for Pakistan. In the absence of a strong and equitable representative tradition, the coincidence of executive and emergency rule and the consequent frequent ouster of fundamental rights have offered opportunities for constitutional autocracy even more than democracy.

The first Constituent Assembly produced a statement of purpose in its March 1949 Objectives Resolution. (It became the preamble to successive constitutions and was incorporated as an operative part of the constitution in 1985.) The Resolution proposed government under the guidance but not the instruction of Islamic principles, acknowledged unspecified autonomy for the units of the federation and guaranteed fundamental rights for majority and minorities alike. It thus tried to combine federalism, democracy and popular sovereignty; according to Prime Minister Liaqat Ali Khan, "the people have been recognized as the recipients of all authority and it is in them that the power to wield it has been vested."[2] The Resolution's generality could not hide profound disagreements about the character of the future constitution or state – for example, its characterization of the role of Islam was made simultaneously prominent, obscure and legally undefined. Its grounding power for constitution-writing has been emotional rather than practical, inertial more than assertive.

The Assembly tried to determine the basic principles of federalism, franchise and judicial powers, and constituted an Islamic advisory com-

[2] Speech on Objectives Resolution in G.W. Choudhury, ed., *Documents and Speeches on the Constitution of Pakistan* (Dacca: Green Book House, 1967), pp. 23–29.

mittee to review this work. The Basic Principles Committees' reports in 1950 and 1952 were received unfavorably by constituencies who objected variously to their recommendations on representation, provincial autonomy, language and secularism. A third attempt yielded proposals for a bicameral legislature and equity among the provinces, provided for legislative sovereignty, guaranteed rights for minorities and introduced state policy directives to prohibit legislation repugnant to the teachings of Islam. These recommendations were approved by the Assembly in September 1954 as a prelude to the constituent Assembly's planned constitution. Before the Assembly could introduce its draft constitution, Governor-General Ghulam Mohammed dissolved that body and offered an alternate constitution that strengthened the hand of the executive and recast the federation to give preeminence to the newly amalgamated province of West Pakistan.

The new Constituent Assembly that followed was organized by the Governor-General to pass his own version of a constitution in 1956. It reiterated the mixed message of dyarchy and democracy of the 1935 Act. Despite Law Minister I.I. Chundrigar's assertions to the contrary,[3] the Governor-General's powers were transferred in thc main to a president whose executive powers outreached those of the elected prime minister, and were echoed in the powers of provincial governors. Like Pakistan's subsequent constitutions, the heads of state and government were separate. Although this division of powers need not necessarily undercut the power of the polity, in Pakistan the military backed the executive with extended emergency powers, thereby limiting parliamentary oversight and powers. In addition, and most formidably, the western provinces were formally consolidated into the "One Unit" province of West Pakistan. One Unit removed the possibility of parity and equity that East Pakistanis required for its version of provincial autonomy; it also concentrated power in the center, which controlled provincial executives in both wings.

More laudably, the 1956 Constitution included justiciable fundamental rights in its body, and provided for extensive central and provincial judicial powers, including specified writ jurisdiction. The Law Minister extolled these protections for rights and judicial autonomy, saying "the independence of the Judiciary is a principle very dear to the people of this country, who believe that they receive justice from the courts of this country and that their rights are safe in the hands of the judges." Writing just before the *coup d'état* that would overturn this constitution, consti-

[3] Speech on presenting the fourth draft Constitution, 9 January 1956, in Choudhury, *Documents*, pp. 281–97.

tutional attorney A.K. Brohi described this constitution as "a Government by the Judges."[4] Since the preeminence of the executive and the relative subordination of parliament was already clear, his comment tried to translate institutional weakness into a virtue. By localizing the previously imperial practice of Privy Council review (already partially altered by the 1949 Federal Court [Enlargement of Jurisdiction] Act and the 1950 Privy Council [Abolition of Jurisdiction] Act), the constitution transformed an instrument of colonial control into a mechanism designed to check the executive. Judicial autonomy brought with it responsibility. The 1956 Constitution placed a greater burden on the judiciary to ensure that workable parliamentary democracy could emerge than the courts could reasonably shoulder.

In the pages of this constitution the seeds of political conflict were sown anew. Claims to provincial autonomy would clash with central power, claims to equitable representation would clash with the limits on participation enforced by consolidating the western provinces, claims to legislative sovereignty would clash with both executive rule and judicial review of laws, claims to an Islamic state would clash with those of secularism, and claims to democracy would clash with constitutional structures of control.

First, however, the *coup d'état* led by President Iskander Mirza and General Mohammed Ayub Khan replaced civilian with military rule. The first victim was the constitution, which was blamed for the travails of the state. Mirza justified taking over the state with a theory of guided democracy that formed the basis for Ayub Khan's rule and his constitutional experiments. It was a theory with deep implications for the state. From an executive-controlled government, Pakistan quickly moved to a martial law state; from its backseat control, the army moved forward to determine the course of administration and to revoke the practices of politics. The 1958 Laws (Continuance in Force) Order replaced the constitution, continued One Unit, but retained superficial resemblance to the constitution in the arena of judicial writs – which were then curtailed by military regulations and military courts. For eleven years, during which Ayub Khan wrote a new constitution (with some minimal rights protections) and empowered a restricted, non-party legislature, the basic configuration of the state persisted.

Ayub Khan's 1962 Constitution envisioned presidential rule without the mask of parliamentary participation. He therefore ended two traditional bifurcations: the conflict between politics and administration was resolved by pushing popular politics deeply underground, and the conflict

[4] A.K. Brohi, *Fundamental Law of Pakistan* (Karachi: Din Muhammadi Press, 1958), p. 39.

between presidential and ministerial powers was resolved by ending ministerial rule. Although the assemblies created by the constitution were able in principle to amend it sufficiently to provide justiciable rights and eventually to amend presidential ordinances, the presidency in concert with the military overwhelmed other government agencies and sources of power. Judicial orders were replaced with declaratory judgments of far less force; the judiciary, feared for its capacity to override legislative prerogative under the 1956 Constitution, could now only counter executive pronouncements with judgments of protest.

More virulent protests, however, developed once limited political activity was allowed: the "decentralized unitarian Government," in Federal Court Chief Justice Muhammad Munir's words, did not work,[5] and neither did the peculiar federalism of One Unit. Neither Ayub Khan nor his constitution survived organized resistance to his rule. In unfortunate parallelism to 1958, Ayub transferred power to General Yahya Khan, who then promulgated martial law regulations anew. Seeking to reduce tensions between East and West, Yahya Khan dissolved One Unit, provided for new elections and proclaimed yet another emergency. Despite his voiced desire for democracy, however, he did not allow civilian instruments to give it birth. The country retained its distrust of military rule and the deep-seated resentments between provinces and peoples that ballooned under martial law. The ensuing war between East and West Pakistan served up the worst of military repression and political conflicts in both wings. Each then found new sovereignties and constitutions.

In the post-war, 1972 Interim Constitution, the structure of the 1935 Act temporarily resumed primacy; while the National Assembly drafted a new document, President Zulfiqar Ali Bhutto assumed presidential emergency powers, some of which extended past the Interim Constitution's life. The 1973 Constitution written by the new National Assembly offered a new configuration of parliamentary power, including universal franchise, direct elections, a bicameral legislature on the federal level and unicameral assemblies for the provinces. The Prime Minister was now stronger than the President. Fundamental rights were again made operative parts of the constitution and the judiciary was empowered to issue

[5] *Constitution of the Islamic Republic of Pakistan, Being a Commentary on the Constitution of Pakistan, 1962* (Lahore: All Pakistan Legal Decisions, 1965), p. 70. After the Bangladesh war, Justice Munir condemned Ayub Khan more strongly, saying "prejudice against the presidential system is due to the parody of a presidential form of government embodied in the 1962 Constitution which had actually set up a disguised dictatorship." "Some Thoughts on the Draft Constitution," in Nazir Hussain Chaudhri, *Chief Justice Muhammad Munir: His Life, Writings and Judgments* (Lahore: Research Society of Pakistan, University of the Punjab, 1973), p. 546.

writs and was promised full separation from the executive. State policy directives, while not justiciable, were accorded serious informal status by members of the constitutional drafting body. For the first time, the military was made subservient to the Prime Minister, strengthening his hand in setting the tone of governance.

Breaches soon developed between constitutional spirit and law. Constitutional amendments restricted opposition to the government and diminished the reach of parliamentary democracy and fundamental rights, and the powers of the judiciary were sharply circumscribed. Prime Minister Bhutto assumed and liberally applied full emergency powers. In early 1973, People's Party Law Minister Mian Mahmud Ali Kasuri had predicted the potential for such abuse under the draft constitution: he warned that, once elected, the federal and provincial heads of government "will be absolutely irremovable ... the Prime Minister will become a virtual dictator ... the President of Pakistan will be like an appendix in the human body."[6] He also cautioned that the center's power to dismiss provincial governments negated provincial autonomy. In fact, by the end of Bhutto's rule, accusations against his appropriation and use of military might – to wage war against provincialists, politicians and opposition political parties – sounded suspiciously like those leveled against past Governors-General and military dictators. His party's legitimacy was compromised by its leader and his use of the constitution, against which reaction became increasingly violent; the state and its constitutional instruments gradually resumed familiar autocratic colors.

Thus, when General Mohammed Zia ul Haq took control of the government and abrogated the constitution in 1977, he found the process of anti-constitutional rule well under way. During his eleven-year rule, General Zia first followed Ayub Khan's model of military rule in civilian costume, and then, facing more serious opposition, developed his own brand of oppression. When political parties protested his rule, he abolished them; when individuals challenged his edicts, he imprisoned them; when courts objected to his use of force, he ousted their jurisdiction. The doctrine of necessity, already prominent through colonial inheritance and judicial precept, was raised to a form of art that would thwart civil society. Determined to Islamize the state, General Zia promulgated ordinances to reorganize the government, and created quasi-legislative, wholly non-representative bodies to approve them. The courts, restricted by prior constitutional amendments and military regulations, were further curtailed by the 1981 Provisional Constitutional Order, an ordinance that almost choked the judiciary and virtually silenced dissent.

[6] National Assembly of Pakistan, *Constitution-Making Debates 1973*, pp. 602–03, 606.

In 1985, after assuring his own tenure through a manipulated referendum, General Zia revived the constitution by ordinance, a process that meant promulgating a presidential constitution atop the 1973 parliamentary outline – a new version of the vice-regal state. It provided an awkward mix that neither the mixed civil–military government under Prime Minister Mohammed Khan Junejo (1985–88) nor the successor civilian governments of Prime Ministers Benazir Bhutto (1988–90) and Mian Nawaz Sharif (1990–1993) were able fully to discipline. When in the political opposition, the People's Party sometimes fought its battles on the field of fundamental rights, but Bhutto's constitutional and political inheritances limited her capacity to guarantee them when she held office. The configuration of presidential and ministerial powers became a subject of political controversy and inconclusive judicial wrangling which did not end when President Ghulam Ishaq Khan dissolved the national and provincial assemblies in August 1990, empowered a caretaker government, ordered new elections for October 1990, and promulgated his own constitutional changes by ordinance. Prime Minister Nawaz Sharif's strategy once he succeeded Bhutto – to duplicate presidential powers for the Prime Minister – served only to complicate the constitutional division of powers offering opportunities for heightened repression; it did not prevent the President from attempting to remove him from office. The conflict between head of state and head of government is inscribed in an internally contradictory constitutional instrument that will continue to thwart political progress until it is rewritten.

This patchwork constitutional progression has been complicated throughout by problems of political transition and legal coherence. Every constitution has been fashioned after the 1935 Act or the modified parliamentarianism of the 1973 Constitution, and every one has given primacy to central, executive power. The political arena, meanwhile, often takes for its language and symbols doctrines of provincial autonomy clothed in reactive nationalisms. Its concepts of federation, articulated in language similar to the 1940 Lahore Resolution, have given the center excuses to redouble repression in the name of security and sovereignty. Civil and military governments have been tied by the enduring laws and regulations they create to buoy their power. Constitutional immunities guaranteed to martial law governments after each bout of military rule have underscored this consistency and shielded the executive from judicial, and, to an extent, popular opprobrium.

Despite differences among these constitutions and the political environments in which they lived, several common conceptual and political relationships have endured. From the beginning, federalism has been defined primarily by the center and provincial autonomy has been limited in this way. Differences in constitutional language notwithstanding, provinces do not cede powers to the center but are granted powers by the center; the principle of devolution keeps the management of inter-provincial relations for the center. The federation is executive-oriented: the center and the executive are often structurally coterminous. National and provincial legislatures, whether under a parliamentary or presidential system, derive their authority from the constitution but their real power from the executive. Legislative autonomy and provincial autonomy, two completely different concepts that express widely divergent structural interests, are nonetheless joined by the opposition to achieve the common political purpose of limiting the executive. This political relationship echoes the character of protest against the colonial state and imbues movements to limit executive prerogatives with the colors of democracy even when they offer only a different location for authoritarianism.

In practice if not in principle, individual rights are also subject to executive discretion. Fundamental rights have had a place in most of Pakistan's constitutions, but their reach has required separate guarantees for judicial powers. When Ayub Khan incorporated non-justiciable rights into the 1962 Constitution, he made constitutionally plain a practice typical of the last three decades. When rights have been protected by the judicial powers, the executive has used constitutional powers to amend the constitution (or administratively to limit judicial authority) in order to limit the potentially disruptive effects of fundamental rights on the political system. Thus, the political meaning of rights and of judicial autonomy – whatever their constitutional rendering – is directly attributable to the executive-dominated state.

Furthermore, Pakistan's constitutions rarely speak to serious ideological questions which form the background for constitutional obedience or protest. Islamizing the state, for example, has come to mean creating institutions whose sources eclipse politics and whose powers supersede both the executive and the judiciary – a haunting prospect for the courts, but virtually impossible for the executive to countenance. The quality of ideological debate takes its limits from the needs of executive rule; movements for ideological change take their cue from other protests against the center. Politics remains highly adversarial but also highly unequal. The state profoundly influences the degree to which peaceful, constitutional, political change can occur.

Constitutions have thus been written to reflect the state that is, rarely the state that might be. This problematic has plagued detractors and defenders of the presidential–parliamentary, civil–military order: the equation of military power and civil control, if not deftly calculated, can bring down any government. The fear of failure has redounded equally to constitutional stability and state sovereignty, and calls into question complex relationships between constitutions, executive, legislatures and courts. When constitutions embody the current state, they help to enforce existing boundaries between classes, religions, territories and ethnic groups; reflecting the state's weaknesses, they establish limits for political or programmatic change. Every major political controversy has been waged on legal and constitutional as well as political fronts and has frequently devolved to the task of redrafting constitutive documents, blaming past constitutions while pressing for new ones which resemble the old. Politics in Pakistan is enmeshed in a constitutionalism which sidesteps and often belies the imperatives of building the state.

Just as questions of law can easily be trivialized into arguments about petty legalisms, so problems of political legitimacy can be transformed into debates about constitutionalism. Those in power have often pursued this political course: to follow the rule of law, to abide by fundamental constitutional precept, has become a good separate from the substance of constitutional law. To establish a process for every act, under civil or military banner, has been a hallmark of both martial law and the bureaucratic state, a triumph of form over content. Apart from a politics of acknowledged legitimacy by the citizenry, however, the rhetoric of constitutionalism almost inevitably devalues the rule of law.

The mixed premises of civic republicanism and liberal constitutionalism – limiting arbitrary government action through individual rights, providing for community improvement through organized decision-making – can be read in judicial decisions on constitutional questions and can be read into much constitutional language, although the state often militates against their attainment. Constitutional debate often has an air of perpetual recreation because the political assumptions of the state and its constitutionalists are sometimes illusory and almost always contested. Pakistan takes its constitutions seriously, but too often suffers from their collisions with an unwieldy state and its reactive, fractious politics.

Contemplating these formidable political inheritances, Justice Muhammad Munir asked after his retirement:

> How is it that with all this experimenting with constitutions, we have not during this long period been able to give ourselves a stable Constitution? . . . Is there something basically wrong somewhere because we have not been able to find a workable constitution for ourselves? Has there been something wrong with the persons who were put in or assumed power to work the previous constitutions? Was there something inherently wrong with those Constitutions themselves?[7]

7 "Reversion to Constitutional Government," *Pakistan Times*, 25 July 1969, reprinted in Nazir Hussain Chaudhri, pp. 116–20, at 116.

Justice Munir himself played an important role in setting the complex meanings of law and constitutionalism at two critical moments in Pakistan's early history, and his legacy is still debated today. More than two decades later, his questions underscore the conceptual inconsistencies and political manipulations of Pakistan's parliamentary tradition. Political habits, entrenched interests and persistent crises have allowed the state's guardians to sidestep primary questions of political organization. Why should the center be allowed to intervene in provincial affairs? Why should parliamentary structure require both President and Prime Minister, Governor and Minister? Why should constitutions be disposable? Were former High Court Justice Kayani's advice after Ayub Khan's *coup d'état* heeded – to scrap the government to see what kind of constitution you might have – what kind of state would emerge? Finally, what kind of justice can emerge from a constitutional system that embodies such structural weaknesses?

## Judgment

One of Pakistan's early foreign advisers cautioned that English constitutional practice assumed democracy to be coincident with democratic institutions.[8] Pakistan's political and constitutional antecedents weakened the prospects for such institutions from the start and created obstacles to their achievement after independence. The task of reconciling these contradictory principles and practices fell to the judiciary, whose jurisprudence has attempted to mold political savvy and legal reasoning in the context of repeated crisis.

When constitutions have not accomplished their tasks – when they have not adequately constituted the state in terms meaningful to their citizens – judges and lawyers have reconstituted the state anew. Given the frequency of constitutional change in Pakistan, its courts have developed rituals of re-creation: not only do they interpret the constitution of the day, but they reread political history and constitutional language to establish their own definitions of political community. These activities lend to judicial proceedings an autonomy only partially written into constitutions, and to their judgments an unparalleled importance in the development of the state.

Each moment of crisis has led to critical judicial decisions. When the first Constituent Assembly was dissolved, its members brought their pleas for reinstatement to the Sind High Court. *Tamizuddin Khan's case*, its

[8] Ivor Jennings, *Some Characteristics of the Indian Constitution* (London: Oxford University Press, 1953), p. 3.

subsequent appeal in the Supreme Court and the government's *Reference* to implement these rulings collectively enshrined methods for judicial appeal, relationships between justices and the state, and a style of prudential judgment that carefully linked the courts to legal philosophies and some of its members to specific political ideologies as well. The substance of these judgments was as important as the fact that they could be offered: the judiciary's discussions of representation and sovereignty refined Assembly discussions, analyzed the efficacy of executive intervention in parliamentary politics, and defined the shape of the new vice-regal state. The courts persuasively argued that they were one bulwark against the possibility of military intercession in politics, but that their existence was nonetheless contingent on a constitutional order that would protect them. They tried to establish an early equation between constitutionalism and justice; less effectively, they proposed an equation between democracy and parliamentary governance.

Yet, under the same Chief Justice the Supreme Court sanctioned a military *coup d'état* just a few years later. Fearful that the chaos of popular politics would threaten the existence of the state, the court used the occasion of *Dosso's case* to rearticulate principles of necessity and efficacy and to establish a jurisprudential basis for army rule. During the crisis of constitution-writing in 1954 the court seemed unequivocally to support civilian government; during the political crisis of 1958, it revised its opinion and in so doing, gave the military an opportunity to restructure the state. The abrogation of the constitution, however, suspended constitutional rule and limited judicial powers for the next twelve years. Rulings during the decade of Ayub Khan's rule showed just how much the courts depended on flexible constitutions: only when justiciable rights were allowed after 1964 were the superior courts institutionally emboldened to challenge the edicts of the presidential state and even then, their reach was restricted by the president.

*Dosso's case* taught Pakistan that without adequate constitutions the polity would be left without power or spokesmen. Rulings during the first days of the Bhutto government underscored this fact by declaring *post facto* in *Asma Jilani's case* and *Zia ur Rahman's case* that General Yahya Khan's regime constituted an illegal usurpation of powers. But these same cases also found ways to countenance specific acts and laws from that period, and thus to bridge the legal vacuum that otherwise would have existed. The courts helped the new government by retaining legal consistency from one regime to the next while firmly supporting the newly drafted 1973 Constitution. The spectre of past martial laws, however, remained in the minds of the judges, who remained tolerant of extensive executive authority in order to preclude another interruption of civilian government.

During this most political of regimes, however, the superior courts took on explicitly political roles. Not only did the high courts turn their eyes away from the Prime Minister's increasing incursions on parliamentary powers, but the Supreme Court concurred with Bhutto's campaigns against his political opponents. In the 1975 *Reference* against the National Awami Party, the court furthered a blatantly political vendetta by ignoring its own rules of evidence, and consequently sacrificed its impartiality. Its judgment expressed confusion about the state's ideological and thus jurisprudential moorings, and was a warning that party rule did not necessarily mean open political debate.

Some of the lessons of *Dosso's case* had receded from active memory by the time of the 1977 *coup d'état*. Although the Supreme Court tried to avoid approving military rule, *Nusrat Bhutto's case* traveled far beyond the petitioner's plea to release the former Prime Minister from prison in order to contest elections. Rather, the court validated military intercession while imposing some limits on martial law. The decision could not stand; by this time, the judiciary should have understood, both historically and logically, that civilian oversight over martial law was a near impossibility.

That the court chose to give the military the benefit of the doubt spoke to the uneven relationship that characterized judicial–executive relations. Fearing for the stability of the country and its own independence, the court wrote a judgment that was self-defeating on both counts. Within a few years, the military had closed the courts for their most important business – enforcing the writ jurisdiction – and thus removed the most effective civil rights protections from a public that might otherwise have been able to resist military rule more energetically. General Zia's martial law state might well have developed as it did had the court not validated his rule; by doing so, however, the court allowed its prudential jurisprudence to become misshapen and, for several more years, ineffective.

Only when the superior courts tried retrospectively to cover this validation by holding the Zia regime to a higher standard of rights protections than his political order allowed did the courts realize the full, negative impact of their earlier judgment. Faced with military tribunals that allowed virtually no protections for petitioners or defendants, the citizenry was left with no recourse to civil courts. Dissent was doubly outlawed, by specific ordinance and by court inaction. Although ways were ultimately found to make this martial law ungovernable, this happened only after years of imprisonments for activists and bystanders, the emasculation of the political party system, and the further entrenchment of those who held financial and political power.

Traveling the maze has proved tortuous for the post-martial law judiciary. Among its difficult tasks are three related problems: the structure of the constitution, including conflicting powers for the heads of state and government; the sweep of the indemnity clauses collected under the eighth constitutional amendment, which affects the entire domain of constitutional law; and the limits to judicial action included in this constitution. The courts have walked a narrow, and in many ways eerily dangerous path. On the one hand, they have tried to reassert their powers by opening their jurisdictions as widely as possible. On the other hand, however, they have been careful not to overstep their assumed bounds, imposing a familiar self-censorship to craft a steady and safe future role. This is a bargain the courts have struck before. Whether it proves secure for the justices or for justice has yet to be determined.

The judiciary's efforts in transitions from martial law to civilian rule, particularly in the post-Zia period, have shown just how difficult the country's mixed political lineages make its task. If the superior courts take explicit account of political trends, their autonomy and impartiality seem compromised, and with it the reach of justice; if they ignore politics, their judgments seem suspiciously suspended from contemporary history and the realities of the state. Moreover, the weaknesses of participatory institutions not only provide the judiciary with full dockets, but serious operational dilemmas as well. If the courts bypass legislatures in order to articulate democratic principles with greater firmness, elected bodies are further weakened; if they wait for parliaments to act, the pace of democratic transition may be compromised and with it, the reach of justice. Political fallibility thus undercuts judicial independence – perhaps not deliberately, but with equal consequence.

The judiciary's extraordinarily high profile has thus been accompanied by its politicization. The role that the courts play has been matched by the political commitments of its members. While it is substantively and methodologically improper to equate every judgment with personal prejudice, many justices have incorporated their preferences into their rulings. Justice Munir, who presided over the Supreme Court in the 1950s, held clear attachments to the center and its Punjabi majority but also to a secular state, beliefs that could not help but influence his judgments. Justice Cornelius, the Supreme Court's only non-Muslim Chief Justice and Munir's main interlocutor, encouraged the Islamic jurisprudence that Munir abjured; it is unclear from his writings whether he meant to impede the growing power of the state, to support alternative venues for justice, or to buttress the incomplete ideology of the professedly Islamic state. Justice Hamoodur Rahman presided with care over the transition cases following Yahya Khan's demise, but then allowed his personal beliefs about the Bangladesh war to affect his rulings in the

*Reference* against the National Awami Party. Moreover, the links between legal and government actors – some of whom have retained private practices while holding government office, others of whom have tried cases before judges over whom they have the power of appointment, others of whom have treated the judicial profession as one of inheritance rather than achievement – have increased in recent years. Even more, however, the arbitrary reach of the executive has been employed against judges. Institutional ties between executive and judiciary have allowed the executive to meddle in judicial appointments and resignations. Judges who incur ministerial or presidential displeasure can be compulsorily retired, denied their seniority and promotions, or arbitrarily transferred among courts; and others still have never had their appointments confirmed, adding a tone of contingency to the judiciary's stature. Peer review agencies like the Supreme Judicial Council have been manipulated by civil and military overseers alike in order to lower the volume of judicial debate.

Public perceptions of judicial impartiality, so important for institutional independence, have therefore been colored by some of the same political influences that taint other political bodies; the courts have been victims of political manipulation far more than coconspirators. Nonetheless, the superior judiciary continues to occupy a unique place – not only historically, but in present configurations of power and privilege that are still seeking an equilibrium between military and civilian rule, and between the powers of the state and of civil society. Their importance can be gauged most clearly in their responses to the crises that permeate Pakistan's politics. Their own words, which introduce this inquiry, reveal just how closely their activities have rendered their institutional, constitutional, and jurisprudential positions.

# 2 Constituting the state (1947–1958)

And sovereignty
Will belong to the people
Which means
You, I, and all of us.

Faiz Ahmad Faiz, "We will see."

Revolutions are not in the contemplation of those who frame constitutions.

Justice Muhammad Munir

Viewed schematically, the political course of independent Pakistan can be seen in microcosm in its first years. Many of the internal structures and external pressures that have come to typify state and society were present at its creation. The uncertainties of its relationship with India – bound so closely in history, ruptured so profoundly while successfully achieving self-determination – deeply permeated the country's political psychology and created the basis for a politics of uncertainty that remains today. Contentious and unstable regional relations influenced the way Pakistan organized its resources, foreign alliances and domestic politics, and quickly created the foundations for a praetorian state. The predominance of the military, even under civilian rule, colored the development of the country's laws and political institutions and equally, the ways its citizens responded to the proclaimed imperatives of the state. Its geographic and economic maps were mismatched and unbalanced: natural resources, capital and infrastructure were organized to fit unpartitioned, colonial India rather than the new state; politics were an awkward overlay on this terrain of nascent centers and multiple peripheries.

Pakistan was truly a product of many imaginations, each with their own visions of political community and state structure. The evolving state was caught between these images, the languages in which they were expressed, and the people who articulated them. For some, Pakistan was the proud culmination of Muslim self-assertion, for others it was the expression of a necessarily Islamic state; for some, it represented successful anti-colonial politics while for others partition meant the failed prospect of a pluralistic, liberal India; for some, independence was the logical outcome of subcontinental politics, for others it was the product of manipulation or historical accident. The state's antecedents, both real and ideal, influenced each attempt to set the strategic and political limits that defined state sovereignty, and also implied judgments about competing political ideals.

The state's provenance made its first decade of governance awkward and sometimes painful. Fundamental differences were immediately apparent between the inherited and often elitist politics of the Muslim League, the mass politics needed to energize a new state and the constitutional structures that facilitated independence. The country's borders were relatively clear (notwithstanding intermittent incidents with India over the accession of princely states and a dispute with Afghanistan over the Durand Line), but its internal structure was not. Who and what would comprise the state, whose expectations were to be fulfilled, on what basis would political representation be organized, what kind of equality would citizenship mean? Competing loyalties among territorial, religious and ethnic groups, among social and economic classes, and among competing political ideologies which only occasionally intersected with other divisions in civil society, left the issue of state sovereignty in question. Clashes among those claiming authority affected the efficacy of inherited political institutions and the success of the constitution-drafting enterprise. At the country's inception, the gap between politics and governance was wide and not fully understood. These were the problems and conflicts that the superior judiciary mediated even before a constitution was written.

## Constitutional politics

The state was established by two Acts of the British parliament, the 1935 Government of India Act, which provided a measure of self-rule to colonial India, and the 1947 Indian Independence Act. Both, but particularly the former, held fast to ideas of strong centralized rule embodied in the British vice-regal state. The 1935 Act was imperial, equal parts autocracy and democracy. It established the office and powers of the Governor-General to represent the British Crown for the purposes of the Government of the Dominion. Section five, which established the structure of governance, operated as Pakistan's constitution until a new one was finally framed. It was supplemented by the 1947 Act, which brought the Constituent Assembly into existence. While the 1935 Act gave pre-eminence to the Governor-General, the 1947 Act gave the Assembly charge of national affairs and the crucial task of drafting the constitution. In short order, relationships between the executive and legislatures in Pakistan came into profound conflict; these contests became paradigmatic for politics for the next several decades.

Although the 1935 Act allowed for legislative representation, historically it had also allowed the Governor-General to dismiss provincial governments at will. The power to dismiss was withdrawn by the British just prior to independence in response to Congress Party pressure; before the Second World War, Congress had objected to this power and had secured promises from the British that it would not be used against it. After independence, however, Governor-General Jinnah reinserted this authority for Pakistan.

Provincial assemblies were largely the domain of political parties dominated by traditionally powerful families and personalities who on occasion elevated personal prejudice to the level of policy. Members of the first Constituent Assembly were elected by the provinces in indirect elections held in 1946; conflicts between the provinces and the center were to be expected once the new central government exerted its authority. Provincial party leaders vigorously opposed the Governor-General's statutory powers and the potential for conflict between the center and the provinces was underscored by the Governor-General's residual powers. He could dismiss ministries, declare states of emergency and issue ordinances of indefinite validity, whether or not a legislature was sitting – powers he exercised liberally and frequently. (Between 1947 and 1956, the Constituent Assembly passed 160 laws, while the Governor-General issued 376 ordinances.) The 1947 Act gave the Governor-General broad discretionary powers to adapt the 1935 Act without the advice of ministers or legislatures. Indeed, the Act vested more powers in the Governor-General than had been invested in the Viceroy. In inevitable executive-legislative battles, the Governor-General was generally helped by the establishment that comprised the state and the military that supported it. Responding to models of governance which resembled autocracy, the enabling acts helped to lay the groundwork for authoritarianism.

The one branch of government that seemed largely autonomous was the judiciary, and the 1935 Act guaranteed its freedom. Judges were often civil servants appointed through the bureaucracy to ensure autonomy from political interference, although this recruitment and appointment procedure also tied the courts to the executive. Many were also drawn from the bar and became members of the judicial hierarchy. In their judicial capacities, however, superior court judges were generally left to their own counsel and their judgments often challenged the exercise of executive authority. All participants in the political arena used the courts to air their views, challenge their opponents and occasionally redress their grievances: a list of superior court cases read like a directory of the country's political elite, all of whom used the courts as ancillary political organs, as they still do. The courts responded with alacrity, and often clarity, when citizen rights were limited. For example, in *Sobo Gian Chandani's case*, Karachi High Court Justice Z.H. Lari (who had been a Muslim League leader in India until after partition) defended the right to belong to the Communist Party. Later, journalists detained under security laws were released by the courts, and when Jamaat-i-Islami leader Maulana Moudoodi was denied a passport, the courts disallowed the government's action. The courts were thus called upon to intercede on behalf of civil society when the legislature was unable to do so, when the constitution-making apparatus was in disarray and when conflicts between the executive and the legislature rendered both moot. Even when the judicial record was uneven or inconsistent, courts provided the only bridge between the political and administrative systems. This role was particularly significant in the process of drafting a constitution.

The Constituent Assembly's obligations were to frame a new constitution for the new state and conduct the business of a federal legislature for the Dominion. The politics of constitution-making and law-making constantly intruded on each other, protracting the business of framing a constitution, muddling the daily affairs of state and lengthening the life of the Assembly. No method for reconstituting the Assembly existed: many members held dual roles in the federal cabinet or served as provincial ministers while also serving in the Assembly; as members died or were removed by intra-party wrangling, new members were appointed by those who remained rather than elected by the public, further removing the Assembly from public opinion and electoral choice. Although the public was aware of the Assembly's continuing inertia, which the Karachi press covered in detail during legislative and constitutional sessions, there was little public display of outrage or concern. Constitution-drafting seemed removed from the process of building and living in the new state.

Given the distance between the Assembly's political roots and the task for which it was empowered, drafting a constitutive document was insuperably difficult; the Assembly long outlived expectations that it would quickly dissolve itself and provide for new elections under a new constitution. After forming several committees to frame basic constitutional principles, the Assembly discovered that the canons of the nation were many and divergent. Its Basic Principles Committee took eighteen months to write a preambular Objectives Resolution that could pass muster with secularists, Islamic modernists and traditionalists alike. The subcommittee on fundamental rights never produced a draft acceptable to all its members, evidencing profound disagreements about the scope of the state, the rights of individuals and the nature of institutions to protect them; the subcommittee on governance found itself deeply divided about the separation of powers; the subcommittee on the electorate never composed a franchise system that successfully resolved representation disputes between the east and west wings. Each committee was plagued by its perceptions of inheritance, contingency and possibility: whether the state was a home for Muslims or symbolized Islamic nationhood, whether citizens of different communities were equal before the law, whether power could be balanced among groups of unequal population and resources, whether power and territory should be coterminous, whether a strong executive would harness or hamper political progress. Most critically, economic, social and political inequalities between the two wings seemed almost immune to constitutional mediation and strained the drafting process.

The constitution-making that began with independence continued without resolution through 1954. The process of drafting the constitution called into question not only the identity and representativeness of those empowered to produce the document, but also the traditional idea that a written constitution would limit government: the obtrusiveness of the Governor-General suggested instead that he would limit the constitution. In fact, after a succession of short-lived parliamentary and executive heads, former Finance Minister Ghulam Mohammed became Governor-General in 1953 and moved to consolidate his powers by proposing his own constitutional model, separate from those of the Constituent Assembly.

In conflicts between Governors-General and the Assembly, battles were fought on the ground of legislative and executive powers. This problem found a crucial focus in the question of the Governor-General's formal assent to Assembly actions. Were assent required to legitimate legislative acts, then the Governor-General could veto particular laws as well as the Assembly's proposed constitution. Because Ghulam Mohammed wanted to retain his own powers and control the bureaucracy and military, such a prospect was certainly possible – risking the Assembly's concept of legislative sovereignty, its draft constitution and the future of constitutional government.

The Assembly rarely brought legislation to the Governor-General for assent. Section 6(3) of the 1947 Act stipulated that the Governor-General "shall have full power to assent to any law of the Legislature of the Dominion," language that opened space between opportunity and requirement. Consistently maintaining that assent was unnecessary, the Assembly had promulgated Rule No. 62 as early as 1948, which provided for copies of bills simply to be signed by the President. From 1949 to 1954, at least forty-six major pieces of Assembly legislation were passed without explicit assent from the Governor-General. Nevertheless, he acted pursuant to these laws and issued orders under them, and the federal courts tried defendants under them. The Governor-General challenged neither their substance nor the procedures under which they were adopted.

When several cases brought before the superior courts indirectly took up the issue of assent, their judgments seemed to assume that legislative acts did not require assent, or that assent was implicit when none was explicitly issued. In *Mohammed Ayub Khuhro v. Federation of Pakistan* (PLD 1950 Sind 49), the Governor-General's attorney, Manzur Qadir, suggested that the 1947 Indian Independence Act did not require assent for Assembly actions undertaken in its constitution-making capacity. The Sind High Court agreed, writing that "there is no limit imposed upon the legislative powers of the Constituent Assembly sitting as a constitution making body." In two contemporaneous cases,[1] the question of assent was not discussed. In a judgment of greater proportion, the Federal Court considered the *Rawalpindi Conspiracy case*, a highly publicized case concerning alleged conspirators against the state.[2] The Constituent Assembly passed a law condemning the alleged conspirators before the courts had so ruled. The Federal Court ignored the absence of the Governor-General's assent when it could have highlighted the tension between the legislature and the executive.

In the same year, the Constituent Assembly set out deliberately to confront the Governor-General and underline its own powers. It amended the 1935 Government of India Act by adding Section 223-A to underscore the power of the High Courts by giving them the power to issue prerogative writs – giving individuals the power to challenge the state through the courts and anticipating individual rights protections planned for the new

1 *Khan Iftikhar Hussain Khan of Mamdot v. Province of the Punjab* (PLD 1950 FC 15), and *Sarfaraz Ali v. The Crown* (PLD 1951 FC 78). *Mamdot* concerned the application of the Public and Representative Offices (Disqualification) Act to the former Punjab Premier and the sovereignty of the federal legislature. In *Sarfaraz* (the Montgomery Murder Case), the appeal noted that "the validity of the [West Punjab Public Safety Act, 1949] and consequently the legality of the trial as a summons case, was impugned . . . on the ground that it had not received the assent of the Governor-General of Pakistan."

On the issue of assent, Justice Muhammed Bakhsh later noted in the first *Tamizuddin Khan* case that "the Federal Court knew very well that no assent of the Governor-General had been obtained to this Act of the constituent Assembly, and therefore it must be taken for granted that the Federal Court did not think that assent to be necessary."

2 *Ex-Major-General Akbar Khan and Faiz Ahmad Faiz v. The Crown* (PLD 1954 FC 87). Discussing this case in the context of rights questions several years later, Justice M.R. Kayani observed that "we neither approved of those prisoners nor disapproved of them, but we released them to maintain a balance of forces in society." "Misfortunes come not alone," Address to Karachi Bar Association, 11 December 1958, in Kayani, *The Whole Truth* (Lahore: Pakistan Writers' Cooperative Society, 1988).

constitution.[3] Like prior laws, the amendment was not sent to the Governor-General for assent. The Assembly passed two additional, confrontational laws. The Deputy President of the Assembly, M.H. Gazdar, reintroduced a bill first submitted in 1951 to repeal the Public and Representative Offices Disqualification Act (PRODA) of 1949, labeling it "a disgrace to the Statute Book."[4] This ordinance was promulgated by the Governor-General to disqualify politicians from holding political office and thus reduce opposition to his rule; its repeal (PRODA Repealing Act, 21 September 1954) limited the Governor-General's powers over individual politicians. He did not object, offering instead to remove the disqualifications he had imposed. The Assembly also amended the 1935 Act to limit the Governor-General's choice of cabinet ministers and to make ministerial advice binding. The amendments, introduced by Law Minister A.K. Brohi, asserted Assembly sovereignty by strengthening its ties to the Cabinet.[5] They required the Governor-General to appoint as Prime Minister a member of the Federal Legislature who enjoyed the confidence of the majority, and further required all ministers to be Assembly members with collective responsibility to the Assembly; ministerial counsel was obligatory, and the Cabinet would lose its authority were a vote of no confidence passed against any of its members.

Although the Assembly's action echoed common parliamentary practice, to the bureaucracy and executive it appeared as political misrepresentation disguised as a claim of legislative sovereignty: by protecting politicians against arbitrary dismissal, writ petitions strengthened their individual and collective hands in contests with the Governor-General. For politicians, however, such laws were essential were the façade of parliamentary sovereignty to be maintained. Frequent arrests in Sind and East Pakistan in 1954 under the Public Safety Acts, the continuing imposition of emergency in East Pakistan (under Section 92A of the 1935 Act), and the dismissal of East Pakistani politicians for agitating for autonomy created an intensely politicized environment in which the central executive appeared to strengthen his powers. The Constituent Assembly confronted the Governor-General on the same grounds that the Governor-General had used in dismissing ministers in the East and West, and the Assembly tried to protect itself and its members statutorily. Politicians continued to argue about whether executive-legislative division strengthened or weakened prospects for democracy, but it became

[3] Government of India (Amendment) Act, 1954, passed by the constituent Assembly on 16 July 1954 as an insertion into the 1935 Act.

[4] 20 September 1954. See National Assembly of Pakistan, *Constitution-Making in Pakistan* (Islamabad 1975), pp. 5–6.

[5] Sections 9, 10, 10(A), 10(B), and 17.

clear that the structure of government and the content of political debate hinged upon political ideas that seemed to admit of little compromise.

On the heels of these two amendments, the Constituent Assembly adopted a new report from its Basic Principles Committee; although only forty of its seventy-four members were present, this move paved the way for the Assembly to consider its draft constitution. In a national broadcast on 1 October 1954, and again on 23 October, the Prime Minister announced that the final phase of constitution-making would be completed by late December.

### Contesting constitution-making

Governor-General Ghulam Mohammed responded swiftly to these measures. On 24 October 1954 he announced that "the constitutional machinery has broken down," and declared a state of emergency. Stating that "the Constituent Assembly as at present constituted has lost the confidence of the people and can no longer function," he effectively (although not explicitly in his Proclamation) dissolved the Assembly and reconstituted the Cabinet with individuals from outside the Assembly. The Assembly hall was closed, its president, Bengali politician Maulvi Tamizuddin Khan, was ousted from his government-assigned house, and a climate of crisis engulfed Karachi. Maulvi Tamizuddin Khan responded with a petition to the Sind High Court for writs of *mandamus* and *quo warranto* to restrain the Governor-General and the new Cabinet from giving effect to the Proclamation and dissolution. This case began seven months of constitutional trials. It was the first of several to examine the nature and scope of executive authority in Pakistan, and one of the few whose decision supported unequivocally the rights of those who challenged it.

#### *Maulvi Tamizuddin's Khan's case*

In *Maulvi Tamizuddin Khan v. The Federation of Pakistan* (PLD 1955 Sind 96) the High Court examined three issues: whether the Governor-General's assent was needed to validate Assembly actions and whether the absence of assent invalidated them; whether the Governor-General had the right to dissolve the Assembly; and whether the writ petitions fell within the High Court's jurisdiction. More generally, the High Court was asked to determine the extent of the Assembly's powers, its relationship to the executive and the judiciary's authority to limit executive authority.

The issue of assent was vital to the Governor-General's argument because the writ petition was filed under Section 223-A of the 1935 Act.

Relying on past judgments and the Governor-General's actions pursuant to Assembly acts without assent, Chief Justice Constantine quickly dismissed this "novel objection," noting that "if accepted [it] would upset a consistent course of practice and understanding." As Justice Muhammad Bakhsh noted, all parties to the dispute had been acting as if assent were unnecessary. The court therefore ruled that assent was not needed for constitution-making; indeed, Justice Bakhsh claimed that the Assembly "could even repeal the whole of 1935 Act." The Constituent Assembly was a sovereign body, the Governor-General's authority was limited in the 1935 Act by the Assembly's constitutive powers, and "both the powers of assent and dissolution are provisions relating to the Constitution." Therefore, the power of dissolution was limited. Proposing that Commonwealth custom required dissolution only "by express provision in the Constitution," Chief Justice Constantine concluded that the "purported dissolution is a nullity in law." Responding to concerns that the Constituent Assembly's tenure seemed unending, Justice Bakhsh noted that the 1947 Act had specifically withdrawn the Governor-General's power to dissolve the federal legislature: "If you need the statutory authority to dissolve a body whose life is only five years, your need of that power is a number of times greater when the life is unlimited."

The High Court decided in favor of legislative supremacy in the constitution-making arena, a decision it viewed as politically progressive. Citing a 1920 ruling of the House of Lords, Justice Bakhsh reiterated a classic statement of the British civil liberties tradition with parliament as protector of individual rights: "The growth of constitutional liberties has largely consisted in the reduction of the discretionary power of the executive, and in the extension of parliamentary protection in favour of the subject."[6] Sorry as the performance of the Constituent Assembly might be, its freedom from the Governor-General and the Crown was most important: "The people of India were given the freedom and the independence to frame any Constitution they liked and to do what they liked with their own Constituent Assembly." Once the High Court ruled unanimously against the Governor-General on the issues of assent and dissolution, it turned to its own authority to overturn his actions. The Sind Court's strong statement that section 223-A provided grounds for its jurisdiction also provided the grounds for appeal to the Federal Court. Chief Justice Constantine was troubled by jurisdictional questions, however, and asked whether the High Court "can . . . issue writs where the authority is within its limits, but the subject-matter lies without its limits?" He concluded that the reach of the federal government superseded explicit authority.

[6] *Attorney-General v. De Keyser's Royal Hotel, Limited,* Law Rep. 1920, App. Ca. 508.

The Sind Court's sympathy for Maulvi Tamizuddin's petition betrayed its strong bias toward legislative sovereignty, however indeterminate. The court discussed theoretical relationships among the Constituent Assembly, federal legislature and the Governor-General, but did not take up the substance of the Proclamation that had precipitated the Assembly's institutional crisis. By concluding that the Assembly, its President and the original Cabinet still existed, the court set aside serious political problems raised by amendments to the 1935 Act and the repeal of PRODA – each of which could lead to further conflicts. The High Court was also silent on the problem of the Assembly's continuing tenure, despite the Governor-General's claim that the Assembly's unrepresentativeness made it illegitimate. The court thus set a course for judicial consideration of future constitutional crises. As standard appellate procedure dictated, superior courts almost always refused to consider the factual merits of the cases before them. Determining whether political crisis was or was not imminent was not a responsibility the Sind Court saw for itself. It was concerned with conceptual issues surrounding the establishment and continuance of state institutions, not with the political environment in which they lived and which of course formed the backdrop for its hearings. The High Court quietly stated a preference for caution that would be raised to the level of doctrine by the Federal Court. The institutional consequences of this attitude became apparent as the appeal proceeded.

Maulvi Tamizuddin Khan's first hearing received strong support for the Assembly and its constitutional duties. The Governor-General disagreed. He was convinced that a political crisis was precipitated by the Assembly and its proposed constitution – equating a diminution of his powers with a national emergency – and with his newly constituted Cabinet challenged the High Court's authority to review his actions.

### *The Federation Appeal*

The Federal Court heard *Maulvi Tamizuddin Khan's case* while the parties to the conflict were jockeying for a non-judicial conclusion to their problems. Parliamentary government in East Pakistan remained suspended, a PRODA case was pending against Chief Minister Mohammed Ayub Khuhro in the Sind High Court, and deposed Sind Chief Minister Pirzada was contesting the Governor-General's right to remove him from office – conditions that the Governor-General equated with the disintegration of the state. The same central Cabinet ministers involved in political negotiations and the Federation appeal were empowered to decide the fate of the provincial government and were involved in the Sind provincial dispute. During the appeal, Chief Justice Munir suggested that the question presented for judicial determination was primarily political and better resolved among the disputing parties instead of "washing their dirty linen in public." Although the court was not a party to negotiations, they were discussed in court as background to the legal proceedings and the justices' interpolations peppered these proceedings.[7] Nonetheless, the respective conditions of both parties were never close enough for compromise: Maulvi Tamizuddin Khan wanted to convene a new Constituent Assembly through direct elections on the basis of adult suffrage; other parties proposed new indirect elections for an Assembly to frame a provisional constitution; and the Governor-General demanded general elections and acceptance of his new cabinet and the constitution he was drafting independently.

In his appeal, the Governor-General had a second opportunity to air his views about his role in Pakistan's government and the Constituent Assembly had another chance to restate its claims of sovereignty. The Federal Court, more sympathetic to the Governor-General than the Sind Court had been, took the occasion to develop a theory of judicial review for Pakistan.

*The Federation of Pakistan v. Moulvi Tamizuddin Khan* (PLD 1955 Federal Court 240) pitted two important constitutionalists against one another for the first but certainly not the last time. In his long tenure on the Federal Court, Chief Justice Muhammad Munir, already known for his service on the Lahore High Court, made his mark defending executive authority and figured prominently in constitutional cases for the rest of the decade. The lone dissenter in the appeal, Justice A.R. Cornelius, offered equally forceful alternative notions of popular sovereignty and constitutional government. The appeal to *Maulvi Tamizuddin Khan's case* offered a view of Pakistani politics in 1955 and foretold sharp political and jurisprudential disagreements to come.

With its determination that the Governor-General's assent was required to legalize Assembly actions, the Federal Court dismissed most of the substantive issues raised in the High Court case. The absence of assent to section 223-A of the 1935 Act meant that it was not law; the High Court therefore had no jurisdiction to issue the writs requested by Maulvi Tamizuddin Khan. If the Governor-General did not acquiesce to

7 This account of the trial and the subsequent *Reference* of the Governor-General, relies in part on reporting in the *Civil and Military Gazette* (Lahore) [*CMG*]. The Federation appeal was covered from 2 March 1955 to 4 April 1955, when the judgment was announced; the *Reference* was covered from 26 April to its judgment on 11 May 1955. See "Appeal against Sind Chief Court decision," *CMG* 8 March 1955, p. 1; and "Tamizuddin Case Appeal," 11 March 1955.

an abridgement of his powers, no diminution could occur. This opinion doomed the writs and the Assembly's draft constitution. The court based its judgment on a close reading of the relationship between the English Crown and Dominion government defined in the 1935 Act, a reading that underscored executive powers at the expense of the Assembly's sovereignty. Because the Governor-General's presence was the Crown's limit on the Assembly's powers, assent was "indispensable" to validate laws.

Justice Cornelius's dissent highlighted conflicts between the 1935 and 1947 Acts. Like the High Court, Cornelius understood the Governor-General's responsibility in the context of the country's independence – "independent dominion" – rather than the more colonial reading offered by the Federal Court majority. Emphasizing the legislature's exclusive right to limit its own actions, he affirmed the Constituent Assembly's broad sovereignty – "a body created by a supra-legal power to discharge the supra-legal function of preparing a Constitution for Pakistan" – and noted that the Governor-General's responsibilities were only "to the Constitution." He therefore argued that Constituent Assembly sovereignty superseded the Governor-General's, whose functions were circumscribed by the Assembly's power to amend the 1935 Act. Cornelius's opinion directly contradicted the majority. He read the Independence Act as a deliberate expression of legislative autonomy "intended to be *absolute*." He derived his concept of legislative supremacy first from the compelling task at hand – framing the constitution and thus making the state concrete – and second from the fact that the Assembly was an elected body, thus linking concepts of legislative powers and popular sovereignty.

Despite its dismissal of the Assembly's challenge, the Federal Court analyzed at length its own views of Pakistan's future government. These arguments are as important as the decision itself, for they address vital issues of sovereignty, representation and democracy.

Chief Justice Munir noted that the 1947 Independence Act offered no guidance "if the Constituent Assembly did not or was not able to make a constitution, or resigned en bloc, or converted itself into a perpetual legislature." He suggested that "if a breakdown came ... it was for the Dominion itself to reset the tumbled down machinery." To explain his method for resurrection, he hypothesized a conflict between sovereign government and democracy: "Since sovereignty as applied to states imports the supreme, absolute, uncontrollable power by which a State is governed, and democracy recognizes all ultimate power as resting in the people, it is obvious that in the case of a confiict between the ultimate and legal sovereign, the latter must yield." This statement suggests that the elected legislature would gain paramount authority, but Munir's reading of Pakistani politics reversed this stance: "An irremovable legislature ...

is not only a negation of democracy but is the worst calamity that can befall a nation because it tends to perpetuate an oligarchic rule." Such sentiment, and the poor record of the long-lived Assembly, grounded many of his questions to Advocate-General Fayyaz Ali. The duration of the first Constituent Assembly might have given his argument a certain force, were it not for the fact that the Assembly was dismissed only after it had completed its drafting tasks. In truth, the Governor-General objected to the Assembly's product, not its membership; the Federal Court, however, allowed this political dispute to move the terms of its considerations away from those framed by the Sind Court. Additionally, Chief Justice Munir did not carry this point to its furthest conclusion. He did not, therefore, take up the parallel question of oligarchy posed by an appointed cabinet acting in concert with an appointed Governor-General for an unspecified period without explicit accountability.

Defining constitutionalism as a limit on the legislature, Munir set the groundwork for executive supremacy and intervention. A constitution, he proposed, organizes and limits the structure of government and "expresses the consent by which the people actually establish the state itself." His outline was neater than reality affirmed. The social contract to establish the state was neither plain nor presumed; indeed, the absence of a universally accepted, popular ideology helped to cause the country's divisive social and political tensions and was reflected in the inadequacies of its state institutions.

Moreover, Chief Justice Munir assumed that "consent" was the duty of the executive to articulate, "as Government is the responsibility of the executive in a constitution." His concept of executive power accompanied a cautionary nod toward legislative limits and the need for "some power competent to dissolve the Assembly." His decision echoed almost fully the Governor-General's case and offered a framework for wide executive authority. This was the setting in which the court required the Governor-General's assent to Constituent Assembly actions. While agreeing that the dominion legislature should be able to remove its restrictions, the Chief Justice wanted to restrict the circumstances under which this was possible: assent expressed the hierarchy of powers within government. He was particularly unhappy with the Assembly's requirement that the Governor-General abide by ministerial advice because it left open the possibility that the Governor-General could be recalled or removed, leaving dominion status uncertain.

The Chief Justice thus wrote his personal predilections into his constitutional analysis, particularly his low opinion of the prevailing political climate: "If the result is disaster, it will merely be another instance of how thoughtlessly the Constituent Assembly proceeded with its business and by assuming for itself the position of an irremovable legislature to what straits it has brought the country." But Munir's reasoning was circular. He already assumed strict limits on Assembly powers, claiming that "it lived in a fool's paradise if it was ever seized with the notion that it was the sovereign body in the State." His preference for an assertive executive led him to castigate the Assembly and propose that the Governor-General purposefully push his position to the fullest extent: "By withholding assent to an unpopular measure he can create a constitutional crisis of the first magnitude, and though eventually he himself may have to go, he can in appropriate cases rivet the attention of the country to the caprice, cupidity or folly of the Legislature." Riveting the country's attention was, of course, precisely what had happened when the Governor-General and the Assembly disputed the question of assent in the first place. Rather than amplify the tensions between the 1935 and 1947 Acts and between the theories of politics which led to the constitutional stalemate, or find a route between them, the Chief Justice came down unabashedly in favor of the Governor-General. The political consequences of this choice, ignored in this judgment, were profound.

Indeed, Munir occasionally interjected his genuine fears were unfettered dissolution not possible. When the Advocate-General asked "what would be the position if it was supposed that the Constituent Assembly got innoculated by Communistic ideas against the wishes of the people," Justice Munir promptly responded, "Revolution with a capital R," to which the Advocate General returned, "Dissolution with a capital D, my lord." This implicit equation of constitutional dissension with political cataclysm, the basis of the Governor-General's presentation, colored the court's view of executive authority and thus its ruling.

Facing political conditions that did not fit the expectations of either the 1935 or 1947 Acts, Justices Munir and Cornelius embodied strongly contrary views about the nature of constitutional governance. Munir saw the government and the Governor-General as one and accepted the Governor-General's actions as a natural response to political exigencies. He assumed that the Governor-General had every right to step between the Assembly and the citizenry when conditions were strained (and when it violated his concept of his office). For Munir, the Assembly's power to make laws did not define its sovereignty; rather, the Governor-General did so by setting limits to its actions. Cornelius, on the other hand, viewed the Governor-General's actions as an extraordinary and improper exercise of executive power that restricted Assembly sovereignty. The rules of the Assembly were reflexive; they could not breach interference from the Governor-General without sharply reformulating the character of the Assembly as a whole and the bargain it could strike with its constituents.

If sovereignty reposed in the citizenry then the Assembly required autonomy from the executive.

In addition, Justice Cornelius stated explicitly what Chief Justice Munir only hinted, and perhaps tried to understate: that power and authority are not the same. The Governor-General's powers included the appointment of provincial governors, military chiefs, diplomats and federal court justices – real powers with tangible consequences for the state. Munir minimized the Governor-General's political weight while simultaneously underlining his legal authority; Cornelius premised his opinion on the Governor-General's structural importance in the state and the need to make such authority accountable. Noting the Governor-General's considerable power and correlate duty to protect the country from imminent demise, Cornelius noted that "his action, when purporting to be taken in exercise of this power and duty, would be above the law, and, consequently, not justiciable." To prescribe a political organization in which the executive was beyond the reach of the courts would be to structure a polity wholly different from that envisioned in either constitutive act, and might well lie beyond the Chief Justice's concept of democracy as well.

The judicial role was thus of principal concern to the court. Both sides agreed that the court should define the limits of the two Acts and ensure that all institutions abided by that definition. (The government consistently announced that it would abide by the court's decision, but never indicated its plans were its case not upheld.)[8] They both interpreted the judicial role as legal rather than political: the Chief Justice stated unequivocally that "the only issue . . . is whether the legal power existed or not, and not whether it was properly and rightly exercised, which is a purely political issue." Munir questioned the judicial role only to criticize the Sind High Court, asking "whether it is a wise exercise of discretion for the judiciary to reinstall in power a deposed government by issuing enforceable writs against a de facto government." His comment dismissed any distinction between *de jure* and *de facto* governance, offering a more explicit nod to judicial prudence than the Sind High Court had expressed. In this sense, the Federal Court may not have wanted to legitimize the Governor-General's actions but thought it necessary to bow to his powers. Later, this precept seemed to demonstrate the court's early predilection to support the government of the day.

Both the majority and minority opinions tacitly acknowledged the serious political problems they claimed were outside judicial jurisdiction. For example, Justice Akram noted that without assent "all the convicts

[8] *CMG* 11 March 1955, p. 8.

and criminals would be released," and proposed that "it was the responsibility of everyone to ensure that no confusion or chaos was created in the administration."[9] The High Court judgment, seconded by Justice Cornelius, would have reinstated Maulvi Tamizuddin Khan and the original Assembly and Cabinet, held the Governor-General to the laws the Assembly passed and conferred upon the Assembly the authority to limit the Governor-General. It would have offered a *modus operandi* between the 1935 and 1947 Acts and among the institutions they created until a constitution was approved. It also could have paved the way for the Assembly's draft constitution. Whether those institutions would have functioned effectively – whether salvation from dissolution would have sobered the Assembly sufficiently to discipline its work, or provided impetus to compromise on its draft constitution – and whether the proposed 1954 constitution would have been workable, given both its genesis and its assumptions, are questions which could neither be raised nor answered by the court. Surely, however, they were in the minds of its members. By upholding the Assembly dissolution and expanded executive powers, the Federal Court resolved limited legal questions but did not resolve the consuming political crisis. When the Chief Justice said that the court's duty "is rightly to expound the law in complete indifference to any popular reaction," he presumed that Governor-General Ghulam Mohammed would try to create a new legislative body, possibly with a new structure and almost certainly with new members.

With this judgment the possibility disappeared that a constitution with limited executive powers would see the light of day, but the Governor-General's role was still unspecified. During the hearing, the Governor-General's counsel, Kenneth Diplock, suggested that the Governor-General was now head of state, "a position much more independent than was held by the Governor-General under the Government of India Act" – an interpretation of the 1935 Act that Maulvi Tamizuddin Khan's counsel, I.I. Chundrigar, energetically contradicted.[10] Such extensive powers would mean that the Governor-General could step into any constitutional breach he perceived without validation from other political or legal authority. (This was the reason Diplock later proposed the maxim "salus populi suprema lex est" to underscore the doctrine of necessity in the Reference that followed this appeal.) Although the dissolution was validated, the court did not explicitly determine to replace representative with appointed government, or legislative with executive institutions.

9 "Chundrigar's Arguments," *CMG* 15 March 1955, p. 8.

10 "Diplock Continues Argument," *CMG* 9 March 1955, p. 1; "Hearing Against Sind Chief Court Judgment," *CMG* 10 March 1955; "Chundrigar Defines the Term 'Law'," *CMG* 15 March 1955, p. 3.

A *Civil and Military Gazette* editorial at the beginning of the trial accurately expressed the situation by its end:

Pakistan's problem is of the nature of a dilemma. If she follows the form of democracy, and lets the common man do with the country whatever he like it is like arming school boys with loaded pistols who are sure to smash the whole show. In case we pursue the substance of democracy, as do those who advocate "controlled" democracy, we run the risk of side-tracking the correct democratic process toward some sort of authoritarianism. It is in the midst of these two perilous paths that our leadership must steer their course.[11]

The editorial set aside the prospect of "full-blooded democracy," noting that the country's "highest interests – solidarity, integrity, security, good government – will have to take precedence of every other consideration." The choice "between the substance and the shadow" was the court's as well.

### *Constitutional interlude*

The appeal left a raft of unvalidated laws and no self-evident method for giving them effect. Almost everything the dissolved Constituent Assembly accomplished was rendered moot by the Federal Court's decision, but neither the court's ruling nor the Governor-General's October proclamation offered a way to convene a new legislature, draft a new constitution or give retrospective authority to the Assembly's work.

To fill the legal vacuum, the Governor-General issued a wide-ranging Emergency Powers Ordinance (IX of 1955) to validate retrospectively the bills passed by the Assembly without his assent, but was prohibited from doing so in *Usif Patel and 2 others v. the Crown* (PLD 1955 FC 387). The court ruled that a 1948 act that extended the Governor-General's power in the constitution-making arena had itself never been validated, so that revisions of the 1935 Act pursuant to it were also invalid. Its *Usif Patel* judgment removed the legal sting from the *Tamizuddin Khan* decision. The court placed the Governor-General on notice that his authority, upheld in the Federation appeal, was still limited. At the same time, the Federal Court prohibited the federal legislature from entering the constitutional field. With undisguised frustration it observed that "a more incongruous position in a democratic constitution is difficult to conceive particularly when the legislature itself, which can control the Governor-General's action, is alleged to have been dissolved." In response, the Governor-General issued yet another proclamation assuming all necessary powers of validation and enforcement to see the country through the

[11] "Pakistan's Dilemma," *CMG* 6 March 1955, p. 4.

continuing preconstitutional period. It temporarily circumvented the court's decision by asserting that the validity of the ordinance was immune to legal challenge.

Concurrently, the Governor-General announced plans for a new Constitutional Convention and heralded a solution to the contentious issue of parity among the provinces. With the assistance of Punjab Governor Mushtaq Gurmani, the Governor-General assumed powers to merge the provinces of West Pakistan to create "One Unit" as a balance to populous, and politically argumentative, East Bengal. The government portrayed this move as an administrative convenience and a political imperative to fulfill the "romance of unity" for the country. Bahawalpur, Khairpur and the Baluchistan States Union lost their autonomy, and the provinces of Sind, Punjab and the Frontier were merged into West Pakistan; only the small frontier states of Chitral, Dir and Swat were exempted from the plan. Many politicians had outlined schemes for zonal federations of various sorts for several years, and a similar plan had been percolating in government circles for some time; most other plans, however, had retained the basic structure of existing provinces that One Unit now proposed to erase.

One Unit was structured to give the Governor-General extensive powers in the new constitution that he planned to promulgate by ordinance.[12] He imposed One Unit imperially, disposed of chief ministers who objected to its promulgation, imprisoned politicians who spoke against it and generally outlawed political organizing.[13] The Punjabi-dominated bureaucracy fashioned the province of West Pakistan along administrative lines similar to the central government, ruling the province as it had the center. The discord and disorder of provincial autonomy was, in theory, harmonized. During a long public relations campaign to sell the One Unit plan, Prime Minister Mohammed Ali castigated the "artificial boundaries" of "provincialism." Claiming that smaller provinces were not justified politically or administratively, he invoked the

[12] The *CMG* reported that, despite objections from "powerful political elements," the Governor-General intended to have the constituent convention pass the constitution "as already drafted by the Central Cabinet." "Constitution through ordinance," 31 March 1955.

[13] Sind Chief Minister Pirzada was dismissed for opposing One Unit and was replaced by former Chief Minister Khuhro, who supported the plan in exchange for ending his protracted contests against PRODA charges. Khuhro was in litigation as of March 1955, when the Sind High Court maintained that PRODA was still operative because the Supreme Court had held the PRODA Disqualification Act invalid in the *Tamizuddin Khan* appeal. Khuhro's attorney, arguing in favor of the disqualification provisions, was Manzur Qadir. The Governor-General also pressured Punjab Chief Minister Feroz Khan Noon to conform to his plans and forced changes in the Frontier government so that it would approve his plans.

rhythms of Jinnah's plea for non-sectarianism in the first Constituent Assembly, saying "within a short time people will cease to think of themselves as Punjabis, Sindhis, Baluchis or Pathans. Instead they will begin to think of themselves as Pakistanis."[14] Not everyone was so inclined. Baluch leaders defied the ban on politics by organizing a new party, Ustoman Gal, specifically to oppose One Unit, and renewed the demands for a unified Baluchistan that had simmered since independence. Later, the Khan of Kalat organized widespread demonstrations and an autonomy movement against One Unit that helped to spur the military's intervention in politics in 1958. Continuing opposition to One Unit led to even greater dissent fifteen years later, culminating in the end of One Unit but also the civil war that led to the separation of East Pakistan from the west.

Majority and minority parties in both provinces nevertheless tried to position themselves for maximum influence in the new constituent body or, like some Frontier politicians, against it. Political scrambling began once the Governor-General issued his order for a new constitutional convention: some parties proposed new methods of representation; others, like the Frontier Awami League and the Khudai Khidmatgars, demanded that the constitutional question of One Unit be popularly validated. The result was predictable confusion. Seeking a route out of the political and legal stalemate, and hoping to impose order upon unruly politicians, the Governor-General took the advice of former Chief Justice Mian Abdur Rashid and requested an advisory opinion from the Federal Court on his plans (*Reference by His Excellency the Governor-General*, PLD 1955 FC 435, Advisory Jurisdiction).

The court now faced the same problems which first brought *Maulvi Tamizuddin Khan's case* to the bench: who should lead the country; on what basis should franchise be organized; how should the institutions of state function; and what role should the judiciary play in answering these questions? The same players acted in this third iteration of the sovereignty dispute but the structure of the *Reference* gave the court occasion for broader analysis. Its arguments offered a range of views about the

[14] Broadcasts of 24 November 1954 and 1 December 1954 published in *Pakistan Times News Digest* (Karachi). The Governor-General's concerns about political fragmentation were reflected in a constitutional draft prepared by Sir Ivor Jennings that would have replaced the parliamentary system with a presidential one "by way of experiment" that "was not intended, as was alleged at the time, to produce an undemocratic system. On the contrary, it was thought that a system in which the nature of the Government was determined by bargains between leaders of political groups, as in France, was likely to be less democratic." In this period of document writing, the causes of political division, particularly between provinces, were left unexplored, "but it was assumed that party lines would cut across the provincial boundaries." See Jennings, *The Approach to Self-Government* (Boston: Beacon Press, 1956), pp. 17 and 112.

relationship between the Pakistani state and the democracy it was trying to establish.

### *The Governor-General's "Reference"*

The *Reference* placed four problems before the Federal Court: the nature of the Governor-General's office; the proper means to validate prior laws; whether the Governor-General had "rightly dissolved" the Constituent Assembly; and the competency of the proposed Constituent Convention. The court was asked to rule on the institutional nature of the pre-constitutional state and to determine whether the declared emergency was both legal and politically appropriate; it was also asked to examine the principles upon which a new constitution-drafting body could be organized. As before, Justice Cornelius raised the most significant challenge to Chief Justice Munir's views. Circling the legalistic tone of the *Reference*, he proposed more comprehensive and politically charged problems: the legal and political status of the Pakistani state, the Constituent Assembly and the Governor-General.

Despite the far-reaching and objective sound of the *Reference* questions, their structure disposed the court toward the executive (the precise questions were jointly determined by the court and the Governor-General); the factual context in which they were answered was fully determined by the Governor-General. The *Reference* noted the virtual perpetuity of the Constituent Assembly, the Governor-General's sense that it was "wholly unrepresentative" and its claim that his assent was inappropriate and unnecessary. Although the Governor-General documented public opinion to support his diagnosis and Maulvi Tamizuddin Khan offered an extensive affidavit challenging this picture of the political environment (which referred only obliquely to the One Unit fracas that dismissed the Pirzada ministry in Sind),[15] the court did not contest the *Reference*'s and thus the Governor-General's claims. Acknowledging that "the answer to a legal question always depends on facts found or assumed," Justice Munir nevertheless noted that "the Reference has to be answered on the assumption of fact on which it has been made." Justice Cornelius, as he had done in *Tamizuddin Khan's case*, provided his own account of the political context, largely at odds with both the Governor-General and the court.

No matter how Munir phrased the court's appointed task, the answers given to the *Reference* questions all had concrete political results; this, after all, was the reason for seeking an advisory opinion. The status of the

[15] The affadavit was printed in full in *CMG* 6 May 1955.

advisory opinion, however, was not plain. It was not binding, the Governor-General's counsel admitting only that it "shall have a very great persuasive force." The court undertook to offer a legal solution to politically intractable problems but understood that an opinion contrary to the Governor-General might not be upheld. This mixed political message affected the court's method to a degree. The justices alternated between strictly legalistic analysis and more politically consequentialist views of their endeavors. When they chose legalism, they sought to limit the role of the judiciary in solving this constitutional crisis, and more broadly, in influencing the course of politics. When they injected consequentialism into their judgments – sometimes tending toward hyperbolic political forecasts that seemed alternately to project the Governor-General as a cause or a remedy for contemplated chaos – they paved the way for direct judicial intervention in determining the design of the state and its political participants. The former led to a reflexive view of politics that was embodied in Kelsenian judgments later in the decade. The latter proved equally problematic for the court as it continued to seek a proper judicial role in the evolving praetorian state.

*Assent and dissolution* The court's advisory ruling at once modified its earlier support for the Governor-General and provided a firmer foundation for his authority. The broad strokes of the second *Tamizuddin Khan* decision were amplified, if not to reflect a nuanced view of contemporary politics then to note the complex details of governance. It was, as Justice Cornelius remarked to the Advocate-General, "a field where there are no rules." Moderating his own language in the Federation's appeal, Chief Justice Munir gave greater weight to the transitions implied in the 1935 and 1947 Acts:

> If the intention had been to transfer to the Governor-General, as representative of the Crown, the prerogative right of summoning, proroguing and dissolving the Constituent Assembly, the elaborate constitutional structure that was built upon the Independence Act, 1947, and the adapted Government of India Act, 1935, could have been pulled down by the Governor-General ... on the very day he assumed his office and before the Constituent Assembly had even commenced to function.

He also stated explicitly that which had been excluded from the *Tamizuddin Khan* appeal, that "in the case of Pakistan, the Indian Independence Act, 1947, contains no express provision empowering the Governor-General to dissolve the Assembly." Although Chief Justice Munir did not accept Justice Cornelius's declaration that denying the constitution-making process denied the autonomy of Pakistan, he agreed that the

Governor-General must coexist respectfully with future legislatures. He seconded the court's declaration in *Usif Patel* that the Governor-General's and the Assembly's powers were not coterminous and that the Assembly, not the Governor-General, framed laws.

Nevertheless, this judgment did not solve several logical problems. Most important, it was silent on the issue of popular sovereignty and left open the possibility that the Governor-General (and his office) might be unpopular. A colloquy with the attorney for the United Front Assembly Party, Bengali politician Hamidul Haq Chowdhry, proved revealing on this point and foretold the extraordinary problem that would face the Chief Justice when he validated military rule three years later. Noting that the opposition still felt that Assembly dissolution must be self-imposed, the Chief Justice engaged in the following debate:

CHIEF JUSTICE: If there is no power of dissolution anywhere, the only means to get rid of an unrepresentative Assembly would be a revolution.
MR. CHOWDHRY: Ultimately, yes, but there are many stages before the last stage is reached.
CHIEF JUSTICE: Could such a revolution be legal?
MR. CHOWDHRY: No revolution is legal.[16]

Yet, Munir's arguments remained consistent with his earlier judgment as he declared that the Assembly dissolution furthered rather than contravened the 1935 Act. To the charge, originally accepted by Justice Cornelius in *Tamizuddin Khan*, that only the Assembly could dissolve itself "by bowing to the force of public opinion or by revolution," the Chief Justice remarked that "revolutions are not in the contemplation of those who frame constitutions." In 1958, on behalf of the executive rather than the electorate, the Chief Justice would seek a form of legality that could justify revolution, idiosyncratically conceived. In this *Reference* he laid the groundwork by conflating legality and legitimacy.

Munir's comment showed not only the court's deep disappointment with the irresponsibility with which it felt the Assembly had undertaken its duties, but also its view of those duties generally. Justices Munir and Cornelius both believed, although for different reasons, that the unamended 1935 and 1947 Acts provided a democratic provisional constitution for Pakistan. Munir also felt that the Assembly's restrictions on the Governor-General were frivolous and ultimately dangerous. His opinions suggest that no acceptable constitution would change the governance structure provided by those Acts. Were one to object that an appointed Governor-General expressed neither democratic nor representative principles, Justice Munir would argue that only a strong executive, modeled

[16] "Rely on the majesty of will of people," *CMG* 5 May 1955.

on the Governor-General's generous powers, could bridge the country's political chasms to produce democracy. The end, democracy, would justify the means. Similar logical fallacies had bedeviled British attempts to adapt their constitutional arrangements to Indian demands for autonomy without an explicit grant of freedom; at some stage, autocracy and democracy must part.

The 1935 and 1947 Acts were preparatory and constitutive, laws to provide interim government until a new constitution was framed. They were not constitution substitutes: they were not designed to help the country confront its massive state-building challenges, and one can argue that their structures could not provide an adequate basis for satisfying Pakistan's needs. The task of writing such a constitution would have to be transformative more than transitional (perhaps even revolutionary) to succeed – by charting relations among government institutions, fashioning an economic system to link a fragmented nation, restructuring recruitment to state service, and examining prevailing concepts of state security. This constitutional process would be almost twenty more years in coming, and then only briefly, inadequately and self-defeatingly. Chief Justice Munir's persistent questions during the hearings reflected serious worries about the prospect of violent upheavals in Pakistan – mostly likely, with images of the 1953 Lahore riots in mind – and he fashioned legal dogma to help preclude this possibility. His assumptions determined not only his ideas about dissolution but served to set a deeper determinism about the Pakistani state.

*Necessity* Validating the Governor-General's dissolution of the Assembly and proclamation of emergency, the Chief Justice took up questions which were to reemerge in Pakistani political discussions in the following decades: when can an emergency justify suspending the normal functioning of state institutions, and who should determine this? Are emergencies defined as the suspension of those institutions, or are they the conditions which cause the suspension? The court was seized with problems at once circular in their presentation and potentially circular in the articulation of their result. If it accepted the political basis of the Governor-General's proclamation then emergency was presumed and only his actions pursuant to it required examination. The Governor-General was not the problem and might be part of the solution; the Assembly was the problem and only could be part of a solution under radically changed circumstances. The court's validation could therefore influence directly the way the Governor-General could or would correct this problem.

Munir accepted the fact of emergency as prior to its declaration rather than precipitated by it: "The validation by the present Proclamation of Emergency is only temporary and the power has been exercised with a view to preventing the State from dissolution and the constitutional and administrative machinery from breaking down before the question of validation of these laws has been decided upon by the new Constituent Assembly." He therefore sought a legal foundation independent of the 1935 and 1947 Acts to answer the *Reference*. The legal principle he invoked was the doctrine of state necessity, which he had embraced in a Lahore High Court judgment two years earlier during sectarian riots in the Punjab.[17] In that judgment, Justice Munir had assumed that the legislature "would assuredly" have approved the Governor's assumption of its powers "if the emergency could have been foreseen," and that history would erase all culpability, "trusting that whatever he has honestly done for the safety of the State will be ratified by an Act of indemnity and oblivion." Not only was the doctrine self-justifying when invoked but it could be made to be so in perpetuity.

The Chief Justice now relied on the Governor-General's good will to frame his actions, stating that "an act which would otherwise be illegal becomes legal if it is done *bona fide* under the stress of necessity, the necessity being referable to an intention to preserve the constitution, the State or the Society and to prevent it from dissolution." In so writing, he accepted the Governor-General's assertion that each declared emergency was caused by different political and economic circumstances, and equally important, that emergency was by definition short-lived. The Governor-General's assumption of legislative powers was limited by only one precept, that it "cannot extend to matters which are not the product of the necessity, as for instance, changes in the constitution which are not directly referable to the emergency." This self-imposed and self-justifying condition, intended to limit the legal scope of the necessity doctrine, was troubling in its indeterminacy. Since the emergency was allegedly precipitated by legislative wrongs – which included the Assembly's lengthy tenure, the kind of laws it had passed, the powers it had assumed for itself and the constitution it had drafted – virtually any constitutional issue, particularly those concerning the division of powers and the nature of franchise and representation, could be "directly referable to the emergency." The wording of the qualification became implicit license, open to abuses that, as it happened, were already known. The necessity doctrine offered the Governor-General latitude that

[17] *Muhammad Umar Khan v. The Crown*, PLD 1953 Lahore 528. Justice Munir underscored the analogous position of a military ruler declaring a military necessity, and a civil ruler declaring civil necessity. Within a short time the two were conflated, as military *coups d'état* were justified on the basis of civil necessity.

he quickly appropriated to redraw provincial rights and responsibilities in his One Unit plan, his prerequisite for approving the 1956 Constitution.[18] Later in the decade, the doctrine was used by military officers and civilian politicians to authenticate their arrogation of power.

*Representation* The court's analysis of the Constituent Assembly's representativeness affected its assessment of a new Constituent Convention. Here, ironically, the court fell prey to arguments from within the Assembly and thus failed to examine adequately the meaning of political representation. If its opinion exhibited a certain political savvy, it failed on the rules of logic. Claiming that dissolution was valid because Assembly representation failed to endure over time, the court repeated its equation of representation, accountability and elections, and the absence of representation with an invalid constitution. The Chief Justice then merged the rights of citizens with those of Assembly members, suggesting that "dissolution does not in any way adversely affect the rights of the members of the Assembly... they can seek re-election to the new Constituent Assembly." Were the same Assembly elected, it would presumably be representative. The power to change the basis of franchise to replace Assembly membership or alter its relative powers was now held by the Governor-General.

How to organize elections and frame the electorate, however, were issues the court deemed outside its ambit, taking refuge in a distinction between legal and political issues to withdraw from a crisis it indirectly helped to mount. Following the lead of the Governor-General's counsel, the Chief Justice placed the responsibility and discretion for convening a new assembly squarely on the Governor-General's shoulders (as opposed, for example, to provincial assemblies, chief ministers, or local councils) who "is bound to take cognizance of... altered conditions." The court declined, however, to discuss the pressing provincial and communal representation problems that caused those conditions. All parties avoided discussion of One Unit and the consequences of its imposition. The issue of parity between the two wings was raised once by Justice Cornelius, but only as an example of executive authority extending its reach.[19] By discussing a future convention or assembly without regard to this political imperative, the court functioned in a voluntary void, again justifying its silence by its law-not-politics distinction. Instead, directly countering Justice Cornelius's suggestion that the new Assembly should conform to the arrangements of the original body, Justice Munir submitted that these

[18] West Pakistan Establishment Bill, 30 September 1955.
[19] "D.N. Pritt's arguments," *CMG* 10 May 1955.

were political issues without relevance to legal decision. "The only legal requirement in setting up a new Assembly," concluded the Chief Justice, "is that it should be a representative body."

Such reticence was sophistry. As Cornelius's dissent hinted, the powers granted the Governor-General by the doctrine of necessity provided a close link between constitutionalism and politics. Although Cornelius did not define his concerns this way, the close relationship between Munir's reasons for validating the dissolution and for mandating a new constitutional assembly formed the logical basis for his objections. He hoped to prevent the Governor-General's over-involvement in constitution-making by finding a basis for dissolution in the constitutive acts rather than in the necessity doctrine.

The court had already decided that it was unnecessary to qualify the powers and responsiblities of the Governor-General, simply by refusing to answer the first *Reference* question. It also seemed to accept Diplock's contention that Assembly arrangements were the province of the Governor-General alone and that these powers were not justiciable.[20] This judgment effectively enabled a principle of representation for the country through One Unit, which was indirectly approved; the *Reference* helped to prevent legal challenges to it. The *Reference* opinion validated the Governor-General's past actions; by ratifying his authority to set the structure of the new Constituent Assembly, the court cemented Pakistan's vice-regal structure and provided a legal basis for the Governor-General's future actions. In a precedent of long reach, the Federal Court determined Pakistan's constitutional structure through the doctrine of necessity.

## Courts and the state

The import of these judicial decisions was grander than the instrumental tasks at hand. On their face, *Tamizuddin Khan's case* and the *Governor-General's Reference* were about specific events, specific difficulties and specific solutions. The Constituent Assembly, in a dispute with the Governor-General, called on the High Court to solve its problem; the Governor-General appealed to the Federal Court, and when its decision left him with more problems than answers, he turned to it once again. The Federal Court's advisory jurisdiction was a godsend for the Governor-General who, without its counsel, would have been forced to resolve his partisan dilemmas in a partisan manner – in that litigious environment, potentially no resolution at all. The way the courts responded to their

20 The *Reference*'s non-binding advisory opinion was subsequently upheld in *Pakistan v. Ali Ahmed Shah*, PLD 1955 FC 522.

charges – in their terms of reference, language and substantive sweep – all framed Pakistan's future political and institutional climate. Yet, the theoretical grasp which encompassed judicial excursions into political principle was, like its practical advice and occasional inattention to facts, prescriptive but not specific, often broad but unclear. This conceptual vagueness influenced the judicial inquiry and judgment on fundamental issues of state.

Underlying judicial discussions in these cases were unarticulated and undifferentiated ideas about democracy. No party to the disputes defined the term, although all used it. When D.N. Pritt raised the subject in the *Reference*, he noted that "even democracy was a political assumption and when the notion was applied to the interpretation of statutes or prerogative rights, the question went out of the realm of law and entered the realm of politics."[21] Jinnah's vision for a democratic Pakistan had been a largely formalistic one and that habit of thinking imbued the courts as well. In their commentaries, the justices referred to democracy as a known concept: an ideal upon which the state was founded, an ideal toward which it should strive, an ideal separate from the "politics" that sidetracked the Assembly, an ideal so clear that definition was unnecessary. Achieving even this ideal – removed as it was from the inequities and inequalities that characterized so much of Pakistan's society, economy and polity – was more complex than incantation suggested.

Democracy seemed clearest to the justices in its negations, although each example demonstrated complexity rather than clarity. The problem was first one of means and ends, second of content. Maulvi Tamizuddin Khan argued that democratic processes were necessary to produce a democratic constitution. The court responded by noting the non-democratic origins and recruitment policies of the Assembly and more important, the absence of substantive results. Maulvi Tamizuddin Khan argued that the Governor-General's dissolution imposed rule from above, an essentially undemocratic action, to force further incarnations of the viceroy on the polity. The court responded by asking how democracy could emerge without being guided. Chief Justice Munir assumed that the public consented to the Governor-General and thereby invested a form of democracy and popular sovereignty in his office. Justice Cornelius, on the other hand, resorted almost entirely to analysis of the procedures established at independence to sidestep any detailed discussion of democratic rule. Neither justice, nor the attorneys in each case, examined the content of the concept, the contradictions posed by the constitutive laws creating the state and the democratic ideal they proposed, or the ten-

21 "Rely on majesty of will of people," *CMG* 5 May 1955.

sions between the language of democracy and the exigencies of Pakistani political life.

### *Sovereignty*

The courts employed several variations on the concept of sovereignty. It was used first to describe the changing relationship between the Dominion of Pakistan and its former colonial ruler, a relationship complicated by the symbolic ties of the 1935 Act and of the Commonwealth. Nationalists themselves, the justices and the country were nonetheless wedded to a system of justice and values inherited from the British and superimposed on the Dominion. Precedents came from the Privy Council, history from kings and Cromwell, constitutional theory from Dicey – not the most intuitively appropriate models for a newly independent state, as the justices knew. Yet, the old order permeated legal and political discourse, reflected in the impatient and occasionally patronizing outbursts of the judges. Justice Sharif reported bitterly that in England "you are talking about a country where people understand democracy. Here the Constituent Assembly was kicked out summarily and nobody said a word even though the members of the Constituent Assembly . . . were representatives of the people."[22] Federal Court queries reflected persistent doubts about just how independent Pakistan really was in 1955 and how long it would take to act like an independent state. One can argue, within limits, that their perception that the Pakistani state was somehow incomplete led the justices to support the appointed Governor-General – as a symbol of the Crown, as a link to the Commonwealth and as a deterrent to the lawlessness symbolized by the legislature.

The courts also used the term to describe the extent to which authority was embodied in each branch of government. In this sense, sovereignty was the court's conceptual handle on a future constitutional separation of powers. Although its subject was the Governor-General's relationship to the Assembly, the Federal Court paid considerable attention to the judicial role. Its construction of those duties profoundly shaped its readings of executive and legislative autonomy; conversely, its diverse renderings of executive and legislative sovereignty affected its analysis of judicial sovereignty. The courts became reluctant mediators, watching political maneuverings but acting without professed politics, espousing neutral political principle as received doctrine, sensing their potential political power but refusing to acknowledge it.

The sources of sovereignty were as important as the exercise of power.

22 "D.N. Pritt's arguments," *CMG* 4 May 1955.

For Justice Cornelius and for the Sind Court, paramount authority resided in the elected Assembly, pursuant to the 1947 Independence Act. This view adapted a doctrine of parliamentary powers which emphasized the sovereignty of the British parliament in framing the Independence Act and the sovereignty of the Constituent Assembly derived from it. For Justice Munir and the Federal Court, sovereignty was defined by the 1935 Act, which it explicated somewhat independently of the 1947 Act. If the textual sources for these constructions seemed at odds, each *Tamizuddin Khan* decision emphasized those differences. The *Reference* brought the two views together in a limited way, underscoring the command of the Governor-General relative to the Assembly but requiring both to stabilize sovereign government. By supporting a strong Governor-General and allowing him to choose the method of franchise, however, the court implicitly questioned the ideas of popular sovereignty that had formed part of *Maulvi Tamizuddin Khan's case*.

The issue of provincial autonomy emerged only indirectly in these cases, but was their crucial unstated political imperative. Its ambiguity, made all the more urgent by the incorporation of One Unit into the Governor-General's solution to the Assembly's sovereignty crisis, partly determined the fate of Pakistan's long succession of constitutions. The constitutional status of the two wings before and after One Unit, and of sectional interests in West Pakistan, provoked the court's discomfort and contributed to its verdict that the Assembly was unrepresentative. Because it did not want to confront the problem directly in these cases it chose to think of provinces in the literal terms of the 1935 Act – as creatures of the Governor-General. The definition of provincial borders and members and interests, and their legal and political significance in the polity as a whole, were among the most pressing issues in the independence movement, the partition process, early attempts to frame a constitution and finally, the 1971 civil war. Its legacy spurred military intervention in Baluchistan in the 1970s and still recurs in calls for Pukhtun nationalism and Sind's provincial battles with the central government. The court's reticence in 1955 on this complex, pervasive issue colored every other notion of sovereignty included in these cases. Pakistan's immediate constitutional future and its long-term political outlook can be partially attributed to this self-imposed limitation.

Construing its role rather narrowly, the court located a place for itself in another concept of sovereignty. It sought to equate its authority and independence with non-partisan politics. As Pritt asked in his *Reference* responses, "what are political parties in a court of law?"[23] The court was

[23] "D.N. Pritt's arguments," *CMG* 10 May 1955.

determined not to favor one political party or another in these cases, although as we have seen, the political context of its decisions influenced its thinking and its outcomes. Given its necessary procedural assumptions, it may have been proper to remove itself from the details of the political fray, but this distance was illusory. The Governor-General finally triumphed procedurally and substantively, by inference if not resolve. The judiciary's neutrality has been questioned ever since.

The totality of these notions of sovereignty reaffirmed the growing distance between government and politics. The Governor-General's actions were approved; far more important, a government contemptuous of political parties received sanction to continue depoliticizing the state.

### *Representation*

The court's interpretation of sovereignty was bound equally to general ideas about representation. Here, all the imponderables of state-building were brought to bear on a crucial concept of political life.

In the first instance, representation referred to the relationship of Assembly members to the citizenry. Because they had been elected indirectly from pre-independence provincial assemblies, by 1954 it was not clear to whom the members were responsible. This confusion contributed to their highly developed self-protection, personal identification with the Assembly, and when that body seemed doomed, quick efforts to cast their fates with a new body. Political parties had only vague identities and rules of membership, based as much on personal and economic loyalties as on political principles or ideology. The slightest disagreements led easily to mass defections; new parties rose and fell with little or no effect on the Assembly. Provincial party links to national parties were tenuous, and provincial elections had no direct bearing on the Assembly in its constitutional or legislative capacities. What it meant to be representative was almost impossible to tell from political behavior. These observations were shared, albeit with different interpretations, by Governors-General, Assembly critics and judges alike.

The court's attention to the idea of representation occurred during a political maelstrom but also in something of a self-imposed political vacuum. It defined Assembly representativeness by highlighting what it was not: it was not an assembly of individuals unfettered by periodic elections, it was not a group of individuals tied only to parties or self-interest, it was not a club of everlasting longevity. The court was reluctant or perhaps unable to define the concept positively, and ended up not defining it at all. At first glance, the key to its judgments seemed to be a concept of representation; a second look betrayed the term's emptiness.

In their attitudes toward Assembly representativeness, the High Court and the Federal Court alike presumed a *laissez-faire* constitutionalism without knowing how to confront an Assembly defined by special interests. The interests themselves – class, religion, ethnicity, ideology, province, party – overlapped to such a degree that accounting for them all would have defeated the most ardent lexicographer. More significantly, to the Federal Court these interests showed no fundamental legitimacy and served no material point: promoting the general welfare was the purpose of the state and therefore the rationale behind constitutional decisions. Buried in their commentaries are two generally incompatible theories of the government: the first vaguely Hobbesian, with individual liberties relinquished to the sovereign as political representative in order to govern the state; the second evoking visions of the common good and thus posed against utilitarianism. Pakistan had been created to solve the problem of Muslim political representation on the subcontinent; now that the state existed, all contributing subsidiary disputes seemed to destroy the original compact. The court took refuge in the presumed impartiality of inherited constitutional instruments without recognizing their deficiencies and structural partialities.

To the courts, a constitution was a self-explanatory life-saver: with a constitution, the state would know what it was and where it could go. To frame a constitution was to legitimize the state, an almost sacred duty that had been frittered away by self-indulgent politicians who did not appreciate the gravity of their task. However, the problems of the state preceded the framing of the constitution, and the court's attitude – combined with its notion of judicial independence – helped to sink the ship it was trying to float. The Governor-General and his allies, with the final backing of the court, tried to remold the country under One Unit to satisfy administrative and personal political objectives; in so doing, they ignored important national political needs and critical distinctions within the polity. The result was a constitution that could not work.

### *Political retrospect*

Did a constitutional theory ground these decisions or their dissents? Yes and no. Although its opinions set the stage for a constitutional set-up that became the 1956 Constitution, the judicial record of the early 1950s does not propound an ideal form of constitution or even clear ideas about the role of a constitution in the state. The courts' concerns were directed primarily to the process of writing a constitution and the pressures on institutions charged with that task, to the incompatibilities between the political environment and institutional mandates, to the vagaries of politicians and political life. Judicial interest was first in the concepts of politics that were to be embodied in the constitution – representation, sovereignty, autonomy, democracy – and second in the institutional arrangements most likely to affect and be affected by the judiciary – the division and separation of powers within the commonwealth and the state and the recognition of judicial independence. Otherwise divided about specific political issues, the courts above all stood for constitutionalism and judicial independence. They wanted to achieve a constitution when it seemed far from reach, and the Federal Court may thus have been willing to settle for less than might have been realized.

The judiciary's dissonant opinions show depth and consistency of purpose, if not result. This is important to remember when reading these judgments retrospectively. Otherwise, it is too easy to read *post hoc* partisanism into Court decisions. The Federal Court's decisions in *Tamizuddin Khan's case* and the *Governor-General's Reference* crucially affected the conduct of politics and the structure of the Pakistani state. Many of those effects were negative; at the least, they did not clarify deep-seated inconsistencies and incompatibilities or stem patterns of political behavior detrimental to developing a democracy. Throughout their consideration of these cases – including detailed examination of foreign constitutions – the courts struggled to define precepts and practices appropriate for Pakistan and standards to incorporate into its future constitution. These efforts were circumstantial, incomplete and misguided, but tenaciously wedded to changing concepts and circumstances of independence and democracy.

Just how to mediate among political conflicts while establishing a tradition of judicial independence, even before a truly Pakistani constitution was written, was therefore the abiding preoccupation of the federal courts in the 1950s. It is evident in their concerns about their appropriate role, about justiciability and about the presumed immunities of the inherited, British-made independence acts. Clumsy and on occasion unsuccessful, it is clear in their attempts to understand and explain politics in ways that would admit the judicial logics to which they adhered.

If the conflict between Justices Munir and Cornelius can be crystallized, it is in their contrasting perceptions of justice and politics. The Chief Justice's concept of political order demanded that courts not pass judgments that could not be enforced. This was an understandable interpretation of judicial self-interest: if a sergeant can interrupt judicial proceedings or remove a judge, as the political climate surrounding the Karachi trial suggested, then judges should choose their legal weaponry with care. Later, it might be difficult for participants or observers to differentiate between caution in the service of the good, on the one hand, and complicity with government objectives on the other. In this period, however, Justice Cornelius viewed justice as an instrument to be applied from a distance, regardless of its political consequences. His idealistic, possibly purist position was in striking counterpoint to the realism with which Munir endowed the court, but also provided a useful comparison to which the Chief Justice never fully responded. Cornelius's position changed in some ways after he ascended to Chief Justice in the following decade, although he never embraced Munir's views. Their conceptual debate had profound practical consequences for the new constitution's configuration of executive and judicial powers.

Perhaps this is why Chief Justice Munir, upon his retirement in 1960, chose to address the West Pakistan High Court Bar Association on the subjects which occupied his court in 1955.[24] His comments offered a fuller picture of his concerns at the time of *Tamizuddin Khan's cases* and the *Governor-General's Reference* than was evident in his judgments, revising some of his earlier statements while affirming their thrust.

Recounting this "sad chapter in the history of Pakistan," Munir suggested that the judiciary faced a country itself on the brink of dissolution. "If the court had upheld the enforceable writs," he submitted,

> I am sure that there would have been chaos in the country and a revolution would have been formally enacted possibly by bloodshed, a far more serious situation than that created by the invalidation of a whole legal system which the new Assembly promised by the Governor-General in his Proclamation could have easily validated.

In his eyes, the choice was not between the Assembly and the Governor-General, but between anarchy and order. He criticized the Sind Court for its blindness to political currents, "completely shutting its eyes to the events that had happened which made it impossible for the writs to be enforced." The primary issue was not the writs or the status of the Governor-General; rather, it was the climate of law and order and the consequent status of law at all.

> Who could say that on 9 February, the coercive power of the State was with the Court and not with the Governor General? And if even a doubt arises as to where such power resides, a doubt must arise as to the very efficacy of the law, and the situation would lie beyond the pale of judicial process ... at that time the possibility of the Court's order not being obeyed was present to the mind of us all.

By resorting to the courts and obeying their injunctions, the Governor-General "saved the country from a revolution."

Unintentionally, perhaps, Justice Munir drew a straight line from the

[24] *Pakistan Times* [*PT*] 23 April 1960.

*Reference* to his later judgment in *Dosso's case* validating the 1958 military *coup d'état*:

At moments like these law is not to be found in the books; it lies elsewhere, viz., in the events that have happened. Where the enforcement of the law is opposed by the sovereign power the issue becomes political or military which has to be fought out by other means and the courts espousing the cause of one party against the other merely prepare the ground for bloodshed.

Power is what power does, and judiciousness meant recognizing its source, location and strength. Only three years after the *Reference*, Chief Justice Munir tested and sanctioned that precept by validating expanded principles of necessity and revolutionary legality.

These are hardly soothing sentiments for populist democrats and were probably greeted with dismay by his audience, in 1960 living under a constitutional order imposed by General Ayub Khan, whose rule owed its judicial support to Justice Munir. His comments, however, accent the precarious role of the judiciary and the law in a contested polity. Only guesses can answer counterfactual questions – what would have happened had the decisions been different, what would have happened had they been ignored – but such queries show simply and forcefully how important the judiciary viewed the related questions of institutional powers and national survival.

The Federal Court's opinions also underscored tensions that mounted in coming decades between the exercise of executive authority and the judiciary's role in questioning or moderating it. (Indeed, before ruling on the dissolution of yet another parliament in 1993, Chief Justice Nasim Hasan Shah spoke forcefully about Munir's *Tamizuddin Khan* ruling, which, he noted, "was still imprinted on the people's mind.")[25] By giving the Governor-General wide berth and offering precedents to uphold executive intervention in constitutional and legislative activities, the immediate consequences of the Federal Court rulings were detrimental for Pakistan's developing polity and particularly for legislative sovereignty. For the longer term, the court established a practice of striking unspoken bargains with those in power so that its rulings would be obeyed and those in power would not feel defied. For a higher purpose – stability, perhaps democracy – the illusion of judicial independence would overtake the reality of its partial domination by those it sought to restrain or influence. At a crucial time in Pakistan's history, the judiciary molded this interpretation of prudence into a precedent from which it would later find it hard to depart.

[25] "Decision on Merit: CJ," *Jang* 9 May 1993, p. 1.

# 3 Confining courts and constitutions (1958–1969)

Flowers are blooming again, you say
Thirsts are quenched again, you say
Wounds are healed again, you say.
I deny your open lies, I contest your looting of minds.

For centuries you have robbed us of our peace of mind.
Your magic will not work on us now.
How am I now to call you a saviour?
A saviour you are not, though some still say you are.
I say no, I say no.

Habib Jalib, "Dastur."

There are quite a few thousand men who would rather have the freedom of speech than a new suit of clothes and it is these that form a nation, not the office hunters, the licenses, even the tillers of the soil and the drawers of water.

Justice M.R. Kayani

The 1956 Constitution ushered in a short period of constitutional rule but the constitution's roots were also its shortcomings, which in turn compounded political instabilities across the country. The Assembly accepted indirect rule, One Unit and the strong executive required by the Governor-General and produced a constitution confirming the structure of the vice-regal state. The constitution transferred the Governor-General's powers to the President, limited parliamentary rule and offered little challenge to the powerful army or the bureaucracy. Fundamental rights were incorporated into the constitution, however, and the superior courts were guaranteed both their independence and the right to issue the full range of writs. As an antidote, the process of constitutional amendment was made quite simple, presumably to overrule the Supreme Court when its rulings challenged the government. Rights protections therefore did little to impede the development of a bureaucratized, militarized state. Politics was progressively separated from government; eventually, depoliticizing the state was elevated to a principle of governance.

The constitution by itself could solve neither the problems of state that it reflected nor the political difficulties the government had to encounter. Crises were common: chronic food shortages, balance of payments arrears which jeopardized an already weak currency, continuing refugee resettlement and land tenure problems, and persistent border tensions with Afghanistan and India. Fragmentation within and between the provinces led to political violence toward the government and repression by the government, and party disputes paralyzed the political system. In East Pakistan, the 1954 elections had produced an unworkable coalition whose members shared only their contempt for the ruling Muslim League's policies, felt to be prejudiced against Bengal. Whether intra-Bengal disputes were purposefully provoked by the center or were derived from local and structural quarrels was not clear. But vituperative provincial appointments and dismissals in East Pakistan between 1956 and 1958 led to the imposition of President's rule and reactive violence in the Assembly itself, where thirty members were injured and the Deputy Speaker was killed. In West Pakistan, the administrative merger of the provinces did not merge political interests. Political parties, including the ruling Muslim League, remained divided along class, ethnic and geographic lines, and new entrants (like Dr. Khan Saheb's Republican Party, which briefly headed the provincial government until his assassination) were often government-sponsored vehicles to manipulate votes in the provincial assembly. The Baluchistan States Union created in 1955 was unstable, with Kalat in particular agitating for autonomy. One Unit also led to growing resentment in Sind and the Frontier against the Punjab, which was seen to have promoted the plan and benefited most from its imposition.

Some of these problems had led to the constitution's founding and were thus impossible to settle under it. Presidential powers were paralleled in the powers of the provincial governors, who mediated – and more often, interfered in – provincial politics. In the name of national unity, the central Cabinet appointed and dismissed provincial governors and thus nullified the autonomy they were to symbolize constitutionally. Equally important, central government emergency powers – another legacy of the 1935 Act transformed into a mechanism of post-colonial executive control – were allowed without parliamentary oversight or approval. Early in the constitution's short life and the equally brief incarnation of civilian constitutional government, central interference in provincial matters and the violation of rights through the imposition of emergency provisions coalesced in the public mind; similarly, the equation of One Unit with autocracy designed to thwart provincial autonomy became one idea in the public conscience in East Pakistan. When constitutional rule was abrogated in 1958, the country was accustomed to frequent appropriations of delegated powers by central authority.

In 1957, Prime Minister Husseyn Shaheed Suhrawardy, an Awami League leader from Bengal, imposed emergency rule in West Pakistan to prevent the Muslim League – one of several parties by then committed to dissolving One Unit – from gaining control of the provincial government and reopening the question of separate electorates. Suhrawardy, unlike many Bengali leaders, saw the end of One Unit as a threat to national unity.[1] The opposition lobbied for the dissolution of the assembly and fresh elections. Instead, President Iskander Mirza referred the issue to the Supreme Court.[2] Chief Justice Munir commented that "on no democratic principle can the power to dissolve vest in the executive unless the exercise of that power is followed by an appeal to the people," and ruled that general elections were to precede rather than follow Assembly dissolution. The effect of the *Reference* judgment, however, was to remove a possible bridge between political and governmental forces.

Regional loyalties remained the guide for party politics, although elections scheduled for 1958 were again postponed. Bargaining among weak parties dominated politics, and intra-party squabbling and conflicts of personal interests militated against party discipline. In a striking piece of political theater, the Khan of Kalat declared independence for his state. His brief movement was quickly repelled – his followers were the only political offenders later executed under Ayub Khan's martial law – and he, too, was placed under arrest.

Iskander Mirza proclaimed martial law on 8 October 1958. Stating that "the vast majority of the people no longer have any confidence in the present system of government," he claimed that the country's integrity was "seriously threatened by the ruthlessness of traitors and political adventurers whose selfishness, thirst for power and unpatriotic conduct cannot be restrained."[3] The Martial Law Administrator, General Mohammed Ayub Khan, continued this diatribe against politicians with "no limit to the depth of their baseness, chicanery, deceit and degradation," decrying that "a perfectly sound country has been turned into a laughing stock."[4] The constitution was made an icon of political failure. Mirza claimed that

> it is so full of dangerous compromises that Pakistan will soon disintegrate internally if the inherent malaise is not removed. To rectify them, the country must first be taken to sanity by a peaceful revolution ... It is said that the

[1] Husseyn Shaheed Suhrawardy, "Political Stability and Democracy in Pakistan," *Foreign Affairs* 35, No. 3 (April 1957): 422–31.

[2] *Reference by the President of Pakistan under Article 162 of the Constitution of Islamic Republic of Pakistan*, PLD 1957 Supreme Court 219.

[3] "Martial Law Proclaimed," *CMG* 8 October 1958, p. 1.

[4] "Democracy 'Is the Ultimate Aim'," *CMG* 9 October 1958, p. 1.

Constitution is sacred. But more sacred than the Constitution or anything else is the country and the welfare and happiness of its people.

In some respects, Mirza may have been correct; certainly, government under the 1956 Constitution was barely working. By his action, however, principles of public order would be determined by martial law authorities, and now superseded constitutional rule. Assemblies and provincial governments were dissolved, political parties were abolished, group meetings were banned, politicians were arrested and martial law regulations replaced the constitution. Military tribunals were allowed maximum powers with few defendant rights to balance them; these courts were designed to punish actions against the state, as well as looting, hoarding and black market activities. Civil courts were prohibited from contesting martial law regulations or matters related to martial law. Writs were allowed, but not against martial law authorities.

Under the Mirza–Ayub regime, democracy was the announced "ultimate" aim, but was no longer advertised as a means to achieve it. Although the constitution no longer operated, the government promulgated the 1958 Laws (Continuance in Force) Order to retain the working of civil institutions. It ordered the country to carry on as much as possible under the 1956 Constitution – paradoxically, the political basis for the constitution was not considered viable but its administrative rules were adequate. Mirza noted his anomalous position: "My authority is revolution ... I have no sanction in law or Constitution."[5] Ayub Khan therefore looked to the judiciary for formal sanction, which he received post-haste. Within three days, he announced that martial law was subservient to the President, and that "in the opinion of the Chief Justice of Pakistan, Mr. Justice Muhammad Munir, the President's position was not affected by the abrogation of the Constitution."[6] According to Ayub Khan, Pakistan was "not under military rule." After several days spent shifting government responsibilities, however, the army's paramountcy became clear. Ayub Khan forced Mirza to resign and unceremoniously, to leave the country, and added the presidency to his own job as Chief Martial Law Administrator (CMLA) while ceding the role of Commander-in-Chief to General Mohammed Musa, who later became Governor of West Pakistan. On the same day, the Supreme Court announced in *Dosso's case* that the usurpation of power to create a new regime was valid.

5 Interview with Mirza and Ayub in "2-man Regime Described," *CMG* 10 October 1958, p. 1.
6 "President's Position 'Not Affected': Ayub Quotes Munir," *CMG* 11 October 1958, p. 1.

### Legalizing the usurpation of power

In *The State v. Dosso and another* (PLD 1958 Supreme Court 533), a suit which examined the scope and functioning of the 1901 Frontier Crimes Regulations (FCR), the Supreme Court ruled on the legality of the usurpation of power.[7] The original cases, now bundled together as one suit, had questioned the reach of constitutional rights guarantees in the tribal areas, where prior to One Unit disputes were settled by applying a combination of tribal laws and the FCR. Each appeal questioned writs against the FCR when the constitution was abrogated. The joint appeal did not require a ruling as broad as one judging the legal character of the new regime; indeed, by taking on the legality question, Chief Justice Munir put aside other interesting problems about regional and national laws.[8] The definition of the court's charge in *Dosso* was an issue of dispute between the majority confirming the regime's legality, led by Chief Justice Munir, and Justice Cornelius as the sole dissenter, who did not discuss the legality issue at all. Specifically, the court ruled on the legal status of fundamental rights after the constitution was abrogated. Equally important, it discussed relationships between legality – which it termed validity – and legitimacy and explicated relationships between power and authority. The majority opinions are interesting not only for espousing a doctrine of revolutionary legality, credited with only partial accuracy to Hans Kelsen,[9] but also for their conclusory tone, which seemed to brook no dissent in substance or method. The court's judgment, however, was questionable for its logic as well as its political assumptions.

The court's primary problem was to adjudicate a constitutional issue in the absence of a formal constitution. Ayub Khan announced that the country would function as much as possible according to the 1956 Constitution although the fundamental rights section of the constitution stood abated, and that civil courts would remain open but could not challenge the government. The court now had to identify the legal basis and scope for preexisting laws under this political order.

The way that Justice Munir defined *Dosso* set the judiciary on an explicitly political path. Given the restrictions imposed on its powers, the

[7] In *Malik Toti Khan etc. v. District Magistrate, Sibi and Ziarat*, PLD 1957 (W.P.) Quetta 1, and *Dosso and another v. The State and others*, PLD 1957 (W.P.) Quetta 9, High Court Chief Justice S.A. Rahman concluded that provisions of the FCR which enabled executive authorities to refer criminal cases to a tribal council (*jirga*) conflicted with constitutional guarantees.

[8] Willard Berry, *Aspects of the Frontier Crimes Regulation in Pakistan* (Durham: Duke University Commonwealth Studies Center, 1966).

[9] Hans Kelsen, *General Theory of Law and the State*, translated by Anders Wedberg (New York: Russell & Russell, 1961).

court could have refused to hear these appeals, thereby igniting a battle between judicial and executive authorities at the beginning of martial rule. It chose to keep its doors open and live within its new limits. Alternately, the court could have removed itself from the political fray by ruling that the suspension of the formal constitution meant that the appeals themselves were no longer possible to judge, a course it also eschewed. Finally, the court could have ruled that appeals filed prior to the 1958 abrogation would be judged according to the 1956 Constitution. The Chief Justice, however, sought a far-reaching determination, perhaps to dispel challenges to the new regime, more likely to retain civil court powers by the simple act of executing them. Munir therefore appropriated some of Hans Kelsen's analytical theory of revolution and law, in which, juridically, "the decisive criterion of a revolution is that the order in force is overthrown and replaced by a new order in a way which the former had not itself anticipated."[10] Coining the doctrine of revolutionary legality as an acceptable mode for contesting a constitutional order, Munir ruled that a successful challenge to power conferred a badge of legality: "Where revolution is successful it satisfies the test of efficacy and becomes a basic law-creating fact."

The Chief Justice read into Kelsen's theories wide justifications for usurping constitutional powers. Kelsen proposed a specific relationship between efficacy and validity, stating that "efficacy is a condition of validity; a condition, not the reason of validity."[11] Justice Munir, however, considered efficacy to be "the essential condition to determine whether a Constitution has been annulled." To Kelsen "a norm is considered to be valid only on the condition that it belongs to a system of norms, to an order which, on the whole is efficacious,"[12] but Munir required neither empirical nor theoretical proof that the norm, in this case the efficacious revolution, belonged to a system of values that was otherwise justifiable. He ignored – whether because he thought it unnecessary, difficult or inconvenient – the crucial distinction between legality and legitimacy. Writing of the doctrine Munir called revolutionary legality, Kelsen had simply proposed that "the principle of legitimacy is restricted by the principle of effectiveness." Munir did not see efficacy as a limitation on legitimacy, but rather as defining political possibility – in his terms, legality.

10 J.M. Finnis calls this a theory of legal discontinuity, since "the content of the post-revolutionary legal system is similar, if not identical, to that of the pre-revolutionary period." His reading of Kelsen more accurately reflects 1958 conditions in Pakistan than did Chief Justice Munir's. See J.M. Finnis, "Revolutions and Continuity of Law," in A.W.B. Simpson, ed., *Oxford Essays in Jurisprudence*, 2nd ser. (Oxford: Clarendon Press, 1973), pp. 44–76.

11 Kelsen, *General Theory*, pp. 41–42. 12 Ibid.

*Dosso* therefore equated force, efficacy and legality: "The revolution itself becomes a law-creating fact because thereafter its own legality is judged not by reference to the annulled Constitution but by reference to its own success." The "new law-creating organ" – the Laws (Continuance in Force) Order – "however transitory or imperfect," and more generally, Ayub Khan's regime, thus validated itself. In Kelsen's language, the source of the *grundnorm* (literally, the grounding principle of state) was the regime itself, the *grundnorm* its subsequent orders. Because the President could change the new order at will and fundamental rights were suspended, laws no longer had to comply with rights to be valid. Defying linear logic, the court relied on a doctrine which in turn required it to assume its result: equating validity with efficacy (and defining efficacy very broadly) was the same as defining power by its exercise. Like the Queen of Hearts, the regime determined what words, or laws or rights, would mean.

The revolutionary legality doctrine was based on a political realism nascent in the *Governor-General's Reference*. Now political realism determined legality. But, as Machiavelli noted centuries earlier, realism can be misplaced and there is reason to believe that Justice Munir's realism was flawed. His judgment was made within days of the usurpation of power, surely too soon to judge the efficacy for which he searched: the absence of public protest could mean many things without giving legitimacy to the regime.[13] To achieve a political result Justice Munir abstained from political analysis; his concept of efficacy, removed from a concept of legitimacy, was politically disembodied. He tried to make revolutionary legality an independent concept when at best it depended on a host of undisclosed factors. Philosophically, his concept of legality was empty; politically, it was dangerous.

Most important were questions left silent. Should the court interpret political events so soon, or at all, for the purpose of legal judgment? Where should the line be drawn between politics and constitutional law, substantively and procedurally? Shortly before the *Dosso* case, Justice Munir had declared poetically that "when politics enter the portal of the Palace of Justice, democracy, its cherished inmate, walks out by the back-door."[14] In *Dosso*, he made politics and legality the same; he interpreted legality as legitimacy, knowing that the regime would use his judgment to validate itself in the public eye. The court's majority accepted

13 American Ambassador Charles Burton Marshall suggested that military courts limited resistance to the *coup d'état*, saying "obviously such formidable sanctions, even held in reserve, would suffice to make claim of contest a jest." "Reflections on a Revolution in Pakistan," *Foreign Affairs*, 37 (January 1959): 255.

14 *Malik Feroz Khan Noon v. The State*, PLD 1958 Supreme Court 333.

the limits on judicial action stated in the first proclamation. The combination of the declaration of usurpation and the revolutionary legality doctrine further diminished the court's powers. Not only was the government immune from direct challenge, but without rights to enforce, courts could not mount or support effective resistance to state encroachments on individual liberties. By applying legal positivism as a doctrine rather than an analytic tool, the court found itself presiding over a six-year absence of justiciable rights in Pakistan.

Justice Cornelius's limited dissent took on both of these issues, although he analyzed only the rights issue explicitly. He too looked for outside authority to prove his views about rights, relying on natural rights theory to validate the continuance of fundamental rights in the absence of positive rights guarantees. Cornelius saw the exposition of fundamental rights in the 1956 Constitution as an act apart from the enactment of the constitution itself, for "essential human rights ... do not derive their entire validity from the fact of having been formulated in words and enacted in that Constitution." Pakistan's only *grundnorm* (although he did not use this term) was a concept of natural rights and the 1956 Constitution was only one iteration of them. Although the abrogation of the constitution marked "a point of no return," rights could not be retracted retrospectively. Constitutions might come and go, but rights remained. Just as Munir's understanding of the violability of judicial powers affected his analysis of positive rights, so Cornelius's arguments about basic rights colored his notion of judicial authority. In the shadow of the sweeping majority judgment, his dissent was remarkably limited. He implied that the role of the court in an emergency should be to protect those rights it was able to protect – a limited but highly political rendering of judicial actions – and to leave the political arena to sort itself out. This was realism of a different mold than Chief Justice Munir's.

The majority and minority opinions in *Dosso* therefore lived as if in separate worlds. The Chief Justice, relying on a legal positivism which included no independent concept of fundamental rights, did not try to refute Justice Cornelius's natural justice arguments. Justice Cornelius assumed a doctrine of natural rights that precluded positivism and ignored the majority's invocation and adaptation of Kelsen. The chasm separating them was so wide and so clear that debate may have seemed useless. The division was tragic for the country; subsequently, the conceptual space between them was occupied by frequent extra-constitutional appropriations of political power.

Moreover, the court did not consider two substantive issues as important as the legality question: first, the identity of the usurpation of power with military rule and the consequent change in the institutional structure of the state; second, the question of One Unit that had provoked the original cases. The "October Revolution" established parallel military and civilian structures to operate at the pleasure of the regime; summary military courts, for example, operated by the rule of courts martial and were immune to civil court questioning.[15] No mention was made of the *coup d'état* or the extraordinary powers invested in the military, even though these dominated daily news reports. Chief Justice Munir, personally familiar with Iskander Mirza's pre-*coup* political travails, also knew that the doctrine of revolutionary legality would legitimize the praetorian state. This was the context for Justice Cornelius's rights-protecting strategy, weak as it might seem in light of the developing military state. These two interpretations of the judicial role – acquiescence versus non-cooperation – framed the poles of judicial opinion for the duration of the regime, much of which included Justice Cornelius's tenure as Chief Justice.

The Chief Justice sought no independent, concrete proof that a revolution had occurred or might occur. If a revolution assumes a determined change in the location of power, none had in fact taken place in Pakistan, nor would it in the following years. Under Ayub Khan, the same combination of military, bureaucratic and feudal interests that had ruled since pre-partition days continued to dominate the political arena and reap economic rewards. It was these interests on which Ayub Khan relied to ensure the longevity of his rule. Only the mechanics of power were altered. By pronouncing the legality of the new regime, the court may have helped to prevent real change from taking place.

The new regime wholeheartedly embraced One Unit; indeed, Ayub Khan took partial credit for the idea.[16] The *Dosso* appeals implicitly questioned the center's justification and right to dictate standards and processes of justice across the country. The majority barely touched on this issue and Justice Cornelius discussed it only to buttress his natural rights arguments. One Unit was upheld indirectly. Because writs against the government were prohibited, no challenges were lodged against it for most of the Ayub Khan era. That the court ruled on regime legality thus offered a mixed message: while indicating formal judicial interest in the structure of the state, it demonstrated judicial willingness to retreat from articulating principles of state in favor of upholding its own limited survival.

Preserving the court's remaining powers, if not a full judicial mandate,

[15] In *Manzoor Elahi v. The State*, PLD 1959 Lahore 243, the High Court claimed jurisdiction over military courts only if they could be proven to have transgressed their own jurisdiction, regardless of the adequacy of their findings.

[16] Mohammad Ayub Khan, *Friends Not Masters*, p. 192.

may have been one of Munir's concerns. A decade later, when the problems of *Dosso*'s inheritance dominated Pakistani politics, he recounted his participation in the 1958 decision to abrogate the constitution, recalling specifically the amendations he offered to the 1958 Order to protect the jurisdiction of the superior courts.[17] The Chief Justice viewed his cooperation as an heroic attempt to save for civil society one mechanism to counter military repression. (One participating attorney in *Dosso*, Yahya Bakhtiar, noted during *Asma Jilani's case* in 1972 that Justice Munir had taken up the legality question in *Dosso* without any notice to appellants, and did not allow responses on the legality issue during the appeal.) If Munir's account is true, then setting the *Dosso* agenda was of a piece with establishing the terms of martial law – an extraordinary and indicting role for a civilian judge. Whatever the other consequences of *Dosso*, it did not ensure that justice would be done, or even appear to have been done. Judicial complicity became a Faustian bargain.

The court provided for itself a unique if somewhat imprecise role. By ruling as it did, when it did, it legitimized the military regime. Doing so by recourse to a doctrine which it claimed was of unimpeacheable integrity and neutrality, the court gave not only its own imprimatur to the regime, but seemingly that of rational, impartial observers. *Dosso* helped to set Pakistan's future for more than a decade because the court helped to legitimate the regime domestically and internationally. Building on the foundation of the *Governor-General's Reference*, which underscored executive authority through the doctrine of necessity, it almost unquestioningly supported Ayub Khan. The illegal usurpation of power was made legal and girded a theory of representation previously endowed by the necessity doctrine. That doctrine – inapplicable in *Dosso* (for it applied only to actions of a legal regime) but equally dismissive of fundamental rights – was held for another day. In 1977, after General Mohammed Zia ul Haq's *coup d'état*, the court would pair necessity and revolutionary legality – the judgments of 1955 and 1958 – to create an even more durable basis for the garrison state.

## Relocating political power

From the beginning of his regime, Ayub Khan distinguished his martial law from strict military rule – a distinction the courts later underlined –

[17] "Days I Remember," *PT* 11–12 November 1968. These articles were prompted in part by the publication of Ayub Khan's autobiography the year before, in which the Field Marshall suggested that Munir was present when the decision to eliminate the office of President was taken. See *Friends Not Masters*, p. 74. These articles were entered into the

and assured the country that civil institutions would continue to function as much as possible as before. The 1958 Laws (Continuance in Force) Order proposed such continuity, and Ayub Khan's public statements suggested that involvement in civilian affairs would be corrupting for the army, which would do well to return early to their barracks. The military, in fact, did not completely take over administrative institutions during Ayub Khan's martial law, instead supplanting them with parallel institutions like military courts, or integrating individual officers into existing structures of civil authority.

In the early years of the regime two principles of government were articulated, administrative efficiency and the negating of politics. The first was accomplished by a flurry of organizational efforts, including dozens of study commissions to restructure laws, land tenure, agricultural and industrial production, the civil services and education. Some commissions managed successfully to reform legal arenas such as family laws; others were ignored when their recommendations contradicted regime interests directly, like the Constitution Commission, or indirectly, like the Civil Services Commission, to which the bureaucracy objected. Each effort linked a concept of political stability with one of economic development to cement the power of the state: Chief Justice Munir later commented approvingly that "many a reform which in the constitutional regime would have been impossible was introduced."[18] The regime also outlawed a broad range of anti-state actions, punishable by summary military court sentences of imprisonment, fines and lashing.

To achieve the second goal, Ayub Khan redefined participation in public life by banning some traditional politicians from public office. Politicians were banned under a revived PRODA, which had been abolished legislatively prior to the 1954 Assembly dissolution. The 1959 Public Offices (Disqualification) Order [PODO] was applied retrospectively to 1947; it disqualified politicians who were found guilty of misconduct by a special tribunal from holding office for up to fifteen years. These two-member tribunals, of which one member was a serving superior court judge, functioned according to the Criminal Procedure Code, and each accused could speak on his own behalf. The 1959 Elective Bodies (Disqualification) Order [EBDO] extended PODO: it was applied to legislative members who had held no other public office, broadened the definition of

record of *Asma Jilani's case* in 1972, when it was argued that complicity in Ayub Khan's plans compromised Munir's impartiality in *Dosso*.

18 *Constitution of Islamic Republic of Pakistan, Being a Commentary on the Constitution of Pakistan, 1962* (Lahore: All Pakistan Legal Decisions, 1965), p. 52. Justice Shahabuddin reported that his advisory commission's critical comments concerning the 1962 Constitution were suppressed by Ayub Khan. See "Recollections and Reflections," in Mushtaq Ahmad, *Pakistan at the Crossroads*, p. 128.

misconduct against which the accused could be judged, and ultimately was used to ban thousands of politicians. EBDO inquiry committees were dominated by the bureaucracy and required the accused to appear before them but did not guarantee them legal aid; disqualification could last until the end of 1966. When these orders were lifted, latent divisions among the thousands of banned politicians extended the fragmenting effects of these laws, although the substance of opposition demands to restore democracy remained remarkably similar during the decade of the 1960s.

To complement restrictions on the uncompliant political elite, the government put into effect a variety of repressive measures that reduced mass voice. Strikes and agitations in schools and public utilities were outlawed under martial law regulations, with punishments of ten years rigorous imprisonment for their violation. When political party activities were once again allowed they were strictly limited, and a wide range of ordinances constrained non-party politics. The government consolidated publications laws in order to maintain control over the media after martial law was lifted, and as we shall see, it sharply restricted media ownership, employment, financing and coverage.

Most expansive was an order promulgated under Ayub Khan's supra-constitutional powers to restructure political representation through the 1959 Basic Democracies Order, announced on the first anniversary of the *coup d'état*.[19] The order provided for a tripartite division of local government, in the words of one of the plan's authors, to be "representative, pragmatic, vigorous, dynamic and basic."[20] The plan's bywords were representation, decentralization, democratization and popular education.

Basic Democracy was a curious endowment of political science to politics. It assumed the transcendence of form over content, emphasized an imposed process of representation rather than the policies of representatives or the interests of constituents, and thus carefully subsumed local interests under the umbrella of the state. It substituted the prospect of accessibility of local office and the benefits of patronage for the possibility of influencing the polity, another way to separate politics from administration. It rested on an analysis of the concept of democracy that was entirely idiosyncratic, not to the "genius of the Pakistani people" as

[19] The Basic Democracies Order was followed by implementing orders, including the 1960 Municipal Administration Order, the 1961 Muslim Family Law Ordinance, and the 1961 Conciliation Courts Ordinance. The Basic Democracies Order was incorporated into the 1962 Constitution, as was the 1965 Electoral College Act.

[20] See Masudul Hasan, *Textbook of Basic Democracy and Local Government in Pakistan* (Lahore: All Pakistan Legal Decisions, 1968).

Ayub was wont to say, but to the requirements of his administrative state:

Democracy is merely concerned with the location of the source of power, and not with the form of organization for the channelisation of power . . . The concept of Basic Democracy is based on the hypothesis that democracy is not an end by itself; it is only a means to an end, the end being the welfare of the people. The concept of Basic Democracy visualises the emphasising of the basic values of democracy rather than its form. The underlying idea is that the democratic order in a State should not be formal; it should be basic in character.[21]

Basic Democracy functioned in the absence of political parties and generally in the absence of debate. On this point, the General was adamant. Addressing a public rally in Lyallpur, he commended his own system, "free from the curse of party intrigues, political pressures and tub-thumping politicians that characterised the Assemblies." He refined his anti-politics into a political philosophy. Theorizing that "democracy does not depend on the counting of votes alone," he proposed the "sensible alternative" of consensus rather than "creating hard and fast cleavages in our ranks based on majorities and minorities."[22]

With time, Basic Democracies acquired a mantle of ideology to justify the state's manipulation of its functions. It was linked theoretically if not practically to economic well-being, and thus to the system of state authority; in Ayub Khan's words, "no democratic system can be complete unless and until political democracy is accompanied by economic and social democracy."[23] Basic Democracies author Masudul Hasan elevated its place in a grand continuum of global politics: "In a Democracy the people are above the State; in a totalitarian order the State is above the people; in a basic democratic order the people and the State are at par and both are subject to a higher purpose. Democracy is ideological disintegration; Communism is ideological despotism; Basic Democracy is ideological democracy." The theoretical truth of this proposition was never tested; instead, Basic Democracies merged with the state as martial law and patronage defined it. Indeed, one of its chief bureaucrats later opined that its combination of localism and the "delegation of authority from the government officials to the elected representatives is the very culmination of democratic decentralization."[24]

21 Ibid., pp. 61 and 63.

22 Address to Lyallpur rally, 12 October 1959, in Jafri, p. 54; Address to Lahore Basic Democracies Convention, 15 June 1960, in Rais Ahmad Jafri, *Ayub: Soldier and Statesman* (Lahore: Mohammad Ali Academy, 1966), pp. 63–64; Broadcast, 26 October 1960, in Masudul Hasan, p. 69.

23 Address to Basic Democracies Convention.

24 Ayub speech in Masudul Hasan, p. 69; M. Aslam Abdullah Khan quote in Presidential Address, *Proceedings of the Third All Pakistan Political Science Conference 1962*, ed. Muhammad Aziz Ahmad (Karachi: University of Karachi, 1962), p. 247.

Basic Democracy offered the appearance of participation while ensuring that it did not interrupt the functioning of government, thus restricting the meaning of representation and reducing the role of public voice in the political arena. As a way to channel popular disenchantment with politicians into an institutional form, it was intrinsic to Ayub Khan's regime without being intrinsic to the bureaucratic-military state. As a mode of representation, it offered a means to enfranchise a new group of budding politicians whose loyalty to their constituencies would never match their fidelity to the regime. It offered parity between East and West Pakistan through equal numbers of constituencies but never addressed the historically crucial questions of representation – separate electorates, population and One Unit. Basic Democracy circumscribed the power of the individual by harnessing collective power to the state. A symmetry would therefore develop between the relative autonomy of the state ensured by the Basic Democracies structure, the autonomy of the bureaucracy and the military who ran the state, and the mandate for rule offered by the courts. To make his plans work, it was therefore necessary to civilianize martial law.

When he took power, Ayub Khan announced that a new constitution would be drafted to replace the 1956 Constitution, which he had earlier called an "amorphous document without a hard core and a solid base." Before promulgating a new one, he took steps to harness the courts to his cause. While formally acquiescing to the notion of judicial independence – telling the Karachi High Court Bar Association that "the courts are . . . the final arbiters of what is legal and illegal" – he in fact assumed the role of executor, judge and enforcer: "If the law declared brings the Government into conflict with what it considers to be its own responsibilities, or if the law so declared has consequences which the Government does not wish to see, then the Government has its own responsibilities, and therefore, the power and the duty to alter the law that the courts have declared."[25] To ensure compliance in the civil sector, judicial appointments were vetted for political propriety and the legal profession was regulated through the Bar Council Order. Although the regime allowed civil courts to function – later heralded as a unique feature of this martial law[26] – the state controlled the law and its relations with civil society. The 1963 Press and Publications Ordinance (which remained in effect until 1988) controlled the management of newspapers, placing information

25 15 January 1959, in Jafri, pp. 34–36.

26 Justice Dr. Nasim Hasan Shah, "The First Martial Law and the 1962 Constitution," in *Articles and Speeches on Constitution, Law and Pakistan Affairs* (Lahore: Wajidalis, 1986), p. 29.

about the state, government and the law outside the reach of most citizens. Moreover, judicial review was sharply curtailed.

Despite constraints on their activities, Bar Councils agitated for an end to martial law. By September 1960, General Ayub Khan was able to report that the harsher aspects of military rule had softened, and the reasons for furthering martial law were weak.[27] Emphasizing the need for an orderly transfer of power, he formally lifted martial law in 1962 while incorporating some of its principles into a constitution for civil–military rule. From the first, Ayub Khan was specific about the public order requirements for this constitution, saying that "it should not admit of political instability under any circumstances."[28] His definition of instability always remained wide, including the exercise of political rights. Two issues in particular influenced his construction of authority for the civilian version of his state. First, he considered martial law constraints upon free expression – political speech – to be fully appropriate. "Freedom of speech," he told a gathering of attorneys, "is a necessary instrument for a specific purpose. It must however, be judged in the context of that purpose. Freedom of speech has never meant an unlimited license to say whatever one likes."[29] His constitution took to heart his distinction between "responsible freedom and irresponsible license" by proscribing criticism of government and generally circumscribing rights by limiting their justiciability. When Ayub was finally forced to agree that rights were important, he separated them from their protection by the judiciary. In this sense, Ayub Khan's civilian state retained the paternalism of his military state.

Second, Ayub Khan underscored the superiority of the executive in relation to the judiciary. The Supreme Court's feistiness reinforced his instincts for constitutional control. His general inclinations were reinforced by an incident in 1961 during which Sir Edward Snelson, British Secretary to the Ministry of Law, was tried for contempt toward the superior courts. Snelson had publicly criticized the superior courts for trespassing the "strictly defined frontiers of the prerogative writs" which he felt should have immunized government from such writs.[30] Asked to summarize his views in court, Snelson referred to "a great deal of disarray in the Government discipline of its subordinate services." The justices took exception to the publication of views which seemed to denigrate

27 Inaugural address to Pakistan Lawyers' Convention, Karachi, 30 September 1960, in Jafri, pp. 70–73.
28 Address to Karachi High Court Bar Association.
29 Speech Karachi Bar Association, 25 September 1961, in Jafri, pp. 88–90.
30 *The State v. Sir Edward Snelson*, PLD 1961 (W.P.) Lahore 78, and *Sir Edward Snelson v. The Judges of the High Court of West Pakistan, Lahore and The Central Government of Pakistan*, PLD 1961 Supreme Court 237.

their capacity to render justice, contrasting Snelson's claim to free speech with the need to maintain accessible courts:

JUSTICE ORTCHESON: If after reading the speech of Sir Edward someone comes to the conclusion that it was no good to approach the High Court because no writ would lie against the Government would that not be interference with the course of justice?

SH. GHIAS MUHAMMAD (for centre): If he says that the judges are inefficient it would be contempt of court.[31]

Somewhat righteously, and directly contravening Ayub Khan's political theory, the court concluded that "the law of the country is what the judiciary says it is."[32]

Snelson's conviction marked a low point in judiciary–executive relations, and probably affected the tone of the courts' future assertion of their powers. It also reinforced Ayub Khan's sense that court powers be limited, leaving the executive to police itself:

> The Judiciary should have the ultimate power of deciding whether the limits of Executive authority have or have not been exceeded. But I do not agree that those limits should be unduly rigid or that within those limits there should be a possibility for the Judiciary to interfere with the acts of the Executive. It has sometimes been assumed that the Executive officers are for ever attempting to break the law and that the Judicial officers are there to put a restraint upon them. Such an assumption gives rise to an attitude of hostility and conflict between the two, which is not healthy.

"Any Government worth its name," he concluded to the Karachi High Court Bar, "should be in a position to control its Executive officers and rectify their errors."

The 1962 Constitution helped Ayub Khan limit the power of civil society. In its quasi-federal structure, the President held overriding authority in provincial matters. Provincial governors were appointed by the President, whose power to dissolve provincial assemblies made provincial ministers ultimately responsible to the President rather than the assemblies. Regional economic disparities favoring West Pakistan and a constitutional structure favoring the central executive were mutually reinforcing factors that exacerbated inter-provincial tensions and helped bring on violent opposition to the President, the constitution, and the federation.

[31] "December 12 Fixed for Judgment," *CMG* 19 November 1960, p. 9. The court responded angrily to the Attorney-General's defense, which it characterized as "tantamount to a threat," saying "if we have contravened the law prosecute us: we will face it." See "Sir Edward Denies Contempt Charge," *CMG* 15 November 1960, p. 1. After finding Snelson guilty, the court refused Snelson's request to expunge language criticizing him contained in the High Court judgment.

[32] "Snelson, Govt. appeals Fail: High Court Decision Upheld," *CMG* 29 April 1961, p. 8.

To support this structure, the powers of the judiciary were circumscribed, limited to reviewing purported interference with enacted laws. Courts could not question the validity of laws which allegedly conflicted with principles of state policy, and only later were given the power to review contraventions of fundamental rights. The constitution also limited the powers of the National Assembly. The legislature had no control over the recurring expenditures that comprised more than 90 percent of the budget, and constitutional amendment required two-thirds majority, three-quarters for resubmission if the President disapproved. Justice Shahabuddin called the 1962 Constitution an instrument of "a despotic rule of the state since there was nothing in it to act as an effective check on the power assumed by [the president]."[33] Moreover, the President's wide emergency powers were not susceptible to challenge. To reduce opportunities for resisting the President, political parties were banned, although they were later restored by the Assembly. Ayub Khan wrote a constitution to centralize his powers – correcting what he felt was the primary weakness of the 1956 Constitution – but maintained the weaknesses of federal organization that had led to political disarray in the mid-1950s. It was a constitution written to perpetuate the alliance between the military and the bureaucracy, and even more, to continue the General's rule.

Ayub Khan's commitment to his form of presidential governance was complete, and until he left office in 1969 he equated opposition to it with anti-state activity. Although political parties were reinstated in 1962, the government tried to suppress the platform of the Combined Opposition Parties led by Fatima Jinnah, a group that contested the first constitutionally sponsored elections in 1965 by proposing the restoration of a parliamentary system, direct elections and universal suffrage, and a democratized constitution; the government-owned media also limited its coverage of COP candidates. Only the successful patronage system of the Basic Democracies saved Ayub Khan from embarrassing defeat. Fundamental rights were withdrawn under the emergency declared during the 1965 war with India and remained suspended until Ayub Khan's departure from office several years later. Their short life nonetheless inspired moments of political excitement: labor unions pressed for the right to strike, the Jamaat-i-Islami called for rights to override overweening executive powers and Awami League activists in East Pakistan agitated for provincial autonomy (and were arrested for their activities).

The absence of provincial rights – particularly the perceived exclusion of East Pakistan from central government – together with the suppression

[33] "Recollections and Reflections," cited in Mushtaq Ahmad, p. 28.

of public demands for democracy, proved Ayub Khan's undoing. The President continued to frame his policies in the language of democratic decentralization, but many Pakistanis came to believe that his vocabulary covered a fundamental lie. Thus, the National Democratic Front, first organized in East Pakistan by Suhrawardy in 1962, pressed for the restoration of the 1956 Constitution and parliamentary government. By 1966, Sheikh Mujibur Rahman articulated the principles that became the Awami League's Six-Point Plan for the restoration of democracy and a redesigned federation – a cause that won him four years in prison. The Democratic Action Committee, an opposition organization created in 1969, also agitated for regional rights and a federal parliamentary system. Although Ayub seemed to accede to some demands in early 1969 in order to retain East Pakistan in the union, the damage to the country had been done. His constitution and rule proved to many in East Pakistan that their presence in the Pakistani state was on sufferance alone. The task of saving or dividing the country was left to his hand-picked, unconstitutionally empowered successor, General Agha Mohammed Yahya Khan.

## Living with *Dosso*

Following *Dosso*, the courts tried repeatedly to fix the parameters of military rule by determining the circumscribed powers of civil institutions within the military state. In particular, the judiciary was asked to resolve persistent questions about the character and compass of its own activities. The courts, now joined in the administration of the martial law state, cast their decisions upon shifting sands of political possibility. The two constitutional periods of Ayub's rule – the years of direct martial law prior to the promulgation of the 1962 Constitution, and the years of indirect military control following the promulgation of the 1962 Constitution and the subsequent addition of justiciable rights in 1964 – provided an intricate byplay between jurisprudence and politics, particularly in the arenas of judicial powers and fundamental rights.

### *Extending the repressive state*

The Supreme Court moved with such alacrity to fill the legal vacuum created by the *coup d'état* that it did not wait for the Laws (Continuance in Force) Order to come into effect and did not include the order's provisions in its decision. *Dosso* was soon challenged in a review of a 1950 East Pakistan provincial law concerning the distribution of rental incomes on religious properties. A 1957 ruling had held that some of these laws conflicted with the fundamental rights provisions of the 1956 Constitution.[34]

*The legal framework* In *The Province of East Pakistan v. Md. Mehdi Ali Khan Panni* (PLD 1959 Supreme Court (Pak) 387) the court considered the depth and breadth of the 1958 Order and reiterated its position that fundamental rights were nullified. The Chief Justice cited the "unfettered legislative powers" of the new regime, which could annul or alter any court ruling. General Ayub Khan held executive, legislative and to an extent, quasi-judicial powers in the new regime, and could undercut judicial authority in any of those capacities. Justice Munir's decision in *Mehdi Ali Khan* rang the true, constricting tone of the Ayub Khan regime.

Despite arguments by the appellants which Justice Munir called both "ingenious and at times far fetched," the court declined to review its *Dosso* decision. Instead, it saw the Order, in the words of counsel for both sides, as "the shortest Constitution in the world . . . a singularly ingenious piece of constitutional legislation." By elevating the Order to the status of a constitution, rather than as a substitute for one, the court set aside conflicts between the order and other constitutional laws. The court upheld the reasoning behind *Dosso* and the full range of its effects.

Although the 1958 Order required that the old legal order would be retained as much as possible, Justice Munir refused to assert potential judicial powers when contradictions in its instructions – between keeping alive undefined parts of the constitution and abrogating the constitution as a whole – were inevitable. According to the Chief Justice, "a more confusing state of affairs in the administration of the laws is difficult to conceive." Efficiency, convenience and the impulse not to offend those in power became canons of justice. The court also retained its construction of fundamental rights in *Dosso*. Asserting that "the argument in favour of the present existence of such rights gets into self-evident contradictions" because of the ban on writs against the government, the Chief Justice considered "their inferential continuance" to be "a complete impossibility." He nonetheless asked abstractly, "are the laws void in the sense of their ceasing to exist once they come into conflict with paramount law or do the laws exist and are in force but have to be disregarded or ignored to the extent they come into collision with paramount law in the decision of a case?" His answer underscored the preeminence of the Order: in conflicts

[34] In *Jibendra Kishore Chowdhury v. Province of East Pakistan*, PLD 1957 Supreme Court (Pak) 9, Justice Munir endorsed fundamental rights in the 1956 Constitution; after the abrogation, he reversed his opinion. Appeals to the 1957 decision were remanded to the High Court in Dacca, which was unable to conclude the cases consistently and returned them to the Supreme Court.

between fundamental rights and properly enacted laws, "the moment the fundamental right was taken away by an amendment of the Constitution the law again became operative." For laws superseded by the Order, the same principle would apply.

Justice Cornelius took a simpler view. Because the first consequence of the order was to quash rights, grounds for this and every other rights-related appeal disappeared. He observed that many provisions of the 1956 Constitution were observed by the regime, although in a new political environment which gave the state "a character of novelty . . . as a form of Martial Rule." The order's assurance to govern substantially according to the old constitution "is immune to legal process to the same extent as the Martial Rule is itself immune." According to Cornelius, basic rights remained valid not only within the framework of the natural justice arguments offered in *Dosso*, but also because they existed in the current legal order – modifying but not necessarily canceling the 1956 Constitution. The difference was one of justiciability, not existence: is implied ought. His analysis foretold a tension in the regime's attitude toward rights that was only partly resolved when justiciable rights were appended to the 1962 Constitution.

For Justice Cornelius, *Mehdi Ali Khan* provided another occasion to try to secure fundamental rights in the military state, and at the least, to demonstrate the close relationship between justiciable rights and judicial powers. Most important, however, was the effect of the judgment on the regime's freedom to pursue its goals. Speaking for the majority, Justice Munir made it clear that no challenges to Ayub Khan would be brooked while the legal structure of the state was premised on these powers.[35] Changes in state structure could only be undertaken by Ayub Khan, the source and executor of the state's legal framework. *Mehdi Ali Khan* exposed the concrete possibilities for the military state to extend its control. By not contesting the absence of justiciable rights, and in consequence accepting severely reduced judicial powers, the court confirmed the new legal order and transposed its own constricted voice to the new regime.

The court was not comfortable with a blanket validation of unknown military intentions, but its latitude was now limited. When the Lahore Court ruled that the 1958 Order did not remove high court writ jurisdiction against orders of summary military courts, were the matter outside

35 Hamidul Haq Chowdhury – himself prohibited from politics by the renewed PRODA – urged the court in 1968 to reassess *Dosso* and *Mehdi Ali Khan* in *Chowdhury Tanbir Ahmad Siddiky v. The Province of East Pakistan and others*, PLD 1968 Supreme Court 185, but Justice S.A. Rahman noted that the issue was still not justiciable.

summary court jurisdiction or "not in accordance with the law that gave the Military Court the jurisdiction to hear cases,"[36] martial law authorities simply proscribed further writs. In 1960, therefore, the Supreme Court qualified its construction of judicial–military relations by confirming the limited authority of the civil courts to question actions of martial law authorities. In *Muhammad Ayub Khuhro v. Pakistan* (PLD 1960 Supreme Court 237), in which the ever-litigious Mr. Khuhro contested charges of embezzlement and corruption, the court ruled that unless expressly prohibited, regulation by regulation, the court could review specific acts of special military tribunals. The court concluded that the special tribunal that had tried Khuhro was not "a criminal Court as established by law," and that its proceedings and determinations were void. The case was a small victory for civil law; it also provided instruction for martial law authorities when constituting future military tribunals.

*Confirming power* Having in the main affirmed the legality and powers of the regime, and having demurred from ruling on the goals of the state or the manner in which they might be achieved, the courts were now asked to review specific exercises of state power. Among the actions they considered were pillars of the regime's political policies – the military's appropriation of the media and attendant violations of free speech – and some of its economic policies – martial law policies to reform the system of land tenure.

The first major problem to come before the courts was the seizure of newspapers. In April 1959, the central government dissolved the Board of Directors of Progressive Papers Ltd. (PPL), a privately held newspaper company whose publications had been outspokenly opposed to the government. (PPL editors Faiz Ahmad Faiz, Syed Sibte Hasan and Ahmad Nadim Qasmi were arrested immediately after General Ayub Khan took power and only released months later at the direction of the Lahore High Court.) It directed the owner's shares to be seized and disposed by public auction, but the buyer was not required to pay full price to the owners.[37] Mian Iftikharuddin, the owner of the company and a prominent, often dissident politician, petitioned to stay the government order (*Mian Iftikhar-ud-Din & Arif Iftikhar v. Muhammad Sarfraz*, PLD 1961 Lahore 842).

The government justified its action on the basis of its amendments to

[36] Language used by Justice Shabir Ahmad reviewing the case in *Gulab Din v. Major A.T. Shaukat*, PLD 1961 (W.P.) Lahore 952, at 977.

[37] See Zamir Niazi, *Press in Chains* (Karachi: Karachi Press Club, 1986), pp. 79–82.

the 1952 Security of Pakistan Act,[38] which allowed it to remove the owners or directors of any news company. Mian Iftikharuddin's counsel, long-time civil rights attorney Mian Mahmud Ali Kasuri, contended that the President could not validly promulgate ordinances which amended laws made prior to the declaration of martial law.[39] The Lahore High Court, however, ruled that *Dosso* gave the President just such powers. Mian Kasuri also argued that the amendment was *mala fides*, retrospective and beyond the competence of the government to effect. Although admitting that the court could declare an ordinance invalid had it "crossed the frontiers within which it had to remain," Justice Shabir Ahmad nonetheless rejected these propositions. Consistent with the order, the High Court dismissed Mian Iftikharuddin's right to speak against the order before it was passed. The court also refused to defy the standing order against legal challenges to the regime, refused as well to accept Mahmud Ali Kasuri's distinction between statutory and constitutional provisions and amendments, and rejected any distinctions between substantive and procedural rights. The High Court thus accepted fully the rights-canceling import of *Dosso* and *Mehdi Ali Khan*.

On appeal, the Supreme Court reconsidered all of these points (*Mian Iftikhar-ud-Din and Arif Iftikhar v. Muhammaed Sarfraz and the Government of Pakistan, and vice-versa*, PLD 1961 Supreme Court 585). Speaking for the majority, Justice Kaikaus determined that the 1958 Order protected "all action taken by the present regime under the Security of Pakistan Act." He distinguished presidential powers exercised under the abrogated constitution, which were subject to constitutional limitations, and those of a supra-constitutional nature, which could override the constitution. (The limits included in the first category were easily revoked by the second category of acts.) Invoking *Dosso*, Justice Kaikaus described the abrogated constitution "as an enactment adopted by the President and subject to his will." Mian Qasuri, however, argued that such powers required accountability:

MR. JUSTICE HAMOOD-UR-REHMAN: Is it your contention that because he says he is a citizen, he cannot exercise any powers?

MR. KASURI: That is why he is calling the country a republic. The President is not an Officer; he has no divine right to rule over us. The President holds himself answerable to the people. He is not like Louis the 14th.

38 Security of Pakistan (Amendment) Ordinance, 1959 (XXIII of 1959), promulgated 19 April 1959; Security of Pakistan (Amendment) Ordinance, 1961 (XIV of 1961), promulgated 22 April 1961.

39 He relied on the decision of the Supreme Court in *Muhammad Ayub Khuhro v. Pakistan*, PLD 1960 SC (Pak) 237, which differentiated between martial law ordinances and regulations. The court rejected this as precedent.

He argued that the power to amend and interfere with fundamental rights did not necessarily cancel those rights. His probable aim was to resurrect the natural justice arguments proposed by Justice Cornelius in *Dosso* and *Mehdi Ali Khan*. Nevertheless, the court judged the issue immune to judicial consideration, for "even if the Central Government did contravene a principle of natural justice, its order would not be liable to challenge in a Court of law."

The constitutional effects of this judgment were broad. Both courts sustained the regime's supra-constitutional authority and accepted the merged legislative, executive and military functions which defined Ayub Khan's office. Both demurred on the question of fundamental rights, retaining the popular belief that rights no longer existed. The judiciary maintained its distance from contentious or potentially explosive legal problems. By example if not dictum, the court agreed with Mian Kasuri that "it was never intended that the Judges may become constitution-makers." Without a formal constitution, the courts were unwilling to stand for an abstract idea of constitutionalism, accepting instead the Kelsenian distinction between form and substance postulated earlier by Justice Munir.

The Supreme Court ruling had profound political effects as well. It removed impediments to government plans to establish paramountcy over national communications; the media were now brought under bureaucratic control. The government created an ostensibly independent umbrella organization, the National Press Trust, to govern the workings of a raft of newspapers (those owned by Progressive Papers among them), controlling policy related to recruitment and hiring, the distribution of newsprint and government advertising and editorial practices. A system of press advice instituted by Information Secretary Altaf Gauhar enabled the government to monitor and in some cases control the content of reporting.[40] In the absence of justiciable rights, press freedom was jeopardised and a long subcontinental tradition of activist journalism was muted in Pakistan.

Nonetheless, the legal status of the 1958 Order remained unclear. *Dosso* validated the abrogation of the 1956 Constitution but it did not decide whether abrogation had to be in favor of an alternative document. By keeping the question open, *Dosso* offered the martial law administration

[40] The publishers and editors of the *Dacca Times* and *Ittefaq* (Dacca) frequently and unsuccessfully sued the East Pakistan government to overturn its prohibition of news coverage of protests against federal and provincial policies. *Toffazal Hossain v. Government of East Pakistan and another*, 17 DLR (1965) 76; *Toffazal Hossain and Motahar Hossain Siddiqui v. Province of East Pakistan and others*, 17 DLR (1965) 498; *Toffazal Hossain and Motahar Hossain Siddiqui and Zahirul Islam v. Government of East Pakistan through Home Secretary*, 19 DLR (1967) 79.

the room it needed to structure the state. *Mehdi Ali Khan* assumed that the abrogation had been in favor of the 1958 Order, but did not explicitly validate it. In 1961, when the Lahore High Court considered the ouster of writ jurisdiction toward martial law authorities, it tried to establish that judicial exclusion was not absolute.[41]

Only in 1963, when a new constitution was already in force, did the court take up the constitutionality of martial law regulations – now largely moot – and the abridgments of judicial jurisdiction they ordered or implied. *Muhammad Afzal v. The Commissioner, Lahore Division and The Estate Officer, Lahore Improvement Trust* (PLD 1963 Supreme Court 401) provided a useful transition to a period of mixed governance. The judgment was not wholly satisfactory for proponents of full judicial independence and fundamental rights, or for advocates of a strong centralized state exemplified by the military regime; at most it implied that the mixed civil–military administration was a dubious enterprise.

The appellants argued that martial law orders inconsistent with the 1956 Constitution were invalid and could not remove rights available under that constitution. These included rights granted to individual citizens, such as property rights, and those granted generally, such as the right to challenge the government in court. Martial law orders had canceled the former and specifically curtailed the latter. Justice Hamoodur Rahman read the 1958 Order to provide an administrative and legislative hierarchy to martial law, with only the CMLA capable of canceling or amending those laws in effect before martial law. He distinguished martial law regulations from actions taken pursuant to them, separated the responsibilities and liabilities of local martial law administrators from CMLA Ayub Khan and ruled that the ordinance under review was not competently made because it conflicted with existing laws and presidential ordinances. He therefore found that local military regulations that conflicted with civil laws were never protected by the 1958 Order and could be found invalid. Most important, he ruled that their validity could be questioned, "if that did not amount to questioning the Martial Law Order itself."

This judgment therefore provided an interesting gloss on the law-giving and law-executing powers of military rule. If Ayub Khan could set the terms of constitutional structure by proclamation but could only administer it directly, his rule would be constrained. In *Muhammad Afzal*, Justice

[41] *Gulab Din v. Major A.T. Shaukat*, PLD 1961 (W.P.) Lahore 952. The court determined that the 1959 Land Reforms Regulation could not be challenged itself but that actions taken pursuant to it could be questioned by the courts. This followed the ruling in *Khuhro* that laws made by the martial law administration were passed under the executive's delegated powers of legislation.

Hamoodur Rahman tried to buttress anti-*Dosso* arguments by limiting the immunity of the regime from judicial investigation and thus limiting the reach of *Dosso*.

From 1958 through 1962, the courts lived with the most restrictive consequences of *Dosso*: a regime perpetuating the vice-regal system under the banner of military rule and the pretence of revolutionary success, a system of civil institutions coexisting unhappily with a parallel system of military institutions. Each parry by civil society was answered with a sharp counter-thrust from the martial law regime. For civil society, the state's prevailing norms produced only structural tensions and systemic incompatibilities. In the short term, the superior courts chipped away at the powers of the military state by confirming incrementally the residual powers of the judiciary. Their rulings were cautious measures against the controlling authority of martial law. In the absence of constitutional rights the judiciary was at a loss to gain ground against military power. Anxious not to withdraw from view, equally concerned not to offer further licence for military rule, the courts seemed to sanction authoritarianism as a middle ground between preferred democracy and feared autocracy. At best, this can be read as a tactical maneuver by the justices to secure their place in the state.

However, their decisions helped indirectly to extend the reach of the martial law state and thus to limit the scope of judicial rulings. Without a formal constitution it was immeasurably difficult to write constitutional opinions. Each small court triumph against military rule was easily undercut by martial law authorities who could with one stroke rewrite the regulations and ordinances governing daily life. Courts and martial law authorities played by irreconcilable rules, calling into question the strategic bargain into which the judiciary had entered. The courts were an undeniable component of the political system, seeking its weakest links while upholding the steel frame of power. This disharmony might have broken down completely had not the military's grip on society gradually loosened, and had not Ayub Khan promulgated a constitution, if a deeply flawed one, in 1962.

## *Confirming rights*

The post-1962 period provided an equally complex scenario for judicial interpretation. Ayub Khan promulgated his constitution unilaterally, paying little heed to the recommendations of his Constitutional Commission. The presidential constitution did little to dispel the fears and critical problems of a divided citizenry. The obeisance to authority and the uncertainties that colored politics remained a material part of public life.

While considering prospects for more democratic rule, politicians also had to decide how to live within bounds still defined by authoritarianism. The same questions about cooperation and complicity, responsibility and autonomy that occupied the judiciary's attention also affected the ways that political parties and individual politicians dealt with each other and with the state.

The courts, however, were back in business, with a national constitution against which they could measure executive actions. Until justiciable rights were added to the constitution by grudging amendment in 1964, the courts were unable to do much more than clarify rules of procedure. Once rights were added, the superior courts were better situated to draw distinct lines of rights and obligations between the state and the citizen, providing an opening for political expression that would find greater voice later in the decade. Having lived with *Dosso*, the courts now tried to find ways, tentatively and incrementally, to revise it.

The judiciary found an early opportunity to rule on challenges to presidential ordinance-making power and in the process to assert judicial authority when Ayub Khan attempted unilaterally to amend the constitution (*Muhammad Abdul Haque v. Fazlul Quader Chowdhury et al.*, PLD 1963 Dacca 669). Ayub Khan wanted members of his executive councils to speak in the National Assembly even if they were not members, and issued ordinances to amend the constitution to that effect (the Assembly was not able to amend ordinances until 1966). One Assembly member brought the matter to the Dacca High Court, asking generally whether a presidential order which conflicted with the constitution would prevail. The Dacca Court held that the presidential order amending the constitution violated the constitution, warning that "it is of the very essence of a written Constitution that it is not susceptible of an easy change." The court also noted that prohibitions against judicial scrutiny of government actions transgressed the spirit of a written constitution, even one, as High Court Justice Murshed wryly suggested, whose provisions "are novel and unfamiliar in the country."

The Supreme Court did not accept an appeal (*Mr. Fazlul Quader Chowdhry and others v. Mr. Muhammad Abdul Haque*, PLD 1963 Supreme Court 486). In his sternly worded dismissal, Justice Cornelius, now Chief Justice, put the government on notice that the written constitution gave the courts powers that they would exercise with vigilance. He affirmed the authority of the high courts to interpret the constitution and the power of the Supreme Court to stand "firm in defence of its provisions against attack of any kind." The constitution, he averred, "is the fundamental law of the State, in opposition to which any other law, or direction or order, must be inoperative and void." The constitution continued the habit of executive paramountcy but was nonetheless to be treated above other laws and orders. Cornelius underscored the preeminence of the constitution, which he called "the master-law." This definitional hierarchy was crucial, for Pakistan had been governed for most of its sixteen years by approximations of constitutional rule rather than by clear constitutional instruments. Cornelius warned that, even if the document itself did not embody democratic principles, the President could not override the constitution he had created.

Describing presidential authority as "just short of constitutional power," Justice Cornelius allowed constitutional modification "not for the purpose of *altering the Constitution itself*, but in order that the Constitution as a whole should be brought into force." The court was determined to hold Ayub Khan to the presidential constitution he had written, weak though it was. Judicial review would continue unless the legislature voted to restrict it. The constitutional source of judicial jurisdiction, in Justice Kaikaus's words, would lean strongly against its ouster.

In *Fazlul Quader Chowdhry* the courts tested three propositions of constitutional rule. Asked which governmental organs could judge the proper use of presidential authority, they concluded unhesitatingly that the courts held final authority under the 1962 Constitution. Asked whether presidential power was unlimited, they answered clearly in the negative; and asked whether the president had exercised his powers constitutionally, they answered with an equally firm "no". *Fazlul Quader Chowdhry* became a landmark in the Ayub constitutional period. In one judgment, it established the right of the judiciary to judge specific presidential acts, general directions for presidential action, and the status of state institutions under the 1962 Constitution. The decision told the country that executive rule was fettered by the written constitution and that the constitution's guardians were the courts.

The courts exercised greater powers after fundamental rights were incorporated into the constitution the following year. Individual citizens were empowered, although in limited ways, to challenge the state. To the extent that citizens could claim rights from the state, the balance of constitutional power began to shift from the president to the polity. This shift was far from complete and was not intended to be so. Ayub Khan's constitution embodied conflicting political interests – civilian versus military, local versus national, East versus West – and his administration, through the Basic Democracies scheme, underlined these tensions. By 1964, Pakistan was ruled by an amalgam of civil and military rules, laws and ordinances, some originating decades before independence, which together comprised a crazy-quilt of inconsistent guides for (and against) political action. Ayub Khan held sway but the justiciable rights he unwillingly allowed, thinking their admission was merely a bargain to retain power, spelled the beginning of the end for the Ayub era by exposing its weaknesses. In this enterprise, the courts became willing collaborators.

From 1964 to 1969, the superior courts ruled in a number of important governance arenas: the role and functioning of political parties, the nature of political opposition, the extent to which government could control political expression and throughout, the judicial role in establishing these limits. A major test of judicial powers came just at the time that rights were added to the constitution, when a contest between the federal government and an opposition political party reached the courts. It is testament to the courts that they traversed the grounds of rights and judicial review amid a sticky conflict of wills and ideologies.

*Political parties* After the constitution came into force the legislature passed the 1962 Political Parties Act, a statute that regulated political party activities. Despite this law, the government dissolved a contentious opposition party, the Jammat-i-Islami, by summarily closing its operations and delegalising it under the 1908 Criminal Law Amendment Act. The Jamaat and its founder and leader, Maulana Maudoodi, had opposed the founding of Pakistan; after independence, the party labored to include its concept of an Islamic state in the first constitution, and often took the role of iconoclast in Pakistani politics. The decision to provoke a legal conflict with the Jamaat highlighted not only the government's own decision to underplay the role of Islam in the state, but its fears that unrestricted political parties might seriously undermine its monopoly of voice and power.

At the time of these suits, the party was actively engaged in public agitations in both provinces, and to some – even those who upheld universal rights – its platform sounded seditious. It was thus a point of some irony that political party rights were tested on behalf of the Jamaat. The Jamaat immediately contested the government action in criminal and civil appeals; the West Pakistan High Court dismissed the criminal petition, while the East Pakistan High Court admitted the civil appeal.[42] Both cases were brought to the Supreme Court in a joint appeal (*Saiyyid Abul A'la Maudoodi, et al. v. The Government of West Pakistan and the Government of Pakistan* and *The Province of East Pakistan v. Tamizuddin Ahmad and The Government of Pakistan*, PLD 1964 Supreme Court 673).

The court upheld the rights of political parties and condemned the

[42] In West Pakistan, Criminal Appeal No. 43 of 1964; in East Pakistan, Civil Appeal No. 19 D of 1964, *Tamizuddin Ahmed v. The Government of East Pakistan*, PLD 1964 Dacca 795.

government for actions designed to deprive the party and its members of their rights. Chief Justice Cornelius confined his court's concerns to three related fundamental rights problems: the nature of limited rights under the Ayub regime, the definition of political parties and political activities protected by fundamental rights guarantees, and the relationships between fundamental rights and judicial review. The case gave full scope to a long debate about political parties between two familiar attorneys, Manzur Qadir for the government and A.K. Brohi for the Jamaat; the court in turn explored the fragility of political organization and the limits of appellate jurisdiction under the 1962 Constitution. The Chief Justice accepted the basis, if not the full content, of Brohi's efforts to justify a broad range of political party rights and activities. Such an argument was not needed to accomplish the Jamaat's goal in court and certainly overstated the degree of democracy intended by Ayub Khan's government; as Justice Hamoodur Rahman noted, "the Act does not say that once a political party has been formed, it shall always be a political party and that it shall not be dissolved except by a decision of the Supreme Court." The Act included many logical lacunae; among other problems, it "prescribed no mode for bringing into legal existence a political party. It merely recognizes its *de facto* existence."

Throughout *Maudoodi*, the court carefully contrasted concepts of public order and individual rights, seeking to determine the boundaries of government intervention in political life and the degree to which they could be challenged. The debate between Qadir and Brohi crystallized the practical and conceptual difficulties of controlled democracy. If rights symbolized freedom to contest rules of political debate, as Brohi proposed, restricting those rights denied the open quality of politics, constrained prospects for truly active parties and challenged conventional understandings of rights. Alternately, Qadir's representation for the central government distinguished the 1962 Act from a "charter of liberty for political parties to operate as they pleased." The central government had the awkward task of defending limited democracy in the language of open political discourse, the Jamaat the easier job of upbraiding the court to defend constitutional rights in the face of a strong government predilection to ignore them.

Justice Cornelius urged an independent judicial investigation into government complaints about the Jamaat-i-Islami's violation of public order. He felt that the court's responsibility was to balance the claims of individual rights against the reasonableness of government actions, a task best accomplished after a separate hearing on the facts of the case. Cornelius may have had in mind cases like *Dosso* in which Pakistan's political future was mortgaged to unverified observations about the political environment. In *Maudoodi*, however, this proposal (which the court did not accept) gave Cornelius an opportunity to expand on judicial review to ensure that constitutional rights were meaningful in substance and procedure. As Justice Kaikaus's opinion confirmed, absolute rights and controlled democracy could not easily coexist, the government's concept of limited rights was internally inconsistent and, perhaps most important, constitutional rights once given can not easily be withdrawn. The absolutist rights grounds on which the court decided *Maudoodi* were connected to tight relationships between legislative sovereignty and integrity, popular sovereignty and judicial review, and the substance and form of democracy.

Justice S.A. Rahman also offered direct political counsel to Ayub Khan. Noting that "the opposition of today may be the Government of tomorrow," he cautioned, "to place an instrument in the hands of the party in power by which they can effectually eliminate from the political scene any opposition, without let or hindrance, cannot be held to be consistent with healthy function of the body-politic on democratic lines." His comments were a warning to Ayub Khan as he prepared for the 1965 elections. Using the language of constitutional rights, the court chose an intensely political method for establishing the role that justiciable rights could play in repoliticizing the Pakistani state.

*Basic Democracies* Accompanying concerns about the substance of political rights were those of administrative organization in the Basic Democracies. In 1965, the East Pakistan High Court was approached with a case that challenged legislative and executive powers under the 1965 Electoral College Act and the division of provincial–central government responsibilities in the Basic Democracies framework. Thirteen writ petitions were filed in Dacca and combined in *Sherajul Haque Patwari v. Sub-divisional Officer, Chandpur* (PLD 1966 Dacca 331). The Dacca Court took up several related issues: the separation of powers in the basic democracies system and provincial–center relations within that scheme; superior court jurisdiction to review aspects of the basic democracies orders; and the kind of democracy implied by such orders. The court supported the petitioners' objections to executive actions, in language so strong that the Supreme Court appeal judgment included a reprimand to Dacca Chief Justice Murshed. whose dramatic judgments presaged his own entry into Bengali politics later in the decade and his inclusion in crucial negotiations prior to the Bangladesh war.

Protesting "the compound brewed in the cauldron of an executive and legislative misalliance," the High Court suggested that the 1965 Act purposefully confused administrative and electoral functions by requiring the provincial government to execute policies which it had no voice in formulating – an "abdication of legislative power" which purposefully confused administrative and political functions. The Act required the legislature to derogate from its duties by allowing electoral bodies to acquire legislative functions indirectly rather than by specific conferment, presumably with limits and discretions. Justice Murshed interpreted the separation of powers in the 1962 Constitution strictly: the constitution enumerated provincial and central government responsibilities, in the words of the court, "to ensure fixty [sic] of legislative machineries and to avoid confusion and laxity in legislative competency." The Act transgressed these boundaries.

The Act's language opened the door for judicial scrutiny. Citing the Supreme Court's judgment in *Fazlul Quader Chowdhry*, the Dacca Court claimed its right to review the purpose of the law. Again, it cast its judgment in the language of legal and political responsibility:

> A Constitution is a sacrosanct document which must guide the machineries of Government. It is of seminal consequence that its provisions must be faithfully and meticulously followed. It specifically places the duty of preserving and enforcing the Constitution upon the Courts. Such duty cannot effectively be discharged if the Courts cannot decide that a Legislature has failed to observe the *mandamus* of the Constitution.

The Dacca Court based its opinion on several assumptions and implications: that legislative responsibility was exclusively the domain of the legislature; that the intentions of a legislative amendment could be read in its wording, even when no legislative history was available to inform that reading; that the separation of powers confined the actions of each branch of government within its written constitutional mandate; that the purview of the courts extended beyond written boundaries to give effect to the overall purposes of the constitution and the judiciary. The 1962 Constitution and the 1959 Basic Democracies Order were to be read to make them consistent in the pursuit of a concept of democracy that was still undefined. Were this not possible, the purposes of both documents would be called into question.

The High Court opinion is particularly important for its arguments against infringements on provincial autonomy. The Dacca Court interpreted central government claims to democracy in the 1959 Basic Democracies Order against related standards of provincial autonomy and the separation of powers. Its ruling was a manifesto for opponents of Basic Democracies and Ayub Khan's administrative state. While the court did not rule on the *vires* of the 1959 Order, its decision resembles a preamble to such an opinion: if the assumptions of Basic Democracies could be proven wrong, then the Order's concept of democracy could also be proven wrong – and with it, the purported purposes of the constitution, and, by implication, the organization of the state.

The Supreme Court reversed the Dacca judgment on all these grounds (*Province of East Pakistan et al. v. Sirajul Huq Patwari and others*, PLD 1966 Supreme Court 854). Chief Justice Cornelius detailed the principles, evolution and current practices of Basic Democracies to remind the High Court that basic democracies were legally mandated and that "a law made in proper form ... is to prevail unless its operation is frustrated by reference to one or more of the accepted rules by which conflicts of laws, under a Federal Constitution, are to be resolved." Constitutional laws were appropriate if properly written. A similarly conservative view determined whether the delegation of powers was excessive, as suggested by the Dacca Court, and whether rights had been violated. Political theory might influence politics, but should influence judicial discretion only when explicitly needed. To act otherwise, Cornelius suggested, would be to propose "a new principle on which all laws, whether new or old, would be placed in jeopardy at the hands of the courts." The Supreme Court's disdain for the Dacca Court ruling can be understood not simply as a challenge to Justice Murshed's opinion, but also as an attempt to retain the powers of judicial review carefully being crafted by the Supreme Court, and even more as a guard against the possibilities of unraveling the state which the High Court found in the Act.

Pursuing similar arguments, Justice Hamoodur Rahman proposed that items not within the specified competence of central or provincial governments should be assumed to be concurrent, a constitutional structure that Ayub Khan had eschewed in writing the 1962 Constitution. He, too, seemed determined to find a reasoned foundation for the Basic Democracies.[43] He suggested that constitutions and ancillary laws were flexible instruments for political change rather than rigid definitions of state structure. In *Sirajul Huq Patwari*, the Supreme Court allowed constitutional laws considerable space while still asserting its right to review legislation and interpret the constitution. It evinced remarkable faith in government's pursuit of the common good. At the least, the judgment suggests restraint in condemning elected government, and in so doing, hampered Justice Murshed's efforts to liberalize a praetorian constitution for Bengal as well as the rest of the country. Reacting against the provincialist spirit of the Dacca Court's judgment, the Supreme Court supported government actions which did not explicitly trespass com-

[43] The Dacca Court also contested Basic Democracies in *Mr. Abdul Hafez v. Government of East Pakistan and others*, 19 DLR (1967) 539, when it announced that the Basic Democracies Order was not a "central law" as one "made by or under authority of central legislatures and includes law made by the President."

monly accepted principles of political practice without judging those principles. *Sirajul Huq Patwari* can thus be read as a vote of confidence in the right of the state to take charge of its administration, if not the underlying principles of the Basic Democracies scheme. When the court took on Ayub Khan, it was for his transgressions of positive rights, not the organization of his state.

*Detention and political expression* Within a year, the Supreme Court again confronted tensions between concepts of public order and individual rights. *The Government of East Pakistan v. Mrs. Rowshan Bijaya Shaukat Ali Khan* (PLD 1966 Supreme Court 286) took up the persistent problem of preventive detention, an instrument often used to control political opposition, in considering a *habeas corpus* petition from the wife of a political activist detained under the 1958 East Pakistan Public Safety Ordinance. In *Rowshan*, the court upheld its strong rights statement in *Maudoodi*, but its judgment reflected deep divisions among the justices about the extent to which rights guarantees should restrict government powers.

Expressing the court's view that "prevention detention ... makes an inroad on the personal liberty of a citizen without the safeguards inherent in a formal trial," Justice S.A. Rahman cautioned that its use must be kept within constitutional and legal confines. He unequivocally defended open political participation: "In a democratic system of Government it is the right of any party not in power to criticise measures adopted by the Government, in order to discredit it in the public eye, so as to oust it from power by constitutional means." To restrict that right – especially without proving that a detainee had dangerous ulterior motives – would deny fundamental rights. Upholding positive rights while optimistically appraising the constitution, he noted that its framers "tried to strike an equitable balance between the rights of the individual and the interests of collective security and personal liberty."

Striking this balance in court, however, proved difficult. The original *habeas corpus* petition argued that the 1958 Ordinance was illegal (as a continuation of earlier illegal laws) and that the grounds for detention were impossibly vague. Justice Cornelius was willing to admit the second charge in principle but upheld the provincial government action and refused to judge the validity of the arrest on procedural grounds. He suggested that "if facts show that the law has been used bona fide and not colourable for mere oppression" the court was not empowered to contest state action – a rare example of reticence on his part in furthering claims of individual rights and extending judicial review powers. Justices Kaikaus and Hamoodur Rahman nonetheless voted to dismiss the case, holding that government actions conflicted with fundamental rights, and Justice S.A. Rahman voted to dismiss the case without citing a conflict with rights.

Troublesome as *Rowshan* was, the court's majority supported individual rights to extend political expression. Justice Cornelius's concerns soon resurfaced, however. When the West Pakistan High Court upheld limits to political speech imposed by the provincial government, the Supreme Court broadened the scope of justiciable rights while confirming limits to opposition political activities. In *Malik Ghulam Jilani v. The Government of West Pakistan* (PLD 1967 Supreme Court 373), the court questioned limits imposed on politics in a controlled democracy, although it also tried to define allowable restrictions on the proportions of political opposition.

The origins of the case struck at the heart of Ayub Khan's regime, which had long justified its praetorian aspect in national security terms. In January 1966, after Pakistan signed the Tashkent Declaration to signal the end of the 1965 war with India, opposition parties convened a conference and organized processions in Lahore to oppose the Declaration, which they felt favored India. They defied the imposition of Section 144 of the Pakistan Criminal Procedure Code by the provincial government prohibiting "direct action" against the central government. Among the political parties attending the conference as a member of the Combined Opposition Parties was the Jamaat-i-Islami. During a rally, Jamaat leader Mian Tufail was reported by police informers to have lambasted Ayub Khan for promulgating a constitution in which "the people had been deprived of their elementary rights and all effective power was placed in the hands of the President, who was responsible to no one." Condemning the 1962 Constitution as inadequate, undemocratic and "an instrument of oppression," the Jamaat resolved to revoke the emergency and change the political system.

Although procession organizers – among them Malik Ghulam Jilani, Sardar Shaukat Hayat Khan and Nawabzada Nasrullah Khan – claimed to have taken no part in the Jamaat's demonstration, the police arrested them all for instigating riots.[44] The High Court upheld police concern for maintaining public order. The Supreme Court, however, found this view too restrictive. Indeed, Justice Cornelius chastized the High Court for lacking "any clear appreciation" of the facts of the situation, reminding the court that "the ascertainment of reasonable grounds is essentially a judicial or at least a *quasi*-judicial function," and that judicial review was

[44] Their detentions were upheld by the High Court in *Malik Hamid Sarfraz v. The Deputy Commissioner, Lahore*, PLD 1966 (W.P.) Lahore 847. All the organizers were politicians of standing who tried to underscore government weakness by courting arrest.

needed precisely to determine the propriety and reasonableness of government actions. Appearing on behalf of Malik Ghulam Jilani, A.K. Brohi had suggested that the actions envisaged by the defendants were in "the legitimate sphere of political activity." Police evidence, accepted by the High Court and by Chief Justice Cornelius, indicated that Mian Tufail intended, in Justice Cornelius's words, to "open conflict with the Government, as by law established." He thought that Brohi's interpretation justified "politicians to play with fire in the hope that they will eventually be able to subdue the conflagration they cause." The court therefore upheld detentions to prevent intrusions of public order.

The Supreme Court's brief judgment was silent on many critical issues. When the Chief Justice declared that "to bring about political changes by Constitutional means alone is legitimate," he did not define such means. More important, he did not discuss, as Justice Hamoodur Rahman had done earlier, the contradictions in a political system that severely restricted the boundaries of political action. Opposition parties contended that the emergency prevented legal political organizing and prohibited political change by constitutional means. In fact, the court's proposed relation between intention and consequence left the concept of constitutional political change extremely unclear. Those who foment rebellion may know the effects of their actions; it can certainly be argued that on other occasions the Jamaat purposefully instigated unrest to prove a political point. The Combined Opposition Parties, however, had legally contested elections against Ayub Khan just the year before and were now using public opposition to the Tashkent agreement to express dissatisfaction with the elected government. When political organizing is outlawed, the results of purportedly illegal gatherings are hard to calculate. All that can be predicted is that their consequences, peaceful or disruptive, will also be illegal within the terms of an emergency. In such situations, where can constitutional political change originate? While the organizers knew well that by their actions they were inviting arrest, the court's emphasis on law and order led it to accept unreasonably high costs.

In *Ghulam Jilani*, the Supreme Court again confronted politics directly, and again took a directly political course for its decision. By the time the court heard this case, however, the political tide had already turned against Ayub Khan; the court's opinion therefore reacted as much to a climate of instability as to the challenges that *Malik Ghulam Jilani* posed to the structure of government authority. While it affirmed the authority of judicial review, it limited the scope of legitimate political action. Ironically, Justice Cornelius proposed in this case what he opposed in *Dosso*: to reduce the meaning of legitimacy in favor of the limited reading of legality sanctioned by the regime in power.

Even though *Ghulam Jilani* supported the government, the government was unhappy with the court's requirement that reasonable grounds must justify detention. Despite further cases upholding the decision,[45] the extended powers of judicial review implied in this judgment were subsequently restricted by ordinance.[46] In *Government of West Pakistan v. Begum Agha Abdul Karim Shorish Kashmiri* (PLD 1969 Supreme Court 14), the province proposed that detainees prove that arresting authorities acted invalidly – presuming guilt procedurally prior to innocence. Speaking for the court, Justice Hamoodur Rahman linked the right of review with the right of citizens to forestall deprivations of liberty. He labeled the amended ordinance "an exercise in futility," warned that no security laws had sanctioned "arbitrary, unguided, uncontrolled or naked power. . . to any authority," and advised that emergency provisions did not create new conditions for interpreting laws, although they could affect the court's judgment about what might constitute reasonableness. The Court thus advanced its review powers in direct contravention of government wishes. The government was by then weakening rapidly, however, and Ayub Khan did not have the opportunity to circumvent the court's ruling on this subject again.

The post-1962 constitutional judgments offered a mixed bag of decisions, confirming constitutional rights and extending the powers of the judicial review on the one hand, accepting state limits on political voice and action on the other. When specific rights were articulated in the constitution, however limited they might be, the courts were willing to relinquish natural justice and natural rights arguments in favor of the positive rights vehicles provided by the state. Chief Justice Cornelius, for example, did not use natural rights pleas to extend political rights or civil liberties beyond the limits set by the constitution. Justice S.A. Rahman, reluctant to protect natural rights, was punctilious in protecting positive rights, judging the law by its letter rather than by independent doctrine or presumed intent.

Although civil liberties were attached rights to the constitution, real rights protections were not necessarily furthered by this addition: limited substantive rights did not, for example, expand the range of political opposition. Even efforts to constrain abuses of power through extra-

[45] The first was *Mir Abdul Baqi Baluch v. Government of Pakistan*, PLD 1968 Supreme Court 313. The Karachi verdict in this case was delivered two months before *Ghulam Jilani* and appeals were again filed challenging the validity of detention. The Supreme Court reiterated its decision in *Ghulam Jilani* and remanded the case to the High Court.

[46] Ordinance No. 2 of 1968 amended the 1965 Defence of Pakistan Ordinance 3(2)(x), under which Malik Ghulam Jilani was originally detained. The amended section declared that "the sufficiency of the grounds on which such opinion as aforesaid is based shall be determined by the authority forming such opinion."

constitutional laws faltered in the face of a strong executive. While Justice Cornelius had praised the Frontier Crimes Regulations in *Dosso*, for example, the regulations were fair only if applied fairly. Ayub Khan, however, employed the FCR ruthlessly to harass his opponents, including the National Awami Party (NAP), whose members he imprisoned; similar provisions were incorporated into the West Pakistan criminal code for similar purposes.

Moreover, the growing distance between East and West Pakistan, reflected in disputes between the Dacca High Court and the Supreme Court, was not solved by the federal court's assertions of national interest. Judicial rhetoric could not mask either the inequities between the wings that Ayub Khan chose not to correct, or the growing perception in East Pakistan that its rights might not ever be respected. The court's belief in the common good thus put off its exact definition for determination under more pliable circumstances. That time, however, never arrived.

The Supreme Court discovered its capacity to extend rights guarantees by looking inward rather than outward, taking opportunities to sustain and broaden the right of judicial review as a vehicle for discussing rights generally. In cases like *Maudoodi* and *Shorish Kashmiri*, its opinions drew a close line between the procedural right of review and the substantive rights such review might protect. In others, like *Ghulam Jilani*, *Fazlul Quader Chowdhry*, and *Sirajul Huq Patwari*, the court differentiated the two tasks, trying to extend judicial review apart from contestable substantive rights guarantees. The court protected procedural rights but viewed substantive politics as an exclusively legislative arena, even when the elected assemblies were weak and constituted within a highly restricted political environment. The justices believed that the route to stronger legislatures was not through judicial action but through active politics. The substance of political change – even when form and content were not conceptually distant, as in *Ghulam Jilani* – was a task apart.

These opinions probably represented a deliberate judicial strategy to retain and where possible augment the parameters of judicial action to retain elements of democracy in the constitution. The superior courts tempered their efforts to restrain the exercise of power legally by continually applying political prudence. But prudence kept judicial purview restricted to the constrained mechanisms for political voice structured by Ayub Khan. It was a strange and twisted compact, as any attempts to build democracy from authoritarianism without revolution must surely be. Therefore, this strategy provided conflicting direction for political opposition. Parties, hastily outlawed in the 1958 *coup d'état*, were partially restored in 1962 and affirmed in the 1964 *Maudoodi* decision. Their activities were circumscribed by the 1965 emergency and were undercut further in 1967 by the *Ghulam Jilani* judgment, when government emergency provisions were amplified more than the rights of political opposition, despite specific standards against which rights violations were to be measured.

Reviews of this strategy were mixed. Writing in 1965 about judicial review of administrative tribunals, one local commentator thought that the courts appropriately balanced public order concerns and individual liberty.[47] Malik Ghulam Jilani thought otherwise. He lamented that "any law which a citizen can invoke in his defense or for his protection is quickly changed ... The so-called constitution finds itself amended and multilated [sic] the moment any court of law appears likely to grant relief to a citizen under its provisions, and the courts accept amendments with obvious satisfaction."[48] "Expression is stifled and dissent is frowned upon," he concluded, adding sadly that "justice is no longer a matter of right."

Superior court decisions allowed a measure of dissent to meet but not permeate the regime, doing little damage to the short-term stability of the state but giving vent to opposition opinions. The judiciary also offered a protected forum in which those opposed to the regime could express their views. In both ways, the court put reform before revolution as an acceptable mode for political change. The judiciary preserved and perhaps strengthened itself institutionally when it might otherwise have found itself stranded in a sea of corruption and imposed state authority. Justice Cornelius exerted a more extreme and provocative presence when he was in minority in the 1950s. In the 1960s, faced with the need to fashion a majority, he seemed to step back to retain the court's independence. His version of prudence, however, did not compromise the character of the state or the judiciary, as had happened in the 1950s. If living with *Dosso* meant living with the state according to Ayub Khan, the court seemed determined to outlive his edicts, if not change the state itself. The pressures of political opposition – partially attributable to the judiciary's protection of fundamental rights – helped lead to the breakdown of Ayub Khan's regime. The court would then, temporarily, have the last word.

### *Political prospect*

All these political and legal currents were evident in October 1968 when Federal Law Minister S.M. Zafar convened a celebration of the consti-

47 S.M. Haider, *Judicial Review of Administrative Discretion in Pakistan* (Lahore: All Pakistan Legal Decisions, 1967).

48 "Times Always Passes," unpublished manuscript, p. 3, cited in Lawrence Ziring, "Pakistan: The Vision and the Reality," *Asian Affairs* 4, no. 6 (1977): 385–407.

tution as part of the year-long festivities commemorating Ayub Khan's "Decade of Development." Retrospectively, reports of the conference read like a handbook for the constitutional crises soon to tear apart the state. The Law Minister cited judicial independence as a hallmark of the regime, boldly characterizing Ayub Khan's respect for the rule of law as "unambiguous and extremely vocal." He was roundly supported by judges, bureaucrats and politicians, and in a paean to the government, *Dawn* lauded the constitution's "pivotal role ... in imparting unity, purpose and vitality to the people and providing the impulse for all-round progress."[49]

Yet, concurrent with these celebrations were the first hearings in the Agartala Conspiracy Case. Citing East Pakistani opposition plans to overthrow the state, the central government initiated the case to discredit those who, like Awami League leader Sheikh Mujibur Rahman, were fighting for provincial autonomy and civil rights. *Agartala* was tried in Dacca by a tribunal consisting of former Supreme Court Chief Justice S.A. Rahman and East Pakistan High Court Justices M.R. Khan and Maksumul Hakim; citing expedience to justify circumventing regular courts, the government operated the tribunal under the 1968 Special Criminal Law Amendment (Special Tribunal) Ordinance, with special rules of evidence to exclude the usual requirements of civil procedure. (These rules were amended during the proceedings – Ordinance VI of 1968 – to take account of some limited defendant objections.) Mujib and his associates challenged the tribunal in a writ petition to the High Court (under Article 98 of the 1962 Constitution) but the court refused it, arguing that under the prevailing state of emergency, the status of fundamental rights was unclear. When General Yahya Khan assumed power, he was forced to repeal the Tribunal Ordinance to end the prosecution so that Mujib could attend the 1970 roundtable conference intended to preclude (unsuccessfully) a post-election war between the provinces, but he did not drop the charges against the defendants.

*Agartala* symbolized everything that government festivities left unspoken: the power of the state constitutionally to imprison political leaders and to convene a special tribunal to hear the proceedings; to extend such a trial for partisan purposes; more generally, to ignore the economic and political demands of the majority province while applauding a decade of purported reforms.

[49] "Text of Zafar's speech at Lahore," *Dawn* 13 October 1968, p. 19; "'Pakistan Constitution backs human rights'," *Dawn* 14 October 1968, p. 3; "N.A. has ample power to check Executive," *Dawn* 15 October 1968; Marghub Siddiqi, "Sovereignty of Legislature in Pakistan," *Dawn* 15 October 1968; "Legislature supreme in Pakistan," *Dawn* 14

The incommensurability of the two events reflected the contradictions of the Pakistani state in the 1960s. Pakistan confronted pressing economic, security and political needs in its second decade, and Ayub Khan claimed that his preferred form of government would satisfy them. His policies exacerbated rather than solved these problems. Although some of his initial reforms took hold, such as the codification of family laws, the basic distribution of resources and capital remained highly concentrated. Ayub Khan allowed his family to amass a considerable fortune under his industrial policies; public funds and the structure of license capitalism also enriched other West Pakistani industrialists, exacerbating not only East Pakistan's sense of relative deprivation but that of other aspiring West Pakistani capitalists. To the extent that a principle of equity was required to undergird economic progress, it was thwarted mightily by the economic policies established by government. Moreover, by the end of the 1960s not only had foreign exchange reserves fallen to a decade low, but foreign aid (and public relations) that previously buttressed the regime had diminished as well. Foreign policy seemed to have lost both its moorings and the full devotion of the army.

For the decade of the 1960s, government was a civilian overlay on military power, its electoral system was an instrument of state patronage and its bureaucracy was removed from the citizenry. The economy expanded to serve the state and its army rather than its citizens, and was organized in highly discriminatory ways. The national security state serviced a military whose interests seemed to militate against popular rule; rights were therefore manipulated as part of a program of political control. Those who reacted against repression were treated harshly while their demands went unmet. Cycles of repression and rebellion defined the state and finally its demise.

In this enterprise, Ayub Khan's constitution facilitated his state. A constitution promulgated by ordinance remained, despite cosmetic improvements, an instrument of authoritarianism rather than constitutionalism and democracy. No constitutional theory supported state sponsored inequities, materially or politically. While an independent judiciary might be a prerequisite for the life and sustenance of a developing country,[50] it could neither create the conditions for equity and development nor guarantee those results. The form of democracy embedded in Basic Democracy was, in reality, no democracy at all but a

October 1968, p. 3; "Remarkable progress in all fields," *Dawn* 14 September 1968; "The Constitution," *Dawn* 19 October 1968.

50 See S.M. Zafar's comment in "Constitution seminar thought-provoking," *Dawn* 15 October 1968, p. 7.

constitutional ruse perpetrated by the praetorian state to sustain itself. Without a constitution committed to a political theory its citizens recognized as democratic, Pakistan's structure and the ambitions of its rulers defeated the possibility of democracy.

# 4 Seeking justice (1969–1972)

Who could have known
that the blood of those words
would drop by drop
become lines that shine?
And now these lines of blood
have in themselves become
a story and a fable.

Ahmad Faraz, "Preface."

A free and uncorrupted right of suffrage does not necessarily satisfy all the demands of liberty. Some of the most menacing encroachments on individual liberty have been made in the name of democratic principles themselves.

Justice Hamoodur Rahman

The authority of executive-dominated government was contested vigorously when Ayub Khan turned over the reins of government to General Yahya Khan. The problems that set the stage for civil war still existed at its conclusion; the impossibility of their resolution in post-election constitution-writing led to war and then the independence of Bangladesh. To clear the way for constitutional rule, the judiciary was asked to take center stage once again. Rulings on the transfer of pre-war power in *Asma Jilani's case* and the conditions for post-war constitutionalism in *Ziaur Rahman's case* arbitrated continuing disputes about federalism and executive powers, and focused deeply rooted arguments about political ideology and conscience.

## Changing the structure of the state

The decade of development, praised outside Pakistan as the result of dynamic civil–military governance, never disguised the political vacuity of Ayub Khan's government. Deposed *Pakistan Times* editor Mazhar Ali Khan accused Ayub Khan "of destroying institutions wedded to the public weall [sic], and of victimising individuals who could not be easily browbeaten or purchased."[1] Ayub Khan was never able to control disintegrative forces that were present at the start of his rule, and far more dangerous by its end: growing tensions between East and West Pakistan that made both the federal structure and its system of representation vulnerable, the inadequacies of the presidential system and its constitution to handle the weaknesses of the basic democracies scheme, and increasing frictions born of repression.

Opposition to the presidential system voiced by the Combined Opposition Parties during the 1965 elections was particularly vociferous in East Pakistan, where the alleged benefits of Basic Democracies and central government economic policies were only illusory. In 1965, Sheikh Mujibur Rahman articulated a six-point program that echoed long-held Bengali claims for equity and soon became the platform for the Awami League and the byword for renewed Bengali nationalism, political autonomy and finally, independence.[2] The left-wing National Awami Party, formed in 1957 to protest One Unit, was strong in East Pakistan but was only able to gain majorities in the minority provinces of Baluchistan and the Frontier. The Awami League therefore joined NAP's opposition to One Unit, protesting its Punjabi economic and political dominance and the military strength of the central government. Through the late 1960s, emergency provisions imposed during the war with India remained in effect, restricting the scope of personal expression and party politics – a reminder to East Pakistan that only the West had been protected during the war, and to West Pakistan that the presidential system was inadequate.

Pakistan thus simmered with frustrations that became the basis for an anti-Ayub movement. Clashes between civilians and the police increased by 1968 in both provinces (and in East Pakistan, between civilians and the army), and public meetings were regularly banned under Section 144. The right to strike paved the way for industrial actions that then provoked army reaction. Student unrest in Karachi, shootings at unarmed students in Rawalpindi, and the arrests of People's Party and NAP leaders led Dacca's *Holiday* to observe the "threnody of violence which reverberated like a dark symphony across the whole of West Pakistan."[3] Police firings increased the civilian death toll in East Pakistan[4] and troop movements were observed in West Pakistan.

[1] "Ayub's Attack on Progressive Papers," *Forum* (Dacca) 7 February 1970, pp. 8–9.

[2] "Mujib's 6-Point: Platform or Diving Board?," *Holiday* (Dacca) 20 February 1966; Rehman Sobhan, "Autonomy and Social Change: West Pakistan," *Forum* 22 November 1969, p. 6.

[3] "The right to an answer," *Holiday* 17 November 1968.

[4] "East Wing lights flame of protest," *Holiday* 8 December 1968. Herbert Feldman cites thirty-nine killings in Dacca in mid-March 1969 alone. *The End and the Beginning: Pakistan 1969–1971* (Karachi: Oxford University Press, 1976), p. 13.

With national elections announced for early 1970, Ayub Khan engaged in energetic but fruitless talks with opposition parties to discover common ground for political peace. Success in these talks presupposed a disposition toward constitutional change, which in turn presupposed successful negotiations – a dialectic between constitution-making and politics that reappeared in the decades after the Bengal crisis. The East Pakistan contingent reiterated its dissatisfaction with the deprivation of civil liberties, pervasive economic discrimination, the absence of Bengali participation in constitutional power-sharing, and the need for autonomy.[5] Ayub Khan could not suppress the movement against him. His departure, ironically and sadly his most damaging bequest to the country, destroyed the state's constitutional and territorial compact, however weak, and then the state itself.

### *The new martial law*

The 1962 Constitution provided formal procedures for a president to leave office, including dissolving the National Assembly, resignation, impeachment or removal for reasons of incapacity. In the end, Ayub Khan did not heed his own constitutional instrument. Instead, on 24 March 1969, concluding that only the military had the capacity to control civil disorder (without him at its helm), he acted extra-constitutionally and "stepped aside," asking General Agha Mohammed Yahya Khan to undertake his "legal and constitutional responsibility to defend the country not only against external aggression but also to save it from internal disorder and chaos." With the constitution effectively abrogated, General Yahya Khan declared martial law, assumed the role of CMLA and on 1 April 1969, declared himself president.

The new martial law reflected the circumstances of its birth. Agreeing to Ayub Khan's transfer of power at the outset reflected Yahya Khan's insensitivity to the foundations of constitutional rule. In some ways this martial law was harsher than the one imposed in 1958, forbidding a wider range of political activities not ordinarily thought to be concerned with state security. Civil servants were dismissed, military courts were given broad powers to try and sentence civilian offenders and civil courts were prohibited from judging martial law actions.[6] The martial law regime also

[5] Kamal Hossain, "Post Mortem on RTC," *Forum* 14 March 1970; Mujibur Rahman's statement reported in *Dawn* (Karachi), 14 March 1969, reprinted in *Bangladesh Papers* (Lahore: Vanguard, n.d.), pp. 33–38. See also *Forum* issue on the Round Table Conference, 14 March 1970, and Hamza Alavi, "The Crisis of Nationalities and the State in Pakistan," *Journal of Contemporary Asia* 1, No. 3 (1971): 42–66.

[6] Martial Law Regulation No. 58 (Removal From Service [Special Provisions] Regulation). The 1969 Courts (Removal of Doubts) Order was promulgated to nullify a High Court

took steps to restructure the state. In his first months, Yahya Khan dissolved One Unit, announced plans for elections and promulgated a plan to draft a new constitution.[7] Although the fact of martial law seemed to dismiss the prospect of civilian rule, Yahya Khan's subsequent actions indicated that he understood some of the sources of conflicts in the state. Yet centralization and devolution, like martial law and democracy, were incompatible. The violence that culminated in civil war was the logical outcome of these two contradictions.

Civil disobedience in West Pakistan was more than matched by anti-government action in East Pakistan. Their similarities – against repression, presidentialism, basic democracies and the suspension of political rights – did not disguise fundamental conflicts between the two wings. To the extent, however limited, that West Pakistan had prospered under Ayub Khan, East Pakistan had been wrung dry, its hard currency earnings absorbed by the West without compensation in foreign aid, investment or development. The demand for autonomy acquired the coloration of internal colonialism by the mid-1960s; economic disparities paired with political dissatisfactions fueled Bengal's politics. Since political parties rarely transcended provincial boundaries, inter-party discussions took on the rigid characteristics of international negotiations.

Bengali politicians insisted to the end that their interest was in restructuring the organization of the Pakistani state; Tajuddin Ahmed, who led the Bangladesh Provisional Government, told foreign journalists in December 1971 that the Awami League's original demand for autonomy "within the framework of Pakistan" was transformed into a campaign for independence in reaction to Pakistan's violent refusal to consider such compromise.[8] It is unclear whether Yahya Khan ever fully understood the basis of these claims. Zulfikar Ali Bhutto, leading the newly formed Pakistan People's Party in the West, later admitted that economic exploitation and political repression in East Pakistan caused the Pakistani state to disintegrate,[9] but the government in the West (and many of its politicians) never fathomed the violence that Bengalis felt had been

ruling in *Mir Hassan and another v. The State*, PLD 1969 Lahore 786, that courts could operate without obstruction.

7 Province of West Pakistan (Dissolution) Order, 30 March 1970. The Legal Framework Order (President's Order No. 2, 28 March 1970) provided for provincial as well as national elections, with direct voting and universal suffrage.

8 Interview with *The Times* (London) 23 December 1971, cited in Hamza Alavi, "The State in Postcolonial Societies: Pakistan and Bangladesh," in Kathleen Gough and Hari P. Sharma, eds., *Imperialism and Revolution in South Asia* (New York: Monthly Review Press, 1973), p. 171.

9 Interview with Walter Berg, German Television, Karachi, 2 April 1972, in *Speeches and Statements*, vol. 4–1 (Karachi: Government of Pakistan, Department of Films and Publications, 1972).

systematically perpetrated against them. Most important, the state establishment – civil bureaucracy and military alike – was so entrenched that it almost instinctively supported policies and actions that would maintain the status quo.

Some of the Awami League's proposals were acceptable to both wings, including a long-standing plea for a parliamentary system with direct elections based on universal adult franchise. Others – including separating foreign exchange, currency, banking and taxation, creating provincial militia or paramilitary forces, and leaving only defense and foreign affairs to the central government – carried the concept of decentralization so far as to call into question the survival of the federal state. Certainly, the confederal structure envisioned by the Awami League would have weakened the central government to a point beyond which its caretakers were unwilling to travel.

Yahya Khan's Legal Framework Order (LFO), designed to organize elections and steer the new constitution, may well have been doomed from the start. Although he recognized the basic issues of constitution-making – the nature of federation, the basis of representation, and the design of the electorate – he provided several obstacles to their resolution. First, the LFO allowed only 120 days to complete a constitution, a requirement aimed at expedience but unlikely to be met. Second, by dissolving One Unit and disallowing the contentious parity principle before the elections, Yahya Khan prejudged, or at least predisposed, the constitution that could be framed – even while responding to the wishes of both East and West Pakistan. For example, Mujib had complained earlier that the parity principle self-defeatingly emphasized regionalism. On this point, Yahya Khan agreed with him. However, regionalism without parity continued to be a decisive element in the NAP and Awami League political strategies.

Third, the LFO enshrined executive power at the expense of legislative authority. The National Assembly to be elected in 1970 to draft the constitution could be dissolved (and reconstituted) if the President refused to authenticate its proposals, the President had sole power to interpret the Order and his constitutional interpretations were immune from legal challenge. In a pre-election speech, Yahya Khan announced that if the election victors did not accept the LFO as promulgated, martial law would continue.[10] Finally, and perhaps most important, the LFO was silent on the question of autonomy. While Sheikh Mujib called the elections "a referendum on autonomy,"[11] Yahya Khan left the question to post-election constitution-drafting. It can be argued that this issue was

[10] "Bengal nearing Decisive Hour," *Holiday* 29 November 1970.
[11] *Morning News* (Karachi and Dacca) 26 October 1970, in *Bangladesh Papers*, p. 101.

appropriately left for the prospective Assembly to debate. However, the meaning of autonomy – variously invoked by Sheikh Mujib, G.M. Syed, Khan Abdus Samad Khan Achakzai, Khan Abdul Wali Khan, Ghous Bakhsh Bizenjo and their parties to connote decentralization, formal devolution within a federal or confederation system, regionalism or reactive nationalism – was never clarified by Yahya Khan, nor is it clear that he understood the concept in terms they accepted.

The call for autonomy in Bengal, which resurfaced in Baluchistan in the 1970s and Sind in the 1980s, became a signal of opposition to central government generally, as well as its particular policies; autonomy was never accorded the status of a full-fledged ideology or constitutional theory by its critics. The Awami League saw autonomy as an expression of Bengali dignity, a right of a higher order than the simple procedural rights included in the LFO. The martial law government dismissed it as one of many opposition ploys to achieve power, never comprehending that autonomy was integral to Bengal's satisfaction in any political order. Yahya Khan thus invited inevitable, stiff reaction to the LFO and to the election results.

The government consistently claimed that martial law was primarily a reaction to political upheaval, intended despite its restructuring proposals only to prevent disorder. In fact, martial law was designed to prevent social and economic developments that could erode the special privileges of the civil–military bureaucracy. Yahya Khan did not offer a theory of democracy or politics to counter People's Party populism or Awami League autonomy programs, nor did the LFO propose an alternative constitutionalism. He recognized that he had no mandate to impose a vision of politics on Pakistan, no matter how disrupted the polity had become. Instead, he responded to selected items on the public docket of discontent while remaining silent on others, leaving the country with innumerable problems and an incomplete (although dictated) agenda for formal politics. The serious substantive issues of an election campaign, particularly the class-ethnic divide symbolized by the PPP and the Awami League, could never be confronted by the military government. Martial law would usher in the elections, judge their acceptability and, if necessary in his eyes, outlive them. As a prelude to civilian rule, it was not a recipe for conciliation but a portent of future tragedy.

### *Elections and war*

Despite their inauspicious provenance, the 1970 elections were the first in Pakistan to be conducted on the basis of universal adult franchise, and were generally regarded as open, fair, free and without violence. Once votes were counted, however, the political situation remained unsettled: the People's Party won 88 National Assembly seats, a majority in the West (NAP won seven seats); the Awami League won 167 of 168 national seats, an overwhelming majority in East Pakistan and an absolute majority of National Assembly seats.

By the rules of normal politics, the League and Sheikh Mujib should have controlled the central government, but neither the People's Party nor the military was willing to concede without a fight. Different ideologies and interests propelled vitriolic disputes between Bhutto and Sheikh Mujib, holding the country hostage to their respective desires to become Prime Minister and write the constitution. The stakes were high. Were the Awami League to prepare a constitution based on its six-point plan, the structure of government would be transformed; were the PPP to write the constitution, the Awami League was convinced that its demands could not be satisfied. The army, whose traditional status and funding would presumably be jeopardized were confederation to prevail, entered the political fray to protect its own interests.

The political parties and the military struggled for months, with the PPP treating the army as an equal bargaining agent while the Awami League discounted its political role. The more the army tried to participate as a legitimate actor, the less the Awami League (and some dissident West Pakistani politicians) was likely to agree to negotiation, distrusting both the military and increasingly the PPP for accepting its seeming patronage. Each party threatened non-participation were its sole claim to office not met. Throughout the struggle the National Assembly did not meet, leaving the military in charge long after elections were held and thus sharpening the terms of political discord. Bhutto claimed that the PPP would not "permit anyone to 'chisel us out' of power" and in March 1971 proposed that power be transferred to both parties separately, leading many politicians to believe that separation was a foregone conclusion of the military establishment.[12] The country was literally stretched by its leaders to its breaking point.

Civil disobedience in East Pakistan began anew: a non-cooperation movement launched there on 1 March 1971 brought down a new Martial Law Ordinance to punish demonstrators, and later in the month, Yahya Khan banned all politics and the Awami League party, imposed complete press censorship and sent the army to restore law and order. (Two National Assembly members were among those killed in early March

[12] Bhutto statement reported in *Dawn* 15 March 1971, reprinted in *Bangladesh Papers*, p. 234. Reactions to this proposal were uniformly negative, and Bhutto later disavowed the statement.

shootings in Dacca.) By late March, the Pakistan army had moved into East Pakistan and war began.

The brutal war sustained images of an army terrorizing its own unarmed civilians, millions of refugees evacuating Bengal's cities, guerillas operating in the countryside, the intercession of foreign powers and intervention by the Indian army, and impassioned pleas for sovereignty in the United Nations by Zulfikar Ali Bhutto on behalf of the martial law regime. These all polarized rather than subdued political tensions. The progression of the war, from occupation to the liberation of Dacca, solidified the Awami League's mass political movement led concurrently by the government-in-exile and rural guerilla leaders.

Until the war's end, the central government justified its intervention, in its ubiquitous phrase, "to preserve the integrity of the country." In truth, the war was its coda to the two-winged state rather than a prelude to a new constitutional order. Actions that exacerbated the conflict, including banning the Awami League, arresting Mujib yet again and renewing counterinsurgency, were only later balanced by efforts toward constitutional conciliation, civilianizing the administration and dismissing the military governor. After nine months of army occupation, East Pakistan viewed West Pakistan as a foreign power. Animosities between political parties, between the central and provincial governments, among ethnic groups and among political ideologies were heightened to a point of no return. The result was army violence and inflamed political rhetoric, destruction in East Pakistan and renewed conflicts with India, a civil war that became a complex international event, and secession.

### *Secession*

In the early 1970s, the Bhutto government predicted the eventual reintegration of the two countries, and repeated its interpretation of the war to every available audience. Reminders of the war continued for years: in 1972 the government commissioned an independent panel under Justice Hamoodur Rahman to investigate charges of army brutality in Dacca (although its report was never released); Mujibur Rahman was detained in Pakistan until January 1972; Indian and Pakistani prisoners of war were not transferred until late 1973 and 1974, considerably after Islamabad and Delhi concluded negotiations;[13] refugees were not repatriated

[13] The government sought a reference from the Supreme Court to allow the diplomatic recognition of newly independent Bangladesh; although Bhutto formally recognized Bangladesh at the Lahore meeting of the Organization of the Islamic Conference, he wanted to preempt legal challenges to his decision. *Special Reference under Article 187 of*

for years after the peace treaty was signed (and some remained in camps in Bangladesh two decades later because Pakistan was recalcitrant in relocating them). Perhaps most important, the effects of the war on Pakistan's political psychology were deep and in some quarters devastating. Relations between the new government and the military were never fully comfortable; indeed, when Zulfikar Ali Bhutto was overthrown in 1977, some of his opponents revisited the events leading to war in their public indictments of his rule.

Secession called into question the ideology of the Pakistani state. Until the war, the intellectual foundation of Pakistan was the two-nation concept that originally impelled partition and that presumed differences between the Muslim and Hindu "nations" that partition was to have solved. The presence of a large Muslim population in India, surely some competition to the ideological basis of Pakistan, was excused as aberration or accident. With secession, however, went the two-nation theory, for what ideology could justify the split, or the presence of two separate Muslim states where there had been one? The war seemed to undermine the conceptual origins of the state and the nature of its founding. West Pakistan now looked to be as much the result of accident as intention.

The next decade proved how difficult it was to overcome the continuing intersection of ethnic nationalism, economic inequity and political instability in the post-Bangladesh era. The governing People's Party never explained its silence on the autonomy issue prior to the war. Political disputes among parties in the provinces – many predating the war, some predating independence – acquired the additional hue of newly interpreted defeat and victory. The People's Party at once inherited the loss of Bengal and electoral victory in the west. It resumed an air of strident patriotism and brooked little opposition to its policies. NAP, long a supporter of the autonomy movement in Bengal, now participated in coalition ministries in Baluchistan and the Frontier that challenged the ruling PPP. Its talk of nationalities was cited by the Bhutto government as subversive; its past Congress Party support and its adherence to Pukhtun nationalism were offered to the public as proof of its separatist tendencies. The PPP, which attained the central government without new polls, soon equated opposition with anti-state behavior, dissent on provincial rights with irredentism, and demands for due process with separatism. The Prime Minister responded to opposition by bringing all the power of the state to bear against it: first intelligence units and paramilitary forces, then civil and military courts and finally, the army. When that

*the Interim Constitution of the Islamic Republic of Pakistan by President Zulfikar Ali Bhutto*, PLD 1973 Supreme Court 563.

army overthrew the Bhutto government in 1977, NAP and its Pakistan National Alliance partners first applauded, only to regret their own loss of political platform and voice under a far harder repression.

At the end of 1972, the Pakistan Muslim League [United] still argued for new elections, but the PPP government chose not to give the country an opportunity to refashion a new post-secession electoral consensus. Resting on a mass political base and populist ideology, the PPP submerged what should have been a serious problem of political process. Bhutto may have been legitimately worried about reopening the emotional wounds of war with the inflamed rhetoric of election campaigns – elections, as he well knew, are unpredictable affairs. But by eliminating the possibility of elections, the PPP actually allowed these wounds to fester. When his government was overthrown later in the decade, his opponents criticized the PPP in court for its reluctance to hold elections after the war; the legitimacy of his government was a question lurking just below the surface of political civility, and came to be connected in the minds of the opposition with the PPP's role in the war and with Bhutto's increasingly authoritarian behavior as Prime Minister.

Enormous misunderstandings about collective and communal rights as well as about political process were therefore set aside rather than confronted, legacies of a past many preferred to forget. The grave results of these strategies during Bhutto's tenure were felt in the Frontier and Baluchistan, and under the military in the 1980s, in Sind. Although the regimes would change from civilian to military and from populist to authoritarian to dictatorial, the questions they posed about democracy and equality were similar. For the moment, however, the parties in the National Assembly were called upon to write a new constitution, to set aside their differences in a new effort to reconstitute the state.

First a bridge had to be built between the future constitution and Bhutto's transitional martial law government. The country began its civilian government with Yahya Khan's martial law intact and Bhutto acting as civilian martial law administrator, a condition that chafed at a public that felt keenly the absence of political freedoms. Although the government convened a constituent assembly and provided an interim constitution based on the 1935 and 1947 Acts, it also used martial law to enforce its political preferences. Civilians were tried before military tribunals and civil courts were still barred from reviewing their actions. The martial law government pleaded as its military predecessors had before, citing the need to maintain order, the absence of a constitution to reflect the changed circumstances of the state, and the desire to retain consistent legal practice. Until the 1973 Constitution was ratified, civilian rule did not mean civil law. The first year of divided Pakistan and the Bhutto government represented a transition to popularly elected government; only with time did it resemble democracy, and then only tenuously.

## Transition to civil law

Although the war between East and West Pakistan ended more than two decades of tensions between the wings, many complex and confused legal issues were left to the courts to resolve, often provoked by conflicts between the Bhutto government and its critics. *Dawn* editor (and former Ayub Khan Information Secretary) Altaf Hussain Gauhar and the indefatigable Malik Ghulam Jilani had both been arrested under martial law regulations.[14] When the Punjab and Sind High Courts dismissed their *habeas corpus* and bail petitions for lack of jurisdiction, arguing that courts were not able to challenge Martial Law Orders, the Supreme Court took on the combined appeal in a landmark constitutional case in 1972.

### *Revoking "Dosso's case"*

In *Asma Jilani's case*,[15] the Supreme Court considered three related issues: the validity of the revolutionary legality doctrine established in the 1958 *Dosso* case; the doctrine's applicability to the transfer of power to Yahya Khan; and the status of his legal framework were the revolutionary legality doctrine judged inapplicable. The court quickly concluded that Yahya Khan had usurped power, that his action was not justified by the revolutionary legality doctrine and consequently that his martial law regime was illegal. By extension, the court considered the validity of the Bhutto government, insofar as it was brought into effect by actions and rules promulgated under an illegal martial law. This last issue strongly influenced the Bhutto government's legal arguments, reflecting its uncertainty about its legal foundation and political mandate. Repudiat-

[14] Malik Ghulam Jilani was arrested initially under the Defence of Pakistan Rules, which he challenged in the Lahore High Court. Before his hearing, the government rescinded its order, replacing it with Martial Law Regulation No. 78, which barred judicial challenge under the 1969 Courts (Removal of Doubts) Order. Altaf Gauhar was arrested under MLR No. 78, and the Government of Sind presented a new arrest order after Jilani's High Court hearing; when the Sind government withdrew its order in July 1972, the federal government issued a new order under the Defence of Pakistan Rules. Gauhar challenged his detention in 1972 (*Mrs. Zarina Gauhar v. Province of Sind and 3 others*, PLD 1976 Karachi 1257). His attorney, A.K. Brohi, maintained that under the Interim Constitution, the Defence of Pakistan Ordinance was not valid law; Attorney General Bakhtiar maintained that fundamental rights could not be enforced by the courts during emergency. The High Court challenged the Sind government nonetheless.

[15] *Miss Asma Jilani v. The Government of the Punjab and another and Mrs. Zarina Gauhar v. the Province of Sind and two others*, PLD 1972 Supreme Court 139.

ing Yahya Khan was one thing; validating Bhutto would be another. The court's attitude toward the Bhutto government in this early case was generous, and continued to be so for several years.

After the wrenching experience of the war, each justice felt impelled to review Pakistan's constitutional history, seeking to understand the effects of judicial actions on politics and to distance the court from actions it now viewed as mistaken. Their judgments of the past were harsh. In Justice Yaqub Ali's words, "the history of the constitutional mishaps which befell Pakistan between 1953 and 1969 bringing ruination, and untold miseries to its 120 million people, forms the overcast background against which the court is required to answer the questions which fall for decision." Paraphrasing Ayub Khan, he concluded that the judgments in *Tamizuddin Khan's case*, the 1955 *Reference* and *Dosso's case* had made "a perfectly good country ... into a laughing stock," and converted the country into "autocracy and eventually ... into military dictatorship." He pointedly criticized the abrogation of the 1956 Constitution, observing that Iskander Mirza and Ayub Khan committed treason and destroyed the basis of representation between East and West Pakistan. "The cessation [sic] of East Pakistan thirteen years later," he commented, "is, in my view, directly attributable to this tragic incident."

Justice Sajjad Ahmad joined this critique of the court and the General with a familiar rebuke for politicians:

> Twice the Constitution was abrogated, the abrogation being preceded and followed by reckless material greed, scramble for power and free run for political ambition and adventurism. On each occasion, the abrogation of the Constitution ... was accompanied by the simultaneous clamping of Martial Law on the entire country, associated with its accursed terror and its potential mischief of coercive action in the destruction of democratic values and civilised pattern of life in the country.

Tipping his hat to the Bhutto government – still seized with a martial law that allowed the arrests of Gauhar and Jilani – he noted that "the very name of Martial Law has become an anathema ... intolerably repugnant to the common people."

The justices vented decade-long frustrations. The 1970 elections, the ensuing war and the detention of Yahya Khan were all, in their different ways, cathartic for the country and the courts. *Asma Jilani's case*, heard while a new constitution was being drafted and decided just before it was ratified by the National Assembly, helped the court place itself on the independent footing it felt was required and deserved. Simple as the decision to condemn the vilified Yahya Khan might seem, the justices still were obliged to work out a new role for the court, to sidestep the minefields of process and substance which they felt had helped to cause (certainly, had not prevented) military autocracy, and finally to develop an understanding of the judiciary's role in popularly elected government. This case was not only an attempt to rectify the wrongs of the General but was also an effort to combine political principle and practical politics, to determine anew the appropriate role of courts in the polity.

*Revolutionary legality and martial law* In assessing the doctrine of revolutionary legality, the court undertook two related tasks: it revoked the doctrine as enunciated in *Dosso's case*, refining its meaning for future reference; and it applied its reasoning to the circumstances of Yahya Khan's assumption of power, judging the regime illegal and its actions invalid. Within a few years, the court would turn aside its own warnings about the necessary connections between law and political legitimacy, but in 1972 its judgment was itself revolutionary, for it sought to challenge assumptions about relations between court and executive, and between state and constitution.

Chief Justice Hamoodur Rahman confronted *Dosso* at conceptual and historical levels, developing the latter in far more detail. *Dosso*, he determined, was never fully justified on Kelsenian grounds: Justice Munir had used the doctrine haphazardly and wrongly, applying analytical precepts as prescription, substituting a vague notion of international acceptability for internal legitimacy, and seeking a *grundnorm* where none could or should be found. For Hamoodur Rahman, a polity could be governed only by deliberate consent which formed the basis of a *grundnorm* and of government. Thus, "if a grundnorm is necessary," the 1949 Objectives Resolution – framed by political representatives, not alien legal theorists – would be more satisfactory than imported doctrine. The hypothetical construction is important here; in a later case, he would emphasize that he was not proposing that Kelsenian argument was necessary, but that more appropriate sources for a *grundnorm* were available than that chosen by Justice Munir. With oblique references to Locke and Harrington, he defined political community: "Government becomes a Government of laws and not of men," he suggested, only when accountability is a fundamental principle of politics, a principle he saw fulfilled by elected legislatures and courts. Asserting that "no one is above the law," the court determined that successive abrogations of constitutions and Yahya Khan's declaration of martial law were all actions wrongly taken.

The court chose its history carefully. The appellants argued that concepts of effectiveness and legality enunciated in *Dosso* had never been established in fact. Yahya Bakhtiar, former counsel in the *Dosso* case and now the Attorney General, had not been allowed to discuss the validity of the 1958 abrogation of the 1956 Constitution when he defended one of the *Dosso* appellants; the Munir Court simply assumed that the 1958 Laws (Continuance in Force) Order was a valid constitutional instrument from which the judiciary derived its authority. Bakhtiar now suggested that if "the yardstick of legitimacy of the source of law" was applied, then the "reign of usurpers" commenced as early as 1953, ending only in December 1971 when the Bhutto government was formed.[16] Nonetheless, all parties agreed that the 1962 Constitution and the actions of the courts pursuant to it gave successive civil and military governments some *de facto* and *de jure* validity. Rather than eschew necessity and revolutionary legality arguments, Bakhtiar contended that *Dosso's case* was now the law of the land and that the necessity doctrine vitiated its continuance. In words he would rue when defending Prime Minister Bhutto's wife in her 1977 challenge to General Zia ul Haq's *coup d'état*, the Attorney General observed that "nothing succeeds like success."[17] Bakhtiar used state security arguments to justify detaining the appellants: that the liberty of the nation was paramount, the liberty of an individual secondary to it, and the political climate a factor in determining the imperatives of state security – all arguments that would be applied against him a few years later.

His subtext concerned the legitimacy of the Bhutto government: once in power, government seeks the firmest mooring. Altaf Gauhar's attorney, Manzur Qadir, argued for an extremely limited reading of the necessity doctrine – "only to prevent chaos and without demolishing and eroding the rights of the people." The Bhutto government, keen to show respect for the courts but far more anxious to retain power, found itself supporting Yahya Khan's regime. The Attorney General argued for the same efficacy principle that had supported Ayub Khan's authoritarianism (against his own counsel), while Qadir, previously in the employ of Ayub Khan, argued for fundamental rights that the government said had disappeared. The doctrine of necessity was neither refined nor limited by either counsel. To achieve judicial approval, the Bhutto government drew lines of continuity between prior military regimes and its own mixed government.

To support the government's martial law without destroying its popular legitimacy, Bakhtiar conflated concepts of legality, efficacy and legitimacy, while the petitioners tried to keep them distinct. Qadir relied on a general notion of morality to sustain his argument: he proposed that "mere effectiveness of a political change or an enduring phenomenon

[16] "Jilani, Gauhar case: Attorney-General opens arguments," *PT* 22 March 1972.
[17] Ibid.

should not suffice," but that the courts should ascertain that efficacy was "in conformity with morality and justice."[18] In effect, he argued that ethics and political legitimacy were dimensions of efficacy. The court accepted his view by defining sovereignty as a principle of political trusteeship.

The court concluded that Ayub Khan had no authority to turn over the government to Yahya Khan, who in turn had no authority to accept power or to impose martial law. If the transfer of power lacked legal foundation, the declaration of martial law was equally wrong; civil government, not the military, rightfully determines when emergency exists. Since the transfer of power was neither a revolution nor a *coup d'état*, the doctrine of revolutionary legality, which the court had already dismissed as an empty theoretical concept, could not be applied to Yahya Khan. Despite Bakhtiar's argument that martial law validates itself by its own coercive force, the court concluded that the doctrine of necessity could not validate an illegal regime. Indeed, the Chief Justice disallowed the possibility that the military could abrogate the fundamental law of a country in the name of martial law:

> It would be paradoxical indeed if such a result could flow from the invocation in the aid of a State of any agency set up and maintained by the State itself for its own protection from external invasion and internal disorder. If the argument is valid that the proclamation of the Martial Law by itself leads to the complete destruction of the legal order, then the armed forces do not assist the state in suppressing disorder but actually create further disorder, by disrupting the entire legal order of the state.

The court therefore decided that the "constitutional and legal duty to restore order" invoked by Ayub Khan for Yahya Khan was more limited than either understood, and could not sanction military rule.

*Judicial authority* The validity of actions taken under martial law remained an equally thorny problem to which the court applied finesse if not determination. Having disavowed *Dosso*, the court could have declared Ayub Khan's regime illegal; instead, it acknowledged that regime's *de facto* validity because the 1962 Constitution had converted it into a constitutional regime. The court could also have offered *de facto* validity to actions taken under the illegal Yahya Khan regime. To do so, however, would have required accepting the limits on court powers specified in the 1969 Courts (Removal of Doubts) Order, restrictions the

[18] "Gauhar, Jilani cases hearing continues," *PT* 19 March 1972. Bakhtiar tried to clarify that he was not justifying martial law as such but only one of its results, President Bhutto's assumption of power. In the end, the court accepted this distinction with reservations.

court refused to endorse. This judgment can be read not only as a decision about the validity of imposed military rule and the sanctity of constitutions, but about the proper place for the judiciary in a rightly constituted state.

In this arena, the court adopted the views of the amicus curiae, A.K. Brohi and Sharifuddin Pirzada, one a past Law Minister, the other a future one. Both argued that the court was the sole guardian of its jurisdiction and that the martial law regime had no authority to limit judicial actions. Calling the *Dosso* decision "a standing menace," Brohi proposed that the Supreme Court could reverse its own decisions, a course he urged for *Dosso*. He argued as much from consequence as from principle: like many others, he was convinced that "the blessings of the judiciary" in *Dosso* helped Ayub Khan to secure his power, and he sought a parallel effect by having the court nullify actions taken under Yahya Khan's (and perhaps Bhutto's) martial law.[19]

All the justices agreed that it was "the exclusive privilege" of the superior courts, in Justice Sajjad Ahmad's words, "to identify laws from what are not laws or bad laws." The 1969 Order was bad law because it struck "at the very root of the judicial power of the courts." Hamoodur Rahman was therefore quick to pronounce illegal the 1969 Order as well as Martial Law Regulation No. 78, which led to the imprisonment of Gauhar and Jilani, because "they were both made by an incompetent authority and, therefore, lacked the attribute of legitimacy which is one of the essential characteristics of a valid law." He then proposed explicit limits on the necessity doctrine: "Recourse has to be taken to the doctrine of necessity where the ignoring of it would result in disastrous consequences to the body politic and upset the social order itself but I respectfully beg to disagree with the view that this is a doctrine for validating the illegal acts of usurpers." Neither law could be sustained on these grounds.

The court then took two further steps. First, it placed the responsibility for ensuring public welfare with the judiciary: necessity could be invoked once usurpers were declared illegal and illegitimate. The acts of usurpers could be condoned legally, in Justice Yaqub Ali's words, "on the condition that the recognition given by the court is proportionate to the evil to be averted, it is transitory and temporary in character." Second, it echoed the legality-legitimacy distinction in the court's interpretation of the public interest by separating condonation (limited) from legitimation (general). Creating a novel link between strict legality and the common

[19] See "Brohi's Argument on Court Jurisdiction," *PT* 23 March 1972, and "Sharifuddin Pirzada Opens Argument," *PT* 25 March 1972.

good, Chief Justice Hamoodur Rahman established a bridge between law and politics – one ignored or destroyed in earlier decisions – to proclaim a strong, central role for the courts.

This judgment was clearly moved by more than institutional jockeying in the new government. The justices were offended by Yahya Khan's crass restrictions on their powers. More important, they were deeply troubled by conventional wisdom, voiced frequently by attorneys on all sides in this case, that the *Dosso* judgment was responsible for the extraordinary tragedies of the following thirteen years. Some justices considered the Munir court's intervention in politics a sorry abdication of the judiciary's primary role as a guarantor of democracy. To take precipitous action when the Bhutto government had still to achieve its promised constitution, however, might again look like political interference. It was for this reason that the court invented its otherwise weak condonation-legitimization distinction. Disallowing martial law regulations which stifled public opinion, the court at once satisfied the appellants and condemned the military regime. By allowing the Bhutto government to continue, even though it owed its existence to an illegal regime, the court was able to calm the Attorney General's worst fears while serving notice to the government that its arguments were neither seemly nor effective.

### *The legitimacy of the transition*

The judgment in *Asma Jilani's case* left unanswered questions. What would happen were the current martial law not fully lifted? What guarantees could be formulated to restrict future military interference in politics? And as a subtext, where should Pakistan seek the ideological roots of its polity in the absence of its Bengali majority, and how should it organize its future politics? Justice Hamoodur Rahman's personal views on the nature of the polity were neither fully developed nor specifically directed to the economic, political and emotional conditions of the "one-winged" state.

Justice Yaqub Ali hinted at these problems of establishing legitimacy, clearly troubled by the prospect that a National Assembly elected before the war was now writing a constitution for the state that remained after the war. He approved the Munir Court's 1955 *Reference* requirement that new elections be held before writing a new constitution. The 1972 Court could have stipulated similar conditions for post-war, post-Yahya Khan Pakistan by requiring Bhutto to provide for a new constituent assembly. Whether from weariness or fear of unknown consequences (including, perhaps, concern about Bhutto's view of a temperamental court), the court ignored this option. It resurfaced nonetheless in *Ziaur Rahman's case*, a contemporaneous challenge to the political transition in which the Lahore court held that the interim constitution was validly enacted.

The years 1971 and 1972 saw continuing political agitation against the government. When a group of journalists and political workers, including the printer, editor and publishers of *Urdu Digest*, *Zindagi* and *Punjab Punch*, were arrested for demonstrating against martial law during the period the court was considering *Asma Jilani's case*, they filed petitions in the Lahore High Court challenging their arrests but were convicted and sentenced before their writs were considered. In *Zia-ur-Rahman v. The State* (PLD 1972 Lahore 382), they argued that the 1962 Constitution was unlawfully abrogated and that the 1969 Martial Law as well as the continuing martial law was unconstitutional. Once again, the government justified its actions by the necessity doctrine and claimed that President's Order No. 3 of 1969 removed judicial jurisdiction to contest state actions.

Although it denied that the 1962 Constitution was in force, the Lahore Court firmly refused the government's plea. In language as direct as the Supreme Court's a month earlier, the court dismissed both the necessity and the revolutionary legality arguments as well as the jurisdiction ban. Reversing the government's argument, it stated instead that martial law and the abrogation of the constitution violated the Objectives Resolution (which it treated as a supra-constitutional document) and that the judiciary "have no jurisdiction to accept such usurpation as lawful and valid." Jurisdiction, judicial powers and the concept of the state were all wrapped under the banner of the public interest and expressed in the language of political representation.

The High Court expressed a more comprehensive and activist view than the accountability function proposed by Hamoodur Rahman. The courts were not only participants in guiding and stabilizing democracy, but were themselves symbols of open politics as well. In Justice Afzal Zullah's words, "when the courts are open and functioning effectively under the normal law, there is no justification for establishing special Military Courts for trial of civilians . . . There was absolutely no justification ever to 'supplant civilian laws and Courts by military orders and Courts'." In effect, he proposed a contextual condition for necessity and for law and order: if the people accept civil court legitimacy, then martial law is unnecessary; if martial law is nonetheless imposed, then it is *de facto* unnecessary (literally and figuratively), and thus unlawful. Since the courts had never closed, the 1969 martial law and its continuance in Article 281 of the Interim Constitution were invalid.

The justices distinguished their own tenure after 1969 from actually joining in usurpation. Their distinction paralleled the equally awkward but workable distinction between condonation and legitimacy. Justice

Afzal Zullah launched an impassioned defence of the judiciary: "Judges . . . are bound by their oath to observe the law; but while doing so they are not oblivious of the necessity of preserving the State, the destruction of which will be the end of the principles and oath, they love and cherish to serve and honour." With these words, the High Court tried to expunge the legacy of *Dosso* and to give effect to the Supreme Court's ruling in *Asma Jilani's case*. Because the decision seemed to explicate a policy role for the courts, an unfamiliar and untested arena for the judiciary, the government appealed the decision to define the legislative–judicial relationship (*The State v. Żia-ur-Rahman and others*, PLD 1973 Supreme Court 49).

As a guide to the legislature in framing a permanent constitution, the Supreme Court considered three issues: the powers of the superior courts, the relationship of these powers to the legislature, and the legitimacy of the interim constitution. Its judgment revealed practical opinion as much as conceptual thinking, reflecting the court's sense that these questions required expeditious resolution.

Citing his own opinion in *Fazlul Quader Chowdhury*, the Chief Justice reaffirmed the supremacy of a written constitution, the responsibilities of the courts under it, and the judiciary's duty "to see that the constitution prevails." Judicial review was a method of accountability; policy-making, however, was beyond judicial ken. The contents of a constitution remained for the legislature – the people – to determine, and the courts could not declare its provisions void.[20] The powers of the sitting legislature were valid by virtue of the Legal Framework Order; despite *Asma Jilani's case*, the terms of political change set by Yahya Khan held the day. First, the order had provided a free and fair election with "a mandate to make provision for the constitution of Pakistan." Denotatively, Hamoodur Rahman provided content for the necessity doctrine: "If there was any act of the usurper which could be condoned on the basis of the doctrine of necessity, then this was pre-eminently such an act."

Second, since Assembly membership was not determined by the order, only the electorate could object to its membership. Since the sitting Assembly did not violate the Framework's quorum provisions, he demurred from ruling on its mandate. Ruling that the Assembly was validly constituted, the interim constitution validly ratified, and the President

[20] Even the Objectives Resolution would hold a lower status than a written constitution unless it were incorporated into that constitution. Elaborating his comments in *Asma Jilani's case*, he affirmed that "the *grundnorm* is the doctrine of legal sovereignty accepted by the people of Pakistan and the consequences that flow from it," but did not equate the Resolution with a *grundnorm*. On the political ramifications of this point, particularly under General Zia ul Haq, see chapter 7.

validly elected, the Chief Justice made clear his intention to cede all questions of legitimacy to the *fait accompli* of the past elections.

Furthermore, the court accepted an additional division between courts and parliament and between law and politics. Referring to the election mandate – which was surely unclear but which he evidently preferred not to clarify – he concluded that limitations on the Assembly were political and therefore outside the judicial jurisdiction. To act otherwise would be to enter the arena of policy and politics, where the courts did not belong. Nevertheless, the import of these decisions was political even if their intentions were not. Rather than address directly the distinctions between politics, policy and law, the Chief Justice set a vague boundary for court jurisdiction.

The court considered the validity of Article 281 of the Interim Constitution precisely because it created an additional ban on its powers. Reading the article carefully, creatively and gracefully, the Chief Justice concluded that its validating of acts "done or purported to be done in exercise of the powers given by Martial Law Regulations and Order since repealed or even in the purported exercise of those powers" could not include those undertaken *mala fide*. The interim constitution was lawful, legislative powers were unsullied, the judiciary retained its full powers – but Article 281 could not enforce some of the detentions included in the appeals. The transition was validated, but the Bhutto government's use of martial law regulations were sharply curtailed by the court's authority to invalidate such actions. Moreover, the court retained the right to review decisions of military courts.

## The judiciary and transition

The effect of *Asma Jilani's* and *Ziaur Rahman's* cases was to assert the right of judicial review and to extend its scope to include reversing the principle of *stare decisis*. The manner of the assertion, however, was as important as the fact. These judgments offer considered arguments about the rights of citizens and the nature of political change, and carefully analyze the judiciary's responsibility to correct its own errors. Underlying them are serious questions about the nature of the transition the courts were witnessing and the judiciary's role in that process.

### *Sovereignty and legitimacy*

For decades, the military or the executive invoked the threat of a legal vacuum during periods of political disruption, regardless of their causes, to justify imposing martial law. The threat had itself become a familiar, periodic condition of political life, restricting the ability of elected government to determine its own fate. Far more substantively than it had done previously, the court now articulated a plain principle of legislative responsibility: the legislature should be the architect for the public interest and, when necessary, the judiciary should protect the public good indirectly. Embedded in this principle was a notion of popular sovereignty that the judiciary employed to distinguish popularly elected legislatures from the repressed voice of the basic democracies, and thus to affirm the electoral basis of the state. These were general propositions; the absence of specificity may have reflected the court's understandable uncertainty about the new government it confirmed.

The courts took advantage of a period of relative freedom to assert procedural rights. Its decision reversed the necessity doctrine and its recent limited appproval by the Attorney General; instead, it sanctioned an equation between legitimacy and legality only to the extent that legitimacy and universal franchise could be joined. The court refined the conditions which defined "competently made" law: unlike the Cornelius court, which defined competence procedurally (which helped it to accept the Ayub Khan regime), the new court tried to anchor the meaning of competence in a system of popular political rule. Chief Justice Hamoodur Rahman combined three separate political judgments in his concept of popular sovereignty: that prior to joining a polity, that framing its constitution, and that of continuing memberships to express constitutional legitimacy. The experience of the Bangladesh war, it would seem, convinced the Chief Justice that the third judgment was a particularly important limit on political power. While not fully describing a theory of popular sovereignty, the court at least vested legitimacy in the popular will.

Judicial assertiveness was tempered by a realism that may have been too protective of the current political mood, leading to decisions taken perhaps too hastily. Just as the 1955 court had given half a political judgment but stepped away from its harder part, so this transition court took the first but not the final steps to protect the democracy it heralded. It had been willing to accept its own validation of the Ayub Khan constitution, and working backwards, Ayub Khan's regime, thereby limiting its revocation of *Dosso*. In addition, the 1970 electoral mandate to which the court repeatedly referred was less apparent than the court or the government admitted. Only the anxious statements of Attorney-General Bakhtiar evinced the government's fear that the 1970 elections might be declared invalid. Certainly, the basis of franchise had changed dramatically with secession, domestic electoral choices after the war could not help but be framed differently, and regional politics were orchestrated on a vastly new footing. The court had the opportunity and the right to propose such a course and a model – the 1955 *Reference* – for so doing. Its silent recourse to mitigating circumstances may not have been in the country's best long-term interests.

Although these judgments concerned the legitimacy of Yahya Khan's assumption and assertion of power, in political terms they were equally about Ayub Khan. The legal framework the court accepted while reversing *Dosso* still allowed it to approve the 1962 Constitution and condone the 1958 *coup d'état* – indirectly validating the military rule that Lahore High Court Justice Kayani earlier called "an apology to the rest of the world and a necessity in the country itself."[21] Indeed, the Cornelius court's judgments in Ayub Khan's constitutional period had consistently assumed that the regime was consolidating, not liquidating its authority. While Justice Cornelius tried to hold that process to an even, less oppressive course, he knew better than to think that keeping Ayub Khan to the letter of his own manipulative law by ensuring limited citizen rights would change the structure of the state. Yahya Khan's ascent, complete with intermittent political detentions, political party bans and newspaper censorship, returned Pakistan to the authoritarianism and anti-politics with which Ayub Khan entered office and, with some modifications, ruled the state.

In design and consequence, the transition court was careful not to overturn too many institutional stools at once; its judgments may therefore have moderated further agitation for popular rule. The strength of its judgments must therefore be viewed not only from the point of its past, but also of its future. Presuming a transition to democracy from the fact of the 1970 elections and the seeming popularity of the People's Party, it was content to judge only one step in its formulative path, the last hurrah of the military under Yahya Khan. Its caution tacitly acknowledged that the transition was still speculative – a political reading that would be reinforced in the short, strained period of parliamentary government under Zulfikar Ali Bhutto.

Indeed, between the first hearing of *Asma Jilani's case* and the final judgment in *Ziaur Rahman's case*, bitter constitutional wrangling in the National Assembly showed the thin veneer of political consensus in the wake of the war, the deep divisions among conflicting parties about the nature of political representation, and equally serious differences about the substance of politics. All these issues had arisen before the war and were reasons the war was fought; they had not disappeared with Bengal.

[21] M.R. Kayani, "Don't Marry Pretty Women," in *Half Truths* (Lahore: Pakistan Writers' Cooperative Society, 1966), pp. 45–46.

Under Prime Minister Bhutto, military action in Baluchistan – incursions provoked by the same problems of ethnicity and nationality, economic equity and political fairness that fostered the anguish of Bangladesh, propelled by the Prime Minister's efforts to unseat the opposition provincial ministry – soon returned the army to its primacy in politics. The central government would clash bitterly with opposition ministries in the Frontier and Baluchistan, as it had with Bengal, provoking similar problems of constitutional jurisdiction and political sovereignty.

In fact, the courts were unprepared for the ways the PPP government would later assert its powers. Their relief at the advent of democracy – or at the least a transition toward it, with the advice and consent of the judiciary – may have prevented them from looking too closely at the resemblances between the Bhutto government and its predecessors. As Prime Minister, Bhutto framed his policies in the language of democracy, but increasingly pursued his goals by ignoring democratic procedures; his populism ultimately was at odds with rights protections that the 1973 Constitution was to guarantee. To remain unsullied by criticism, Bhutto legislated around its possibility, most dramatically by amending the constitution to prohibit judicial interference with his policies. The judges' efforts to maintain the triumvirate of legislative-executive-judicial authority existed in a partial political vacuum, created nonetheless by the best of intentions. Only the Prime Minister and the parliament could enforce judicial judgments, and only they could ensure the autonomy of the courts. The persistent dilemmas of Pakistan's judiciary – ones that underscore its weaknesses in its strengths, and sully its conceptual arguments with practical politics – were thus played out on the shaky foundations of the post-Bangladesh stage.

Perhaps most important, if any constitutional issue required precise theoretical grounding, it was secession, for underlying Pakistan's perpetual discomfort with the 1971 war is an uncertainty about which wing seceded from the other. Secession and separatism became the unspoken issues against which popular politics was judged but not measured. The fears of military intervention, renewed war and national disintegration were overwhelming political preoccupations for the country and the courts.

### *Politics and policy*

Similar interpretative difficulties surround the court's ruling on separation of powers. In *Ziaur Rahman's case*, the court intended to establish the primacy of the electorate, hitherto prohibited from participating in politics. Ironically, the court's language resembled, in tone if not purpose,

Ayub Khan's warnings against judicial interference in matters concerning principles of state policy. Having posited a conceptual division between the legislative and judicial branches, the courts purposefully distanced themselves from politics. Although the 1962 Constitution had made clear the coincidence of the President's power and policies, no such standard, however inappropriate, was available to the courts during the transition. The court was primarily interested in removing politics from the administration of law by separating the spheres of justice and politics. This meant more than providing the appearance and substance of justice; it meant separating the state and the government – a distinction previously impossible to draw and now hard to implement.

This desire to depoliticize the courts continued a pattern set although not followed by Justice Munir in the 1950s. By the time of *Asma Jilani's case* and *Ziaur Rahman's case*, the court stringently and explicitly preferred to distance itself from politics – perhaps a hint to the new government that it would prefer not to spend its time hearing *habeas corpus* petitions – and to see the new constitution reconstitute the political state. Without defining the limits of politics and policy, however, this distinction was theoretical at best. Fearing the known consequences of bald interference in politics, the court preferred the unknown consequences of reserve, a calculus of uncertain consent.

The court's definition of policy and politics was as speculative as its definition of the polity. The Supreme Court might have confronted this truth boldly, molding rather than dismissing the High Court's strident opinions or offering minimal directions for its later consideration. Instead, it refrained from articulating substantive standards and limits, feeling that these tasks belonged to the legislature. Later this reticence would be reinterpreted, for the National Assembly also found itself prey to the wishes of an increasingly powerful executive, and then, once again, to the army.

Additionally, if the judgment in *Ziaur Rahman's case* could be variously interpreted by the courts in deciding what would or would not be a political case, it could also be used by the government for broader purposes than was intended. Seeking the broadest interpretation of Article 281, Attorney General Bakhtiar unwittingly foreshadowed the Bhutto government's concerns with executive prerogative in either civilian or martial law garb. Bhutto would shortly amend the 1973 Constitution to manipulate the judiciary and justify violence against the civilian population in the name of democracy. The courts would not protest these actions. Additionally, within two years the Supreme Court transgressed its voluntary boundaries by ruling on explicitly political cases, including a *Reference* against the National Awami Party.

Such questions were exceptionally difficult to address, and the courts could not predict the unknowns of politics at the beginning of a new constitutional and electoral era. The confusions implied in these transition cases persisted beyond the Bhutto period. More important for the superior courts was a change of perspective and habit. The Cornelius court had created a special role for itself, protecting the status quo when the alternative seemed greater repression, acting as a window for those agitating against the Ayub Khan regime. The superior courts were mediators between unpopular government and an unchanging state structure; if they could not make the state equitable, they would try to make the government respond to minimal conditions of fairness.

The transition judiciary faced the problem of restructuring its relationship to the state while the state was just beginning to restructure itself. Two basic characteristics of governance had been altered. First, the state was changed by the war: Pakistan was literally not the place it had been. In this sense, *Dosso's case* and the 1955 *Reference* were overtaken by events, if not formally overruled by the courts. Second, the polity no longer necessarily perceived government as an enemy, since the People's Party promised sweeping changes in the political and economic structure of the state. The discourse of politics had therefore moved into a new era. Imagined optimistically, the courts might also reconceive their mandates under a new constitution: guarding against abuses of authority but not interpreting every government action as dangerous for rights, not countering every assertion of executive power with a judicial reaction, not searching for justiciable rights in an unjust political system. The transition cases can be read as a final gasp against the autocracy of the 1960s, but also as a response, if incomplete, to the promise of democracy.

With time the judiciary would learn whether it protected itself adequately within this democracy or from future incursions against it. The court's reactions in the transition cases crossed the analytical divide between politics and law. Previously, the court equated legal competence and properly constituted authority; it sought to demonstrate whether the rules for determining competence were followed when laws were made, but not to judge their internal soundness or the assumptions on which they were based. Examining the sources and purposes of power were outside legal bounds, although judicial decisions might affect the progress of politics. In the 1972 cases, the court ventured tentatively into political philosophy, discussing the purposes of government and the foundations of the state. But unlike the Munir court, this court removed itself from the formulation of policy. As the Bhutto government gained power and later limited rights, such distance – which resembled Chief Justice Cornelius's crafting of his court's purpose – proved a valuable reminder to the judiciary of its proper role.

In the Lockean theory of political consent articulated by Hamoodur Rahman in both *Asma Jilani's case* and *Ziaur Rahman's case*, the court remained apart from politics. The Chief Justice heeded political theorist Harold Laski's warnings about the fatal confusion of law and morality. Attorney General Bakhtiar, however, might have done well to invoke Laski's caution about popular sovereignty, remembering that "the announcement of its desirability in nowise coincides with the attainment of its substance."[22] The justices knew the perils of Pakistan's newest experiment with representative government, and soon saw their handiwork in its results.

[22] Harold J. Laski, "The Foundations of Sovereignty," in *The Foundations of Political Sovereignty and Other Essays* (New York: Harcourt Brace and Company, 1921), reprinted in 1968 by Books for Libraries Press, Inc., p. 231.

# 5 Testing courts and constitutionalism (1972–1977)

How can you think
the coming storm a mere illusion?

Kishwar Naheed, "Speech Number 27."

The greater the importance of safeguarding the community from incitements to the overthrow of our institutions by force and violence, the more imperative is the need to preserve inviolate the constitutional rights of free speech, free press and free assembly in order to maintain the opportunity for free political discussion, to the end that the Government may be responsive to the will of the people and that changes, if desired, may be obtained by peaceful means.

Justice Sardar Muhammad Iqbal

The years of People's Party government reflected the accumulated fears, dreams and contradictions of Pakistani political life. Despite protests against the PPP's ascendance to power – for allegations of its manipulating elections results, its partial culpability for the war and its refusal to hold new polls – the country held high hopes for a new constitution. Sadly, it was soon sullied by the way the government used it; restrictions on constitutional rule negated aspirations for participatory democracy.

The PPP held power from December 1971 until July 1977, but its short rule encompassed tremendous progress and forceful regression: national programs were hindered by party factionalism, divisive and destructive as ever; feudal interests dominated debate on taxation, land tenure and industrial policy, slowing whatever progress might have been achieved by careful nationalization and appropriate tax policy; rivalries among the provinces, fueled by the Prime Minister's continual quest for power, reached new intensity, dominating foreign and domestic policy debate alike. Institutions like the press and the judiciary, which presumed to criticize government as a matter of right, were confined by new laws and emergency provisions that removed the executive from public scrutiny.

Instruments of state power – the bureaucracy, the army, the exchequer – were partially harnessed to the ruling party. Socialist programs were soon eroded as the inertia of political habit – the relative autonomy of the military and the bureaucracy, which retained its large share of the national budget and thus insulated its institutional power – superseded the ideology of the party's foundation documents. Although its ideological moorings might have suggested an attempt to triumph over the military state it inherited, the People's Party government transformed itself instead, taking on the attributes of its martial law predecessors rather than changing the state structure. Yet, state institutions were never fully politicized, leaving the politicians and the army at loggerheads. The seeds of democracy planted by the party were left unnourished as the government began to look and sound authoritarian. In this period, the judiciary confronted problems about its institutional identity and the political consequences of its judgments as serious and difficult as any it had hitherto experienced.

## Between dictatorship and democracy

In the immediate post-war period, the government orchestrated limited political catharsis: treaties were written and prisoner exchanges concluded with India, the emotional issue of Bangladeshi sovereignty was resolved for Pakistan by finally recognizing the new state, the trial of Sheikh Mujibur Rahman was ended and he was sent home, and Justice Hamoodur Rahman headed a commission to investigate the role of the army in the East Pakistan conflict. During this time, the country was governed first under martial law and then under a temporary constitution. The 1972 Interim Constitution returned Pakistan briefly to a constitutive document on the model of the 1935 Act. People's Party leader Zulfikar Ali Bhutto – transformed by the war and secession from minority to majority party leader – held the presidency as well as the position of CMLA for four months after the war, giving the executive extensive powers under emergency security laws that had held sway during the war. Minority party opposition, similar to that against Ayub Khan after the 1965 war, finally forced him to lift martial law.

The National Assembly was empowered to draft a new constitution that it later boasted was Pakistan's first to depart from the Westminster model to evolve "a genuinely Federal Constitution."[1] The amending sessions were frequently acrimonious, with opposition and PPP members alike seeking to vindicate their personal records in light of changed political circumstances. More important, accord among the People's Party, the National Awami Party and the Jamiat-ul-Ulema-e-Islam was

[1] Comments of Khurshid Hasan Meer in National Assembly of Pakistan (Constitution-making), *Debates: Official Report*, 10 April 1973, p. 2424.

contentious and precarious; minority party members periodically boycotted amending sessions as their agreements with Bhutto about personnel and powers waxed and waned.[2] Nonetheless, a new constitution was written and approved by a directly elected Assembly for the first time since independence.

### *Constitutional politics*

The 1973 Constitution elevated the status of the Prime Minister while reducing the status of the President and incorporated provisions presumed to deter the army from interfering in politics. It protected political rights, in part by underscoring the writ jurisdiction of the superior courts, including the power to grant interim relief.[3] However, wartime preventive detention laws and security rules remained in force for most of Bhutto's tenure; the government cited continuing acrimony with India and domestic terrorism to justify imprisoning political dissidents. Speaking two years after the constitution's passage, the Prime Minister told the country's lawyers that these "abnormal laws" were set in an "equally abnormal . . . situation in which there is resort to terrorism and indulgence in anti-State and subversive activities," but suggested that justiciable rights could hold law enforcement bodies in check.[4] His assurances notwithstanding, the long reach of executive authority and the extent of rights protections remained issues of sharp divide from the time of constitution-making to the end of PPP rule. Justice Hamoodur Rahman affirmed similar sentiments, asserting to the same judicial conference that "the basic human rights . . . which our Constitution has conferred upon the people cannot be taken away or curtailed by any law save as permitted by the Constitution itself. The Constitution, therefore, also determines the limits of the encroachment permissible."[5] Yet, concerns about the weakness of these guarantees in the constitution and the party's recalcitrance in strengthening them led civil libertarian Mahmud Ali Kasuri, a member of the constitution-drafting committee and the PPP Federal Law Minister, to resign his committee post and Cabinet position. Kasuri was particularly concerned about the head of state's "uncontrolled power" to dissolve the National Assembly.[6]

2 *Debates*, pp. 2369–2372, 2421. 3 *Debates*, p. 2425.

4 "Inaugural Address to Second Pakistan Jurists' Conference," 9–12 January 1975, PLD 1975 Journal 4–8. Attorney General Yahya Bakhtiar, who complained publicly to the first jurists' convention about the continuing emergency, adopted the Prime Minister's stand after the government's 1975 reference against NAP, telling a gathering of Lahore attorneys that "we do not like Emergency, but we have been left with no alternative but to continue it." PLD 1976 Journal 270–74.

5 Presidential Address to Second Pakistan Jurists' Conference, PLD 1975 Journal 8–12.

6 "Provision to check parliamentary vacuum: Kasuri's plea," *Dawn* 13 November 1972.

Democratic principles included in the 1973 Constitution were sharply restricted in subsequent amendments to that document, which rewrote the definitions of legislative sovereignty and judicial autonomy. The amendments not only called into question guarantees for substantive civil rights and independent courts, but also sharply heightened the institutional and political power of the Prime Minister.[7] In sequence, they limited freedom of association guaranteed in Article 17; limited the rights of members of the Ahmadiya sect; widened the scope of preventive detention; removed the National Assembly's obligation to approve extensions of emergency proclamations; amended Article 199 by seriously restricting the High Courts from granting interim relief to detainees; and prohibited the courts from ordering the release of prisoners awaiting trial or already convicted by tribunals. While Article 8 of the constitution declared void all laws conflicting with fundamental rights, the fifth amendment declared laws pursuant to emergency proclamations "to have been validly made and shall not be called into question in any court" due to conflicts with fundamental rights. In addition, the National Assembly amended the Defence of Pakistan Rules in April and May 1976 to give special tribunals exclusive jurisdiction over offenses punishable by the Rules, and to allow cases under civil review to be transferred to such tribunals.[8]

The Prime Minister used these amendments to refine the constitutional separation of powers by removing legislative and judicial oversight from his personal and party programs. Appointments to the superior courts had always required government confirmation, but in the Bhutto period these were often postponed or withheld, leaving many judges with only interim appointments; the fifth amendment also specified the length of service for chief justices, who had previously held lifetime appointments. (Sardar Muhammad Iqbal, Chief Justice of the Lahore High Court, cited this retrospective constraint in his resignation speech soon after the amendment was passed.) Referring to the fifth amendment, Bhutto suggested that "the judiciary should not adopt the role of a parallel Executive

7 The courts distinguished the roles of party leader and Prime Minister even when they were blurred in practice. See *Muhammad Aslam Saleemi, Advocate v. The Pakistan-Television Corporation and another*, PLD 1977 Lahore 852, requiring an equal time/equal treatment provision for election coverage.

8 The Defence of Pakistan (Amendment) Bill and Defence of Pakistan (Second Amendment) Bill constituted tribunals which could proceed *in camera* without the presence of the accused and without full evidence or cross-examination. Only one of its three members was required to have the qualifications of a High Court judge. The Defence of Pakistan (Third Amendment) Bill 1976 allowed one appeal to the High Court, but without bail reduction or sentence suspension. Special courts constituted under the Suppression of Terrorist Activities (Special Courts) Act 1975 consisted of one High Court judge, and were to provide speedy trials of individuals suspected of sabotage; the accused were considered guilty unless proven innocent.

by misinterpreting the law," continuing "if the judiciary had not transgressed into the Executive's functions, there would have been no need to bring it."

No party or faction was fully satisfied by the governance structure created by the constitution, even though it received unanimous approval from the National Assembly. To achieve the goals of the socialist program included in the party's 1970 electoral platform, federalism was tempered with executive privilege and government centralization, which displeased the strong assertions of provincial autonomy voiced in NAP. At the same time, ideology was too muted for the tastes of some PPP members whose socialism predated their party membership.[9] However, the most serious problems for Pakistan were those feared by Mian Kasuri: constitutional changes promulgated unilaterally by the Prime Minister, whose diminishing respect for parliament was matched by his contempt for the judiciary's prerogative rights.

### *Provinces and parties*

Most divisive, both before and after the constitution was ratified, was the issue of provincial autonomy. It was a problem that figured repeatedly in the constitution-drafting debates and in public statements from the National Awami Party. Pressing the autonomy issue during constitutional debate, NAP leader Wali Khan had trumpeted: "When we wanted our rights in the past we were dubbed as traitors, but now the situation had changed. Now we shall take our rights and not beg for them. And if anyone tries to oust us from Pakistan then he should remember that we are not Bengalis who separated."[10] Rhetorical passion occasionally dictated the content of debate, with NAP and the PPP equally keen to curry favor with voters, gain the political advantage over its rival, and extend its power.

Bhutto lifted the ban on the National Awami Party shortly after coming to power in order to orchestrate a constitutional settlement. To avoid further disputes between the parties, the PPP negotiated a hard-fought agreement with NAP and JUI, giving the minority parties provincial ministries in Quetta and Peshawar. The Baluchistan ministry was dissolved by the federal government in February 1973, however, and its ministers, imprisoned a few months later under the Defence of Pakistan

[9] See *Debates*, 3 April 1973, pp. 2145–27.

[10] "No denying rights to Pakhtoons, Baluchis," *Dawn* 20 April 1972. However, Baluchistan Governor Ghous Bahksh Bizenjo observed that "the country wanted not only stable Government but stable democracy." "Autonomy formula accords with NAP stand, says Bizenjo," *PT* 23 October 1972.

Rules, remained in jail for the duration of the PPP government. Further arrests of NAP members in the next years occurred in a climate of civil disruption, with government forces firing on political demonstrations, and intermittent bomb blasts in the Frontier, one of which killed a PPP minister in Peshawar. Most serious for NAP was the killing of civilians, presumably by the para-military, para-police Federal Security Force at a United Democratic Front coalition rally at Liaqat Bagh in Rawalpindi on Pakistan Day 1973, shortly after its ministries were dismissed.[11] Amid growing insurgency against central government actions in Baluchistan – actions of manifold cause that the Bhutto government put at the feet of NAP – hostilities heightened on all sides.

As part of its program to modernize Baluchistan, the federal government tried to abolish the system of feudal political influence and landholding (the sardari system), but in a heavy-handed manner that made political alliances all the more difficult to conclude. Political party loyalties and ideological battles were superimposed on family and tribal disputes of far longer standing. Conflicts in the Pat Feeder and Las Bela areas of Baluchistan were at once inter-tribal and anti-government conflicts; encounters between central government armed forces and tribal lashkars and police were as much the results of traditional turf battles as they were jurisdictional disputes among provincial and government agencies. (Ironically, after a string of unworkable provincial ministries, the Prime Minister found as his ally in Baluchistan the former Khan of Kalat, who in 1958 had so violently resisted integration with Pakistan.) These events lent unusual virulence to anti-government campaigns and government retribution. The credibility, for example, of government allegations that NAP imported Russian armaments through the Iraqi embassy, and the convenient apprehending of anti-government saboteurs during the 1975 Supreme Court case against NAP, were suspect in these contexts as attempts to internationalize the consequences of anti-government actions.

For NAP, any reconciliation with the PPP to promote constitutional rule was deeply compromised by the peremptory dismissal of its ministries, particularly any concessions on the "quantum of provincial autonomy" which the PPP insisted was settled in the 1973 formulation. For the People's Party, the issue was one of political power and inter-party dispute, with the victor entitled to set the terms of political debate both domestically and internationally. For NAP, the issue involved tribal dignity and rights, the nature of the Pakistani federation and the limits that it felt should attend PPP power. Their interpretations of politics were

[11] The formation of the UDF is discussed in Wali Khan's written statement for the 1975 *Reference* hearing against NAP, p. 52. See also *KM* reports, February 1975.

incommensurable: while NAP constantly emphasized a continuum of federal–provincial conflict from Bengal to Baluchistan, implying a veiled secessionist threat, the PPP sought to establish its control over the entire country and particularly those issues sensitive to foreign policy; while NAP looked to those whose traditional power bases were disappearing in the PPP's efforts toward national integration, the PPP looked to its electoral mandate to establish its national political and economic policies.

Both sides were right and wrong. Electoral victory did not entitle the PPP to bludgeon its opponents but did entitle it to pursue its agenda; insults to provincial rights entitled NAP to express its dissatisfactions but did not sanction violence against the government. At the same time, constitutional disputes were as much about the personalities holding power as the power they held. Later, after his release from jail by General Zia ul Haq, NAP leader Khan Abdul Wali Khan reversed his position about the substance of NAP demands, suggesting that the constitution provided an adequate amount of provincial autonomy.

Participatory politics was seriously compromised by the government's response to threats to its undiluted power. The PPP government's increasingly brutal repression against its critics helped them to organize an effective if not democratic opposition. Legislators were frequently disregarded in policy-making, removed from Assembly sessions when they disagreed with the Prime Minister, and harassed mercilessly if they parted company with the party, which used the resources of the state to impose its will.[12] At times, only violence – like that which broke out in Sind in 1972 when the PPP provincial government under Mumtaz Ali Bhutto enforced a law making Sindhi the official language in Sind, despite a plurality of non-Sindhi speakers in the province – convinced the government to change direction. Dismay with the PPP mounted, even though the government had come into office with popular good will generated by relief at the war's end and the installation of an elected Prime Minister.

Ultimately, the Bhutto government did not absorb the crucial lessons of the Bangladesh war. The war was not about bringing the PPP to power. Rather, it concerned the critical nexus between self-determination, provincial autonomy and civil liberties, the necessary incorruptibility of government institutions and the required freedom for them to function, and the overwhelming importance of open political speech in establishing constitutional democracy. In this strained environment, the PPP did not realize its own strengths. Bhutto, who would often warn his colleagues that elections are not arithmetic – that they raise the possibility of all

[12] Government of Pakistan, *White Paper on the Performance of the Bhutto Regime*, Vol. III, Islamabad, 1979.

manner of uncontrollable impulses in the polity and society – approached the 1977 elections as if planning for war, and the opposition did the same. The result was fiasco. Neither side was likely to acknowledge the victory of the other, provoking inevitable post-election confrontations when the Pakistan National Alliance (PNA) boycotted provincial assembly polls in favor of anti-government demonstrations, and then the equally inevitable martial law to control them. The army decided that intervention in politics was a better route to stability than the cacophony of indecisive politics, particularly since the civilian government had set a pattern of using the army extensively, if not effectively, to impose civil order. Military action against civil government, thought only a few years earlier to have been prohibited in the constitution, was as simple and direct as it had been before. By misinterpreting history, the Prime Minister helped to renew the praetorian state.

## Rules, rights and reference

Uncertain democracy confronted emergency provisions in the judiciary's arena for most of the Bhutto period. Maintaining judicial autonomy became increasingly complex between the passage of the constitution in 1973 and its abrogation in 1977. Superior court dockets in the Bhutto years reflect contradictory pulls upon the polity: between economic centralization and partial political decentralization, between democratic constitutionalism and statist emergency powers, between the unitary state and reasserted communal ties. The courts tried to separate actions taken by or against the government from those undertaken for political or partisan purposes. The People's Party often did not differentiate between the two, acting as if citizen rights were no more than another set of obstacles in the path of political power.

### *Military rules, civil courts*

Changing political winds were reflected in breaches of personal liberties. For the courts, this meant frequent *habeas corpus* petitions, challenges to preventive detention and censorship,[13] resistance to the continued use of Ayub Khan's war-era laws, and accusations of official mistreatment and torture in prisons. As open fora the courts were unwitting accomplices to these disputes when the government and its opponents brandished litigation as a weapon of politics. Government efforts to silence critics often

[13] For example, *State v. Yusaf Lodhi*, PLD 1973 Peshawar 25 and *Fakhre Alam v. The State and another*, PLD 1973 Supreme Court 525; *Maulana Musahib Ali v. The State*, PLD 1975 Karachi 909; *Kanayalal v. The State*, PLD 1977 Karachi 675.

provoked legal challenges which led to renewed repression and further litigation. Circularity did not mean substantive equality before the law, however, for the power of the state far exceeded that of the individual. By 1977, the government had lodged hundreds of cases against politicians and party members (as well as their families and other non-combatants) on matters sometimes only distantly related to politics.

As the laws varied under which emergency detentions were enforced so did the capacity of the courts to redress grievances. It was easier to uphold individual rights under the 1960 West Pakistan Maintenance of Public Order Ordinance than under the Defence of Pakistan Rules, which explicitly restricted available remedies. Nonetheless, in its 1973 cases, the Karachi High Court supported citizen rights even when it could not offer relief. Taking up petitions filed after language riots in Sind in 1972, the High Court reminded the government that "an infringement of the rights of liberties of the citizens, should be strictly construed," and suggested that statutory interpretation should, whenever possible, favor the citizen.[14] Judging a group of sixteen *habeas corpus* petitions from the same period, Justice Agha Ali Hyder reminded the government that "in *Jilani's case*, the detenu would have been disqualified for exercising his political rights but for the judgment of the court."[15] In matters concerning its own powers, the Supreme Court cautioned the government that "the jurisdiction conferred on the Supreme Court by clear terms of the constitution itself cannot be whittled down on considerations of policy or convenience."[16] Clearest in its judgment against the government's use of emergency provisions, however, was the Peshawar High Court. In a warning that soon resonated in cases against many Frontier opposition leaders, Justice Shah Zaman Babar stated:

> It is a misconception to think that either under the Defence of Pakistan Ordinance or the rules framed thereunder any arbitrary, unguided, uncontrolled or naked power has been given to any authority. These provisions only confer a power which is coupled with a duty. The power can only be exercised after the duty has been discharged in accordance with the guidelines provided in the statute and the rules.[17]

This judgment released an unlawfully detained prisoner in June 1973. Later that year, NAP leaders were less fortunate.

[14] *Liaqat Ali v. Government of Sind through Secretary, Home Department*, PLD 1973 Karachi 78.

[15] *Zafar Iqbal v. Province of Sind and 2 others*, PLD 1973 Karachi 316. See also *Abdul Hamid Khan v. The District Magistrate, Larkana and 2 others*, PLD 1973 Karachi 344.

[16] *Khan Muhammad Yusuf Khan Khattack v. S.M. Ayub and 2 others*, PLD 1973 Supreme Court 160.

[17] *Fida Muhammad v. Province of NWFP through Home Secretary, Peshawar*, PLD 1973 Peshawar 156.

The Lahore Court also relied on the letter of the constitution to transmit the spirit of law and order when it ruled on government transgressions of rights and rules. Justice Sardar Mohammad Iqbal reminded the government that preventive detention was allowed under the constitution only when used with discretion.[18] Ruling on the detention of a Jamiat-ul-Ulema-e-Pakistan (JUP) politician, the court noted that "the law is . . . extremely chary of the deprivation of the liberty of a citizen at the hands of the investigation agencies." As it would do increasingly, it reminded the government of due process rights, including the right of the accused to be informed of charges against him and the responsibility of the police to act expeditiously.[19] The Supreme Court later noted that "even during the Proclamation of Emergency, the executive is precluded from taking any action which is not covered by the authority of law."[20]

The Lahore Court interpreted citizen rights broadly. Ruling on a writ petition challenging a required monetary deposit to publish a newspaper, the court submitted that "the concept of freedom of expression would imply that every citizen is free to say or publish what he wants, provided that he does not trample upon the rights of others."[21] With time, its language became more insistent. When it heard one of dozens of writ petitions filed by opposition politician Chaudhry Zahur Ilahi (against whom the government filed dozens more), the court decided that the 1971 Defence of Pakistan Ordinance included certain rights protections.[22] "The word 'liberty'," said Justice Ataullah Sajjad, "carries with it a wider meaning of a citizen following fully his course of action in matters of his private life . . . The mere existence of a law enabling the public functionaries to impose restraints on the liberty of a citizen is not enough to justify the action taken thereunder . . . There is a duty cast on the public functionary . . . to act impartially and reasonably." He responded to government immunity claims by defending judicial review, writing that "it is the duty of the superior judiciary to review the actions of the Executive, otherwise the constitutional guarantees given to the citizens would be vain and illusory."

From the time he assumed office, Prime Minister Bhutto held military

18 *Begum Nazir Abdul Hamid v. Pakistan (Federal Government) through Secretary Interior*, PLD 1974 Lahore 7.

19 *Maulana Abdus Sattar Khan Niazi v. The State*, PLD 1974 Lahore 324. Due process matters were also considered in *Nawab Begum v. Home Secretary, Government of Punjab, Lahore*, PLD 1974 Lahore 344; *Mrs. Habiba Jilani v. The Federation of Pakistan through Secretary, Interior Ministry*, PLD 1974 Lahore 153; *Kh. Muhammad Safdar v. The State and another*, PLD 1974 Lahore 200.

20 *Federation of Pakistan v. Ch. Manzoor Elahi*, PLD 1976 Supreme Court 430.

21 *Muzaffar Qadir v. The District Magistrate, Lahore*, PLD 1975 Lahore 1198.

22 *Ch. Zahur Ilahi v. Secretary to Government of Pakistan, Ministry of Home and Kashmir Affairs*, PLD 1975 Lahore 499.

and civil power concurrently. By extending this dual executive capacity in emergency proclamations, he prompted frequent jurisdictional questions. Bars to civil court jurisdiction in the Defence of Pakistan Ordinance and Rules meant that tribunals established under those laws frequently usurped otherwise normal judicial duties. At the least, remedies provided by those tribunals had to be exhausted before the civil judiciary could begin to exercise any authority.[23]

A serious challenge to the intersection of civil–military conflicts in law came within a year of the passage of the 1973 Constitution. Retired military officers accused of fomenting a conspiracy against the state filed a writ petition in the Lahore High Court challenging court martial proceedings against them. Overruling their objections, a court martial in Attock Fort convicted the officers while they awaited judgment on their writs, provoking further petitions contesting the validity of the Army Act in proceedings against civilians, and the validity of extended emergency provisions invoked against them. The High Court dismissed the writs in *F.B. Ali v. The State* (PLD 1975 Lahore 999), holding that a challenge to laws on the basis of conflicts with rights was equivalent to an attempt to enforce fundamental rights, action barred during an emergency. It also ruled that the first constitutional amendment ousted High Court writ jurisdiction,[24] that court martial jurisdiction under the Army Act covered civilian offenses, and that legislative extensions of the state of emergency were valid.

The Supreme Court appeal clarified the status of emergency provisions and the scope of the Army Act (*F.B. Ali v. The State*, PLD 1975 Supreme Court 506). In a carefully worded opinion, Chief Justice Hamoodur Rahman dismissed the appeal, although he disagreed with some of the High Court's statutory interpretations and took issue with the absence of certain due process guarantees for the accused. Specifying the relationship between the civil and military courts under emergency, he nonetheless underscored the validity of court martial powers over civilians established by Ayub Khan in 1967 and later confirmed by the legislature. Indeed, the "pith and substance" of the law was to prevent "the subversion of the loyalty of a member of the Defence Services of Pakistan," a service "as essential as the provision of arms and ammunition." The Chief Justice rehearsed the court's earlier equation of legislative competence

[23] For example, *Indo-Pakistan Corporation, Ltd., Lahore v. Government of Pakistan through Secretary, Ministry of Political Affairs*, PLD 1975 Lahore 1058.

[24] Justice K.E. Chauhan cited *Abdul Ghani Khan v. Government of West Pakistan and others*, PLD 1068 Lahore 1244, on the fundamental rights question. The court limited the ouster of writ jurisdiction in amended Article 199: "If a case does not fall within the four corners of the jurisdiction-ousting conditions, then writs therein can be issued by this Court."

with validity. Citing *Asma Jilani's case*, he reminded the appellants that "courts cannot strike down a law on any . . . higher ethical notions nor can the courts act on the basis of philosophical concepts of law." Law, according to Justice Muhammad Yaqub in the same case, "postulates a strict performance of all the functions and duties laid down by law." Establishing that the Army Act was competent law, the court ruled that under specified conditions the Act covered civilians.

While agreeing to the scope of the court martial, the Supreme Court upheld its own powers. Referring to its opinions in *Fazlul Quader Chowdhury* and *Sirajul Haq Patwari*, the court repeated its responsibility to examine the constitutionality of laws, admitting an ouster of jurisdiction on questions of validity "only on the ground of the lack of competency of the Legislature." In this way the court distinguished its proceedings from military courts. It proposed that where criminal courts and courts martial had concurrent jurisdiction (over persons subject to the Army Act), the military could decide in which forum to try the case. It also reiterated a bar on judicial review of courts martial on strictly procedural grounds. The operative distinction between civil and military court powers was the status of the accused: those subject to the Army Act could be left largely to the discretion of military courts.

*F.B. Ali* tested two critical questions for civil society: whether civil law would override military and quasi-military legal practices of the previous martial law and emergency; and whether the judiciary would retain its powers against constitutional limits on its authority. The court drew jurisdictional lines for the Army Act to ensure that even during civilian-imposed emergencies military courts did not extend their powers beyond those specified in the Act: no confusions were to develop between civil and martial law. The justices also distinguished civil and military judicial authority, claiming for superior courts the traditional arena of judicial review while allowing courts martial the extended jurisdiction mandated in recent constitutional amendments. In effect, *F.B. Ali* recognized the legitimacy of Assembly actions under the new constitution without relinquishing an inch more of the court's own powers than seemed absolutely essential.[25] Its judgment, while not overtly political, was eminently politic.

25 A few days before this Supreme Court judgment, a writ petition contesting a summary military court conviction was heard in the Lahore High Court (*Sh. Rehmat Ullah v. Government of Pakistan*, PLD 1975 Lahore 1513). The High Court acknowledged Constituent Assembly intentions to give "blanket cover" to martial law orders and actions under Article 281 of the 1972 Constitution. (The Supreme Court reconsidered the problem in *Sh. Karamat Ali v. The State*, PLD 1976 Supreme Court 476.) Its judgment barred judicial inquiry into military courts and gave the Assembly wide berth in its constitution-making capacity. *F.B. Ali* affirmed this pattern.

*Dissolving NAP*

*F.B. Ali* set standards of non-interference for the civil and military sectors that were easy to ignore. Between 1975 and 1977 it was frequently cited by the superior courts but rarely heeded. For the present, it had little effect on the fate of imprisoned Frontier politicians, anti-government activists in Baluchistan or other politicians imprisoned for their opposition to the People's Party. The government's evolving practice of limiting political debate was reflected in the passage of the first constitutional amendment restricting free association, which covered the dissolution of the National Awami Party two days earlier, and the imprisonment of many of its leaders. The only restriction on this gag rule was its requirement of judicial validation. The government therefore referred its declaration of dissolution to the Supreme Court in *Islamic Republic of Pakistan through Secretary, Ministry of Interior and Kashmir Affairs, Islamabad v. Mr. Abdul Wali Khan MNA* (Reference No. 1 of 1975). While the court considered the reference, government intelligence agencies collected information for a special court trial conducted in Hyderabad Central Jail in which the proceedings of the *Reference* were used under special rules of evidence.[26] Taken together, they provide an intriguing view of the Supreme Court's relationship to the Prime Minister and to the government's special courts. Equally important, in addition to the personal vitriol expressed between Prime Minister Bhutto and NAP leader Khan Abdul Wali Khan in the NAP *Reference* – and the problems of reconstructing political history from the adversarial statements of a trial – the case shows the depth of Pakistan's constitutional difficulties in the post-Bangladesh period. In its advisory opinion, the court argued that NAP had sought "to destroy the concept which formed the very basis for the creation of this country . . . and even suggesting that after the secession of East Pakistan the concept had disappeared or been drowned in the Bay of Bengal." It also accepted the Attorney General's characterization of NAP's nationality policy as "the sowing of the seed of secession as we have had the misfortune of experiencing from the course of events that took place in East Pakistan in the recent past."

The government's reference, upheld by the court, cited the NAP dissolution for "operating in a manner prejudicial to the sovereignty and

[26] The Hyderabad trial was constituted under Criminal Law Amendment (Special Court) Ordinance 1975, later replaced with Criminal Law Amendment (Special Court) Act (XVII) 1976. The Supreme Court was aware of case preparations for Hyderabad, as evidenced in its questions to Lt. General Ghulam Jilani, Director General of Inter-Services Intelligence, about the use of his testimony in future court martial proceedings. "Intelligence Reports on NAP's Activities Presented," *KM* 9 July 1975.

integrity of Pakistan," fomenting "large-scale terrorist and subversive activities in the country," "creating hatred and disaffection against various sections of the people and inciting the people to bring about a change of Government established by law through violent and unconstitutional means," and establishing links with the Daud government in Afghanistan. The charges were almost impossible to refute, less because of their inaccuracy than because of their peculiar proximity to truth. In documents filed by the government, witness responses during the hearings, and statements filed by NAP officials, hyperbole accompanied incisive political analysis in equal portions. The issues underlying the dissolution were the meaning of political loyalty in a changing polity; the ideological basis of the Pakistani state and the nature of its constitution; opposing concepts of nations and nationalities, autonomy and self-determination, and civil and political rights; and finally, the frank pursuit of power. Unfortunately, the contexts of the *Reference* and the succeeding Hyderabad trial, in addition to recent wars and decades of dispute, made it impossible to resolve these questions in court. The *Reference* judgment took stands on some of these issues but hardly settled deeply felt controversies.

*Judicial powers* The question of procedural jurisdiction influenced the court's determinations. The Bhutto government wanted the court to judge narrow questions and limit NAP's opportunities to voice political disputes in a judicial forum. Attorney General Yahya Bakhtiar asked the court to consider only whether the government had followed proper procedure in declaring the party dissolved, invoking the familiar competence-legitimacy distinction of earlier cases.[27] He distinguished validity – acting in "a legal and proper manner" – from the legitimacy or rightness of such an action. To do this, he invoked the separation of powers: submitting that the burden of responsibility for determining if NAP's actions were prejudicial belonged with the legislature, he suggested that the court should not take "purely political" decisions, that the courts were to remain above politics, and should function as "supragovernment and supracabinet" during the *Reference*. He also argued that rules of evidence should be suspended in matters of urgent national import.

The court, however, accepted the advice of *amicus curiae* Sharifuddin Pirzada, who proposed that the Supreme Court held original jurisdiction in this *Reference*, which in turn required an inquiry of wider scope. A strict reading of the constitution, he proposed, required that only the

[27] "Political Parties Act Legal – A.G.," *KM* 17 July 1975.

court, and not the government, could dissolve a political party. The court considered deciding the government's limited reference and letting NAP seek relief in the High Court, but was clearly troubled by this alternative – not because it extended litigation, but because it felt that allegedly prejudicial party activities could then continue after the government's declaration, causing "incalculable harm."[28] Partly for this reason it determined that its powers in such a reference were "not merely confined to the judicial review and affirmation of an executive act but to the judicial determination of the question as to whether the party is or is not acting in a manner prejudicial to the sovereignty and integrity of Pakistan." It then took as a political reference point NAP's earlier acquiescence in constitution-making and ratification, the very concords which NAP now disavowed in reaction to the government's dissolution of its provincial ministries.

The court's assumptions about politics and the party's assumptions about constitutionality conflicted sharply. The court concluded that freedom of association was subject to "reasonable restrictions"[29] that did not necessarily conflict with fundamental rights: "While the right of assembly is a very important right for the preservation of a democratic political system yet it cannot be denied that no State can tolerate utterances or actions which threaten to overthrow the Government established by law in that State by unlawful or unconstitutional means." It reminded the government that the power to restrict must "prevent arbitrary action or abuse of power or the destruction of the democratic fabric itself." Again, the court relied on procedure to determine substance, proposing that judicial review of dissolution reasonably and adequately protected the party and its members.

Nonetheless, the *Reference* judgment indirectly upheld the first constitutional amendment by agreeing to its substantive terms, despite the decision in *Ziaur Rahman's case* to refrain from deciding the validity of constitutional provisions, and as articulated in *Sirajul Haq Patwari*, leaned in favor of constitutionality. When NAP declined to participate in the proceeding, the court continued to hear evidence from government

28 "6 Legal Points: Pirzada argues in reference," *KM* 15 July 1975.

29 Both Pirzada and Bakhtiar cited *Maudoodi's case* on the relation of fundamental rights to party restrictions under the 1962 Political Parties Act to buttress virtually every element of any argument, an interesting idiosyncracy given the court's firm decision in that case (see chapter 3 above). Pirzada also referred to two contemporaneous Indian cases, *Golak Nath's case* and *Kesavananda Bharati's case*, concerning the question of legislative limits on fundamental rights. References to these cases appeared intermittently in Bhutto era judgments by all sides to contests, either to support the sanctity of fundamental rights, to support legislative incursions on rights (when *Kesavananda* modified *Golak Nath*), or to deny the relevance of the comparison by citing *Ziaur Rahman's case*. See chapter 8 below.

sources. The court acceded to some of NAP's demands for financial and physical resources to press its defense, and consistently distinguished the *Reference* from a criminal trial, but its proceedings and judgment never fully separated the party dissolution from a trial of its leaders, all of whom were imprisoned.[30] NAP's withdrawal, therefore, may have been an expression of pique – the court's preferred interpretation – or an attempt to highlight confusion and malice in the government's case.

The court's decision on the procedural issue gravely influenced the substantive outcome of the *Reference*. It asserted its right to determine the scope and terms of the case contrary to the government's wishes. It took on the government at the same level at which the government, in its constitutional amendments, had begun to take on the judiciary. The court then went further by deciding a question far beyond that which it was required to judge. To support the declaration of dissolution, it could have decided in favor of the government without determining the substantive merits of the case, leaving the government to fix – as it did in any case – the range of subsequent actions. Alternately, it could have decided against the government on procedural grounds by citing conflicts with the right of free association – thus restoring the party and leaving future disputes to political negotiation, the arena from which the Attorney General was so anxious to remove the court.

Instead, the court fell prey to the same temptation of extended reach that had afflicted the Munir court in 1955 and 1958. It issued a long substantive judgment beyond its call, as happened in *Dosso's case*, validating in a judicial forum government actions that probably belonged outside the courts. It took up the *Reference* on the government's political terms, accepting its diagnosis of prevailing political currents to prove its point, thus echoing its actions in *Tamizuddin Khan's case* and the *Governor-General's Reference*. The court expanded its jurisdiction beyond the government's pleasure, but did not subject the government to thorough or impartial scrutiny.

*Ideology and rights* Once resolving to judge substantive arguments for dissolution, and doing so without defence witnesses, the court heard several months of government allegations of NAP anti-state actions. To prove its case, the government read selectively the history of

30 *Written Statement of Khan Abdul Wali Khan* submitted to the court in June 1975. For a review of NAP demands and court responses, see *Pleadings and Orders in Supreme Court in Government's Reference on Dissolution of NAP*, Rawalpindi 1975, and *Khyber Mail* reports, June–August 1975. The court also refused a request from the United Democratic Front coalition to participate in the proceedings. "UDF plea rejected: SC asks Wali to apologise," *KM* 16 July 1975.

Pakistan, accusing NAP of anti-patriotic actions even before the formation of the Pakistani state. Parading long memory to frame a case, the government betrayed both its fears and its weaknesses. It charged NAP with long-term collaboration with Afghanistan against Pakistan, and alleged pro-Indian (and thus purportedly anti-Pakistan) policies initiated in the Congress Party days of Pukhtun Khudai Khidmatgar leader and NAP founder Khan Abdul Ghaffar Khan. (The court ignored NAP's verifiable counter-accusations of People's Party meddling in Afghanistan's affairs, noting only that NAP ideology and not PPP policy was under inspection.) The government's case rested on its conviction that NAP had violated the ideology of Pakistan – a concept never explained by the government or the court except by vague reference to the two-nation theory that NAP felt was destroyed by the Bangladesh war, but that the People's Party claimed was the ideological grounding for the state. The court apparently agreed. By seeking "to create doubts about the people's belief in the ideology of Pakistan," the court decided that NAP leaders "who were never firmly wedded to the Ideology of Pakistan" were guilty of actions coincident with treason. The NAP *Reference* was thus transformed into a tribunal not merely on the 1970 elections, as Khan Abdul Wali Khan suggested, but on the theory of the Pakistani state.

At issue was NAP's concept of a multi-national state. It recalled the same arguments that had fueled constitutional debates since independence and provincial autonomy disputes well before 1947: whether the state was a creation of the provinces or the center, whether a unitary state nullified the ethnic ties of provincialism, whether the provinces could remove themselves from the union when faced with central government policies contrary to their perceived interests, and, as always, who was to speak for the voter. Following the 1971 war, and unworkable relations between the central government and its hand-picked provincial governments after 1973, NAP remained vociferous in its program for national rights, greater provincial autonomy than the 1973 Constitution provided and justiciable civil liberties for its political leaders. Although Wali Khan, Jam Saqi and Ghous Bahksh Bizenjo used different language to express their views in lengthy written statements to the court, NAP nationalities doctrine was recognizable and clear.

The People's Party, however, reiterated that "the quantum of provincial autonomy" had been decided in the constitution and refused to re-enter debate on the subject. For the central government, to espouse national rights was to jeopardize the concepts of citizenship and rights enshrined in the constitution and thus to threaten state sovereignty. NAP accused the government of trampling on the rights of minority provinces and violating the 1972 PPP–NAP–JUI tripartite compact, fundamental rights and the constitution itself. Questioning the legitimacy of the People's Party government, NAP proposed to rework the constitutional foundations of the state once again; recognizing a powerful challenge to its authority, the PPP understandably refused and then tried to neutralize its opponents.

The court took the words of the constitution at face value and did not judge government actions pursuant to them. Instead, Chief Justice Hamoodur Rahman took the possibility of secession – quoting the government charge of NAP's "thinly concealed expression of secessionist intentions" – as necessarily entailed in the concept of autonomy. He noted that

> no Constitution has so guaranteed that the provinces should be constituted on ethnic, linguistic or cultural basis nor has any Constitution guaranteed that each ethnic, linguistic or cultural group living in Pakistan will have the right of self-determination. If it did so it would be recognizing what is practically the right to secede and perhaps the NAP and its leadership could then have had some justification for claiming that these are fundamental rights guaranteed by the Constitution.

"If by providing autonomy is meant the right of self-determination with the right to secede," he continued, "then the phrase 'provincial autonomy' is either a meaningless term or deliberately intended to be misleading and deceptive."

While trying to refute the confederal theme of the NAP nationalities theory, the government also argued that NAP's program for a greater Pukhtunistan was a menace to Pakistan's international boundaries and sovereignty. The government's case was shaky; frequent references to the issue notwithstanding, its evidence was Radio Kabul interceptions, foreign newspaper clippings and non-contextual excerpts from NAP speeches. The government viewed irredentism as the political counterweight to domestic insurgencies and used the prospect of one to buttress the fact of the other; that both issues concerned sovereignty seemed to be the only apparent link in the judgment. (The government, of course, could blame foreign interference for its own internal instabilities.) Here again, the court accepted fully government evidence and conclusions, responding to the language of national instability and violence rather than to pristine logic.

The *Reference* judgment did not enlighten the issues it addressed. Indeed, the adversarial proceedings may have hardened Bhutto's stand on the autonomy issue; open parliamentary debate on this and related questions – by this time the exception rather than the norm – might have moderated all sides in the dispute. The judgment generally accepted the government's case and remained atypically silent concerning tortured and occasionally absent argument. NAP was at once equated with demands for secession and for national expansion. The ever-elusive issue of national ideology was treated as part of the nationalities question, which was in turn treated as part of the question of provincial autonomy. Both were then encircled by the historical experience of Bengal secession and used to reaffirm the two-nation theory more as a matter of creed or convenience rather than actuality. In fact, all these issues were related and exceptionally important, but the Court's opinion neither clarified their intersections nor resolved their contradictions.

The judgment is equally perplexing for what it did not discuss. The questions of nationalities and provincial autonomy were not treated as constitutional issues but as disturbing symptoms of a manufactured and false political unrest; NAP's electoral constituency in the Frontier was not mentioned. Configurations of power reflected in federal, zonal, confederal and consociational governance were never examined, and were discussed only to be disparaged. NAP allegations concerning the denial of individual and party rights were recognized by neither the government nor the court. Democracy was presumed to exist in Pakistan and evidence to the contrary was laid entirely at the feet of NAP.

The historical and political contexts of the *Reference* became the most profound determinant of its judgment, as it was in the Hyderabad tribunal which followed. The trauma of the 1971 war was an undercurrent of Bhutto's government tenure and later figured in the judicial verdict on his demise. In this sense, the case against the National Awami Party can be seen as an attempt by the People's Party government to resurrect a consensus on national ideology by removing from formal politics those who most explicitly castigated the PPP for its role in the war, and who most loudly proclaimed the failure of the two-nation theory. The Bengal NAP and Awami League – the PPP's most articulate opponents until 1972 – were the absent enemies against whom the *Reference* was waged and, in a way, to whom the court directed its opinions.

This reading of the political environment, however, was incomplete. The end of One Unit provided the smaller provinces an opportunity to claim their rights against the central government. Their assertion was accompanied intermittently by a provincialism expressed in combative language, to which the central government responded in tones of equal belligerence and far greater power. In response, disputes hardened. The rhetoric of provincialism spread under the force of repression, and violence within the provinces and against the central government escalated.

If the government thought that eradicating NAP would establish tranquility, its prognosis was mistaken. The court acceded to the government's wishes by dissolving NAP, and the special court in Hyderabad Central Jail used *Reference* testimony to prosecute an endless case against fifty-five party members and associates. Domestic harmony was not restored, however. Instead, the government faced two incompatible and ultimately unsustainable consequences. First, not only did army action in Baluchistan contradict the claims of democracy and stability for which the PPP wanted to be known, but the army resumed its ascent in Pakistani politics after its Baluchistan experience, threatening the uneasy balance of forces within the state that had shifted slightly toward civil society with the elected government.[31] Second, the central government confronted more instability rather than less, making it all the more difficult to enforce order democratically. Imposing order on resurgent communalism did not work. The government therefore employed emergency laws with increasing frequency, rarely with the full participation of the legislature and usually without the approval of the courts. The fragile equation of elected government with democracy had barely a chance to survive.

The Supreme Court played an important role in these evolving events. While the superior courts on the whole tried to meliorate the effects of executive power when it transgressed its boundaries, the 1975 *Reference* Court applied more indignation than critical sensibility to its judgment. The justices may have found conclusive the evidence provided by the government, and may also have been offended by what they interpreted as NAP's blatant disregard for the court and the constitution. The sum of its long judgment, however, was to endorse the Prime Minister's contempt for political opposition. The court's message did little to succor conservatives concerned about national stability or liberals worrying about citizen rights. Instead, the left and right wings joined in a coalition that proved fatal to the Bhutto government in the 1977 elections and their divisive aftermath.

The immediate effect of the Supreme Court's extended jurisdiction and judgment came in the *Hyderabad Conspiracy Case*, which began directly after NAP was dissolved. The Attorney General cited a charge of "conspiracy to disintegrate Pakistan" in a letter to Amnesty International, claiming that the special court was a reasonable successor to the *Reference*:

> As the National Awami Party and its leaders had walked out of the Supreme Court during the hearing of the case about the dissolution of this party, therefore it was considered necessary that these leaders and other accused may have proper opportunity to rebut the evidence that may be brought before the Special Court in support of the findings given by the Supreme Court.[32]

31 A.B. Awan suggested later that Bhutto was most concerned about NAP, and Baluchistan simply got in his way. If so, the justice ministry prepared a case that barely corresponded to this end. Awan, *Baluchistan*, pp. 263–302.

32 19 August 1976, cited in *Islamic Republic of Pakistan: An Amnesty International Report* (London, 1977). Bakhtiar asked government officials and private citizens to refrain from

The absence of due process guarantees – under special rules of evidence, the government could add charges any time before judgment was pronounced – cast a long shadow on the government's allusion that the court was convened for the benefit of its defendants.

By the time it was terminated by General Mohammed Zia ul Haq in 1977, the case had become a catch-all for the government's most irksome critics. Some defendants had been detained since the August 1973 dissolution of the NAP–JUI ministry in Quetta, others were arrested after the case was in progress. While some were office-bearers of NAP, others were dissident People's Party officials, including Mairaj Mohammed Khan[33] and Ali Bahksh Talpur. They were arrested on various charges that were amended with time, but which conformed generally to the *Reference* charges against the National Awami Party. The Hyderabad case emphasized the vendetta quality of the *Reference* and retrospectively colored the Supreme Court's decision. The *Reference* cast a long shadow; only the *coup d'état* in July 1977 arranged for its end.[34]

cooperating with the organization; he called its report on imprisonments under the Maintenance of Public Order Ordinance and the Defence of Pakistan Rules "dishonest, mischievous and malicious." PLD 1976 Journal 270–74.

33 In *Mairaj Muhammad Khan v. The State*, PLD 1978 Karachi 308, Justice Fakhruddin Ebrahim condemned in camera proceedings saying "where there is no publicity there is no justice."

34 In August 1977, the Hyderabad Court criticized the Bhutto government by holding in contempt the editor and publisher of the government-owned *Pakistan Times* for publishing an editorial prejudging the outcome of the Hyderabad tribunal and claiming that those who advocated the Wali Khan's release were unpatriotic. (*State v. Abdul Wali Khan and others*, Special Court (Central Prison) Hyderabad, PLD 1977 Journal 315.) General Zia ul Haq released the Hyderabad prisoners in 1978 after ignoring requests to transfer the case to the High Court. Wali Khan's disdain for Prime Minister Bhutto was evident in his conciliatory comments about the military government's stand on provincial autonomy, which he called a "settled issue." After his release, Wali Khan contested the use of the *Reference* ruling in the Hyderabad Tribunal. Speaking in 1978, he suggested that the *Reference* was not a judgment "in the strict sense of the word," because it was later submitted as evidence before a court lower than the Supreme Court. "Wali absolved from contempt charge," *Dawn* 25 February 1978.

Later, Bhutto said that he had planned to release the Hyderabad detainees in April 1977 "but for a fundamental political quid pro quo from Afghanistan which had no direct relevance on the merits of the legal issues before the Tribunal." His distress with NAP was compounded by its allegedly undisclosed agreements with the military:

> But on what considerations has the regime unilaterally disbanded the Tribunal? The question has become more relevant in view of the recent statement of Attaullah Khan Mengal, in which he has said that the Baluch leaders have complied with their part of the agreement but that the regime has not . . . The nation is entitled to know the contents of this agreement. Its disclosure is inherently important not only to follow the mustery but to evaluate the future of Pakistan's fragile unity.

Zulfikar Ali Bhutto, *Response to White Papers in the Supreme Court of Pakistan*, Criminal Appellate Jurisdiction, Criminal Appeal No. 11 of 1978, p. 159.

*Civil law attrition*

If *F.B. Ali* did not confront the problems facing civilians in martial law tribunals, the *Reference* and the Hyderabad case enlarged this legal lacuna. Judgments from the early Bhutto years had decreasing precedential force when faced with constitutional amendments curtailing the superior courts and ordinances empowering special tribunals. The courts still tried to order the release of illegally held detainees and the Lahore Court reminded the government that even during an emergency, "the powers vested in or exercisable by High Court could neither be assumed nor suspended either in whole or in part by the Federal Government or by the Government of Province under the direction of the Federal Government." Justice Gulbaz Khan added that "when a right of a person is to be taken away, that can be taken away only by express legislation and not by implication."[35]

By 1977, the effect of constitutional amendments and ordinances promulgated by the Prime Minister under the emergency began to affect substantive rulings of the courts. In 1975, Justice Hamoodur Rahman had been able to report with general accuracy that the judiciary had "consistently avoided any interpretation which might lead to chaos in the country but at the same time it has safeguarded the rights of the citizen within the limits guaranteed by the Constitution."[36] Security laws now made it difficult for rights to be protected and the law itself was contributing to instability.

Despite claims that their powers were undiminished,[37] the courts were now forced to acknowledge the declining scope of their rulings and the increasing authority of the executive. Dismissing an appeal against detention under the Defence of Pakistan Rules, Chief Justice Yaqub Ali conceded that a 1976 amending ordinance to the Rules gave special

[35] *Begum Parveen Malik v. The State and 2 others*, PLD 1977 Lahore 1017. See also *Mahmud Ali Kasuri, Bar-at-Law v. Punjab Government through Secretary Home Affairs*, PLD 1977 Lahore 1400; *Saifullah Saif v. Federation of Pakistan and 3 others*, PLD 1977 Lahore 1174; *Begum Shaheen Ramay v. The State and 2 others*, PLD 1977 Lahore 1414; *Dr. Aijaz Qureshi v. Government of the Punjab through Secretary, Home Department, Lahore* PLD 1977 Lahore 1304; *Iqbal Ahmad Khan, Advocate and 51 others v. The State and 2 others*, PLPD 1977 Lahore 1337. In *Raja Muhammad Ashraf v. District Magistrate, Rawalpindi*, PLD 1977 Lahore 1006, the High Court ruled that the government did not properly distinguish between punitive and preventive detention, noting that "the possibility of a grudge . . . cannot be overruled."

[36] "Presidential Address to Second Pakistan Jurists' Conference," 9–12 January 1975, PLD 1975 Journal 8–12.

[37] In *Federation of Pakistan v. United Sugar Mills Ltd., Karachi*, PLD 1977 Supreme Court 397, Justice Mohammad Gul asserted that the fourth constitutional amendment was not designed to make substantive changes in the constitution and thus did not remove court jurisdiction.

tribunals virtually exclusive jurisdiction over offenses under those Rules, jurisdiction that admitted no review or appeal.[38] His regretful conclusion summarized the court's growing apprehension about the power of civil law:

Power to grant bail is of minimal significance if in the final event superior Courts cannot give redress against the sentence of imprisonment extending to a day less than ten, however erroneous the decision of the Special Tribunal may be on facts and law. Courts of law including Special Tribunals are not infallible ... To provide a remedy against it the constitution specifically conferred on the court the power of review. The complete negation of the right of appeal and revision in majority of the cases arising under the Defense of Pakistan Rules is, therefore, a matter of considerable concern.

By transferring civil cases to tribunals or special military courts with powers that paralleled courts martial, government authorities acting in their emergency capacities set aside many court rulings that interfered with their political agendas. Additionally, law-enforcement agencies increasingly ignored court rulings.[39] The Supreme Court expressed its own dismay and weakness:

Apart from a wilful disobedience of the High Court's order to which they confessed in a written statement, the appellants compounded the offense by allegedly subjecting a citizen to torture ... Article 14 of the Constitution guarantees the dignity of the citizen and declares in clear terms that no citizen of Pakistan shall be subjected to torture. The Supreme Court here faced with a situation where members of the law enforcing agency, who are charged with the duty to protect the citizen, have themselves perpetrated upon their ward acts of inhuman torture. Words are not adequate to express our sense of horror at this outrage.

Words, however, were the court's only weapon.

With the role of the armed forces in civil society expanding, the relationship between the civil and military sectors resumed the outline of its Ayub Khan days. The line between civil and martial law justice dimmed, quasi-judicial institutions gained importance and individual rights lost many constitutional protections. The courts faced a crisis of identity and confidence.[40] This was strikingly apparent by the spring of 1977, when post-election riots in Karachi provoked renewed emergency provisions and brought in the army, which fired on demonstrators. A petition filed in the Karachi High Court (*Niaz Ahmed Khan v. Province of*

[38] *Ch. Zahur Elahi, MNA v. The State*, PLD 1977 Supreme Court 273.

[39] *Sher Ali and others v. Sheikh Zahoor Ahmed*, PLD 1977 Supreme Court 545.

[40] By early April opposition crystallized in Punjab when police attacked demonstrators outside the Punjab Assembly. Through the spring it was reported that nationwide 250 people were killed, 1763 injured, at least 16,863 arrested, and 4290 anti-government processions were held. Maleeha Lodhi, "Pakistan in Crisis," *Journal of Commonwealth and Comparative Politics* 16, 1 (1978) pp. 60–78.

*Sind and others*, PLD 1977 Karachi 604) called the fatal shooting of civilians "improper, unjustified and without lawful authority," and challenged the imposition of a law suspending the right to ask courts to enforce fundamental rights.

The court reluctantly concluded that it could not question emergency powers (commenting wryly that the constitutional meaning of sovereignty was often used in a "political rather than in a strictly legal sense"). Nonetheless, it optimistically read the letter of the law against its contrary spirit:

> By its very nature the curtailment of High Courts' jurisdiction cannot be of lasting nature, for, the express words "for the time being" signify beyond doubt that the Makers of the constitution did not mean to deprive High Court of its jurisdiction for any length of [*sic*] period which may be viewed as permanent or even semi-permanent.

While not fully persuaded that the court's jurisdiction had been canceled, Justice Agha Ali Hyder noted that the amended Army Act was now enlarged "even beyond what passed muster in the case of *F.B. Ali v. the State*." He therefore offered a face-saving calculus of relative authority: were the army to stay within its designated authority, the courts would lose jurisdiction; but if the military transgressed its assigned boundaries, the courts would regain their jurisdiction. Justice Fakhruddin Ebrahim (who would face similar problems as Governor of Sind in 1990) offered familiar phrases:

> The Armed Forces cannot abrogate, abridge or displace Civil Power of which Judiciary is an important integral part . . . The Armed Forces . . . can certainly apprehend those who disturb or threaten to disturb peace and tranquility, but such persons . . . can only be tried by ordinary civil Courts which have admittedly not ceased to function.

These sentiments haunted the judiciary when General Zia ul Haq took power a few months later, and resonated more bitterly when he drastically reduced civil court powers.

The Cartesian cry of the judiciary assumed sadly mistaken premises: that the Prime Minister fully controlled the military, that the electorate accepted the 1977 polls, and that law and order could be balanced with the same emergency provisions that had kept civil disturbance at uneasy bay in years past. None of these assumptions proved true. The persistent use of extra-constitutional authority masked as valid law had worn away the seams of civil society, and traditional boundaries between civil and military institutions were no longer meaningful.

The superior courts were left to confront two incompatible courses of action: to protect fundamental rights as they were whittled away from above, they tried to read the law creatively, searching for sources of judicial power beyond executive transgression; to do so, however, they also had to prolong the myth that democracy was still alive. Were they to announce that the emperor was no longer cloaked in democratic laws, not only would the courts seem inaccessible to those seeking to redress grievances against the state but the judiciary's survival might be jeopardized.

The Lahore Court recognized these conflicting impulses when it supported fourteen writ petitions challenging the spring 1977 martial law in Lahore, and revised security laws purporting to oust court jurisdiction and give the army additional powers. *Darwesh M. Arbey, Advocate v. Federation of Pakistan through the Law Secretary and 2 others* (PLD 1980 Lahore 206) was decided just a month before General Zia ul Haq assumed power; its written judgment, issued after the *coup d'état*, is a stern lecture to both the deposed Prime Minister and the General. Noting that the civil laws placed the army "in a position superior or dominant to that of civil power," Chief Justice Aslam Riaz Hussain spoke sharply against their effects: "Such sweeping amendments, bringing the entire civil population of the province . . . within the ambit of the Pakistan Army Act and making it subject to its provisions is totally against objects and reasons for which that Act was enacted." The court protested the transfer of civil court powers to military courts: "Instead of acting in aid of the civil power the armed forces are acting in supersession and displacement of the same." More generally, Justice Shameem Hussain Kadri asked: "Can it be said that the executive and judicial authorities while acting in aid of Supreme Court divest the Supreme Court of all the judicial powers or replace it by their own authority? The plain answer is 'No'." The Chief Justice termed such law "a fraud upon the State."

Strongly admonishing the government, he suggested that the imposition of martial law in Lahore was less for the common good than for "an ulterior purpose." Justice Karam Elahee Chauhan cautioned that the constitution "does not authorise a political government to rule through armed forces so as to clothe them with such powers and jurisdiction which purport to replace the civil power." The constitution prohibited army intervention in politics precisely to preserve the integrity of civilian rule, protect minority rights and "save those who oppose government policies from the wrath of the group in power."[41]

[41] His pointed comments were elaborated by Justice Kadri, who reacted against the PPP government's constant equation of Lahore disturbances, the Baluchistan insurgency and the NAP *Reference* in its presentations in this case. By the time martial law was declared in Lahore, the government decided that the entire country was gripped by a common emergency and premised its rule on emergency powers. Three other court decisions issued

The Chief Justice spoke to the new regime as well, using words that General Zia later took to heart. The 1973 Constitution prohibited the imposition of martial law.

However, if the Constitution is abrogated, set aside or placed in state of suspended animation or hibernation, it might be possible to impose Martial Law *outside* the Constitution. Such an action may or may not be justified by the doctrine of necessity.

There is a paradox in his hypothesis: to preserve the constitution it might be necessary to place it in abeyance. This was precisely the strategy General Zia used to justify the army's intervention in July 1977 and to continue military rule for eleven years.

Until 1977, the People's Party government gradually took on the character of martial law without its official imprimatur: the army guaranteed the continuance of civil governance, but did so under constitutional rule. By the time of the elections, however, blatant power rather than delegated authority had governed political life for too long; in the wake of the polls, the direction of power changed. When the army moved against the government, it little mattered to the Chief of Army Staff whether prior negotiations among political parties had concluded successfully, or indeed what their content included.[42] General Zia ul Haq, like Iskander Mirza and Ayub Khan before him, saw familiar signposts of civil disarray and political chaos, and determined that only the army was suited to take full control.

## Necessity revived

When the army under General Mohammed Zia ul Haq took power on 5 July 1977, the court was not immediately called to judge the validity of the *coup d'état*, although cases continued to be heard on the effects of earlier emergency provisions on individual rights.[43] Political activities were completely banned and People's Party members were now detained under martial law regulations which recalled the days of Ayub Khan and Yahya Khan; the regime emphasized law and order and national security in its frequent public pronouncements. Nonetheless, General Zia ul Haq

after the July *coup d'état* confirmed the judiciary's disagreement with this assumption and attempts to use Bhutto-era cases to instruct the new regime. See *Jehangir Iqbal Khan v. Federation of Pakistan and 3 others*, PLD 1979 Peshawar 67; *Asfandyar Wali v. The State*, PLD 1978 Peshawar 38; and *Abdur Rahman Mobashir and 3 others v. Syed Amir Ali Shah Bokhari and 4 others*, PLD 1978 Lahore 113.

42 Among the issues supposedly agreed upon in the multi-party discussions was the removal of constitutional restrictions on the judiciary. See discussion of *Mumtaz Bhutto's case* in chapter 6.

43 *Begum Shaheen Ramay v. The State and 2 others*, PLD 1977 Lahore 1414.

announced new elections for October 1977, in which all political parties, including the People's Party, planned to contest Assembly seats. In the interim, the martial law government embarked on a campaign to expose corruption in the Bhutto government. Under martial law regulations, special courts investigated fiscal improprieties by individuals and party-related organizations like the People's Foundation Trust of the PPP, which in turn challenged these government actions in the Sind High Court prior to its appropriation by the government. In addition, Mr. Bhutto was accused of planning the murder of a disaffected PPP National Assembly member, Ahmed Raza Kasuri, whose father was killed in Lahore two years earlier.[44] The murder case commenced in the autumn of 1977, at the same time as the Trust trial, other cases lodged against Mr. Bhutto, and a constitutional petition against the army.

### *Validating martial law*

When Zulfikar Ali Bhutto and ten other People's Party leaders were reimprisoned by General Zia in September 1977 and threatened with trial before military tribunals, his wife filed a petition in the Supreme Court challenging the validity and legality of the martial law regime and alleging that the purpose of the arrests was to prevent PPP participation in the elections (*Begum Nusrat Bhutto v. Chief of Army Staff and Federation of Pakistan*, PLD 1977 Supreme Court 657).[45] The latter accusation proved true in effect if not purpose: on the fourth day of court hearings, General Zia promulgated new curbs on political activities and "to save the country from a dangerous crisis," postponed national elections indefinitely, eliminating what was to have been a principal ground for the case. General Zia cited his confidence in the freedom and impartiality of the judiciary, its familiarity "with the demands of justice and . . . with the conditions within the country and dictates of democracy."[46] The court's decision, which supported the martial law government on the basis of the necessity doctrine, reconsidered the Governor-General's *Reference*, *Dosso's case* and *Asma Jilani's case*, finally pronouncing a judgment of greater scope

[44] *State v. Zulfikar Ali Bhutto*, PLD 1978 Lahore 523.

[45] Attorney General Sharifuddin Pirzada first tried to remove the case from the Supreme Court by proposing that the martial law government was immune from prosecution, and that in any case the High Court should hear such a case. *Application under Rule 6 Order 4 of the Supreme Court Rules*. The court accepted the writ petition, although it could have demurred from the case.

[46] "Elections Postponed: Ban On all Political Activities," *Dawn* 2 October 1977, p. 1. "Zia's Speech," p. 10. The following week, the General announced that no elections would be scheduled until the resolution of unspecified court cases, presumably meaning the constitutional petition and murder trial. "New polls date after verdicts of courts," *Dawn* 9 October 1977, p. 1.

than they had offered. Sidestepping methodological pitfalls in earlier constitutional cases, newly appointed Chief Justice Anwar ul Haq issued an opinion giving the military government free rein to hold power as it wished and offering General Zia warrant to retain that power. *Nusrat Bhutto's case* confirmed a legal foundation for a decade-long military government that made deep inroads into the civil society and orchestrated a legal system that endured well beyond General Zia's death in 1988.

The charges issued by former Attorney General Yahya Bahktiar on behalf of Begum Bhutto echoed some of the National Awami Party's accusations toward the PPP government two years before. NAP had accused the PPP government of violating the constitution and discriminating against opponents by infringing on their rights, and concluded that the sum of these actions jeopardized the legitimacy of the PPP government. Bakhtiar now argued that General Zia's *coup d'état* was tantamount to treason, that his martial law was therefore illegal, that the arrests of PPP leaders was discriminatory and that the martial law government had no authority to transgress the 1973 Constitution or to violate fundamental rights. To support the army, if only in the short term, the court took refuge in the doctrine of necessity.

*Interpreting politics* To avoid charges that this case suffered from incompleteness, like *Dosso's case*, the court met for twenty-one days, hearing personal testimony from Zulfikar Ali Bhutto and Abdul Hafeez Pirzada and receiving lengthy written statements from them and Mumtaz Ali Bhutto. It felt compelled to pass judgment on the political environment, agreeing with the military that election corruption and political disruptions after the 1977 elections had so compromised the PPP government that it could no longer represent the electorate. The Chief Justice concluded that post-election violence challenged not simply the efficacy but the legitimacy of the civilian government – proven by the government's imposition of local martial law in urban areas – and that civil disruptions posed "incalculable damage to the nation and the country." As evidence, the court cited the PNA's apprehension that the failure of multi-party consultations could cause "a terrible explosion beyond the control of the civilian authorities." It used the PNA to justify the supposedly independent actions of the military and assumed the possibility (but not the probability) of further civil unrest to support military rule: "It can only be a matter of conjecture at this stage, whether an accord between the Government and the Pakistan National Alliance would have finally emerged if the Army had not intervened . . . it has become abundantly clear that the situation was surcharged with possibilities of further violence, confusion and chaos." Anwar ul Haq anticipated unknown and unmeasurable political disruption, seen through the eyes of its instigators, to defend the army's right to usurp power, and ignored the fact that PNA agitation had ended several weeks before the case began.

These conclusions followed the court's practice in *Dosso's case* and also departed from it. Like the Munir court, it affirmed the government of the day without fully examining the causes of prior disturbances; this time, however, it heard testimony from both sides before issuing its findings. In neither case did the court question its authority or capacity to judge political facts or define independent, non-accountable standards of judgment. (Only Justice Qaiser Khan questioned judicial jurisdiction, and he was more inclined to ignore rather than review the political situation in favor of a Kelsenian reading of the law.) Because the court determined that civil disturbances merited army intervention it repeated military allegations against the People's Party but ignored the defendants' views, the violence which greeted military takeover, and alternative constitutional negotiations that could be invoked.[47] The court perceived no conflict between justifying army action by reference to PNA views and the military's claim to neutrality, referring confidently to the "total *milieu*" that provoked the change of government to blame the PPP government for its own downfall. As a result, it endorsed the act of taking power and the politics that justified it.

*Necessity* When General Zia took power, he placed the 1973 Constitution "in abeyance" and proclaimed his rule as temporary, with new elections scheduled within the ninety days constitutionally guaranteed after the assemblies were dissolved. Although he then postponed them – canceled, in effect, since ninety days became nine years – his legal case presumed a martial law of short duration "to provide a bridge to enable the country to return to the path of constitutional rule."[48] Indeed, prior to issuing the judgment, Justice Anwar ul Haq asked Sharifuddin

[47] Some of these negotiations concerned the withdrawal of the army from Baluchistan and the status of the Hyderabad special court, talks in which General Zia was involved. The deposed Prime Minister described at length his efforts to conclude a settlement with the PNP, which he maintained had been achieved the night before the *coup d'état*. *Rejoinder of Zulfikar Ali Bhutto to the Written Statement Filed on Behalf of the Respondent*; "No rationale for armed forces' intervention: Bhutto's statement in Supreme Court," *Dawn* 23 October 1977. Bhutto's complete statement before the court was reprinted in *If I Am Assassinated* (New Delhi: Vikas Publishing House, 1979). During the *Nusrat Bhutto* hearing, the National Organising Committee of the Pakistan National Democratic Party demanded the disbanding of the Hyderabad court, a action General Zia ul Haq would finalize by the end of the year. "Disbanding of Hyderabad Tribunal urged," *Dawn* 12 October 1977.

[48] *Written Statement on Behalf of Respondent No. 2* in *Nusrat Bhutto's case*. See also "M.L. was imposed to help bring back constitutional rule" and "Text of Brohi's statement in SC," *Dawn* 11 October 1977.

Pirzada – now speaking for the government – when elections would be held, and was told that they would soon be scheduled. The court took the government at its word, the Chief Justice slavishly suggesting that "it would be highly unfair and uncharitable" to disbelieve General Zia's intentions and statements. Consequently, the conditions it placed on his confirmation were weak, although Justice Dorab Patel and others proposed that the pattern of the 1955 *Reference*'s call for new elections be followed. The court could not have ensured that elections were held but imposing that requirement might have modulated its posture of malleability and subservience to the army – a page from *Dosso's case* that became all the more poignant when General Zia removed virtually all constitutional jurisdiction from the superior courts in 1981.

Chief Justice Anwar ul Haq discarded the revolutionary legality argument of *Dosso's case* because the constitution was not formally abrogated and "the breach of legal continuity [was] of a purely temporary nature and for a specified limited purpose."[49] Instead, the court broadened the 1955 necessity ruling. The court declared military intervention to be necessary and validated all actions pursuant to military takeover. These included: constitutional suspension, new oaths for the judiciary, the promulgation of martial law orders, regulations and constitutional amendments; "all acts which tend to advance or promote the good of the people ... [and] required to be done for the ordinary orderly running of the State"; and all actions "which have been consistently recognized by judicial authorities as falling within the scope of the law of necessity." The court did not object, in whole or in part, to the 1977 Laws (Continuance in Force) Order which administered martial law. The "extra-constitutional" *coup d'état* was thus unfettered.

*Judicial powers* Surprisingly, the court ignored the serious strictures that the 1977 Order placed on its operation. It believed that its continued functioning was an important signal that martial law had not destroyed the constitutional order or the constitution. The Chief Justice claimed

> that the superior Courts continue to have the power of judicial review to judge the validity of any act or action of the Martial Law Authorities, if challenged in the light of the principles underlying the law of necessity ... Their powers under

[49] Writing in 1980, one commentator suggested that acts validated by the necessity doctrine would have only interim validity and that the judgment "represents a clear, and bold attempt to minimize legal recognition of revolutionary change." Neither the language of the judgment nor the force of history support such claims. Dieter Conrad, "In defence of the continuity of law: Pakistan's courts in crises of state," in Wolfgang Peter Zingel and Stephanic Zingel Ave Lallemant, eds., *Pakistan in the 80s: Law and Constitution* (Lahore: Vanguard Books Ltd., 1985), pp. 157–58.

Article 199 of the Constitution thus remain available to their full extent, and may be exercised as heretofore, notwithstanding anything to the contrary contained in any Martial Law Regulation or Order, Presidential Order or Ordinance.

Although he referred to the absence of pressure on the judiciary after the *coup d'état*, Justice Qaiser Khan bluntly reported that "we were directed to take a new oath or to quit."

The court's statement of the judiciary's condition is remarkable for its omissions. First, General Zia removed only those restrictions on Article 199 imposed by Bhutto directly before the trial, despite the new regime's accusations of "unilateral and arbitrary amendments in the constitution ... introduced ... with a view to curb the powers of the superior judiciary ... [and] attempts to cause dissension within the judiciary by persuading [sic] an arbitrary policy in relation to judicial appointments."[50] The same limits on judicial powers that provoked the court's vocal anxiety earlier in the year were not even mentioned now, although there was little reason to think that the judiciary would be able to operate unhampered under government regulations of much wider scope. More urgently, the 1977 Laws (Continuance in Force) Order blatantly removed judicial review from the superior courts. Although the order mandated "the exercise of their respective powers and jurisdictions," it took away court powers in two significant ways. First, fundamental rights and all ongoing cases to enforce them were suspended without qualification because the political environment was judged to be equivalent to emergency. Second, regime immunities were complete; neither its rules nor its acts could be questioned in any court.

The court's attitude was therefore comprehensible only as an effort to conform means and ends. The Chief Justice maintained that the 1977 Order was valid under the doctrine of necessity. At the same time, he maintained that as "an offspring of necessity" the order did not in fact prohibit judicial review. To circumvent the awkward contradiction of validating an order that nullified the authority of the validating body, he simply ignored its most basic provision. Perpetuating the myth of continued authority would later require action supporting it. When, contrary to the 1977 Order, courts did judge regime actions, General Zia issued a Provisional Constitutional Order in 1981 removing those powers retained in the 1977 Order.

The court found the crucial logical step for its reading of the 1977 Order by rejecting the revolutionary legality doctrine. The imprint of *Asma Jilani's case* was deep. Begum Bhutto's legal challenge relied on the court's declaring General Zia a usurper. Attorney General Pirzada and

[50] *Written Statement on Behalf of Respondent No. 2.*

Federation counsel A.K. Brohi energetically refuted this accusation by returning continually to succession questions surrounding the 1970 elections and subsequent party negotiations – the same questions raised in *Ziaur Rahman's case.*[51] Although their arguments establishing relationships between necessity and revolutionary legality differed, both counsels argued that the whole of Bhutto's rule, presumably including the 1973 Constitution, was illegitimate. For the court to agree to this proposition, however, would have meant declaring martial law a new legal order, readopting Kelsenian arguments rebuffed in *Asma Jilani's case* and leaving the status of the popular 1973 Constitution unclear. In fact, the prior legitimacy of the 1973 Constitution – accepted and approved by elected representatives – saved the court from fully separating the concepts of legitimacy and necessity. Only Justice Muhammad Akram came close to articulating the relation between popular sanction and legitimacy, saying "morality cannot be divorced from law." In addition, he suggested that the court followed a weak standard for judging emergency, noting that at the least, its reasonableness "necessarily depends on the alternatives available." He nevertheless joined the majority.

None of these options attracted Justice Anwar ul Haq. He would have been forced to assess the new regime's efficacy, which Mr. Brohi encouraged, without persuasive evidence to support this decision – thereby repeating the mistakes in *Dosso* that Hamoodur Rahman so roundly criticized in *Asma Jilani's case*. Perhaps more crucially, the court might then have concluded that an immediate new election under civilian rather than army supervision was required, a decision outside the military's political agenda. Instead, the court refrained from discussing the critical jurisdictional issue posed by Yahya Bakhtiar: that a decision about legitimacy did not reside in the courts but in the legislature and, in its absence, with the voters.

The court's institutional history thus influenced the structure of its judgment. To achieve a decision, necessity could not be paired explicitly with revolutionary legality. To avoid the Munir court's errors while recalling its conclusion – supporting the government in power – the court took a direct if unnuanced path to necessity. By ignoring doctrinal inconsistencies it rediscovered a legal means to justify an intensely political end. But revolutionary legality triumphed in the end. According to at least one former Supreme Court justice,[52] when General Zia canceled civil court powers in 1981 the *Nusrat Bhutto* judgment was also canceled, and the country was once again ruled by the decision in *Dosso's case*.

51 *Dawn* 12–13, 20–22, 25–27 October 1977.

52 Justice Dorab Patel interview with Wahab Siddiqui, *Mag* (Karachi) 22–28 March 1984, and Wahab Siddiqui, "Justice Patel on 1973 Constitution," *Mag* 31 January–6 February 1985.

*The proof in the pudding*

The judgment in *Nusrat Bhutto's case* was received more positively in 1977 than retrospection now recommends. At the time, the country could take heart in the court's upholding the 1973 Constitution, rather than casting it aside as it had in 1958. Even a weekly journal sympathetic to the PPP editorialized,

The Supreme Court . . . has protected the 1973 Constitution from attack and has maintained the supremacy of the judiciary. This provides important safeguards for the country's future governance. For one, this seems to rule out any attempts to amend the Constitution; and it has been laid down that any citizen may approach the courts to seek redress of grievances against any action that is not considered justified by the Law of Necessity, whose application is limited to the objectives for which Martial Law was proclaimed.[53]

It cautioned, however, that "in the light of Pakistan's tortuous history, it is clear that a higher, more imperative Law of Necessity demands the earliest possible restitution of the people's democratic rights."

Pakistan will never know whether a fully negative ruling on the military regime would have changed its political course. The court's judgment was written with all eyes trained on the military, with the hope that the country would return to civilian government through peaceful elections. Such restrained optimism was not consonant with military ambitions or with political conditions at the time of the judgment, although in the year following the *coup d'état* the public seemed to believe that elections would be held and that postponements were as much the fault of political parties as the army.

In the long term, the court's detailed exertions proved unnecessary. Although high courts reviewed and criticized military court decisions in the next years, General Zia treated the necessity judgment as if his regime's efficacy had been enthusiastically validated. He did so partly because the court acquiesced in the diminution of its powers, allowed if not dictated by the 1977 Order. In the years following *Nusrat Bhutto's case*, the martial law government eliminated its political opponents by imprisonment, punishment and death sentences; relying on a verdict condemning Bhutto for complicity in murder, it executed him in April 1979 despite grave popular misgivings and international appeals for his life. Press freedoms were eliminated, military courts assumed most of the responsibilities of civil courts, the CMLA unilaterally extended his own tenure and postponed even limited elections until 1985. After amending the constitution, General Zia and Sharifuddin Pirzada, by then Minister

[53] "Salus populi suprema est lex," *Viewpoint* 13 November 1977.

for Law and Parliamentary Affairs, even found in *Nusrat Bhutto's case* a legal rationale to immunize the regime's long rule against legal challenge when martial law was formally, but only partially, lifted at the end of 1985.

These characteristics invite a reading of *Nusrat Bhutto's case* as the judicial prelude to the decade of General Zia ul Haq. Certainly, the judgment sanctioned the fact, form and substance of military governance. Its text offered General Zia ul Haq a combination of assertion and silence to create a new, complex and enduring state structure. The court gave the army a perfect legal vacuum in which to restructure the state. *Nusrat Bhutto's case* differs qualitatively from the major constitutional cases that preceded it: while they all affirmed a known plan for the state, this judgment confirmed only uncertainty. In 1977, the Supreme Court turned over responsibility for the state to the military.

At the same time, the judgment retrospectively colored the Bhutto period. However impressive the political achievement of the 1973 Constitution, constitutional rule was not able to absorb the Prime Minister's incursions on it, making the return to army rule all the easier. Public disaffection with the Bhutto government, culminating in civil–military confrontations after the 1977 elections, had many causes. Popular expectations for participatory government had been thwarted by the government's gruff manipulation of state institutions, by its gradual conflating of constitutionalism and legalism through laws creating a security state apparatus, and by the government's refusal to entertain alternative political viewpoints. This judgment can be read as the end of the incomplete transition to democracy under Bhutto, evidence of the peculiar mix of populism, personalistic politics, unmanageable party discipline and ungainly authoritarianism that never found equilibrium and tainted the structure of the state.

The Bhutto period therefore underscores the persistence of the executive–legislative divide that has plagued Pakistan since the 1950s. That democracy was again thwarted, this time under a populist party, invites retrospection about the separation between state and society, and the diffidence that characterized government's relationship to its constituents, even under a self-proclaimed populist party. Conflicts between the establishment and the PPP led to the bureaucracy's protecting its own interests; this in turn led to Bhutto's determination to seize the state regardless of the incursions on the same liberties that his constitution was to have protected. He misread the army's loyalties and its ambivalence to his own mixed messages; ultimately, he was overtaken by forces he thought he had neutralized and had in fact re-empowered.

To the extent that state institutions, including the judiciary, had been assaulted by Bhutto's political ambitions, the court now had an opportunity to show its mettle against him.[54] Were the justices able to imagine the way repression in the 1980s would silence them, they would probably have preferred life under the People's Party to the military. Nothing under previous martial law regimes had prepared the country for the brutality that General Zia ul Haq's military government later unleashed against civil society. The experience of military rule under Ayub Khan and Yahya Khan may have given the court reason to believe that martial law could be controlled in response to judicial or public opinion. The justices may well have thought that extreme prudence, to the point of self-denial and illogicality, could help return civil rule, and therefore that the court could discipline the People's Party before its likely return in new elections.

None of these speculations, if accurate, excuse this judgment, but they do point to the complex conditions that helped to produce it and the equally intricate environment it helped to create. The justices remained on the bench when Bhutto restricted their powers and they remained as well when required to take an oath under the 1977 Order, confident that a limited judiciary was better than no judiciary at all. This case thus raised the same questions about power that were so difficult to answer in earlier cases: how much executive power is too much, how much judicial power is too little, who is to determine the ratios and what should the court do when, once again, the constitution is set aside?

In the context of these pervasive questions, in *Nusrat Bhutto's case* the court knowingly assumed center stage in judging Pakistan's past and determining its future. It both adjudicated and entered the political arena, and allowed itself to become an explicitly partisan political institution. Perhaps most important, the judgment indirectly called into question the durability of elected government when the Supreme Court, in consequence if not intent, dispensed with the formalities of democracy that it had hitherto upheld. The distance between civilian and military government, so long to achieve in the path toward democracy, became far easier to shorten on the return to autocracy.

[54] Upon his elevation to Supreme Court Chief Justice in September 1977, Anwar ul Haq described the judiciary's period of "extraordinary stress and strain" under the Bhutto government. Citing "uncalled for amendments in the 1973 Constitution coupled with an aggressive attitude on the part of the Executive," he decried the insecurity that such laws instilled in superior court judges, "thus impairing and inhibiting their ability to do justice without fear or favour." PLD 1977 Journal 253–58.

# 6 Silencing courts, muting justice (1977–1988)

But I, in the clamour
of breaking bones and spurting blood
had buried the corpse of my hearing
before I could hear
the sound of firing!

Ahmad Nadeem Qasmi, "Firing."

Constitutional Martial Law is a contradiction in terms.
Martial Law means no law.

Justice Karam Elahee Chauhan

General Zia ul Haq assumed power coincident with regional events that proved vital for his regime's tenure. India's Congress Party was voted out of office after allegations of repression and corruption that resembled those lodged against Mr. Bhutto and the two new governments warily recast Pakistani–Indian relations. Iran's peacock throne was overthrown, the Shah dispatched overseas while revolution engulfed the country. The American withdrawal from Iran and the initial successes of the Islamic revolution helped provide political focus for General Zia, who added a strong Islamist tone to his policies while courting favor with the United States after its unhappy interlude with the Bhutto government's policy of foreign policy autonomy. Equally critical, revolution and instability in Afghanistan resulted in the Soviet army's incursion there at the end of 1979, starting a decade-long war whose refugees, guns and drugs would occupy Pakistani society and realign international backing for its military leaders.

These external forces reinforced abrupt changes in Pakistan itself. Despite his protestations to the contrary, General Zia took quick action after the *coup d'état* to alter the structure of the Pakistani state. Military rules promulgated in the regime's first weeks were more thorough and comprehensive than those issued by previous martial law governments, emphasizing not only government accountability and citizen compliance with economic and political policy, but personal and religious behavior as well.[1] Although many observers (including the courts) were inclined to believe the General's initial statements that the regime was a cleansing interlude between elected governments, and that his plans changed only after investigations revealed the extent of the Bhutto government's corruption, early military regulations set a durable foundation for long military rule. They also defined the strictures that confined the courts during and after the military regime, and established a course for the parliamentary system that emerged at its end.

## Enforcing necessity

The first months and years of Zia ul Haq's regime established a complex dialectic between judicial and political power. The civil courts took seriously the judgment in *Nusrat Bhutto's case*, finding in its differences with preceding necessity cases a lease on their jurisdiction and a conceptual handle on their relations with military institutions. The Supreme Court had judged the military government's validity in part by recognizing the latent powers of the judiciary to mold, if not control, its shape and breadth. By translating the doctrine of necessity into standards to judge the necessity of government actions, the courts secured a place in the new configurations of power. In this limited sense, they could argue that military power had not overruled individual rights and that in the absence of organized political parties (which were soon formally outlawed), individual voices could still be heard. Judicial presence and power, in this view, offered continuity with habits and patterns established since independence. The courts could not substitute for political organs, but might provide alternate avenues for political expression in its absence, as they had for three decades. Only when the courts, too, lost their authority did the essential weaknesses in this equation become clear: the absence of a constitution gravely compromised the judiciary's claims to authority, and in the end, power was left entirely in the hands of the army. Significantly, when judicial authority was revoked, underground political parties began to emerge.

The Supreme Court's efforts notwithstanding, *Nusrat Bhutto's case* sounded a death knell for civil government. The effect of the judgment was most immediate in the cases against Mr. Bhutto himself.[2] In an

1 *Martial Law Regulations, Orders and Instructions by The Chief Martial Law Administrator and All the Zonal Martial Law Administrators*, 4th ed. (Lahore: Law Publishing Company, 1983).

2 *Mr. Zulfikar Ali Bhutto v. The State*, PLD 1978 Supreme Court 40; *State v. Zulfikar Ali Bhutto*, PLD 1978 Lahore 523; *Mr. Zulfikar Ali Bhutto v. The State*, PLD 1978 Supreme Court 125; *Zulfikar Ali Bhutto and 3 others v. The State*, PLD 1979 Supreme Court 38; *Zulfikar Ali Bhutto v. The State*, PLD 1979 Supreme Court 53; *Zulfikar Ali Bhutto v. The*

eighteen-month period, he was convicted for complicity in murder and engaged in manifold appeals to change the Lahore High Court's judgment, to replace the justices who tried him and to alter charges framed against him. All these appeals failed, the Lahore court's conviction stood and he was executed in April 1979. Bhutto's conviction caused profound public dismay with the civil courts for years after their verdicts. It was assumed that the military government had found a way to eliminate its most profound opposition by influencing the justices and judicial decision. The stridency of civil court judgments against the regime after Bhutto's execution can be read in part as an attempt by sympathetic justices to vindicate the courts from public opprobrium.

The most important constitutional effect of these cases was established in Bhutto's objection to the composition of the High Court bench, specifically to Justice Mushtaq Hussain, whose animosity Bhutto presumed as a consequence of his own prior actions against him.[3] Overruling the challenge, Supreme Court Chief Justice Anwar ul Haq took the opportunity to extend his ruling in *Nusrat Bhutto's case*. His interpretation clarified the long-range meaning of the necessity doctrine. "Once an extra-Constitutional action or intervention is validated on ground of State or civil necessity," he averred, "then, as a logical corollary it follows that the new Regime or Administration must interpret and be permitted, in the public interest, not only to run the day-to-day affairs of the country, but also to work toward the achievement of the objectives or the basis on which its intervention has earned validation." The terms that the martial law regime established in its constitutional defense constituted the rationale for its continuance; by extension, the broader the rationale it offered to the court, the broader its future powers. The Chief Justice thus gave Zia ul Haq greater authority than he had received in *Nusrat Bhutto's case*. He also established informal guidelines for judging future regime actions. Building on the categories of necessity listed in the constitutional judgment – acts that would have been valid under the 1973 Constitution, amendments to that constitution, acts to promote public good and those required to run the state – he proposed that they be used as standards of judgment: "If it can be shown that the impugned action reasonably falls within one or the other of the enumerated categories, then it must be construed as being necessary and thus held valid under the law of necessity." Lest the regime be held too closely to specific standards, Anwar ul Haq defined necessity "as a term of art." Indeed, he advised

*State*, PLD 1979 Supreme Court 741. Cases were also registered against Mr. Bhutto in special courts.

3 PLD 1978 Supreme Court 40.

that actions be judged against "the prevailing circumstances and the object with which the action has been taken."

The superior courts took the court's ruling as instruction for judicial decorum. The Supreme Court thus played two crucial but contradictory roles. On the one hand, by insisting that civil courts were open for business, it gave citizens opportunities to try to redress grievances against the military regime even while fundamental rights were formally suspended. The courts searched for ways to ensure the conceptual survival of rights, if not their enforcement. In a curious exposition of political epistemology, Lahore High Court Justice Gul Mohammad Khan proposed that during emergency "Fundamental Rights are there but there is no remedy available."[4] The superior courts took Justice Anwar ul Haq at his word and scrutinized regime actions, particularly decisions of military courts. On the other hand, the Supreme Court gave tremendous credence to General Zia's rule in *Nusrat Bhutto's case*, established its validity according to his own standards and provided loose criteria to allow it to be sustained. In contests between the state and civil society the burden of proof was on the citizen rather than the state. When the courts questioned military judgments and occasionally overturned military convictions – that is, when they acted like real courts rather than puppet tribunals – the regime reacted by severely restricting their purview to only the most neutral cases.

Challenges to the regime, particularly those concerning the transfer of civilian cases to military courts and convictions in those tribunals, began during General Zia's first year. High courts tried to establish their right to review regime actions, whether or not they upheld them.[5] Their rulings were creative and careful. Responding to charges that military courts were unnecessary when civil courts still functioned, the Quetta High Court cautioned that "it would indeed be perilous for the Courts to embark upon an enquiry which by its very nature will be subjective to find out if a necessity existed for the taking of any action."[6] Necessity might be relative, but under martial law – "essentially law or rule of force" – the

[4] *Province of Punjab through its Home Secretary and 3 others v. Gulzar Hassan, Advocate and 3 others*, PLD 1978 Lahore 1298.

[5] The competence of military courts and of the regime generally was upheld in *Ali Asghar v. Chairman, Summary Military Court and 2 others*, PLD 1978 Karachi 773; *Nazeer Ahmed v. Lt. Col. Abbas Ali Khan, President, Special Military Court No. 10 and 2 others*, PLD 1978 Karachi 777; *Saeed Ahmad Malik v. Federation of Pakistan*, PLD 1978 Lahore 1218; and *Rustam Ali v. Martial Law Administrator, Zone "C" and 3 others*, PLD 1978 Karachi 736. Additionally, the Quetta High Court distanced the actions of officers from the regime. This ruled out challenges to the regime on the basis of local actions. *Ghulam Mujtaba Khan v. Martial Law Administrator, Zone "D," Quetta and 5 others*, PLD 1978 Quetta 199.

[6] *Khudiadad v. Deputy Martial Law Administrator, Zone "D," Baluchistan and another*, PLD 1978 Quetta 177.

military alone would determine its application. Nonetheless, the Quetta Court echoed the Karachi Court's pre-*coup* judgments, proposing that when military courts did not comply with mandatory provisions in martial law orders, "the High Court would readily correct the finding": superior courts would review tribunal decisions that were procedurally weak or seemingly arbitrary.[7] Elaborating the boundaries of jurisdiction, however, did not mean assuming extensive powers. When the former Northwest Frontier Governor alleged that military courts did not meet the criteria for necessity, the Peshawar High Court responded with a close and limited reading of *Nusrat Bhutto's case*: "To say that it is the duty of this Court to judge in exercise of its Constitutional jurisdiction, the political implications of this or that action will be an argument to which we cannot subscribe subject to law."[8] According to Chief Judge Abdul Haleem Khan, "all that we have to ensure is whether an impugned action reasonably falls within any of the categories enumerated in Begum *Nusrat Bhutto's case*."[9]

The strain on the judiciary to protect due process without jeopardizing its own survival was apparent by the end of 1978, when the courts began to issue judgments sharply critical of military power. Objecting to their continuing detention under renewed emergency provisions, former Sind Chief Minister Mumtaz Ali Bhutto and former Federal Minister Abdul Hafeez Pirzada contended that *Nusrat Bhutto's case* did not suspend rights completely, and thus that the validity of the martial law regime was limited. In a sweeping judgment against the army, the Karachi High Court took on both the structure and substance of military rule.[10] It warned that detention without trial on the instruction of the executive "is virtually making the same authority both the prosecutor as well as the Judge and this anomalous state of affairs inherently tends to arbitrariness." The court recalled that the constitution – which the regime still insisted was not abrogated – proscribed rather than prescribed limits on rights, even during emergency: "The negative language imposes a limitation on the power of the State and thus declares corresponding guarantees of the individual to those Fundamental Rights. The limitations and the

[7] *Imtiaz Bashir v. Special High Powered Committee and 4 others*, PLD 1978 Quetta 131.

[8] *Major-General (Ret.) Nasirullah Khan Babar v. Chief of Army Staff and another*, PLD 1979 Peshawar 23.

[9] The Lahore High Court used identical language when Malik Ghulam Jilani unsuccessfully petitioned to restrain General Zia ul Haq from confirming Mr. Bhutto's sentence. It also supported the President's Succession Order (Presidential Order No. 13 of 1978) as a step "to achieve one of the objects of Martial Law, i.e. holding of General Elections as early as possible." *Malik Ghulam Jilani v. The Province of Punjab and others*, PLD 1979 Lahore 564.

[10] *Mumtaz Ali Bhutto and another v. The Deputy Martial Law Administrator, Sector 1, Karachi and 2 others*, PLD 1979 Karachi 307.

guarantees are complimentary [sic]. The limitation on the State action couched in negative form is the measure of protection of the individual." The court placed the regime on notice that its words and actions would be examined as one. It questioned contextual judgments for determining the scope of the necessity doctrine, noting that the detaining authorities had mistakenly heeded "'the present political situation', rather than the legal considerations that are to be borne in mind in the making of an order of detention under the law."[11]

Finally, and perhaps most important, the High Court refined the necessity doctrine by defining its attitude toward the categories enumerated in *Nusrat Bhutto's case*. Attorney-General Sharifuddin Pirzada argued that any one category of action was sufficient to invoke the necessity doctrine, placing a vast range of executive actions out of judicial reach. The Karachi Court reacted vehemently against this proposal:

> If we are to agree on such interpretation then the power that has been conferred on the Chief Martial Law Administrator to amend the Constitution would virtually operate to confer on him the power to do anything that he may think best and render the power of judicial review nugatory. That would mean he was the only Judge of his actions.

Justice Fakhruddin Ebrahim added that the government's position would contradict the *Nusrat Bhutto* decision on which it relied, remarking that "even the Supreme Court does not appear to have followed the principle that once there is nexus between the impugned measure and the permissible actions, there is no need for any further inquiry."

Other high courts soon followed suit. Determining that the transfer of a civil case to a special military court had no legal effect, the Quetta High Court set aside a conviction on that basis, and the Karachi Court did the same.[12] The Peshawar High Court questioned the structure of the necessity doctrine and the empowerment of martial law tribunals.[13] Two years after the *coup d'état*, the Lahore High Court, acknowledging the executive's sole discretion to detain, nonetheless released the president of the Rachna Mills labor union after deciding that the grounds for detention were improper and did not conform to the minimal standards set in

[11] The Karachi court reasoned similarly the following year when it accepted writ petitions challenging convictions under military court, and affirmed its power of judicial review: *Aizaz Nazir v. Chairman, Summary Military Court, Sukkur and 2 others*, PLD 1980 Karachi 444; *Saleh Muhammad v. Presiding Officer, Summary Military Court, Karachi and 2 others*, PLD 1980 Karachi 26; *Muhammad Ismail v. Summary Military Court, Mirpurkhas and another*, PLD 1980 Karachi 47.

[12] *Syed Essa Noori v. Deputy Commissioner, Turbat and 2 others*, PLD 1979 Quetta 189; *Anwar Ali v. Chief Martial Law Administrator and 3 others*, PLD 1979 Karachi 804.

[13] *Satar Gul and another v. Martial Law Administrator, Zone "B," N.W.F.P., Peshawar, and 2 others*, PLD 1979 Peshawar 119.

martial law ordinances.[14] Chief Justice Abdul Hakeem Khan firmly set aside a series of military court convictions, commenting that open civil courts should be sufficient to ensure the public good. His judgment presaged a problem that would increase in scope and frequency in the next years, as he wondered aloud whether "the welfare of the people will be advanced or we will be nearing it if Courts presided over by technocrats are to be replaced with Army Officers." General Zia ul Haq soon replaced civil court judges with military officers acting on their own authority and police who determined independently the tribunals to which detainees were remanded and the laws under which they were tried.

Although these rulings placed the courts at odds with the martial law government, the judiciary continued to prompt the regime gently to loosen its hold on the civil society and return the country to civilian rule.[15] Ruling on faith, the Karachi Court underscored the regime's transitory character:

> There is no doubt that sooner rather than later elections would be held and the State institutions would be reborn. Martial Law will therefore, have to be lifted and the Military Courts recalled . . . Even the present amendments in Article 199 of the Constitution are transitory by their very nature, for if Martial Law itself is lifted the Military Courts automatically cease to exist.

Its optimism proved wrong. General Zia tightened restrictions on superior courts in June 1980 because earlier constitutional amendments had not achieved the regime's purpose "as civil Courts started issuing stay orders on the judgment of the army Courts."[16]

Tense relations between the courts and the martial law administration began to invade the dialogue among justices themselves. The Karachi Court entertained the first petition against General Zia's constitutional amendments and his amending power a few weeks after further limits were placed on the courts.[17] The majority judged the amendments valid, again holding that the constitutional trichotomy of powers was not violated because martial law was temporary. Justice Zafar Husain Mirza, however, argued passionately that the majority misread *Nusrat Bhutto's case*, that "on no principle of necessity could the power of judicial review

[14] *Master Abdul Rashid v. Sub-Martial Law Administrator, Sector 2, Rawalpindi and 3 others*, PLD 1980 Lahore 356.

[15] *Haji Abdullah v. Presiding Officer, Summary Military Court No. 9, Karachi*, PLD 1980 Karachi 498.

[16] Broadcast, 3 June 1980. The new restrictions were included in Martial Law Regulation No. 77.

[17] *Yaqoob Ali v. Presiding Officer, Summary Military Court, Karachi*, PLD 1985 Karachi 243, concerning amendments to Article 199. Significantly and unusually, the regime's counsel refused to argue the government's case, agreeing only to respond to questions in his personal capacity.

vested in the superior Courts under the 1973 Constitution, be taken away." He concluded with the petitioner that the regime could not promulgate "in the shape of constitutional amendment a permanent constitutional measure to outlive itself resulting in perpetuation of military dispensation of justice after restoration of democracy," and found the amendments unreasonable.

Justice Mirza's minority opinion showed the depth of debate within the judiciary about fundamental issues of governance. His reading of the constitution absorbed arguments about government structure that had plagued the judiciary since *Ziaur Rahman's case*; this time, he articulated the long-term political consequences of structural change on the basis of the evolving configuration of martial law. His conclusions partly followed the arguments presented by petitioner's counsels Khalid Ishaque and Abdul Hafeez Pirzada, but departed from their view that fundamental rights were not part of the constitutional structure because emergency powers could override them. His reading of the political climate and the durability of constitutional change was more prescient than his colleagues. Not only did General Zia ul Haq soon promulgate an ordinance to remove superior courts from decisions affecting the structure of military rule, but the amendments produced during martial law restructured the kind of governance possible when martial law was finally lifted.

For three years, the high courts subjected the necessity doctrine to serious scrutiny. Because they could not revoke the Supreme Court's judgment validating the regime, they took steps to dissect the doctrine and define its limits, largely to mitigate the effects of *Nusrat Bhutto's case*. At each opportunity, the necessity doctrine was tested against concrete actions of the martial law regime. This strategy helped to soften the absence of fundamental rights, although it may have given the doctrine more importance than the courts would have liked. The regime prosecuted citizens in military tribunals while maintaining that the civilian judiciary was an operating instrument of the state; the courts took up the challenge by keeping their doors open and ruling on each case. To do so kept the martial law state open to judicial dispute.

General Zia's initial efforts to depoliticize Pakistan by outlawing its political organs and censoring political expression were restrained by the courts – institutions whose integrity and self-concept were contingent on their distance from politics. Under previous governments, judicial decisions had consequences for the constitutional structure of the state, the activities of its political classes and opportunities for the citizenry at large. Under General Zia, the courts took up similar issues of structure and function, but the context had changed: their dockets now included intensely political problems that they were forced to confront with an unabashedly political agenda of their own. The survival of civil and politicial liberties, conceived in even the most limited ways, seemed coterminous with the survival of the courts.

The situation presented a devil's dilemma for the courts. The judiciary took General Zia at his word: if the constitution were simply in abeyance it would act according to principles set in that document. There was little reason to think that the cumulative results might not resemble those under Ayub Khan's constitution – a game of cat-and-mouse with the government, but on the whole a process of give and take within a discourse set by conventional procedures. However, the delicate coexistence between the military and the judiciary established by the court in *Nusrat Bhutto's case*, perhaps always illusory, was impossible to maintain under conditions in which the military did not feel secure. Equally, the equilibrium orchestrated by a judicious rendering of the necessity doctrine could not be upheld when the regime saw the judiciary speaking for its enemies, by extension becoming an institutional enemy of the state. For the courts, the necessity doctrine was a judicial limit on state action; for the regime, it was a mandate to extend its rule.

The courts did not reckon with General Zia's concept of power. By testing the necessity doctrine they gave General Zia time, and in his perception, provocation to refine the terms and quality of his power. In this sense, the judiciary's decisions courted a disaster unimaginable under earlier military rule. Interceding for the citizen where untrammeled political power was likely to be most damaging, the courts helped to locate civil society's pregnable points; the regime then acted against them. Among the most vulnerable became the courts themselves, and General Zia took pains first to protest their decisions, then to limit their jurisdiction and finally to cancel their powers.

## Revoking constitutionalism

Like military rule under Ayub Khan, General Zia's regime fell into constitutional and non-constitutional periods, but their relative positions were reversed. The grip of the 1958 martial law loosened as power concentrated in the hands of the military, leading to a new constitution that furthered the designs of the military state but allowed some political discourse and institutional flexibility. The courts could review executive actions, albeit in limited ways. Explicit repression was reintroduced only when limited freedoms created growing demands for even more.

The dynamics of power under General Zia ul Haq were quite different. Whatever satisfaction People's Party opponents felt at Bhutto's demise diminished sharply as the political arena was closed to almost all political parties except those that might embellish and legitimate the regime. The expectations of civil society also differed under this martial law. Despite Bhutto's ruthlessness toward his enemies, Pakistanis had grown accustomed to raucous and open politics and bitterly resented renewed military rule. The nexus of support for the regime, a coalition of "military, merchant and mullah," in the words of veteran newsman Nisar Osmani, was neither broad nor deep enough to keep protest at bay. Instruments of the state – particularly the army and police – were viewed as enemies of popular sovereignty rather than vehicles to restore it. The longer the regime stayed in power, the greater the opportunity for citizens to suffer at the hand of increasingly corrupt law-enforcing bodies. Although political parties were muted, local level opposition remained constant, keeping the police and military tribunals active and preventing General Zia from fully consolidating power.

By 1981, General Zia had dismissed the gloss of transition from the military regime and stopped scheduling phantom elections. In the absence of popular backing, he promulgated far-reaching orders to concentrate his rule. Most effective, and consequently most destructive to the civilian state, was the 1981 Provisional Constitution Order (PCO). Issued "for consolidating and declaring the Law and for effectively meeting the threat to the integrity and sovereignty of Pakistan," and because "doubts have arisen . . . as regards the powers and jurisdiction of the superior Courts," the PCO extinguished judicial powers.[18] Its timing coincided with a proposed Supreme Court conclave on the constitutional amendments discussed in *Yaqoob Ali's case*; it was issued directly after a Pakistan International Airlines plane was hijacked to Kabul, allegedly by the exile group Al Zulfikar, an organization deemed a terrorist threat whose purported members were mercilessly persecuted until martial law was lifted. The judiciary's disapproval of the regime was unmistakable and its decisions blunted the sharp edge of military oppression for many detainees, in turn creating space for political opposition. Judgments against military rule led to confrontations with the military that the courts could not win; the PCO was General Zia's victory proclamation.

The 1981 Order was a profound weapon against civil society. With it the 1973 Constitution was effectively abrogated. The PCO was offered as a substitute (and unratified) national constitution, but it was less a constitutive document than an instrument to preclude democracy. It placed virtually all power in the hands of the executive, provided extensive emergency provisions to extend military rule and gave the President

[18] Preamble, *Provisional Constitution Order, 1981* (C.M.L.A.'s Order No. 1 of 1981) (Lahore: Civil and Criminal Law Publication, 1983).

and Chief Martial Law Administrator retrospective power to amend the constitution. All orders and actions taken by the regime were considered to have been validly made, and "notwithstanding any judgment of any Court" could not be called into question "in any Court on any ground whatsoever." Were political parties revived they were to conform to registration standards determined by an Election Commission subordinate to the CMLA.

The PCO excluded the judiciary from hearing a broad range of cases. Members of the armed forces were made fully immune to civil prosecution. High courts were barred from ruling on preventive detention, providing interim relief to detainees under preventive detention, taking action on any case registered in civil or military courts or tribunals or interfering with cases registered at police stations. Pending cases were immediately suspended. In addition, civil courts were barred from entertaining any proceedings concerned with military courts, their pending cases or their sentencing. The Chief Martial Law Administrator had sole power to "remove difficulties" in these matters.

The effects on the judiciary were debilitating. In one stroke, the martial law government declared its intention to remain in power and resist change. The prospects for renewed constitutional rule diminished to an undisclosed vanishing point, leaving the judiciary in its most awkward situation to date. In the 1950s and 1960s, and under Bhutto's "awami" (people's) martial law, the absence of constitutional governance was always treated as a temporary phenomenon. No such understanding could be culled from the PCO. This left the matter of oath-taking, for example, a personal and political decision of considerable reach. To punish and embarrass them further, superior court judges were required to take a new oath to uphold the PCO; not all were invited to do so and not all who were agreed to attest loyalty to the military state. Were the entire judiciary to resign, military tribunals, whose arbitrariness and harshness were now well known, could vastly extend their jurisdiction. To continue in office, however, meant accepting a political and judicial order that rendered political justice an oxymoron.

Judicial review was effectively canceled. Prior to 1981, such review could limit the coercive apparatus of the state, albeit in piecemeal ways. The PCO rendered this control mechanism vacant. Attempts to attract judicial attention were allowed only if the issues involved were not touched by the order's restrictions.[19] Otherwise, the courts were forced to

[19] In *Nisar alias Nisari and another v. Government of Pakistan and 2 others*, PLD 1984 Supreme Court 373 (Shariat Bench), the Registrar of the court refused to entertain two direct Shariat appeals: "The appellants were tried, convicted and sentenced by a Special Military Court. Therefore, the appeal is not entertainable under the provisions of the

return petitions with neither comment nor action, a stamp indicating only that it was "hit by PCO"; the regime instructed court registrars to return petitions raising martial law matters without referring them to a judge. Unfettered by an independent judiciary, the regime reorganized the discourse of politics and the structure of the state by refining the principle of divide and rule. The martial law regime was transformed into a martial law state. Excluding civil court review of executive action, the regime was free to impose power on its own terms, and punish society collectively for the acts of individuals.

### *Rights*

Citizens were now subject to an ever-expanding list of martial law regulations and orders, resulting in the detention of thousands of civilians during the regime's life. Although Zia ul Haq maintained that military courts were used only to combat threats to national security, both summary and special military courts were used extensively and without oversight. The premise of these military courts was autonomy. Neither records, reasoned judgments nor representations were maintained to facilitate later scrutiny; the regime did not always respond to *habeas corpus* petitions and frequently applied death sentences for political acts. In one Baluchistan case, murder charges against a detainee were changed several times when it was discovered that the presumed victim was still alive; the defendant was nonetheless convicted and hanged. High Court Chief Justice Mir Khuda Bux Marri resigned after this incident. In other cases, charges were not framed until sentences were passed. By 1984, the government formally removed itself from the careful standards set in *F.B. Ali's case*, maintaining publicly that military law, including the 1952 Army Act, applied to civilians.[20]

The regime also took the legal profession to task. The freedom of attorneys and bar associations was sharply curtailed in 1982. The 1973 Legal Practitioners and Bar Councils Act was amended to remove peer review from licensing, giving the councils less power than had been granted in the 1926 Indian Bar Councils Act. Further amendments in 1985 gave regime-appointed judges, rather than bar groups, power to

Provisional Constitution Order, 1983." Appeal was allowed only if it did not challenge a military court decision.

20 Exercise of the Right of Reply by the Pakistan Representative in Discussion on Agenda Item 12, United Nations Human Rights Commission, 12 March 1985; correspondence between Lawyers Committee for Human Rights (New York), Political Prisoners Release and Relief Committee (Lahore), and the United States government. See Paula R. Newberg, *Zia's Law: Human Rights under Military Rule in Pakistan* (New York: Lawyers Committee for Human Rights, 1985).

suspend the right to practice before the courts, granted the regime greater latitude in judicial appointments and strictly banned members of bar councils from politics. The amendments were retribution for the national council's expulsion of lawyers who joined the Federal Advisory Council after the PCO was promulgated; a similar expulsion had taken place against PPP members after the 1977 *coup d'état*. Subsequent to the amendments, the regime transferred judges indiscriminately or as punishment for anti-regime judgments, and refused to confirm some judicial appointments; Presidential Order No. 24 of 1985 required judges to accept transfer or be summarily retired.[21]

Individual rights violations were compounded by the regime's efforts not only to neutralize but if possible to destroy opposition as well. Acting on a presumption that General Zia ul Haq shared with his military predecessors, that political parties were divisive forces, parties were prohibited once the pretence of early elections was put to rest. Their leaders were persecuted, imprisoned, tortured and exiled, and many party members were subjected to equally brutal treatment. When civilian opposition did not cease, the government resorted to long-term political trials in special military courts formed under retroactive laws, constructing elaborate cases against alleged anti-state conspiracies that remained unproven after years of imprisonments, and puppet trials conducted with special rules of evidence.[22] President's Order No. 4 of 1982 (Criminal Law Amendment Order), promulgated more than a year after arrests were made in conspiracy cases, allowed the courts to refuse to call defendant witnesses "if the tribunals or court is satisfied that the accused intends to call or examine such witness to cause vexation or delay or to defeat the ends of justice," and sanctioned secret proceedings that could proceed without the presence of the accused. It also prohibited the publication of information about the proceedings without the express permission of the court, presuming that anyone possessing such information was guilty of offences under the 1923 Official Secrets Act. The government underscored this message with continual instructions to newspapers, already engaged in self-censorship after many journalists were arrested, to omit coverage of a wide range of stories.

After the 1981 PIA hijacking, the military government accused many detained PPP members of complicity with the alleged terrorist organi-

21 See Mahmood Zaman, "Lawyers fighting regression," *Viewpoint* 11 April 1985, pp. 18–19, 32; Abdul Hakeem Khan Kundi, Address of Welcome, Fifth Pakistan Jurists' Conference, 28 March 1986, PLD 1986 Journal 301–5.

22 See Amnesty International, *The Trial and Treatment of Political Prisoners Convicted by Special Military Courts in Pakistan*, London, 20 November 1985; and Newberg, *Zia's Law*.

zation Al Zulfikar, using the organization as pretext for instituting society-wide anti-terrorist measures – arbitrary arrests, interrogations, torture, road-blocks and searches, and the use of external intelligence agencies for internal surveillance – designed to frighten the country into compliance with the regime. Non-party members were also persecuted, sometimes randomly: medical school students traveling to a meeting in Sind were shot and viciously beaten by the military in 1984 and then imprisoned and tried before a military tribunal. The court was still constituted long after Interior Minister Aslam Khattack admitted that the government had no case.[23]

To underline its Islamization program, the law of evidence was rewritten and new penalties were established for religious crimes.[24] The regime organized new religious courts and created a Federal Shariat Court (FSC) to review legal compliance with Islam; ironically, when the FSC judged the 1963 Press and Publications Order and the 1952 Security of Pakistan Act incompatible with the precepts of Islam, the government appealed the decision because it thwarted its political programs.[25] These laws did less to establish an ideological system of justice for an ideological state than to provide further instruments of state oppression. Each revision of religious law rigorously distinguished among sects, culminating in a criminal and martial law bar on the practices of the minority Ahmadiya sect – subjecting its members to official harassment more injurious than ever before in its many contentious conflicts with mainstream Sunni *ulema*.[26] When

23 *Bloodbath of Sindhi Students: Report of Fact Finding Commmittee in Respect of the Tori Railway Crossing Incident appointed by the Karachi High Court Bar Association*; "Military trial of Thori case stopped," *Muslim* 10 July 1985; "Mily. court continues to hear Thori case," *Muslim* 25 August 1985; "Body to strive for Thori case detenus release," *Muslim* 30 September 1985.

24 The Establishment of the Court of Qazis Ordinance, 1982 was "to provide for speedy and inexpensive dispensation of justice"; the 1980 Constitution Amendment Order (President's Order No. 1 of 1980) established the Shariat Court; the 1984 Qanun-e-Shahadat Order restructured the law of evidence along purportedly Islamic lines, reducing the legal rights of women and minorities. See *Hadood and Tazir Laws with Rules and Ordinances* (Lahore: Civil and Criminal Law Publication, 1985). Other presidential ordinances were promulgated to bring property laws into conformity with the regime's Islamization programs.

25 *In re. Islamization of Laws*, PLD 1984 Federal Shariat Court.

26 President's Order No. 8 of 1982, Amendment of the Constitution (Declaration) Order, reaffirmed the minority status of the Ahmadiya group. Ordinance No. 20 of 1984, Anti-Islamic Activities of the Qadiani group, Lahore group and Ahmadis (Prohibition and Punishment) Ordinance 1984, gave the regime power to restrict their religious practices, and section 298(c) of the Pakistan Penal Code incorporated these restrictions in criminal law. Contests to the ordinance (*Majibur Rahman and 3 others v. Federal Government of Pakistan and another*, PLD 1985 Federal Shariat Court 8) were not upheld. See also "The situation in Pakistan," United Nations Economic and Social Council Commission on Human Rights, 27 August 1985, E/CN.4/Sub.2/1985/L.42; and Gustaf

disputes between Shias and Sunnis led to urban violence, law and order agencies did not intercede, leading an Islamabad newspaper to accuse the regime of misrepresenting such problems "to make them appear inconsequential."[27]

*Provinces*

The trend toward centralized authority continued as the military dominated civil institutions. The unavoidable presence of the military in all aspects of collective life created reactive acrimonies that rivaled the Bangladesh period, but without any mechanism for voicing protest. Military practice overrode legal precept. Military administrators superseded civilian governors and martial law regulations transcended the hierarchy of federal–provincial relations; the only functioning legislatures were local bodies reelected under highly restrictive rules in 1983, and an appointed Federal Advisory Council (Majlis-i-Shoora) with neither constituencies nor real power. (When some Shoora members tried to act independently of the military, the government let the system languish, abandoning it in favor of elected assemblies in 1985.) The national treasury was devoted to enforcing martial law and supporting a military and intelligence apparatus already growing in importance due to involvement in the war in neighboring Afghanistan. The martial law state, born of a desire to control civil society with a strong hand, was not flexible enough to exercise control peacefully; instead, its repression led to tensions it neither recognized nor comprehended.

The "quantum of autonomy" established in the 1973 Constitution had been inadequate for some provincialists since ratification, but proved to be generous compared to its counterpart under the military. With increasing national debt, the provinces were left to compete with each other for resources, revenues and relative power. Provincial governments balanced their budgets with additional borrowing from the central treasury.[28] Bhutto-era nationalization policies were haphazardly revoked to favor unregulated private interests, leaving necessary national planning for basic services – water, power, energy, land use, education – without focus. Resource policies appeared to benefit some provinces or populations at the presumed expense of others, but the martial law government stalled in

Petren et al., *Pakistan: Human Rights After Martial Law: Report of a Mission* (Geneva: International Commission of Jurists, 1987).

27 *Muslim* editorial, 19 October 1984.

28 See Shahid Kardar, "Provincial Autonomy: The Issue of Financial Independence," in *Provincial Autonomy: Concept and Framework* (Lahore: Group 83 Series, 29 November 1987).

the face of any divisiveness that might impinge on its claims to universal power. This weakness on the part of the state, however, was not captured by its opposition, indicating some regime success in realigning national political forces. With no consensus on political questions, no national political parties to voice political or economic concerns, only punitive action from the center and no judicial authority to mediate conflicts between center and provinces, the provinces took the offensive against each other.

The tone of inter-provincial relations reflected growing animosities among dominant ethnic groups and vastly different views about the country's perennial constitutional problems of representation and autonomy. A two-tiered system of politics developed in response to autocracy. The first included realists who encountered the military state on its own terms, seeking economic and political profit from its engagements and its disinterests, leading to extraordinary fragmentation at local and national levels. It was a politics of reaction, but one willing to circle rather than confront the evolving state structure, to ignore weakened state institutions in favor of renewed feudal relations and to live in a local rather than a national environment. Through the 1980s such politics led to violent ethnic confrontations in the urban centers of Sind amid high monetary stakes driven by the narcotics and armaments trades; to clashes between refugee and local drug traders, each with their own tribal and military patrons in the Frontier; to paralyzing conflicts among Frontier, Punjabi and Sindhi agriculturalists about the future of dams and waterways; to renewed clashes between Baloch and Pukhtun settlers in Baluchistan reacting to disruptions in their ethnic, economic and sectarian balance in refugee settlement areas; and to confrontations between Sindhi farmers and Punjabi landowners endowed by the army in Sind. These responses, all plausible in local terms, reinforced the military's law-and-order justifications for continued rule.

The second tier, equally reflexive, was committed to a traditional landscape of political parties, national in scope but no less inward-looking in vision. Its chosen field was constitutionalism phrased in a language of federalism harkening to the country's origins. Conceptually the problem of provincial autonomy was couched as a debate between the 1940 Lahore Resolution and the 1973 Constitution, between a compact among autonomous units and a nation with powers devolved to those units. Politically, however, the landscape of constitutional controversy had been altered by the 1973 Constitution, and politicians – seeking constituencies without formal parties, expounding politics while formally banned from doing so – often drew on elements of both philosophies by using the idea of federalism very broadly. Veteran Baloch politician

Ghous Bakhsh Bizenjo, leader of the banned Pakistan National Party, claimed in 1984 that "we want equal rights for all provinces on the basis of the 1940 Resolution," adding "Pakistan can be kept alive and stable through federal democracy." His concern was as much for the vehicle of expression as its resolution, for he feared the repoliticization of the autonomy question.[29] He therefore proposed a multi-party agreement on provincial issues prior to elections, a plan never effected by the parties.

For confederationists, the terms of constitutional discussion were starker, viewed through the lens of military oppression as well as federalism. Observing that the provinces were united "only through the brute force of the Military," the Sindhi–Baloch–Pushtoon Front concluded by 1985 that "the covenant between the constituent units has been broken and Pakistan has been turned into occupied territory":

> The Federal system, notwithstanding all the safe-guards provided therein, has failed to prevent Military adventures from destroying its sanctity and undermining Civilian supremacy . . . it has now become incumbent on the smaller Nationalities and their suppressed Peoples, to demand and strive for the Political arrangement, on the promise of which, they joined together to form the State of Pakistan.[30]

As an alternative mechanism to adjudicate disputes between the provinces and the center, the Front developed a confederal proposal premised on a right to secede in the face of unchecked central military powers.[31] General Zia's attitude toward confederationists was expectedly harsh, warning that "all such persons will have to erase such wayward ideas from their minds and become Pakistanis first," and arresting Front leaders for delivering speeches which "vehemently criticized the ideology of Pakistan and promulgated [a] 'Confederal System'."[32]

[29] "Bizenjo for congenial climate," *Viewpoint* 8 March 1984, pp. 15–17. He also objected to all amendments subsequent to the original 1973 Constitution, foreshadowing post-martial-law conflicts about constitutional structure.

[30] Khalid Laghari, A. Hafeez Pirzada, Mumtaz Ali Bhutto, Sardar Ataullah Mengal, Afzal Bangash, "Sindhi-Balouch-Pushtoon Front Declaration," London, 18 April 1985.

[31] "A Confederal Constitution for Pakistan and Outline by The Sindhi Baloch Pushtoon Front," August 1985. See also Makhdoom Ali Khan, "Provincial Autonomy: The Constitutional Impediments," in *Provincial Autonomy*; and interview with Mumtaz Bhutto in *Today* (Karachi) 30 November 1989, pp. 26–30.

[32] For Zia's comments, see *Viewpoint* 23 February 1984. On arrests, which continued after the lifting of martial law, see: *Syed Siraj Hussain, DSP v. Sher Khan and 7 others*, Complaint before Special Court constituted under the Suppression of Terrorist Activities Act, 1975, at Karachi; *SIP Ghulam Muhammed Memon v. Aftab Ali Shah and 6 others*, Complaint in the Special Court in Sind, Karachi, Government of Sind, 1987; *State through Khamiso Khan Memon v. Mumtaz Ali Bhutto and 8 others*, Complaint before the Special Court Sind at Karachi, Case No. S.H.9/87; and *Abdul Hafeez Pirzada v. Government of Sindh, through Secretary Home Department, Karachi*, Constitutional Petition No. 285 of 1987 for enforcement of fundamental rights. See also Government of Sind, Home Department Order, 23 December 1986.

To non-provincialist observers, the center–provinces question symbolized the deterioration of constitutionalism. Inteviewed in 1985, retired Supreme Court Justice Dorab Patel blamed a pattern of executive interference in provincial affairs for the growing impasse among the provinces, citing the center's use of emergency provisions dating back to the 1935 Act. His pessimistic interlocutor conceded that "a total destruction of a Constitution ... is at least as real and potent a threat to democracy and provincial autonomy as an abuse by the Centre of its emergency powers."[33] The same issues that dominated the Bengal dispute and PPP–NAP conflicts under Prime Minister Bhutto thus grew in acerbity if not strength under a more repressive regime, straining the weak ties that bound the state. The Front was important less for its specific proposals than for the strands of political frustration it wove together: the intersection of provincialism and ethnic nationalism, the superimposing of the military over national and provincial development, the invocation of national history as a compact among provinces rather than an expression of national will. In different forms, each issue had resonated under every previous government and surfaced again when martial law was formally lifted. Neither the Front nor its foes, however, reinforced respect for constitutionalism in the powerful political classes it represented or in the army.

### *Partyless politics*

Political parties were banned in September 1979, before court powers were reduced. When the PCO took away judicial powers no forum to air hostility toward the military government was available. By the end of 1981, an underground Movement for the Restoration of Democracy (MRD) was organized by a changing roster of banned parties (benignly labeled "defunct" by the government) whose only common concern was to end military rule. Until martial law ended, the MRD was riven by competing economic interests and political factions, by differing attitudes toward cooperation with the military and by vastly different histories and approaches to politics. Its members were primarily small parties to the right and left of the dominant People's Party, which itself wavered on the comparative advantages of MRD participation because the coalition allowed smaller parties equal voice. The MRD could not mediate the deep-seated disputes about provincial rights, military power, foreign policy and constitutional structure that divided the parties; indeed, the movement itself often disagreed about internal democratic procedure.

[33] Malik Mohammad Jafar, "The crucial question of provinces' rights," *Viewpoint* 12 September 1985, pp. 9–10, 33.

Still, the MRD provided a focus for popular action. In August 1983, General Zia proposed to lift martial law by formally extending his rule, an action he described as an effort to balance ministerial and presidential powers, and "to revive democracy and representative institutions in accordance with the principles of Islam." The country was shaken by MRD-organized anti-government demonstrations that were cruelly quashed by the army; troops deployed in Sind unrelentingly killed unarmed civilians, bringing Sindhi nationalist feeling to a head, while elsewhere thousands of activists were detained. The 1983 demonstrations not only escalated civil–military confrontation but also pointed to changes in the political environment. Although anti-military sentiment was strong, some politicians were ready to orchestrate a *modus vivendi* with the military in order to re-enter politics. Building on this division, the regime pursued two tactics. It persecuted opposition political parties with a vengeance, detaining and torturing their leaders, establishing scores of summary military courts and continuing special court trials. Concurrently, General Zia spoke of lifting martial law, elections and cooperation with civilian leaders. At the end of 1984, he conducted a referendum equating his Islamisation program with his continued rule to deliver himself an additional five-year term, and scheduled national and provincial assembly elections for early 1985.

The elections banned political party participation, constrained campaigning and restricted individual candidates. These restraints provoked a debate in the MRD about electoral participation that paralleled the judiciary's concerns about limited jurisdiction under earlier regimes. To participate might legitimize the regime and the constitutional structure created by the PCO; to abstain risked exclusion from a government that might keep power for many years; to lose would be an insurmountable blow to party politics. The half-hearted MRD boycott proved these fears. General Zia, who retained his position as Chief of Army Staff long after martial law was lifted,[34] was given an extended political life in which the newly elected assemblies were complicit; many military-backed candidates, including Cabinet members, did not win, but familiar political party elites were split between those who ran independently (some successfully) and those who boycotted elections and were thus absent from the new government. The assemblies proceeded to weaken the role of political parties in future politics.

The 1985 elections shrewdly reinforced General Zia's power. Not only did they provide a new forum for his perpetual state restructuring

34 A later constitutional challenge to General Zia's holding both offices was repelled on the basis of protections in the new constitutional set-up: *Abdul Ghaffar Lakhani v. Federal Government of Pakistan and 2 others*, PLD 1986 Karachi 525.

exercises, but they also gave him an opportunity to split his political opposition between parliamentary and extra-parliamentary arenas, creating political divisions and overlapping political–military alliances that outlasted his rule. Together they made prospects for untrammeled civil rule seem remote.

### Lifting martial law

In the month between the elections and the time the assemblies took office, General Zia ul Haq "revived" the Constitution by issuing an order to alter its structure once again (President's Order No. 14, 1985, Revival of the Constitution of 1973 Order, 1985 [RCO]). Most important of its provisions were those strengthening executive power, recasting the powers of the President and Prime Minister to reduce political influence and reducing provincial government fiscal and decision-making authority. Although assembly members had not been elected under this constitutional instrument and could conceivably have rejected the RCO, none refused office. The National Assembly ratified substantial revisions in the 1962 Political Parties Act to reduce party freedom while the government recreated an official Muslim League Party to provide a political front for its power.[35] For the most part, the National Assembly endorsed General Zia's laws and orders, accepting the promised lifting of martial law as a carrot to avoid the ever-present stick of renewed military intervention in legislative affairs.

By far the most comprehensive constitutional amendment wrought by the military regime as a condition for lifting martial law was an indemnity clause, Article 270-A refashioned as the Constitution's eighth amendment. The amendment gave continuing legal effect to martial law regulations and orders at the sole discretion of General Zia; endorsed constitutional changes promulgated under martial law, including those reducing legislative power by requiring a two-thirds majority to override General Zia's constitutional changes; and perhaps most vital, provided immunity for all acts and actors involved in the military government since the *coup d'état*. In addition, General Zia's powers to promulgate new military ordinances, and the ordinances themselves, were also immunized. It was an indemnity of unprecedented scope in Pakistan's history which

[35] On the 1962 Political Parties Act, see *Asseff Ahmad Ali v. Muhammad Khan Junejo*, PLD 1986 Lahore 310. One commentator later called the constitutional amendments prior to lifting martial law a "cruel joke upon the theory and practice of the concept of the sovereignty of the Parliament," and noted that the configuration of the parties act strengthened feudal representation in the assemblies. Rasul Bahksh Rais, "Elections in Pakistan: Is Democracy Winning?" *Asian Affairs* 12, 3 (Fall 1985): 43–61.

changed the essential character of the Constitution. S.M. Zafar, formerly Ayub Khan's Law Minister, accurately predicted that the change would move the government "from a black-out to a brown-out,"[36] converting military rule to civilian martial law. Despite evidence that a transition to real democracy was unlikely and that legislative powers would be limited, the Assembly approved the amendments, and martial law was formally lifted at the end of 1985.

### *Courts*

Indemnity had consequences in every sphere of national life, but none more significant than in the judiciary's relationship to civil society. The country was governed by a constitutional document that incorporated military regulations and retained military tribunals, and gave legal cover to all actions taken pursuant to those laws and courts and to unknown future enactments. While the PCO was technically void the judiciary was still barred from ruling on challenges to past regime actions. Military court convictions and sentences could not be revoked, no matter how absurd or draconian. The 1985 All-Pakistan Lawyers Convention unanimously condemned this policy, strongly denouncing "the validation of all sentences passed by Military Courts and rejects the blanket indemnity of all the excesses, torture, and violence perpetrated by the regime and its Civil and Military functionaries during the past eight years."[37] The following year, the annual jurists convention resolved that "every person, high or low, should be answerable to the Court," adding that superior court jurisdiction should be enlarged rather than limited.[38] In response to these public pronouncements and the international attention they received, Prime Minister Mohammad Khan Junejo told the European Parliament that special military court sentences would be reviewed by civil courts, a commitment he was powerless to keep.[39] Although independent National Assembly members called for the release of political prisoners, the government promised only to establish a committee to look into the issue; its report was ready only as the assemblies were summarily dismissed two years later.

The courts were petitioned nonetheless as citizens sought some public forum in which to attest their views and redress grievances against the state. When retired army officers involved in the Attock Fort Conspiracy

36 Aurangzeb, "Validation Bill to bring civilian M.L.," *Muslim* 17 September 1985.
37 Lahore High Court Bar Association, 28 November 1985.
38 Declaration, Fifth Pakistan Jurists' Conference, 30 March 1986, PLD 1986 Journal 306–7.
39 Comments to Claude Cheysson, Commissioner of the European Economic Community, unofficial transcript of 12 March 1986 meeting of European Parliament, cited in Amnesty International, *Pakistan: Special Military Courts, Unfair Trials and the Death Penalty*, London, February 1987.

Case fought their special military court convictions in the first year of mixed government, Attorney-General Aziz Munshi responded that Article 270-A conferred a stamp of good faith on all such convictions, and that Assembly validation acted "as an embargo in relation to any inquiry by any court ... because the legislature was supreme and sovereign to enact such a provision."[40] Straddling the shaky constitutional fence, the Lahore High Court reserved judgment.

Civil courts continued to receive petitions from martial law detainees and released prisoners, not only to challenge the regime, but also because convictions prevented former prisoners from fully re-entering civilian life and barred them from state employment. New arrests brought thousands of detainees before the lower courts. PPP leader Benazir Bhutto, newly returned from exile, led MRD demonstrations against the government in August and September 1986 that met harsh police, paramilitary and military action that resulted in serious injuries and civilian deaths. The demonstrations had been banned by the government in response, it alleged rather circuitously, to purported opposition plans to disrupt such bans. In a climate of contradictory government signals and public uncertainty, courts acted on few *habeas corpus* petitions and prison releases were still determined at the government's pleasure. Provincial governments also reinforced their powers over courts and detainees. The Sind government, for example, amended the Pakistan Prison Rules to exclude espionage and anti-state actions convictions – familiar to many who survived military tribunals – from remission, except under its direct orders.[41]

General Zia's government cemented its post-martial law power by capitalizing on corrupt and fragmented local-level politics, constructing alliances between the military, paramilitary forces, police and feudal landlords to break the MRD and the PPP in Sind. Individuals were detained for raising party flags in their villages or for living in villages with PPP supporters. Political demonstrations were not banned; instead, law enforcement agencies attacked processions in progress. Entire villages were assaulted and burned.[42]

[40] "A-G argues against civil courts' jurisdiction," *Dawn* 10 July 1986; "Arguments against conviction heard," *Dawn* 9 July 1986; "LHC reserves judgment on jurisdiction issue," *Dawn* 11 July 1986.

[41] Government of Sind, Home Department, Notification, 7 July 1986, included as Rule 214-A of the prison rules. The Sind High Court was forced to admit the force of the notification in *Mst. Amina M. Ansari v. Government of Sind and 2 others*, Constitutional Petition No. 966 of 1986.

[42] For example, affidavit of Bhai Khan of Village Ahmed Khan Brihmani, Taluka; *Mohammad Khan v. Abdul Sami*, Petition to Additional Sessions Judge, Dadu, P.E. No. 31 of 1986, and *Mohammad Khan v. Abdul Sami and 14 others*, Court of Civil Judge and First Class Magistrate, Dadu; *Abdul Moula Shah v. Province of Sind and 2 others*, Court of Senior Civil Judge, Tando Mohammad Khan; *The State v. Abdul Rehman Bhatti, Sub-divisional Magistrate, Tando Mohammad Khan*; *Allah Dino v. Muhammad Malook and 7 others*, Civil Court petition.

The force of numbers took its toll on the courts. The Karachi High Court initially held martial law orders and regulations immune from questioning.[43] In March 1987, however, it carefully reassessed indemnity in *Bachal Memon's case*.[44] Observing that "in order to facilitate the revocation of the proclamation of Martial Law it may be necessary to retain some of the Martial Law Orders and Regulations," the Court suggested that after 1986 such orders were amendable by the legislature, thus changing their legal status. Relying on the Supreme Court judgment in *Ziaur Rahman's case*, the Karachi court concluded that constitutional immunities were not complete. In its unanimous order, the court concluded that some challenges to military court convictions could be heard by civil courts and that petitions under martial law orders provided neither remedy nor hearing for those convicted by military courts. The court concluded with a note of singular approbation for the government:

> In view of the scores of challenges made by aggrieved persons on innumerable grounds against convictions by Martial Law Courts, it may have been more conducive to public confidence, particularly after the revival of the constitution and restoration of Fundamental Rights, if some sort of opportunity of hearing had been provided to the aggrieved parties to ventilate their grievances before an appropriate tribunal.

This decision was a judicial sign that mixed governance could not endure fully in General Zia's image.

Three weeks after *Bachal Memon's case*, responding to seven additional petitions challenging the judgments and sentences of special military courts, the Lahore High Court offered a judgment of greater reach, one that set the tone for further challenges and appeals.[45] Two decades of contradictory politics and their inadequate judicial resolution came to the fore in *Mustafa Khar's case*. Its premise was that martial law inroads into judicial autonomy and jurisdiction violated the necessity conditions articulated in *Nusrat Bhutto's case*, thereby transforming General Zia into a usurper whose actions were liable under the terms established in *Asma Jilani's case*. With a realism reminiscent of the post-Yahya Khan period, counsel Aitzaz Ahsan proposed that actions purportedly taken in the public interest under the veil of necessity be condoned but not validated. The Attorney General predictably sought broad immunity for the regime, contending that necessity vitiated extreme martial law measures which were themselves justified by a principle of efficacy. Justice Muhammad Afzal Lone vigorously contested this reading of *Nusrat Bhutto's case*: "Necessity can confer on a de-facto ruler at the most the same power as

43 *Nazar Muhammad Khan v. Pakistan and 2 others*, PLD 1986 Karachi 516.

44 *Muhammad Bachal Memon v. Government of Sind through Secretary Department of Food and 2 others*, PLD 1987 Karachi 296.

45 *Malik Ghulam Mustafa Khar and others v. Pakistan and others*, PLD 1988 Lahore 49.

exercised by a de-jure functionary, but not beyond that. We are, constitutionally bound by law laid down by the Supreme Court and feel no inhibition, in holding that the Martial Law Regime was not vested with the powers to amend the Constitution freely." The regime, he concluded, "had to act within the bounds of necessity."

The terms of the Lahore Court's judgment were delineated by its reading of *Nusrat Bhutto's case*, and prudence demanded careful adherence to its conditions. The court rebutted contests to the validity of the 1985 Assembly on the basis of distinctions between legislative and constitutive powers, noting that such objections had "political assumption rather than a legal significance." Instead, Justice Lone offered his own efficacy argument. He suggested that the parliament that passed Article 270-A continued to function, its election validated under the same constitutional clause and its sovereignty endowed by the participating electorate. Law was not politics: judging the "exercise of constituent power unduly or against the wishes of the people, is a political question which cannot be subjected to judicial scrutiny." With General Zia still in office, the court was not willing to walk down the path of challenge it divined, leaving future legislative or judicial bodies to enter that domain. Nonetheless, the Lahore Court examined the content of Article 270-A to clarify its jurisdiction. It extended the limits of judicial review proposed in *Bachal Memon's case*: military court sentences would be reviewed on the merits of specific cases. In the Federation appeal, restricted to the issue of judicial review, the Supreme Court supported the Lahore court's reading of necessity.[46] Its judgment was, by this time, subject to political currents. Although the appeal was heard in March 1988, the decision was not issued until October, two months after General Zia ul Haq's death and just prior to general elections. Mustafa Khar, former Punjab Chief Minister and PPP leader, was free to contest elections.

The martial law government thus set the rules for its legal demise. By emasculating the courts under the PCO and flagrantly violating the generous terms of *Nusrat Bhutto's case*, Zia ul Haq gave the judiciary ample cause to call the government to account. By keeping citizens away from the courts, the government gave the judiciary every reason to want to reestablish its accessibility. Judicial protestations notwithstanding, *Mustafar Khar's case* was not simply limited to establishing the limits of judicial review. The justices used it to rework the range of superior court jurisdiction in the post-PCO period, on terms of their own making. The

[46] *Federation of Pakistan and another v. Malik Ghulam Mustafa Khar*, PLD 1989 Supreme Court 26. The appeal was argued in October 1988, after General Zia's death and the judgment in *Benazir Bhutto's case*, discussed below; the scope of the appeal was limited by the decision in that case.

separation of powers so often invoked in constitutional cases thus took a new turn. With time, the Supreme Court increased the scope of judicial review to include legislative as well as executive action, cementing its renewed powers with rulings on substantive rights as well as procedure.

### *Politics*

Peace was hardly the byword of post-martial law politics. Divisions among ethnic groups, classes and provinces were deepened by rampant inflation, severe unemployment, and an economy weighed down by military expenditure. The availability of imported consumer goods and capital for the wealthy masked the failure of a debt-ridden economy barely paying its way. Moreover, the sources of capital, often ill-gotten and illegal, were the causes of increased social violence that corrupt and unsupervised law-enforcement agencies could not correct. Neither the center nor the provincial governments could solve the problems plaguing the society; each blamed the other for their neglect and defeats. The result was government that did not govern, heightened provincialist rhetoric, and local political organizations and parties with little concept of cooperation and strong feelings of deprivation. In post-martial law Pakistan the state was stronger than civil society but it little understood how to use its powers.

As Ayub Khan had discovered twenty years earlier, partial freedom under military guidance is a practical impossibility. Limited political expression almost invariably exerts popular pressures on politicians that can only be satisfied by increased liberties. For Ayub Khan, however, to increase political freedom was to relinquish power, contradicting the political and conceptual foundations for basic democracy, just as similar pressures redounded against Prime Minister Bhutto's concept of democracy in the following decade. In an undemocratic, unrepresentative political order, the imperatives of power for those who hold it and the quest for that power by those who do not are rarely compatible. In the 1960s these structural tensions led to political conflicts that no government institution could solve. Zia ul Haq encountered similar problems as civilian institutions weakened under his rule. His power arrangements caused greater political disarray and social disintegration than they could manage, creating a constitutional order that only he could manipulate.

On the surface, the post-martial law state bore remarkable similarities to Pakistan in preceding decades. Weak state institutions were matched in their hesitancy by unruly political parties with little common purpose and slight involvement with their supposed constituencies. The government's zeal in countering civilian opposition was matched by political party failures to mobilize and even more, sustain their opposition. The assemblies seemed to do the General's bidding, the economy seemed to work in spite of its structural deficiencies and society persevered even while it crumbled. Politics continued on the path of least resistance and most noise, providing entertainment for few and succor to fewer.

Appearances can be deceiving when the prospect of elections, however restricted, reemerges. After two years of relative complacency, the National Assembly realized that without significant accomplishments – apart from lifting martial law and legalizing parties, activities that could be interpreted as primarily self-interested – its members might lose elections and began to listen to complaints in the districts. The results became noticeable in 1987. First, the divide between disenfranchised political parties and parliamentarians lessened slightly as each side realized the advantages of limited dialogue. The parties, particularly the PPP, tried to maintain distance and singularity while experimenting with possible electoral alliances. The Assembly simultaneously began to realize how deeply the country was politicized; determined to retain title, its members reacquired political color. Second, the National Assembly responded negatively to constitutional proposals to limit further its legislative powers. Both the proposed 1985 Shariah Bill and the 1986 Constitution (Ninth Amendment) Bill created government structures superior to the legislature. The Shariah Bill would have created non-legislative bodies to oversee an Islamization program; the ninth amendment would have enlarged the powers of clerics and in some versions would have made the appointed Federal Shariat Court the supreme government body.[47] Despite firm and constant pressure from Zia ul Haq to endorse these laws, the Assembly withheld (but did not deny) action on these bills.

The vehicle through which discontent was voiced was muted anti-militarism toward General Zia and public dismay with Pakistan's involvement in the Afghanistan war. The Assembly sought control of the economy and forced the government to withdraw its budget until it was marginally civilianized. By 1988 its voice turned distinctly belligerent. Prime Minister Junejo, other Assembly members, and opposition politicians outside parliament spoke out against government policies, military responsibility for social problems and Pakistan's dependence on the United States as its military patron. With General Zia committed to fight in Afghanistan, concord was not possible.

Equally, the Assembly protested executive disregard for legislative initiatives and prerogatives – prerogatives that General Zia ul Haq

[47] See Chaudhry M. Altaf Husain, "Ninth Amendment and Shariat Bills – some aspects," *Dawn* 21 October 1986.

thought he had dismissed in his revived constitution. Significantly, the Prime Minister did not represent dissatisfied independent parliament members, who were themselves vocal, but the Muslim League mainstream to whom General Zia ul Haq had given renewed life and which he thought supported his version of parliamentarianism. To forestall an Assembly fight on his programs, General Zia like many Governors-General and military officers before him, exercised his constitutional trump by abruptly dismissing provincial and national assemblies in May 1988.

### The martial law state

One month after the dissolution, Pakistan's ambassador to the United States offered a long list of reasons for dismissing the Prime Minister: "a sense of drift and indecision," the breakdown of law and order, a deteriorating economy and a hostile external environment. Citing the path toward democracy as "irreversible but delicate," he offered as evidence of the free political climate a recent Supreme Court ruling to allow party-based elections, and emphasized that dissolution was fully constitutional.[48] Parliament was thus blamed for woes only partly in its purview, let alone its control, while General Zia's position was untouched.

Both the constitutionality and political wisdom of the dissolution would soon be challenged in the courts. But it was impossible to judge General Zia's intentions before or after the Assembly dissolutions; he and many of his senior military command died in a military transport plane explosion three months later. Later reports suggested that he might have used the legislative vacuum to rewrite the constitution by ordinance or, alternately, to use the occasion of partyless elections to form a constituent assembly to do the same – in either familiar version, to promulgate a new document to enforce a presidential system of governance. Although there is no way to prove these speculations, they conform to General Zia's professed leanings and to the direction that his policies were taking him.

In his brief encounter with civil–military government, General Zia discovered, as did the Pakistani people, the profound difficulties of mixing praetorian laws and institutions with popular politics and parliaments. Politicians who participated in government discovered that satisfying the imperatives of martial rule and autocratic politics – even when softened by the revived constitution – was awkward and, when mixed with a portion of populism whose precise formula was outside their control, contradictory. Those proscribed from the assemblies found the

[48] Letter from Ambassador Jamsheed Marker to Lawyers Committee for Human Rights (NYC), 28 June 1988. For a discussion of the 1988 Political Parties Registration Act case, see chapter 7 below.

long silence of partyless politics equally hard to endure; they were beyond the corridors of power, fearful that inertia would bind the existing assemblies to the citizenry and even more, that public aspirations for alternatives would pale in contrast to known compromises.

Most of all, those holding ultimate power were still those most removed from popular politics. However the equations of civil praetorianism are formulated, their content inevitably grates on a society whose voice is muted not by self-restraint drawn from a shared concept of common good, but by the fear of sanction amid common fate. From 1986 to 1988, a façade of open politics disguised thinly the frustrations of a political society that could not fully test the limits of the government that spoke on its behalf. Violence gained an upper hand both as official response to political organizing and as accompaniment to the tribulations of daily life. For those in power – and particularly for General Zia, whose signature graced all plans of state – avenues for dissent were already too broad and varied; for those who tried to traverse them, their paths were too few and their destinations limited.

Through this period, new generations of politicians were born and trained, schooled in a language of political control, ignorant of the ways of open politics, and nevertheless responsible for coping with the legacies of military rule. Others, long excluded from the halls of power and justice, would have a brief, interrupted and only partly successful encounter with PPP government in the late 1980s. Their contrary experiences formed the poles of oppositional politics in the post-Zia period, both in the manner of their political organizing and the substance of their policies.

The eleven years of General Zia's rule are therefore crucial for understanding both the cumulative direction of Pakistani political history and the specific instance of post-Zia politics. Although General Zia's regime often resembled past military governments, his rule represented the most sustained period of martial law the country has known. His policies – particularly those restricting fundamental rights and access to the courts – penetrated the psychology of the society and the character of politics in the awkward federal state. His constitutional experiments determined the shape of the state and provided the groundwork for future iterations of mixed rule when open elections were restored in late 1988. These in turn exposed more clearly the constitution's tensions and contradictions.

If the post-Zia period can be viewed as a transition toward somewhat more democracy, then its direction and contours were drawn by the legal structures of martial law, by the regime's efforts to moderate those laws, and by reactions to them by the army, the establishment and politicians. Taken in tandem, the revived constitution, presidential ordinances and statutory laws changed the state by altering the power relationships that defined it. They enhanced the military's role in government and solidified its relationships with other government institutions; this affected foreign policy and domestic politics alike. They also removed the foundation on which the judiciary had previously stood and thus weakened the protections it could offer to individuals and to society at large; this determined the character of political discourse. These changes have together anchored the quality of political and constitutional choice and defined the ways that political institutions could survive the constitutional structure. It was left to General Zia's political successors and judicial observers to decide how enduring the legacies of the martial law state would be.

# 7 Reviving judicial powers (1988–1993)

What parents sowed, the children reap.
Who's the benefactor? Who the thief?
When the corn came in, the knives came out;
Brother fought brother for every sheaf.
One sinned, another bears the grief.
What parents sowed, the children reap.

Bulleh Shah, "Heritage."

Courts do not exist in isolation. Judges are part of the society in which we all live.

Justice Dorab Patel

From the time that martial law was formally lifted at the end of 1985, the transition to mixed civil–military governance was complicated by constitutional structures that General Zia had hoped would simplify his post-martial law tenure. He tried to achieve a balance between military rule and limited civilian participation in government, relying on constitutional amendments, implementing laws and selected military regulations rather than the full force of martial law. Although General Zia absorbed some lessons of past transitions – including providing immunity from prosecution for government officials once the protections of military rule was gone – establishing control over the pace and content of change was virtually impossible. Petitioners and courts alike soon realized that these same laws provided the means, although occasionally tortuous, to unravel the web of restrictions covered by the eighth amendment. The courts therefore became vehicles for altering the relationship between state and citizen under a constitutional order otherwise inaccessible to challenge; individuals sought relief from the courts when none was available elsewhere. Cumulatively, their petitions helped to refine the practice of politics through the courts and thus incrementally to refine the shape of the post-martial law state.

Between the lifting of martial law and elections following General Zia's death in 1988, the courts faced political problems of retrospect and prospect. They were petitioned both by victims of military rule, and after

August 1988, by General Zia's political heirs trying to regain power. The Supreme Court was also asked to review laws written or amended during martial law to reform the processes of politics. Both kinds of cases gradually shifted the balance of power. Were military sentences overturned, Zia ul Haq's opponents – particularly the PPP – could resume political organizing. Equally important, overturning military-written laws opened a Pandora's box of constitutional and statutory possibilities that would occupy the courts for years.

These cases were unusual in Pakistan's legal history. Although the judiciary had reviewed *coups d'état* and judged regimes that were, in judicial parlance, past and closed, never before had the courts participated in a transition specifically obstructed by the reigning constitutional order. Keen to exorcise the ghost of the PCO and equally imperative, to survive the indemnity the regime had bestowed on itself, the judiciary took up these challenges.

## Reviving politics

Political parties had been agitating for party-based elections for years, and by late 1987 had turned their attention to the elections that would be held to renew assembly terms. Observing that the assemblies had garnered some favor with their voters simply by their willingness to govern, if only minimally, the PPP and its MRD compatriots hoped to open elections to party participation by forcing the government to accept a legal challenge to its party prohibition. The PPP therefore filed a writ petition in the Supreme Court to overturn General Zia's amendments to the 1962 Political Parties Act and thus to reopen the political arena to party organizing. The petition filed in late 1987 was heard in February 1988 but the court waited until late June, after the assemblies had been dismissed, to hand down its decision. Whatever the reasons for delay, it provided an exquisitely timed judgment: by striking down the amendments, the court pushed General Zia to announce an election date and to leave open the question of party participation, rather than prohibit it out of hand.

In *Benazir Bhutto v. Federation of Pakistan and another* (PLD 1988 Supreme Court 416), Chief Justice Muhammad Haleem cast a stone against the advertised inviolability of General Zia ul Haq's laws under the 1985 indemnity provisions. Although his judgment could not redraft constitutional powers written during martial law, it offered a precedent for attacking the General's laws; later cases attempted to revise, if not reform, the confused constitution that was Zia ul Haq's pernicious legacy to the country. The Chief Justice swept away the concept of executive discretion which operated with such depth under the PCO and RCO. Interpreting the revived constitution, he announced, "must receive inspiration from the triad of provisions which saturate and invigorate the entire Constitution, namely, the Objectives Resolution (Article 2-A), the Fundamental Rights and the directive principles of State policy so as to achieve democracy, tolerance, equality and social justice according to Islam." Constitutional democracy and government responsibility to implement its guarantees were to override the tangled military–civilian procedures of the past decade.

Although directive principles were not in themselves enforceable by the courts, they became indirectly enforceable to "bring about a phenomenal change in the idea of co-relation of Fundamental Rights and directive principles of State policy." General Zia might point to the Objectives Resolution, now incorporated into the body of the constitution, as a guiding principle to achieve an Islamic society, but Justice Haleem cited both the Resolution and other constitutional principles to demarcate state goals. Procedurally the court moved the terms of political debate away from the terms set by the General. Moreover, the courts were to help the polity realize these goods, for law "has to serve as a vehicle of social and economic justice, which this Court is free to interpret."[1]

Haleem expanded the concepts of justiciability and justice to carve out a sphere for judicial interpretation under the constrained constitution. Referring to Indian constitutional debates concerning state policy, fundamental rights and legislative authority, he directed that no principles of state policy could contravene rights and that all legislative limits on rights should be strictly construed. His interpretation was practical rather than theoretical. The recent and incomplete reassertion of justiciable rights could ill afford to be sacrificed to the long-term designs of rulers unwilling to submit to an electorate. From this view, it was only a short step to establish the need for political parties in a constitutional, parliamentary electoral process. The court's decision implied two important judgments: that without party-based elections the constitutional order was negated; and that Zia ul Haq's counterposing an Islamic polity to one ruled through political parties suffered from logical inconsistency or hypocrisy. The justices took explicit exception to the organization of executive and legislative power under the 1985 RCO, criticized the 1985 non-party

1 The Supreme Court took its own advice and accepted original jurisdiction in a case concerning the treatment of bonded laborers. *In the Matter of Enforcement of Fundamental Rights Re: Bonded Labour in the Brick Kiln Industry*, PSC 1988 1171. Pursuant to this issue, see also Bonded Labour System (Abolition) Act, 1992 [Act III of 1992].

elections and the assemblies they brought to power and invited challenges to the government in these arenas.[2]

This judgment was a signpost that, according to the superior courts, political rights were to be accessible, substantive and enforceable. If the door to elected government were not opened fully, the parliament could not be considered fully to function. The court called the General's bluff: were open elections not scheduled, future laws could be held unconstitutional and the façade of mixed governance would be exposed. Provided the government followed the decision – a tentative but necessary hypothetical – the court could itself become the usher and guarantor of a transition to popular government through party-based elections. However, the court could not resolve the question of where dictatorship stopped, transition commenced and democracy began. The Chief Justice appeared to believe that democracy commenced after open elections, but Justice Nasim Hasan Shah dated the transition earlier, claiming that the democratic process was restored in 1985. Although the court did not know it at the time, the autumn 1988 elections would offer opportunity to reassess this critical question.

In addition, "the ultimate repository of the power to take any final punitive action against a political party," in the words of Justice Afzal Zullah, who would soon become Chief Justice, was to be the Supreme Court rather than the federal government. After an absence of many years, the courts were back in the business of protecting rights, even if constrained by a difficult constitution. Unless or until the constitution were reworked, possibly by a newly elected National Assembly, Justice Haleem's court could at least aspire to the role of Justice Cornelius's court twenty-five years before: watchdog for civil rights in a constitutional order that recognized their conceptual if not actual existence.

Strong as its impact might be, the Supreme Court's judgment in *Benazir Bhutto's case* was reasoned and reasonable. Despite grand language, it did not overstep the boundaries of the petition, treating the overarching problem of General Zia's political legitimacy only in passing and only as a

[2] Regarding future cases arising under the Political Parties Act, Justice Shafiur Rahman explained that "this Court is keeping to itself the final power of interpreting and applying these provisions." The PPP took up this invitation a few months later in a suit to enforce the Representation of Peoples Act for the November 1988 elections. In *Benazir Bhutto v. Federation of Pakistan and another*, PLD 1989 Supreme Court 66, the court accepted the party's submissions that the use of election symbols, proscribed by the appointed Election Commission, gave substance to the fundamental right to free elections, and ruled that the administration of elections should not override the right of parties and voters to participate. Further challenges to a requirement that voters produce government identity cards persuaded the government to loosen the rule. See *Aitzaz Ahsan and others v. Chief Election Commissioner and others*, PLD 1989 Lahore 1, and *Federation of Pakistan v. Aitzaz Ahsan* 1988 PSC 1283.

means to confront the specific issues at hand. Similarly, it did not take on the indemnity clause, knowing that the constitutional problematic of Article 270-A would soon surface. The Chief Justice's version of prudence concerned the complexion of politics rather than the nature of court powers. Rather than discuss imposed limitations on judicial jurisdiction and powers, he instead structured a decision to circumvent the institutional problem in favor of a limited, solvable quest. His plan, adopted in spirit by the superior judiciary in subsequent cases, gave judicial prudence a new tone in the post-Zia period.

*Benazir Bhutto's case* posed political ironies as well as opportunities. Noting the similarities of this case to Maulana Maudoodi's 1963 petition against government control of political parties, the court nonetheless upheld the concept of party regulation and supported requirements for parties to maintain Islamic ideology, morality and public order – innocent-sounding stipulations that bound parties to sensibilities written both by General Zia and the Bhutto government. Indeed, the PPP's complaints against General Zia's use of the Political Parties Act echoed the spirit of NAP complaints against the PPP government in 1975; referring to the cases against Wali Khan and NAP in 1975–76 obliquely reminded the petitioners of those unfortunate collusions between court and ruling party (although both the PPP and the court persisted in thinking the *Reference* judgment correct). This time the People's Party was out of power, seeking a legal route and judicial sanction to return to office. Its strategy to use the judiciary to achieve the goals of opposition politics influenced its attitude toward the courts when it unexpectedly resumed power in late 1988.

The court's reach was lengthened by dramatic events in the summer of 1988. Until May 1988 General Zia seemed confident of his rule, weathering criticism in his sanctioned institutions and occasional street opposition with sufficient force to remind the country of his power. He continued his unsuccessful quest to Islamize the constitutional order, and was rumored to contemplate a presidential constitution when his five-year term expired in 1989, in part to achieve this goal. The dismissals and his hesitancy in setting an election date within the constitutionally prescribed time fueled rumors of renewed emergency governance or martial law.

General Zia's death in August 1988 and the unobstructed transfer of power to Acting President Ghulam Ishaq Khan, who allowed party-based elections the following November, abruptly changed the political landscape although it did not transform the structure of constitutional politics. Nonetheless, the administrative powers of the state required clarification, and the courts were asked to pave the way for a smooth bureaucratic transition. To retain the previously announced November election date, which would form a government after the constitutionally mandated ninety-day period for elections, Acting President Ghulam Ishaq Khan submitted a reference to the Supreme Court to continue fiscal operations in the interval. With practiced finesse, the court concluded that the May dissolution was not valid until it was judicially recognized – a date later than May – and that the elections fell within the prescribed period for these purposes. The court felt it had little choice. Confronted with a true crisis, the court responded decisively on the basis of written constitutional instruction and refused to enter into discussions of political alternatives offered by the contributing counsel. The court reiterated its views that legislative and executive powers required sharp distinction, that the power of governance lay with the electorate and that dissolution was an unpleasant act of necessity.[3] Additionally, the Quetta High Court cautioned that dissolution must be justified on "definite reasons provided by the Constitution," and that the "extraordinary powers of dissolution ... must be exercised carefully, faithfully and in accordance with the provisions of the Constitution."[4] These words would later instruct the President when he fashioned the instruments for further dissolutions in 1990 and 1993.

The Lahore High Court later noted that Ghulam Ishaq was "the first person to come to power under a Constitution made not by him or under him but by the people of Pakistan."[5] The People's Party contested national and provincial elections against an amalgam of politicians and parties – many associated with the late General – loosely configured as the Islami Jamhoori Ittehad (IJI). Campaigning in the shadow of recent military rule, the PPP won the center by a slim margin as well as the Sind provincial government, although it lost to the ethnically based Mohajir Qaumi Movement (MQM) in the urban centers of Karachi and Hyderabad. The PPP joined a coalition with the Awami National Party (successor to its old rival, NAP) in the Frontier. Its defeats in Punjab and Baluchistan,[6] however, influenced its attitudes and performance in its first year far more than its victories. With little to distinguish elected Assembly members but their recently acquired party labels, the PPP characterized its political opposition as an obstacle to the democratic state. It thus

3 *Reference No. 1 of 1988, Made by the President of Pakistan Under Article 186 of the Constitution of the Islamic Republic of Pakistan*, PLD 1989 Supreme Court 75.

4 *Muhammad Anwar Durrani v. Province of Baluchistan through Chief Secretary and 10 others*, PLD 1989 Quetta 25.

5 *Khawaja Muhammad Sharif v. Federation of Pakistan through Secretary Cabinet Division and 18 others*, PLD Lahore 1988 725 at 761.

6 After dissolving the Baluchistan Assembly within weeks of taking office, the Prime Minister referred the matter to the Supreme Court; the court returned it to the Baluchistan High Court, which then returned the Assembly to office.

proceeded on a collision course with the IJI that threatened the integrity and viability of government institutions, an early and unfortunate repeat of the 1970s.

Without a two-thirds majority in the National Assembly the new government's powers to amend the constitution and pass significant legislation were limited. It therefore ignored parliament in favor of energetic local campaigns to expand its voting bloc and vitriolic public relations offensives against the IJI, which more than matched it in malice. This strategy failed. Early by-election bids were unsuccessful, shaving the PPP's parliamentary margin even closer. The PPP–MQM alliance of convenience crumbled: absent concrete political programs, profound distrust on both sides – based equally on communal misunderstanding, class differences and disagreements over political strategy – the PPP helped pave the way for serious, violent disputes on the streets of Sind province, and a later alliance between the MQM and the IJI that proved, in part, the PPP's downfall just eighteen months later. The Frontier coalition with the ANP, a party which itself splintered, weakened as well. Although the government survived a bitter vote of no-confidence in the autumn of 1989, its small margin limited its legislative and political flexibility. Unsure of its strengths, overly sensitive to its weaknesses, wary of the army and unaccustomed to holding office, the PPP found the encumbrance of General Zia's constitution precisely the obstacle to its governance that its authors intended it to be.

The constitutional order was admittedly troublesome. Superficial appearances suggested that the 1973 Constitution held sway despite military amendments, but the post-1985 Constitution was in fact almost a new document. The basic structure was clear to the PPP: the powers of the Prime Minister were reduced in relation to the President, the army's role was greater than that envisioned in the 1973 Constitution and martial law amendments were difficult to erase without an Assembly majority greater than it possessed. Political parties regained their standing to contest elections after the 1988 Supreme Court ruling but their internal organization and political influence were constrained by inheritance and ambition. The PPP therefore took regular recourse to the courts to try to solve its political problems and also found itself confronting its opposition in trials initiated before it assumed power.

## Surviving indemnity

Upon attaining office, the PPP government faced its constitutional legacy through two sets of problems related to indemnity: the legality of General Zia's dissolution of the assemblies, actions taken by his post-dissolution government and the PPP's capacity to reorganize government institutions; and the scope of martial law courts and the power of military laws under the new regime. Taken separately, each problem was a symptom of post-military adjustment; taken together, they formed a legitimation crisis for the new government, the rule of law and the durability of the transition from military to civil rule.

### *Dissolution*

Although the May 1988 Assembly dissolutions were not contested at the time, General Zia's death and the announcement of new elections inspired petitions from members of the former assemblies and cabinet for reinstatement. The Sind High Court dismissed the first challenge to the dissolution's constitutionality in September 1988,[7] observing the petitioners' opportunism in light of scheduled elections. A petition in Punjab met with greater consideration and temporally, a life that extended long past the elections. Although the Lahore High Court ordered that "no interference" was to be brooked "in the process of bring[ing] about democratic polity,"[8] the court's reasoning gave the petitioners ample opportunity to appeal the decision. The court held that the grounds for the 1988 dissolution were "so vague, general or non-existent that the orders are not sustainable in law." Although Chief Justice Abdul Shakarul Salam meant his diagnosis to sustain the electoral process, his words were later used to challenge the new government. The Chief Justice suggested that presidential discretion did not mean extending discretionary powers "on illusions, fancy or whim." He indirectly reminded General Zia's political heirs that Islamic government, too, presumed humility before its electorate.

The court dismissed arguments to justify dissolution, including incomplete efforts to Islamize the state, with rhetorical appeals to recent history:

> Who does not know what were the objects and purposes for which Pakistan was created? That it will be independent free democratic country in which the majority will be Muslims and they will be enabled to lead their lives in the best traditions of Islam. Have these objects and purposes been fulfilled? Has not the country been subjugated by Martial Law or remained under its threat for a large part of its life? Have we gone more astray from Islam than before? Can anybody in his right senses say that since objects and purposes of Pakistan have been fulfiled [*sic*], let it be dissolved?

7 *M.P. Bhandara v. The Federation of Islamic Republic of Pakistan through the Secretary, Ministry of Justice and Parliamentary Affairs*, Constitutional Petition No. 893 of 1988.
8 *Muhammad Sharif v. Federation of Pakistan*, PLD 1988 Lahore 725.

Its conclusion that "it would be the perversity of the highest order" was linked to its assessment that the petitioners were "not acting bona fide in pursuing the legal remedy," but were seeking political gains, an endeavor in which "they cannot hope to make the courts their instruments." According to Justice Sidhwa:

> Between a tussle of those that try to seek and secure naked powers, out of a system that lays down its parameters and limits, and those whose duty it is to ensure that such rules and limitations are observed, in which one or the other parties will succeed from time to time, the inviolable obligation of the seekers of the power is to abide by and respect the Constitution.

Phrased simply, in all political disputes the courts would side with the constitution.

The problem was, of course, which constitution? The majority opinion solved only the dissolution question and then only abstractly. Most troublesome to court and government alike, the petitioner's position on the division of presidential and ministerial powers – an irritant that was elevated into pitched political and legal battle between the Prime Minister and the President – became part of an argument concerning the validity of the caretaker cabinet formed after the dissolution. The summer cabinet functioned directly under Zia ul Haq and thus without a Prime Minister. The court advised that, without a Prime Minister, the validity of cabinet actions could be questioned legally and politically, for "questions relating to the Constitution cannot be refused on the ground that it may lead to consequences requiring political action."

Ruling that the dissolutions were unconstitutional, the Lahore Court nonetheless refused to reinstate the former assemblies, holding the prospect of elections to fulfill the ends of constitutional governance. The Supreme Court entertained appeals in October 1988 in *Haji Saifullah's case*.[9] Its judgment took the problems of indemnity in a more difficult direction, examining the staying power of the RCO, the nature of presidential and ministerial powers and the role of the judiciary in mediating political disputes.

The justices firmly supported limits on presidential powers. Although the Court believed that the President could act without advice from the Prime Minister, Justice Nasim Hasan Shah suggested that "the real question is as to whether the said discretion is as uncontrolled as it is claimed." (The Attorney General had argued that stipulated presidential powers, blessed by the Objectives Resolution, gave the president transcendent authority.) He concluded that the caretaker cabinet was incom-

[9] *Federation of Pakistan and others v. Haji Muhammad Saifullah Khan and others*, 1988 PSC 338.

plete without a Prime Minister, whose office was to be a check on presidential power. Noting that the National Assembly had vigorously criticized unlimited presidential powers before passing Zia ul Haq's constitutional amendments, he advised that presidential discretion concerning legislative dissolution "has to be exercised in terms of the words and spirit of the Constitutional provision" – and that such exercise must be objectively measurable.

More difficult, however, was granting relief. Like the High Court, the Supreme Court judged individual interest – reinstatement – subordinate to collective good – elections. Its view was procedural rather than substantive: the court did not understand the national interest to be a certain kind of political society but a path away from General Zia's polity. The judgment nonetheless raised serious questions about judicial interpretation and the use of political facts. The Attorney General argued that the suit raised political questions which were always, in Justice Shafiur Rahman's words, "outside the pale of judicial review." However, the court assumed a necessary connection between political consequences and constitutional interpretation, particularly when the constitution was violated. Political actions would be judged through a lens of constitutional compliance.

Every constitutional reading presupposes political ideas and political consequences. The High Court imputed a consequentialist reading of recent political history, a judgment with which the Supreme Court concurred. The courts selected political facts to suit their judgments and then assumed two unproven counterfactuals: that reinstating the assemblies would thwart the election process because assembly members would refuse to relinquish their seats or contest elections (tacitly assuming behavior similar to the 1950s Constituent Assembly); and that interrupting the election process was politically infeasible. Most signficantly, the Supreme Court felt compelled to guarantee elections, holding that "the bane of our society has been that elections have not been held with any degree of regularity after reasonable intervals."[10] It therefore made the announced election dates a binding part of its judgment, although the consequences of non-compliance were not specified.

The times determined in no small measure the outcome of justice. In a sense, the courts validated the *status quo ante*: the dictator was dead, campaigns were in progress and popular sentiment strongly favored elected government. Yet, until the courts ruled, elections were to be held at the behest of an acting President and an appointed Chief of Army Staff

[10] Short order, *Federation of Pakistan and another v. Haji Muhammad Saifullah Khan and others*, 1988 PSC 315.

– each acting in his constitutional, but in some ways, personal capacities Had either objected to elections or experienced a change of heart, th entire process might be jeopardised. In *Benazir Bhutto's case* and *Ha Saifullah's case*, the courts were crucial in sanctioning the process o transition; and although the elections produced a PPP government, th Supreme Court bowed before no political party or personality, findin credence only in a written, if somewhat mutilated, constitution. Althoug these cases can be read as a victory for elections, in a more importan sense they were a public triumph for the idea of constitutionalism, n matter how weak the constitution.

### *Constitutional powers*

The benign effects of *Haji Saifullah's case* were muted by their interpreta tion by the government. Attorney General Yahya Bakhtiar and Prim Minister Benazir Bhutto took the court's judgment to mean that action taken by the caretaker cabinet – including judicial appointments mad after the elections but before the new government took office – wer invalid. In March 1989 the government abruptly issued a press notic suspending the appointment of judges made in the caretaker period. Th court angrily refused to grant relief – several members of the bench wer among those purportedly suspended – and instructed the government t delete its order.[11] The government pursued its course with unexpecte belligerence toward the court and asked that three judges affected by th press notice be removed from consideration of the issues involved.[12] Wit *Snelson's case* an unarticulated background presence, Justice Shafiu Rahman objected to the government's order and chastized the govern ment's stubborn pursuit of a goal that "defeats the very object . . . tha justice should not only be done but should manifestly and undoubtabl appear to be done."[13] As the PPP reacquired its earlier reputation fo meddling with the justice system, the court dismissed the petition.

In a separate opinion, Justice Afzal Zullah suggested that the require ments for judicial appointment, particularly the need for ministeria advice, were contestable.[14] These cases thus returned the court to issue

11 *Muhammad Akram Sheikh, Advocate v. Federation of Pakistan and others*, PLD 198 Supreme Court 229.

12 *Federation of Pakistan v. Muhammad Akram Shaikh* and *Haji Muhammad Saifullah Federation of Pakistan*, PLD 1989 Supreme Court 690.

13 Abdul Jabber Khan, "President cannot appoint Judges – Yahya," *Nation* 17 Novemb 1989, p. 1.

14 The question was compounded by a petition to require the government finally to separa the executive from the judiciary. Citing public interest concerns as well as the need assure fundamental rights, the Karachi High Court ordered that a plan be written an

with which it had been seized in 1954: the terms of governance after parliamentary dissolution, and the role of ministerial advice in government appointments. In 1954, the absence of a constitution gave the judicial debate a peculiar flavor that was temporarily managed, if not settled, with a new Constituent Assembly. In 1989, however, the problem was the constitution itself and the Prime Minister's attempts to assert powers amended and restricted by General Zia. Although these cases concerned past actions and appointments, Prime Minister Bhutto's attempt to replace the Chairman of the Joint Chiefs of Staff, contravened by President Ghulam Ishaq Khan, placed the problem of appointments squarely within the ambit of current presidential-ministerial rivalries.

These disputes remained in the courts. Shortly after the elections, attorney M.D. Tahir proposed that the Chief Justice should have been consulted before appointments were finalized during the caretaker period; disagreeing, the Lahore High Court dismissed his petition.[15] By the time the appeal reached the Supreme Court a year later, *Haji Saifullah's case* was completed, casting a different light on the original petition and expanding its scope. Through November and December 1989, the President and Prime Minister continued to fight publicly about their relative powers and the arenas in which they could be exercised. Additionally, the Punjab government opposed the PPP by supporting petitioners trying to strengthen presidential powers and engaged General Zia's Law Minister, Sharifuddin Pirzada, to argue for the provincial government. In an address to the nation while the case was pending in the Supreme Court, the President reasserted his powers as chief executive, a situation characterized by one commentator as a "peculiar constitutional conundrum."[16] Only the prospect that the Prime Minister might lose the protracted battle – leading to a new crisis of power and legitimacy – led the government to withdraw its case.

The end of *M.D.Tahir's case* – which required excising a paragraph of the Lahore judgment, dismissing the appeal and requiring the President and Prime Minister to enter "mutual discussions" on points of conflict – did not solve the overarching problems facing the government. It was still

implemented. *Sharaf Faridi and three others v. The Federation of the Islamic Republic of Pakistan through Prime Minister of Pakistan and another*, PLD 1989 Karachi 404. Additional writ petitions on the same subject were entertained by the Lahore High Court in *Salman Taseer v. Federal Government*, *Khan Mohammed, Advocate v. Federation Government* and in the Peshawar High Court in *Mohammed Khalil Yusufzai, Advocate v. Federal Government*. "SC adjourns hearing of Fed Govt appeal," *Frontier Post* (Lahore) 24 November 1989.

15 *M.D. Tahir v. Federal Government and 12 others*, 1989 CLC Lahore 1369.

16 D. Shah Khan, "Constitutional enigma of who is more equal," *Muslim* 12 December 1989.

unclear how and where political disputes were to be settled, and indeed, what was to define a political, as opposed to legal or constitutional, conflict. Fearing that the court would become reactively and protectively politicized, some commentators pleaded that similar problems be removed from judicial consideration in favor of presidential-ministerial summitry.[17] Such proposals were bound to be halfway-houses during this politically uncertain time. Were conflicts about executive powers solved only through negotiation, resolving fundamental problems would rest with personalities subject to intense political pressures – neither a lasting nor a predictable means toward constitutional peace. Were such problems sent to the courts, the constitution would be left to the judiciary to rewrite, leaving the legislature – the body formally assigned such responsibilities – in the cold. Although the Prime Minister gave the judiciary a limited show of support, saying that "the Supreme Court is the proper forum to determine what the law is," her conclusion was simplistic.[18] Not only the formal separation of powers, already confused by the executive powers debate, but the principles of parliamentary democracy, would be neglected. The distance between elections and constitutional government had yet to be fully bridged.

Thus, when Prime Minister Benazir Bhutto announced in late 1989 that "we don't like this Constitution, but this is the Constitution we accept," acquiescence seemed far from her mind.[19] The weak PPP reinforced the constitution's disdain for party rule; the constitution in turn diminished the prospects for the ruling party to gain control of government. Fearful of belligerent opposition from provincial governments with which she seemed unable to compromise, Bhutto blurred the edges of constitutional obedience. What it meant to govern according to the constitution was as unclear as the distinction between law and politics. The Sind High Court turned its attention to these issues in a group of cases concerning the eighth constitutional amendment.

The *Eighth Amendment case* contested the validity of that amendment within the ambit of the 1973 Constitution.[20] As in *Mustafa Khar's case*, the petitioners contended that neither General Zia nor the National Assembly could legally amend the constitution beyond its original intent. Further complaints cited the PCO as abrogating the constitution, the

17 Makhdoom Ali Khan, "Litigating political questions," *Dawn* 17 November 1989, p. 1; Sabihuddin Babar, "Power Bench," *Newsline* December 1989, pp. 55–6.

18 Ahmed Rashid, "Interview with Prime Minister Benazir Bhutto: Opening too many fronts was a mistake," *Nation* 24 November 1989, p. 7.

19 Ibid.

20 Heard collectively in the Sind High Court as *Haji Ahmed v. Federation of Pakistan through Secretary, Ministry of Justice and Parliamentary Affairs and 88 others*, Constitutional Petitions D-76, 163, 168 of 1989.

1984 referendum and 1985 partyless elections as illegally constituted, and claimed that Zia ul Haq had stretched the doctrine of necessity beyond the limits recognizable in the concept of condonation. The Karachi Court dismissed the petitions but its hearings offered opportunities to broach more detailed constitutional investigations, including the definition of "the touchstone of necessity" and its validating reach; the powers of the executive and legislature in the martial law and mixed-government state; the definition of valid and competently made laws; the relationship between judicial powers and government validity; the status of fundamental rights in transition governance; and generally, the role of the courts in promoting political change.

Although ruling against the basic challenge, the High Court updated its reading of judicial powers and the judiciary's role in politics. Chief Justice Ajmal Mian proclaimed that the instrumental role of the 1985 National Assembly in lifting martial law militated against retrospectively declaring it illegal and thus refused to direct its actions invalid. He elevated to principle the legal doctrine of *de facto* authority to reassert not only Assembly actions, but General Zia's presidential powers at the time martial law was lifted. His reasoning inverted the relationship between legal principle and political effect: to further a transition to democracy and regularize constitutional authority meant accepting asserted power as legal and setting aside questions of legitimacy as irrelevant to the current task. He identified a starting point – in this case, 1985 – from which to reach a viable, governing goal. The Chief Justice reminded the petitioners that the 1988 elections were held on the basis of the same amended constitution they now eschewed. With a recognizable consequentialist flourish, he warned, "if I were to declare certain amended provisions of the Constitution as violative of the Objectives Resolution or of the basic structure of the Constitution, it would disturb the basis on which the present structure of the democracy is grounded. It will be difficult to demarcate a line, where to stop." The end of democracy was to justify the means to achieve it – political judgment cast as legal expedience, repeating a strategy employed by the superior courts throughout this and earlier transitions. The High Court would therefore say only that "the natural corollary" of holding the indemnity clause to be competently enacted was to "provide protective cover to the assailed constitutional amendment." Without excluding its own jurisdiction, the Karachi Court refused to declare the amendment unconstitutional on the basis of "higher ethical notions or of philosophical concepts of law or of the basic structure."

The Chief Justice recognized that this controversy embroiled constitutional jurisdiction in issues that were themselves politicized. Weakly distinguishing political cases and political questions by the accessibility of jurisdiction – "a political case may be subject to adjudication by the court but a sensitive political question may not be subject matter of adjudication" – he offered a parallel distinction:

> The challenge to the Eighth Amendment on the ground that it was not passed according to the Constitution is not a political question and, therefore, it can be adjudicated upon though the case relating to it may be termed as a political case. In contrast to it the question, what should be the balance of power inter se between the President and the Prime Minister is a sensitive political question of the nature which is not suited for adjudication by a Court but can be resolved by the Parliament or by the people.

His lesson: the courts cannot replace the constitution-making place of sovereign, elected bodies.

The High Court took up the issue of separate powers, the justiciability of constitutional amendment and limits to judicial powers. It resolved none. In a season of reasserted superior court authority, the Karachi decision moderated this exuberance. Because the *Eighth Amendment* judgment did not solve any of the issues it raised, and because the court refused to enter the debates it entertained, problems of constitutional structure and most seriously of conflicting political legitimacies, lingered. The Chief Justice articulated the negative consequences of deciding against the amendments but did not elaborate the equally negative consequences of deciding in favor of its constitutionality. The structure of General Zia's state was proving remarkably resistant to change. In the absence of a contrary decision by the Supreme Court, these problems were by default left to the politicians to unravel.

### *Dissolution again*

If the state seemed immovable, solving political problems seemed an impenetrable task for the federal government. Its weak relations with provincial governments were heightened in Sind, where despite a PPP majority the provincial government could not stop a deteriorating law and order situation made more violent by heightened political competition. Civil authority was ineffective, but neither Bhutto nor her Governor and Chief Minister could orchestrate an agreement with the military to provide adequate patrols and punishments without renewing the specter of martial law, particularly among Bhutto's Sindhi supporters. To combat dacoity, drug trafficking, kidnappings and political violence, the army demanded that superior court writ jurisdiction be suspended under the constitution so that emergency tribunals – under the military – could rule with despatch. Bhutto, however, having campaigned against military rule and military courts for ten years, wanted the army to patrol "in aid of civil power" without overtaking civil court functions, ultimately a weaker policy. The feud between the army and civilian government about the reach of military involvement in civil affairs had an ironic reach: violence after the 1977 elections had provoked Zulfikar Ali Bhutto to amend the 1973 Constitution to allow just such military patrols. This new dispute fueled popular apprehensions that the government – still preoccupied with the endless war in Afghanistan and renewed tensions with India about Punjab and Kashmir – was not in control, and that *rapprochement* between civil and military authority might be resolved in favor of the army.

The coincidence of perception and reality was never tested. Assuming that public fears were potent enough to withstand an assault against Bhutto in the name of preserving civilian government, the opposition was spurred to actions that skirted the boundaries of constitutionality. In August 1990, the President invoked his expanded powers under the revised constitution and dissolved the assemblies, reconstituted a caretaker government headed by parliamentary opposition leader Ghulam Mustafa Jatoi (once a senior PPP member and now leader of the small National People's Party), and called for new elections. The dissolution order claimed that political failures and weaknesses – including provincial disputes, urban violence, undocumented "contempt for the Constitution," and the alleged misuse of government funds – required that the PPP government be dissolved without recourse to a vote of no-confidence.[21] Citing rampant corruption and incompetence in the Bhutto government, the President also revived laws from the era of Mr. Bhutto that allowed him to convene special tribunals headed by High Court Justices[22] in order to air complaints of corrupt practices against the deposed government and potentially to disqualify its members from future electoral politics.

The PPP filed suit against the dissolutions. Protesting the "shoddy manner in which the N.W.F.P. Assembly was dissolved," the Peshawar High Court declared the dissolution of the Frontier Assembly invalid and

[21] One interpretation of these events suggested that the establishment prevented Bhutto from governing appropriately; see Maleeha Lodhi, "Why Benazir Bhutto Fell," *The News* 6 August 1991, p. 6.

[22] Holders of Representative Offices (Prevention of Misconduct) Act 1976 and Parliament and Provincial Assemblies (Disqualification for Membership) Act 1976. The revised version of these laws ensured the right to legal counsel, mandated punishment of up to ten years imprisonment and fines; additional regulations stated that should the accused fail to appear, "the special court shall be entitled to draw an adverse presumption." Thus, although the PPP preferred "ordinary courts under ordinary law," its leaders faced additional sanctions were they to boycott these tribunals.

ordered its restitution.[23] In a pointed concurrence, Acting Justice Qazi Muhammad Jamil took exception to suggestions that presidential powers could supersede ministerial authority. (The President then refused to confirm Justice Jamil's permanent appointment three days later, prompting one former NWFP Advocate-General to lament that "after this, nobody would be inspired to become a judge."[24]) Despite its principled language, the High Court decision was based on a technicality, and the Supreme Court quickly stayed the order in favor of announced October elections. A challenge to the dissolution in Lahore had a similar effect. The Lahore Court ruled the President's dissolution order validly passed.[25] Citing *Haji Saifullah's case*, it determined that by citing specific (if unproven) reasons for dissolution, the order was valid. Like rulings in earlier courts, the court took its direction from political winds and refused to examine the soundness of the President's arguments or the sufficiency of his claims. In fact, much of the order really concerned the inadequacies or biases of constitutional structure, as well as issues that deserved parliamentary debate or prior judicial scrutiny.[26] The shortness of time prevented an appeal, however, for elections took place within days of the initial hearing.

The caretaker government organized elections within the prescribed three month period. With remarkable deftness, it managed an overwhelming victory for the IJI coalition in the national and provincial assemblies, including the usual PPP stronghold in Sind. In fact, the margin of popular votes was quite narrow, but the Constitution's winner-take-all framework gave a huge majority to the IJI. The PPP objected to specific election results, and suggested that an identifiable number of seats were inappropriately won.[27] This conclusion was supported in part by

23 *Aftab Ahmad Khan Sherpao, President of Pakistan Peoples Party, N.W.F.P., v. The Governor, N.W.F.P.*, PLD 1990 Peshawar 192.

24 Cited in *Friday Times* 4–10 October 1990, p. 1.

25 *Khwaja Ahmad Tariq Rahim v. Federation of Pakistan and others*, PLD 1990 Lahore 505 short order. The Supreme Court appeal (*Khwaja Ahmad Tariq Rahim v. The Federation of Pakistan through Secretary, Ministry of Law and Parliamentary Affairs, Islamabad and another*, PLD 1992 Supreme Court 646) upheld the President's discretionary power to dissolve the National Assembly, saying "once the evil is identified, remedial and corrective measures within the constitutional framework must follow." At the same time Justice Rustam S. Sidhwa cautioned against grounding dissolution on trivial examples of misrule because "it would be conferring on the President and the Governors sweeping powers, almost creating some form of Constitutional autocracy."

26 According to one foreign observer, the caretaker government and army explicitly preferred a presidential to a parliamentary system, and devolved powers to localities to weaken political parties. David Housego, "Preparing the demise of Benazir Bhutto," *Financial Times* 21 August 1990.

27 The People's Party and its electoral alliance alleged massive vote-rigging and other election fraud that involved the President's office and the caretaker government. Se

some foreign observers who felt that the caretaker government exercised undue control over election structures and personnel.[28] The People's Party, while issuing complaints to the Election Commission, did not appeal the results in court.

The affirmed dissolution order (and presumably its restatement of presidential primacy and cooperation with the military) became, according to the new government's Law Minister,[29] a *grundnorm* for future governance. Technically, of course, this was true only insofar as the IJI's exercise of power became its own justification. In fact, it was the absence of an acknowledged *grundnorm* that made it possible for the army and the parliamentary opposition to organize the dissolution without encountering significant public opposition. The confusions of the Constitution, the PPP's shaky grasp of its own authority and the military's proximity to power all combined to create a political situation that gave the appearance of constitutional sanction.

Prime Minister Mian Nawaz Sharif, elevated from his prior position as the Muslim League's Chief Minister in Punjab to national leader of the IJI, came to power with a parliamentary majority that should have allowed him considerable legislative latitude. However, he also inherited the same flawed constitution that plagued his predecessor. Although hidden at first beneath seeming agreement between the President and the ruling coalition, the inherent conflict between presidential and ministerial powers resurfaced within his first year in office, and was later raised to pitched battle and ultimately another dissolution in the spring of 1993. First, however, the field of contest was the courts.

## Surviving dissolution

Although the 1990 transition survived a change in leadership, the same political problems that occupied the Zia, Junejo and Bhutto governments now confronted Nawaz Sharif: strident ethnic disputes and conflicts about sovereignty and rights; the disposition of scarce resources in the absence of a unifying political and economic ideology; the feared instabi-

People's Democratic Alliance, *How an Election was Stolen: PDA White Paper on Elections 1990* (Islamabad 1991).

[28] Outside observers criticized the integrity of the election process. An American-sponsored group upheld the election results despite their criticisms of rights violations during the election period. See National Democratic Institute for International Affairs (USA), *The October 1990 Elections in Pakistan* (Washington DC, 1991). Others, including the Paris-based International Federation for Human Rights and a monitoring group sponsored by the South Asian Association for Regional Cooperation (SAARC), were more critical of specific practices.

[29] Statement by Syed Fakhr Imam in National Assembly, 1 January 1991.

lities of regional and global politics; the role of the military in a purportedly civilian state; and the inappropriateness of the constitution to problems of state. As a matter of policy, however, the government in its first year was unabashedly preoccupied with remaining in office, and interpreted this as a task apart from identifying and solving social woes, or even coming to a compromise with its small but strident PPP opposition. The Prime Minister followed Zia ul Haq's political script by trying to eliminate opposition through patronage or force; in Sind province, for example, IJI Chief Minister Jam Sadiq Ali (formerly a PPP colleague of Zulfikar Ali Bhutto's) embarked on a campaign throughout 1991 to eliminate the PPP from the political landscape, and allowed his political allies to terrorize those who criticized his policies. The number and kind of rights abuses documented during Nawaz Sharif's first year resembled those of prior military, not civilian governments.[30]

The authoritarian aspect of these transitions is one that the constitution sanctions if not encourages, as it has before, but that mass politics may finally find objectionable. Like the PPP before it, the IJI coalition confronted a devilish dilemma: to lean toward authoritarianism was to erode the civilian basis for its parliamentary rule; to commit itself fully to civilian, parliamentary government, meant a clash either with the army, backed by the confusing Constitution, or with the President, thus risking its tenure. Ultimately, the second route canceled prospects for fulfilling even the most limited promise of parliamentarianism: Nawaz Sharif survived the dissolution of Bhutto's government but his government risked dissolution the same way and for strikingly similar reasons. This vulnerability represents a profound political-constitutional problem that inhibits parliamentary rule: when Nawaz Sharif tried in early 1993 to marshall parliament to amend the eighth amendment – albeit tentatively and incompletely – he found political support for change mixed and suspicious of its intent. Indeed, his proposed revision – initiated after he, like Benazir Bhutto, wanted stronger powers of appointment, in this case after the death of the Chief of Army Staff in January 1993 – became a bargaining chip between the IJI and the PPP and between the PPP and the President. The attempted challenge to the President's power later cost the government its life.

The persistent imbalance between presidential and ministerial powers means that government continues to operate along two only partly compatible axes that together diminish parliamentary rule. The power of dissolution remained the President's certain trump, but is only the most

[30] See Human Rights Commission of Pakistan, *State of Human Rights in Pakistan 1990* (Lahore, 1991).

obvious structural impediment to democratic transition. As long as the President asserts his power by issuing ordinances on a vast range of issues – almost forty in 1991, far more since the 1990 dissolution – the National Assembly need not face tendentious governance problems that desperately require resolution. The strength and durability of an elected parliament cannot be tested unless it is wholly responsible for such decisions. In its short life, the IJI parliament accomplished as little as its PPP predecessor while the President, with the army's apparent acquiesence, continued to anchor the state. Ghulam Ishaq's attempted dissolution of Nawaz Sharif's government dramatically reinforced the weakness of the state – not only by superimposing presidential power over ministerial prerogative, but by using the lure of future powers to divide Pakistan's many political oppositions. His clear intention was accompanied by the unabashed political ambitions of others: the President's partner in his attempt to dismiss the IJI government was Bhutto's People's Party, while Nawaz Sharif, like his predecessor, was sent packing to the courts. (The only difference was that Ghulam Ishaq lost this second round – technically, when the Supreme Court restored the IJI government, and politically when he, as well as Nawaz Sharif, was forced to resign a few months later.) Not only does this configuration of power dilute political authority and by default strengthen the military's role, it inevitably creates further tensions in the society and, unless quieted by ever-increasing demands for patronage that reinforce a neo-feudal state, in the assemblies as well. Under such conditions, politics cannot help but be degraded.

The events of early 1993 reinforce this diagnosis. Although Ghulam Ishaq Khan failed formally to dissolve Nawaz Sharif's government, he did succeed in highlighting the power vacuum and venomous politics that the constitution both encouraged and allowed. After months of disputes that began over the appointment of a new army chief in January, the President dissolved Sharif's government. He assumed that the courts would follow their past pattern by condemning the idea of dissolution but allowing the fact to stand. The Supreme Court, however, appropriated the case in original jurisdiction (which limited appeals) and then decided against the President – building its argument on the logic but not the results of its prior dissolution judgments, and citing the President for his "incorrect appreciation of the role assigned to him."[31] When Nawaz Sharif resumed office, however, he found himself combatting political forces allied with the President, resulting in a stalemate that was resolved

[31] *Mian Muhammad Nawaz Sharif v. President of Pakistan and others*, Constitutional Petition No. 8 of 1993.

by the army rather than the courts. The Chief of Army Staff, General Waheed, orchestrated an administrative restructuring rather than a *coup d'état*. In mid-July, he persuaded the People's Party to halt its street demonstrations against the IJI, forced both the President and the Prime Minister to resign, called for new elections, and appointed a caretaker Prime Minister to govern until those elections were held in October.

The force of the court's restoration order became merely heuristic: while it erased the chasm that had hitherto existed between its past reasoning and its judgments, the result it envisioned was negated by General Waheed's decisions. The caretaker government led by former World Bank official Moeenuddin Quereshi quickly made plain its contempt for the policies it inherited – all resulting from the same misappropriations of power that the court identified and the subsequent corruption that had come to define the state. Its efforts to reform the economy and restore a semblance of the rule of law underscored both the opportunities available to Pakistan and the deep problems endowed by its governments.[32] The nexus between the inequitable constitution and the institutions that supported it, and political avarice and resulting anarchies, were made clearest to Pakistanis on the eve of elections that nonetheless returned to office many of the same politicians who had for so long helped to taint the integrity of the state.

### *Politics*

Although his government did not fully confront the constitution's inadequacies until its abrupt dismissal and rapid reinstatement in 1993, during his first term Prime Minister Nawaz Sharif took up two issues that underscored how tightly the political and constitutional spheres are bound to each other, and how directly they affect transitional governance. First, to fulfill campaign promises to the ulema, the National Assembly passed the Enforcement of Shariah Bill in May 1991, a version of a bill that had been passed by the IJI controlled Senate (with little PPP comment) the year before.[33] The bill, intended to ensure the continuing process of bringing civil law into conformity with Islamic injunctions, functions as a piece of enabling legislation, and its provisions are open-ended to allow considerable latitude for implementing laws. Its full

32 For an analysis of the contradictions of caretaker rule, see Paula R. Newberg, "Dateline Islamabad: Bhutto's Back," *Foreign Policy*, No. 95, Summer 1994: 161–74.

33 One commentator called it "unconstitutional in its more important provisions and inconsequential in others," while another cited its internal inconsistencies. Anwar H. Syed, *Nation* 4 July 1991, and Justice (Retd.) Gul Muhammad Khan, *Nation* 4 August 1991.

meaning, therefore, is not apparent. The same interpretive and sectarian difficulties that prevented the passage of such a law for so long have not been solved in this version, but have been temporarily bypassed.[34] If symbol is to triumph over substance, however, the message is skewed. Rather than heralding an era of Islamic governance, the lessons that can be drawn from this bill are as contradictory as its content may prove to be: that political promises are kept only to select, influential groups; that legislative compromise can be orchestrated only with proven political allies – power-dealing rather than power-sharing; and that truly divisive social issues will not be admitted for parliamentary debate.

The Shariah Bill undercuts the authority of the civil courts and may limit them more in the future. The superior courts are responsible in the first instance to the constitution; the Shariah Bill, however, holds the prospect of lessening the legal status of the constitution and diminishing the authority of the justices to interpret its reach. Institutionally, an intermittant process of surrounding the superior courts and insulating Islamic injunction from civilian purview has continued for some time: various incarnations of Islamic advisory councils and shariah courts and benches had already created inroads into the scope and functioning of civil law and reorchestrated relationships between civil and Islamic laws. Until the passage of the 1991 bill, however, the courts had managed, albeit somewhat inconsistently, to retain most of their authority and thus maintain the supremacy of secular law and civil rights protections. The new bill creates the possibility of a vastly altered legal framework that undercuts accustomed jurisprudence and that most judges are not trained to handle.

These changes are difficult to assess in absolute terms. In the absence of thorough parliamentary debate and consensus about the legal and political foundations of the state, however, they highlight acute problems for which neither statutory nor constitutional law provides adequate guidance. Although the Prime Minister's office proudly proclaimed that the forty-five-year debate about national ideology and the Islamic state was now resolved,[35] its passage bespoke far more dissent than unanimity. *De*

[34] According to one constitutional lawyer, the Prime Minister would be unlikely to control the process of Islamizing the country once the ulema took advantage of the bill's open-ended language. See Makhdoom Ali Khan, "Paying the Bill," *Herald* June 1991, pp. 26–28. The problems of defining the Islamic element in Pakistani constitutionalism were rehearsed in *Mirza Khurshid Ahmad and another v. Government of Punjab and others*, PLD 1992 Lahore 1, and *Nasir Ahmad and another v. The State*, PLJ 1992 Cr.C (Lahore) 427, in which the Ahmadiyya community once again contested restrictions on their community's practices as violating fundamental rights.

[35] Hussain Haqqani, Press Assistant to the Prime Minister, cited in a Pakistan Press Institute report published in *Nation* 5 May 1991.

*jure*, the bill is to test civil law conformity with religious injunctions; *de facto*, it appears to function as an informal theory of the state, but its procedural inadequacies challenge this notion. By grafting legislation based on one set of norms to a constitution based on others – even more confusing when the Objectives Resolution is added to the constitutional mix – government has created jurisdictional and ideological contradictions for the judiciary. Whether the nature of governance has changed, or only some of its rules, is not clear from parliament's actions; although the burden of discovering the difference might normally lie with the courts, their freedom to do so is constrained by the bill itself.

The IJI's parliamentary majority disguised serious divisions within the coalition that reflected divisions within society. Intricate problems of sectarian practice and minority beliefs have not been fully explicated in law. Their often violent persistence in the society – all the more visible after a series of political-sectarian assassinations in recent years that form part of a "menace of intolerance"[36] – points to tricky but untutored problems for judicial scrutiny. Women's rights and minority rights, already threatened by earlier laws, can be jeopardised further under the aegis of this bill without an understanding of alternate protections; the scope of fundamental rights protections may be limited for the purposes of interpreting statute law; press freedoms can be constrained under its expanded definition of defamation.[37] Finally, in the absence of judicial autonomy and parliamentary sovereignty, future legal and social conflicts seem more likely to be settled by dictate than democratic process. Without other constraints on his powers, the President's hand is likely to be strengthened, in practice if not by law, well beyond the boundaries envisioned by either the original 1973 Constitution or even General Zia's constitutional structure, in turn threatening the future of parliamentary government. The links between procedural and substantive rights are drawn all the more clearly by their potential violation.

The second constitutional question that the Prime Minister brought to the fore was the authority for identifying and punishing those who violate law and order. In July 1991, with virtually no notice to parliament, he submitted for a vote a constitutional amendment designed to increase his emergency powers and diminish civil court powers in this arena. The problem of confronting civil emergency was not necessarily constitutional; Pakistan has laws aplenty to handle such problems, should government choose to enforce them. The complex political situation surrounding this issue – dramatically illustrated by the concurrent iss-

36 Karrar Husain, "Religious intolerance in Pakistani context," *HRCP Quarterly Newsletter* July 1991.

37 Asma Jehangir, "On the Offensive," *Herald* June 1991, pp. 29–30.

uance of several related presidential ordinances[38] – indicated that the Prime Minister's first interest was to provide for himself emergency powers equal to those allowed to the President.

In addition to resurrecting the intractable contest between presidential and ministerial powers, the amendment also compounded continuing debates about the definition of emergency powers. The vague wording of the amendment can increase the Prime Minister's powers beyond those explicitly contemplated in the amendment; similarly, limits on civil court powers and justiciability can be redrawn as the definition of emergency is incrementally broadened. Like the Shariah Bill, the twelfth amendment was written to suit the incumbent's will.

The Prime Minister thus heightened the stakes in the presidential–ministerial debate and also changed its terms. From the 1950s onward, conflicts between heads of state and government were represented by their parliamentary protagonists – however optimistically – as conflicts between representative and dictatorial politics, and between parliamentary and presidential or vice-regal government. The current constitution, however, paves the way for certain competition between executives and pretenders, thereby formally confusing the meaning of parliamentary rule. The manner of the amendment's passage confirms this interpretation. The text was discussed only in party conference – even that step was justified as an expansion of intra-party democracy by its members – and parliamentary debate was simply disallowed. Written copies were not distributed until voting began and the Speaker of the National Assembly refused PPP members and IJI dissidents the opportunity to speak. By eliminating minority voice, parliament was transformed into a rubber stamp typical of autocratic rather than democratic states, and the parliamentary sovereignty sought by the Prime Minister was significantly diminshed. To try to undercut the President by duplicating authoritarian powers risks society's freedoms and the state's flexibility by extending constitutional weaknesses; to add this twelfth amendment broadens the reach of the eighth amendment without confronting its fundamental jurisdictional dispute.

[38] Including the Terrorist Affected Areas (Special Courts) Ordinance (No. XXIV of 1991) and the Speedy Courts for Speedy Trial Ordinance (No. XXV of 1991). The first ordinance grants extraordinary powers to the police and civil armed forces; it empowers special courts (which can sit *in camera*) in areas determined by the President, without consultation, to require such measures. Similar provisions for special courts are embodied in the second ordinance. Special courts are also mandated by the 1976 Criminal Law Amendment Act and the Suppression of Terrorist Activities Act. On the use of anti-terrorist laws to prosecute alleged criminals as part of a campaign of political harassment, see *State v. Syed Qaim Ali Shah*, PLJ 1992 SC 625. On the use of the Special Courts of Speedy Trials Act (XV of 1987), see *Muhammad Nazir alias Pappu v. The State*,

The amendment is a symptom of the strictures placed on parliament, the starkly constrained political choices presented to those laboring under it, and the potential havoc it can wreak in the polity. The first draft proposed providing emergency powers to civil forces without formally declaring an emergency and suspending judicial writ powers – the same kinds of policies that Justice Cornelius's court tried to forestall twenty-five years ago. Benazir Bhutto discovered to her peril in 1989 that the army considered writ authority a critical obstacle for establishing law and order, while the PPP considered it a crucial guarantor of political rights. The IJI coalition took the army's position on this issue but discovered that some of its own members were reluctant to suspend this rights protection; a strategy meant to overwhelm the PPP opposition (and potentially threaten its members, particularly in Sind, once the amendment was passed) created fissures within the coalition itself. Even in its weakened form, the amendment is an unwieldy appendage that complicates the constitution, pressures the courts while lessening their status, and weakens party rule. Equally important, it helps to solidify the developing equations between governance and emergency, and between politics and crisis.[39]

Nawaz Sharif's government and its political forebears, however, took the lead in violating rights in the name of state security and thus in skewing the legal order to require obedience to imperatives defined by the ruling elite. The responsibility for the character of violent social schism, if not for every action pursuant to it, lies with those who want to establish political control by fashioning a new version of civil praetorianism. Government failures – not only to see how closely political contest is tied to civil unhappiness, but also where criminals part company with political opponents – are compounded by reducing the process of governance to seizing control rather than developing the state. This strategy is self-destructive. While the police try to ford the streams of political alliances and selective illegality, equally harsh incursions into public safety are allowed to continue, so that criminality is determined by the identity of perpetrators rather than the nature of the crime. The denial of fundamental rights weakens rather than strengthens government and each time government falls, its members look for protection to the same courts whose powers they have tried to curtail.

The events of the post-Zia period have thus been deeply influenced by

PLD 1992 Lahore 258. See also Ordinance XVI of 1992, amendment to Code of Criminal Procedure 1898 (Act V of 1898).

39 See I.A. Rehman, "Sense and nonsense about heinous crimes: order through police terror?" *Frontier Post* 1–5 August 1991.

opportunities to thwart democratic transition made available by a constitutional construction oriented toward the executive and away from parliaments and courts, and at the same time, by the virtual necessity of appealing to courts to right the wrongs of executives. Pakistan faced similar dichotomies of rule from its beginning: tensions between those who execute policy and those who judge it, elected bodies more concerned with self-interest than with participatory government and representative rule, ambivalence about the mosaic of nationalities and minorities that belong to the society but increasingly not to the state, and confusion about political ideologies that take on the colors but not the content of constitutional governance. Their cumulative effects become more damaging with passing decades. The social consequences of constitutional inadequacy and bias have become more brutal and the division between state and society more graphic. Constitutional law and the judiciary's role as its guarantor are more contested and contestable than they have been in the past, and violations of judicial autonomy and constitutional supremacy are far harder to correct. Those holding power find it useful to amend the constitution, promulgate laws under the guise of participatory politics, and retain control over state institutions; when these mechanisms finally fail to work, however, then this constitution may too become a victim of politics. The disjunctions between constitution, government and politics illuminate Aristotle's distinction between right and wrong constitutions and, at the least, argue for urgent constitutional revision.

### *Courts*

The road from imposed to elected government was neither straight nor direct. Apart from specific problems of constitutional interpretation, including the powers and functions of the executive, the transition period between 1985 and 1991 helped to focus recurring, deeply rooted problems in the polity. Crucially, early judicial cases reformulated questions about the role of the superior courts in parliamentary democracy.

In their separate opinions in *M.D. Tahir's* appeal, two justices highlighted their discomfort with the case's attenuation, particularly uncertainty about the status of judicial appointments and actions taken by those judges, and questions about judicial responsibilities in such cases. Justice Zafar Hussain Mirza questioned whether "consent of parties, or adjusting the controversy according to a consensus" was an appropriate reason for the court to withhold judgment; Justice Abdul Qadir Shaikh referred more generally to the court's "primary and sacred function" to resolve constitutional controversies.[40] Both views imply specific political and analytical understandings from the courts: first, that they take their cues from the constitutional questions posed and not the parties posing them, and then seek resolution rather than temporary measures to bypass uncomfortable political situations; second, that they assume that fundamental constitutional disputes will resurface, and that efforts to elude them are fruitless.

Both justices were undoubtedly correct in principle. Given the obstructive effects of the 1985 Constitution, it was probably impossible, and probably ill-advised, for the superior judiciary to ignore the political environment that produced a constitution, or the climate in which it is exercised. The weaknesses and strengths of governments and oppositions in the post-martial law period betray confusions and equivocations about the nature and limits of parliamentary rule. All sides may require judicial intervention to clarify their powers, establish their political boundaries and orchestrate a workable interpretation of the constitution. This will require, in turn, a more open interpretation of judicial powers than has ever existed in Pakistan, or that may be possible to reconcile with its current government.

Taking on such a role means the courts will encounter the dangers articulated by the Karachi court in the *Eighth Amendment case*. The case upheld the amendment only by judging the competence of its writing, not its political and legal effects. At the same time, the majority undertook indirectly to criticize the broad role which Supreme Court Chief Justice Haleem was establishing for the superior courts. The Karachi Court's caution is well-taken. The courts have been more accustomed to blinders on their powers than blank checks for their opinions. Their long-established practice of tempering their judgments is almost doctrinal: to exercise prudence is to prevent government dissatisfaction and thus to forestall limits on jurisdiction and power. Even were such care not the norm, the pitfalls of judicial activism during transition are clear enough, for Pakistan's constitutional politics are accompanied by other well-practiced political habits. If government finds the courts unsatisfactory, it can ignore their findings, change their personnel and lessen their weight among the triad of powers. This process is already in progress, and in the absence of a stronger articulation of judicial principle it is likely to continue. If the opposition objects to the government's use of political power or even to judicial decisions, it can submerge the courts in largely unresolvable constitutional litigation to make up for its weak parliamentary showing. Such are the lessons of history.

[40] Cited in Wajid Shamsul Hasan, "Role of judiciary in developing democracy," *Morning News Magazine* 15 December 1990.

Recent history – particularly in 1993, when history seemed to encircle itself more than once – also provides instruction about the relationships between constitutional structure, judicial power and political choice. Although the constitution tilts toward the executive rather than the courts, the transition has nonetheless been influenced by the judiciary's role and equally important, the role that the public believes it to have played. This issue affected the stability of Benazir Bhutto's government and indirectly helped to end it, and was at the root of Nawaz Sharif's troubled relationship with Ghulam Ishaq Khan. It remains a thorny problem, symbolizing critical institutional incompatibilities that can defeat democratic transition. Ultimately, it was underlined by the Supreme Court's judgment on the dissolution of the Sharif government, when – despite some public skepticism – the court rather unusually sought to correct its own precedents.

Although public attention was trained on the decision to restore the Sharif government, the court's jurisprudence was more interesting and important. Embedded in its ruling was not only a reversal of prior judgments, but admissions that earlier courts had not followed their own reasoning, and that the chasms between juristic rationales and rulings had been misguided and their results unfortunate. In a related judgment, the Peshawar High Court noted that a firmer basis was needed for judging whether the President's actions were correct than the 1990 decisions had offered.[41] The Supreme Court, led by Chief Justice Nasim Hasan Shah, provided a formal rethinking of the tortuous path from *Haji Saifullah's case* to the 1993 dissolution, saying that "on hindsight . . . after having found that the action of dissolution of the National Assembly was not sustainable in law, the Court . . . ought to have restored the National Assembly." More generally, he suggested that fundamental rights should be "construed in consonance with the changed conditions of the society and must be viewed and interpreted with a vision to the future." He thus offered the public reason to rethink as well the role that the courts had played in determining the course of recent politics, and the part they should play in reconstructing the polity.

The logics of constitutional jurisprudence were matched in the very social fabric that the court cited to support its new opinion. The ways that General Zia removed judicial autonomy affected the judiciary's sense of its independence once martial law was lifted. Although the suspension of superior court powers was the most obvious consequence of the 1981 PCO, equally pressing effects remain visible in the subordinate judiciary.

[41] *Nawabzada Mohsin Ali Khan, etc., v. Government of NWFP*, Writ Petition No. 395 of 1993.

During the 1980s, the government created deliberate confusions among the lower courts so that different codes for judgment – military, religious, civil – could be applied by the police and the military at their own discretion. Justice became a matter of bribery, corruption and contingency. Relationships among the police, the courts and local politicians – those who could either require or stave off corruption – became a crucial nexus in local government's relationships to national political parties and movements. Under the protection of the military, individual rights were violated to achieve government ends and the judiciary was employed to cement these policies. Such practices did not end when the Junejo government took office. By the end of the 1980s, in some localities – particularly Karachi and Hyderabad – the Bhutto government seemed simply to ignore rather than violate the rights of its opponents, hoping that local courts would comply with its wishes. This practice continued under the IJI but was accompanied by gruff political manipulation by the police, the army and civilian politicians alike, and resulted in another army action in Sind beginning in 1992. Such policy creates enemies from the ashes of friends, and becomes another step away from open politics and open courts. From these deteriorating standards it is only a short step to replacing a national justice system with personalized, retributive justice, and this happens in parts of Pakistan today.

Official inroads into the justice system are difficult to repair; conditions of political instability help government to justify limits on justiciable rights and on the courts. When political violence destroyed law and order in Sind in 1988 and 1989 the subordinate judiciary bore the brunt of this violence. When courts released prisoners on *habeas corpus* writs, judges were accused of accommodating political patrons; when prisoners were not released, judges were accused of accommodating military or opposition party desires. Either way, the courts were viewed as dependent rather than independent institutions, and judges were seen as participants in a corrupt political game rather than neutral arbiters. Once again, process and substance, and concept and strategy, converged on the heels of political dispute.

Government has built on similar public perceptions by representing legal order as a good that only it can restore, and then only through crisis management. This led to the reimposition of martial law in Sind in 1992–93.[42] But such policies have neither solved nor even neutralized the problems of political instability. Pakistanis witness growing local disrup-

[42] Although the courts freely granted writs of *habeas corpus* writs during this period, which led to a signficant number of releases of political prisoners, the army rearrested some of these detainees under the Army Act under charges of treason, which cannot be contested in civil courts. See *Rule of Law*, I, 3, Supp. 1 (Karachi: August 1991).

tions spanning a range of public discontents – sectarianism, class conflict, corruption (official and unofficial), party competition and generally, a diminished respect for government's capacity or, more indictingly, interest in solving the country's woes. Indeed, government's seeming incompetence in encircling divisive forces and reducing violence is viewed in some quarters as its excuse for accumulating greater central executive powers without public opposition.

Moreover, as Nawaz Sharif discovered, it is almost impossible to maintain public respect for law when government obeys it selectively and restricts the meaning of due process. Political schisms, given even partial reign, are always hard to control. While it is clear that not all laws are good laws – and certainly some of Pakistan's laws are unjust and unjustly applied – it is even clearer that the rule of law cannot be credibly enforced when only some of the people follow it some of the time; its invocation becomes ironic at best. When government does the violating, its claims that writ jurisdiction is intrusive and destabilizing are difficult to justify, particularly for citizens for whom writs become established protections against the state's own lawlessness.[43] Writ jurisdiction is also vital for the state to maintain its multiple roles as political representative, society's umpire, and the guarantor for a governable state.

Adding political insult to constitutional injury, President Ghulam Ishaq Khan implicated the judiciary in its efforts to eliminate opposition in the references filed against the former People's Party government – in the words of one commentator, "hammering a few more nails into the judiciary's coffin."[44] If success is measured by a high judicial conviction rate, then these efforts failed: some cases were dismissed by presiding judges for lack of evidence, most were postponed, and no references resulted in conviction. But if success is measured by the way these references weakened political parties through quasi-judicial maneuvers,

[43] The Lahore High Court reiterated the need for writ jurisdiction in a judgment in late 1991 that repeated a Supreme Court injunction written before the transition began: "Even the Writ Jurisdiction conferred upon the High Courts by the Constitution is discretionary. But the right to apply for a writ is certainly not a privilege. On the contrary, it is one of the most valuable rights that can be conferred upon a citizen." *Muhammad Siddiq Khan v. District Magistrate*, PLD 1992 Lahore 140 at 150, citing *Karamat Hussain and others v. Muhammad Zaman and others*, PLD 1987 Supreme Court 139.

[44] "Mockery of justice," *Friday Times* editorial 4–10 October 1990. Additionally, Benazir Bhutto's husband was incarcerated without bail for two years, suspected of being an accessory to criminal actions although the alleged main protagonists were released on bail; his imprisonment was extended by the promulgation of special ordinances that were finally withdrawn. On the issue of presumption of innocence, see *Asif Ali Zardari v. Special Judge (Suppression of Terrorist Activities) II, Karachi and 2 others*, PLD 1992 Karachi 430. Addressing the unfettered actions of law enforcement agencies, the Lahore High Court also reminded police that illegal detentions were "an offense." *Mst. Rehmat Bibi v. S.H.O. Police Station Samanabad, Lahore and another*, PLJ 1992 Lahore 193.

then this strategy worked, if only temporarily. Perhaps most important, however, the courts have been included in a government strategy that – even more than PRODA, PODO and EBDO of years gone by – pairs criminal indictment with political affiliation, mixes political purpose and civil law, and confuses the sources of official crime. When Justice Nabi Khan Junejo was killed in Karachi in 1991, therefore, many assumed that his role in hearing political cases under special rules was the ultimate if not the immediate cause of his death. Judges are at risk, and justice has been obstructed by the state that envelops its pursuit.

### *Justice*

In Pakistan's fifth decade, the dialectic between courts and parties – and between the formal organization of power and the practice of politics – assumes a complex form. The courts provide routes for resolving the problems of weak parties in an uncertain, disputatious polity. This is a heavy burden for the judiciary to bear and one with potentially paradoxical consequences. If superior courts successfully mediate problems that are best confronted by political parties, they can reinforce the weaknesses of party rule by giving important issues non-parliamentary resolution; government can then chose whether or not to follow their judgments. To demur from this task in order to strengthen parliamentary democracy can prove not only troublesome, but can also remove from the superior courts their reason for being – to air and resolve the problems of constitutional rule.[45] Pakistan's judiciary has inherited an uncomfortable institutional profile far higher than may be practicable, and certainly more contested than it might wish.

These conundra may be resolved by political imperatives rather than judicial imagination. If government satisfies its constituents, parliament may be able to alter the terms of constitutional rule within the mechanisms prescribed in the revived constitution. If the judiciary requires the government to rework the constitution, the parliament must be persuaded that court sanction is a useful vehicle to promote its own interests; then, the problems of separate powers might be resolved. Parliament must therefore also believe that clarifying the terms of power will enhance its authority: if, for example, presidential ordinances so weaken

[45] The judiciary's strict adherence to the trichotomy of powers was reiterated more forcefully as the transition proceeded on its rocky road: "The independence of judiciary is a most sacred pillar . . . and no inroad into the fundamental rights . . . can be made by the executive. . . The Legislature can regulate the exercise of such rights guaranteed in the Constitution but in light of the independence of the judiciary." *National Industrial Cooperative Credit Corporation Ltd. and another v. Province of Punjab/Government of Punjab, through Secretary, Cooperative Department and another*, PLD 1992 Lahore 462.

parliamentary sovereignty that individual reelection seems impossible in fair polls, or if the consequences of political violence are economic failures that alienate voters from the governing party and the party from its commercial supporters, then the assemblies and the courts might both gain, despite inevitable presidential objections. If all major parties determine that their collective interests will be served by dismantling those parts of the eighth amendment that strengthen presidential powers, then the distribution of constitutional authority and the stature of parliament may be enhanced.[46] But if civilian government neither alters the terms of power nor operates adequately within inherited constitutional structures, it too may lose office and the prospect of regaining it.

Having opted to retain the revised constitution, all post-martial law governments have tried simultaneously to maneuver within its strictures, exploit its weaknesses and evade its provisions. In the long term, these modes of political behavior are self-defeating – logically, practically, constitutionally – and sufficiently problematic to provoke Benazir Bhutto to base her choice for president, Sardar Farouk Khan Leghari, in part on his commitment to revise the eighth amendment. But every government has continued to adhere to an idea, if not the essence, of a constitution. Their dedication to a concept with many rhetorical, if few actual, champions speaks to a collective recognition that in the idea of constitutionalism, however indeterminate, lies a key to legitimacy and stability. Conceived only instrumentally, however, constitutionalism employs a language too vague and perhaps superfluous to the conduct of politics, particularly if its vocabulary is manipulated by those holding power only in order to retain it.

A constitution can endow government with political legitimacy only if that government already has a sure sense of its sources – when state and society share a political language, use it with the same sensibilities and accept and understand the consequences of its use. Political insecurity and occasional connivance have jeopardised such understandings and thus risked citizens, governments and the state itself. It is the judiciary's job to help explicate this language, articulate the accords they represent, and then interpret their possibilities – it is in fact the first purpose for which it is intended. For a transition to move from military to civilian rule, and hence toward democracy, the country requires an impartial and unimpaired judicial conscience and a clear sense of the place and predilections of civil society. It therefore also requires a legislative – indeed

[46] In January 1992 former PPP Attorney-General Yahya Bakhtiar tabled a constitutional amendment in the Senate to repeal parts of the constitution that were covered by the eighth amendment and revoke powers of the Shariah courts. See "Return to Democracy," *Viewpoint* editorial 23 January 1992, p. 5.

constitutional – foundation that ensures the judiciary an autonomous place in the state. Although the courts have helped define this process, a grounding has yet to be firmly established.

# 8 Judging the state

> The tyrannical ruler who is well-versed in power
> builds about himself a fortress made up of edicts;
> while falcon, sharp of claw and swift to seize,
> he takes for his counsellor the silly sparrow
> giving to tyranny its constitution and laws,
> a sightless man giving collyrium to the blind.
> What results from the laws and constitutions of kings?
> Fat lords of the manor, peasants lean as spindles!
>
> Muhammad Iqbal, "Divine Government"
> The Sphere of Mercury, *Javid-Nama*

> The judiciary cannot fight the dictators. We require strong political institutions which are lacking in the country.
>
> Justice Qazi Muhammad Jamil

In Pakistan's first decade, establishing good government meant refining received traditions: concepts of rights, representation and authority were reiterated in their untarnished, ideal forms for the new state. The exercise failed from its inception because its authors refused to understand that such concepts were meaningful only when applied consistent with the intended structure of power, and that a constitution autocratically conceived cannot be popularly legitimate or democratic. From its first decade, the country has therefore shouldered the burdens of constitutions unequal to the task of governing the Pakistani state. The 1950s Basic Principles committees comprehended the need to provide a principled grounding for the future constitution but did not accommodate its diverse sources and applications. The second Constituent Assembly shared these problems under the influence of the Governor General and the army, who were anxious to defuse challenges to their power. In the constitutional equation of the 1950s, neither an agreed goal nor a means to achieve it, two crucial variables for sustaining the state, was made manifest.

Justice Munir's court supported the Governor-General's intercession in the constitution-making process and then the military's intervention in politics. *Tamizuddin Khan's case* and the 1955 *Reference* reflect the visions and myopias of their time. By refusing to examine the national political structure and the constitutional requirements for political change, the Supreme Court helped to cement power relationships between the bureaucracy, army and the political classes, and thus undercut the very constitutional concepts it hoped to encourage. By declining to provide meaning to the concept of parity in the *Reference*, for example, the court laid a jurisprudential groundwork both for the 1958 *coup d'état* and the demise of the two-winged state in 1971. By insisting on strong central, executive power, the court helped to reinforce patterns of governance, party roles and provincial politics; it thus helped to restrict the scope for political change.

During the early 1960s, the superior courts had few opportunities to alter this thinking. Although the High Courts occasionally countermanded executive orders or echoed local interests against the center, the courts generally were forced into retreat. Justice Cornelius's Supreme Court agitated for a constitution and upon receiving an inadequate one, agitated for its improvement. With government determined to write law only to sustain its own power, however, judicial activism was only specific and piecemeal. In a decade that witnessed the fragmenting of the state, the courts neither objected nor acted to curb that disintegration: they took their language and philosophy from ideas of democratic governance that they thought the state was to have originally embodied, tempering their judgments with the government's interpretations of political imperatives. However, habitual dichotomies – the vice-regal and administrative state juxtaposed to those of the federal, participatory state – became confused in the public mind, in constitutional instruments and finally in judicial decisions. When the state began to collapse, the judiciary was immersed in ideals about constitutionalism that found little place in politics.

Only after Ayub Khan violated his constitution and the country was divided after brutal civil war did the courts begin to change their views of their purpose. Dismayed by the war and its indirect role in that process, the post-Yahya Khan judiciary initially tempered its respect for unbounded executive powers. Given the opportunity in *Ziaur Rahman's case* to influence directly the writing of the 1973 Constitution, the Supreme Court refrained, insisting instead that the doctrine of separate powers be respected to support an independent judiciary and popularly elected legislatures. Their incantations on the separation of powers did little to modify Prime Minister Zulfikar Ali Bhutto's abuses of authority under the 1973 Constitution, but their judgments in the constitution-drafting period reflected a new critical awareness of the judiciary's influence on state organization. The Supreme Court lamentably departed from this insight when it validated General Zia ul Haq's *coup d'état* but the superior courts tried to recover their ground after *Nusrat Bhutto's case*. The courts accurately assessed their power to articulate alternative political opinions, but they were too late. Post-*Nusrat Bhutto* decisions troubled the army sufficiently to provide the 1981 Provisional Constitutional Order, which nullified crucial judicial powers for the duration of martial law.

After martial law was lifted at the end of 1985 and popular rule with party-based elections returned in 1988, the courts combined idealism and pragmatism to untangle the post-martial law constitution and their own independence. Deciphering the legal ruse of indemnity and immunity demanded judicial imagination and care. Post-martial law judgments nevertheless resemble those of preceding decades – eschewing politics while judging it, moderating exhortative moralism with selective history, modifying their enthusiasm for judicial autonomy with caution derived from periods of enforced silence. These patterns of judgment embody strategies for retaining judicial independence based variously on theories of institutional organization, political philosophy and impulses for self-preservation. Each has lent context and focus to cases that have determined crucial political outcomes. While the courts have not always given expedience primacy of place, their opinions have always been sensitive to ways in which their decisions may influence their future capacities to act. To think this way is both to acknowledge and determine the judiciary's uncertain place in the political arrangement of the state.

The courts thus confront two worlds concurrently. Their role is to interpret the state's constitutive framework for the polity and to provide citizens with the opportunity to voice their opinions and redress their grievances – a responsibility in the first instance to the polity. Were the source of state sovereignty firmly based in the people, this role would be primarily hermeneutic, deciphering meaning from contexts of intent and effect. But because the polity has so often been divorced from the state, the judicial role has been more conflictual than judges would like or occasionally are willing to recognize. The meaning of constitutions, proto-constitutions and pseudo-constitutions has generally not been derived from popular sovereignty but variously from executive will, military intervention and the embedded interests of the state.

Jurisprudence therefore assumes intrinsically political meaning because it affects profoundly the dimensions and organization of political power. The Supreme Court's adherence to the doctrines of necessity and revolutionary legality testifies to the impact of legal reasoning on specific political events, and also to the contingency of judicial rulings. While the early court may have held sway against the state before new constitutional instruments were drafted, its subservience to the Governor-General and then to the military confirmed judicial hesitancies and fear for the courts' institutional lives. When the superior courts later challenged their own precedents, their primary audience was not the polity but the state, their subject not the constitution but the army.

The courts have added to this political mix by the content of their judgments. Even when their decisions have rested on technical grounds, the superior courts have often given their findings based on the merits of a case and have thus furthered their interpretive reach. Although this process can be construed as a gesture toward the public interest – taking on the political without calling it by name – it means that the courts assume a mantle of political authority that can inadvertently undermine popular efforts to confront the government of the day, or take on the state. However consonant these judgments might be with popular, anti-repressive forces, they may not always be at one with their long-range interests. Political climate and state structure thus serve to confuse the sources and ends of procedure and substance.

In such environments the judiciary is forced to become an intensely controversial institution in a state in which controversy is often proscribed and political scripts are written by the state. Judicial judgments that contradict these determinations challenge implicitly the sources and meaning of power. Moreover, if the state outlaws courts, it appears to acknowledge its own uncertain legitimacy. While courts can act as bridges between state and polity, they also reflect the state's distance from political society. Judges and executives therefore live in uneasy synchrony: the courts rule within boundaries established by the state, which in turn accepts rulings that are incremental and unthreatening. If the judiciary violates this unwritten patronage agreement, its jurisdiction is jeopardised; if the executive oversteps its extensive territory, court judgments expose the limits of his rule. Even when written constitutions establish institutional parameters, the judiciary remains the weaker partner. Its power lies in the absence of coercive capacities and in the polity's agreement to restrict its challenges to the state to the judicial realm. If civil society finds the judicial–executive relationship wanting – because court rulings do not support popular sentiment or because the executive ignores or restricts the court – its political choices lie in popular politics, which the state often does not sanction and in which courts do not participate.

Political power thus means many things. Power vested in the state is potentially and often actually coercive: state institutions can force civil society to conform to its plans because the state and not the polity controls military and economic resources. Civil institutions exist at the behest of such power and exercise their own authority because the state allows it. The resulting disproportions of economy and opportunity become part of the same state structure and thus all the more difficult to contest and remedy. Judicial power is the power of judgment, of open proceedings and accountable rulings. Although the courts are literally accountable to the state, which can close their doors, they can also choose to close them themselves – a choice they prefer not to take but which forms a backdrop to their most constrained deliberations. When the polity cannot fully choose the state, the courts offer a semblance of political participation by providing a forum for political debate. The force of their rulings will necessarily be limited, but they provide an institutional example of alternative political discourse and thus help to strengthen the role of civil society within the state.

## The metaphor of the state

The effects of judicial rulings have reinforced the state in fundamental ways, not only by tacitly supporting the government of the day but also by confirming the structure of the state. In Pakistan's jurisprudence, the concept of state structure indirectly illuminates the limits and possibilities of politics but is rarely discussed directly. This silence like many others is almost an interpretive method: the courts have approached the concept of the state circuitously, joining a curious admixture of theories and concepts to approximate its substance. Equally important, and in part because of this long habit, the courts have found it difficult to work with the concept of structure or to approach the problems of politics structurally. The courts substitute assumptions about political behavior for thorough analysis of constitutional structure, parsing philosophical concepts rather than analyzing enduring political forces. The flawed interpretive discourse of the early independence years still permeates judicial behavior and affects the way the state can be built.

### *Basic structure and judicial review*

The courts have found it difficult to judge the idea of constitutional structure or the related notion of basic state structure when it has been raised in constitutional cases. Their approaches to constitutional problems have changed, if only incrementally, as the state has evolved. The *Eighth Amendment case* reiterates concerns that have been raised in Pakistan's courts since the Bangladesh war, and far longer among its politicians. Does the separation and division of powers offer the key to state structure, or does that structure emerge from pre-constitutional consensus? Should constitutional directive principles reflect the state that might be, or the state that is: what relation should directive principles of policy bear to justiciable rights, and should policy principles themselves be justiciable?

These questions – the answers to which define principle, policy and process – almost paralyzed the first Constituent Assembly, caused major breaches between General Ayub Khan and his appointed Constitutional Commission, sharply divided legislators drafting the 1973 Constitution, and indirectly occupied General Zia ul Haq's constitution-revising exercise in 1985. They were given modern voice in *Ziaur Rahman's case*, when the courts faced the twin problems of state reorganization and political legitimacy. Choosing reticence over assertion, the courts did not take up the fundamental issues of structure that had already divided the state and that could be equally divisive in the future.

By the time the superior courts heard major cases under the 1973 Constitution, the Indian Supreme Court had ruled on similar questions in ways that Pakistan's courts found important but difficult to absorb in their own experience. In *Golak Nath's case* and *Kesavananda Bharati's case*,[1] the Indian Supreme Court reworked issues of constitutional structure and responsibility. Its rulings on legal standing to allow collective rights suits, on the relative constitutional status of directive principles and fundamental rights, and on legislative and judicial powers to amend and enforce constitutional guarantees for rights and social welfare were heard loudly, if not clearly, across the border. From the 1975 NAP *Reference* on, these decisions were cited by Pakistan government representatives and their challengers to address a vast array of constitutional issues. When the Supreme Court reviewed these cases, however, it reiterated its familiar version of the separate powers doctrine rather than extend the scope of its deliberations to specific structural considerations.[2] Each citation reflected the weaknesses in Pakistan's constitutional heritage and the judiciary's ambivalence toward the transformative capacities of constitutions.

In India, state policy directives clashed with fundamental rights guarantees over economic policy questions, in particular the state's right to redistribute property against individual rights to own and inherit prop-

[1] *I.C. Golak Nath v. Punjab*, AIR 1967 Supreme Court 1643 and *His Holiness Kesavananda Bharati Sripadagalvaru v. State of Kerala and another*, AIR 1973 Supreme Court 1561. These issues were reconsidered in *Minerva Mills Limited v. Union*, AIR 1980 Supreme Court 1789, in which the majority basically upheld *Kesavananda*. Early considerations had subordinated directive principles to fundamental rights (*State of Madras v. Champakam Dorairagan*, AIR 1951 Madras 120, Supreme Court 226); later cases tried to integrate both the substantive and procedural interpretations of these concepts. See K.C. Markandan, *Directive Principles in the Indian Constitution* (Bombay: Allied Publishers Ltd., 1966).

[2] See Justice Haleem's review of constitutional history in *Fauji Foundation and another v. Shamimur Rehman*, PLD 1983 Supreme Court 457, appealed from *Shamimur Rehman v. Government of Pakistan and others*, PLD 1980 Karachi 345. The judgment's rendering of recent political history, including the validation of martial law regulations, provided precedents for the *Eighth Amendment case*.

erty.[3] The Indian Supreme Court's first major judgment on the subject, *Golak Nath's case*, deemed fundamental rights immune to parliamentary amendment. While its ruling seemed at first glance to outlaw the revision or diminution of rights, in fact the court placed the definition and scope of rights in its own, and not the parliament's purview. Its denotative version of fundamental rights required judicial intercession to determine the strength of those rights. The court therefore offered a new view of parliament's legislative and constituent roles, and relations between parliamentary and judicial powers.[4] A contest about rights and policy was interpreted as a dispute about the separation of powers in which, for the moment, the judiciary matched itself with rights guarantees.

In *Kesavananda Bharati's case*, the Indian court choreographed a similar equation between policy principles and rights: through the medium of a basic structure doctrine, the court tried to ensure progressive policy while retaining judicial right to oversee parliament's interpretation of that policy. To provide flexibility in the name of sacrosanct constitutional principles, the *Kesavananda* court appropriated the power to determine not only the content of rights, but also what the basic structure of the constitution was, and thus how and when constitutional amendment could be enforced.[5] Asked what the basic structure of the constitution and the state was or should be, the justices could respond only in the general terms of republicanism, federalism and democracy; their judgment therefore gave the courts considerable power to reconsider basic structure issues. But *Kesavananda* offered two potentially contradictory premises: the need to allow constitutional and thus political change, and the inviolability of the constitution.[6] Whether or not a basic

[3] For an analysis of the *Kesavananda* court, see Rajeev Dhavan, *The Supreme Court of India and Parliamentary Sovereignty: A Critique of its Approach* (New Delhi: Sterling Publishers Pvt Ltd., 1976). See also K.K. Mathews, "Supreme Court and Policy Decisions," in *Three Lectures* (Lucknow: Eastern Book Company, 1983), pp. 1–23.

[4] See Upendra Baxi, "Some Reflections on the Nature of Constituent Power," in Rajeev Dhavan and Alice Jacob, eds., *The Indian Constitution: Trends and Issues* (Bombay: Tripathi Private Ltd., 1978), pp. 122–43; and Rajeev Dhavan, *The Indian Supreme Court and Politics* (Lucknow: Eastern Book Company, 1980).

[5] *Kesavananda* was unhappily received by all sides, and given force only by political events. While it was pending, parliament passed the 39th amendment to restrict superior court review of election disputes involving senior government officials. Raj Narain argued the amendment's invalidity because it violated the constitution's basic structure. To reject the doctrine would have been to uphold the amendment; *Kesavananda* gained legitimacy contextually rather than doctrinally. See S.P. Sathe, "Limitations on Constitutional Amendment: 'Basic Structure' Principle Re-examined," in Dhavan and Jacob, *Indian Constitution*, pp. 179–191.

[6] Similar issues have been raised in a basic structure case in Bangladesh. In *Anwar Hossain Chowdhury v. Bangladesh and Ors, et al.* (1989 BLD [Spl]1), Justice Kamaluddin Hossain used the precedent of *Fazlul Quader Chowdhury's case* to reverse a constitutional amendment which would have restructured the country's judiciary.

structure could be identified, state actions were both limited and given meaning by the judiciary.

These Indian cases discussed constitutional structure in terms of parliamentary sovereignty and judicial powers, and have been interpreted as conflicts between executive-oriented authoritarianism and court-oriented liberalism.[7] In Pakistan, liberalism and authoritarianism also framed judgments about state policy, but were far closer in concept and practice. From Justice Munir onward, many (though certainly not all) superior court judges viewed them as mutually supportive political principles and therefore tried to match the vice-regal state to quite discordant representative principles. While the Indian cases discussed constitutional structure in terms of parliamentary sovereignty and judicial powers, in Pakistan these concerns have been translated into familiar problems: the breadth of executive powers, the nature of rights, the ideological cum religious basis of the state and prospects for representative, democratic governance. With the accumulated history of civil unrest and social tensions, the language of law has become more deeply ingrained in formulating these problems, if not resolving them. In their 1953 report on the Lahore anti-Ahmadiya riots, Justices Munir and Kayani could speak with some authority of the primacy of secular, civil law in healing the cleavages among parties and religious groups. Democracy was the process of solving disputes and its secular vision was the goal that right-thinking citizens would approve. Justice Shahabuddin echoed similar sentiments in his 1960 Constitution Commission Report, and they reappeared in Justice Hamoodur Rahman's judgments on the Yahya Khan interregnum.

But Justice Hamoodur Rahman added a new twist to the constitutional question of state ideology. His judgments in *Asma Jilani's case* and *Ziaur Rahman's case* reopened the issue of ideology precisely by trying to remove the content of the *grundnorm* from the inconclusive analyses with which the courts had been seized since Justice Munir's *Dosso* decision. Were the *grundnorm* identified as the Objectives Resolution and, as later cases determined, were the resolution given operational force by incorporating it into the constitution, then the state might be said to have a justiciably identifiable ideology.[8] This question, which occupied the Basic

[7] See Lloyd I. Rudolph and Susanne Hoeber Rudolph, *In Pursuit of Lakshmi: The Political Economy of the Indian State* (Chicago: University of Chicago Press, 1987), p. 109.

[8] Confusion about moral and political consensus has affected judicial methodology. Kelsenian positivism was an attractive choice for Justice Munir precisely because it imputed no moral or political evaluation; indeed, it gave the revolutionary legality-efficacy doctrine the appearance of moral choice without its substance. Justice Munir would thus read Kelsen's statement that "the function of a constitution is the grounding of validity" in a functional, rather than moral context. Justice Hamoodur Rahman, however, eschewed both positivism and its revolutionary legality consequences when civil society felt the need

Principles committees with only the most tenuous resolution between secularists and Islamicists, was not resolved in the 1973 Constitution. After bloody inter-provincial war, and with the concept of federation still disputed among West Pakistan's provinces, the Assembly was ill-prepared to do battle on ideological dimensions of secularism. The Bhutto government indirectly and expediently endorsed the notion of an Objectives Resolution-*grundnorm* in its 1975 *Reference* against Khan Abdul Wali Khan in order to locate a standard against which the offending NAP could be indicted and sentenced; Justice Hamoodur Rahman concurred.

Thirty years of civil and military authoritarianism gave General Zia ul Haq's efforts in the 1980s to reorganize the state a different tone. Dissatisfactions with provincial organization and the whole texture of the secular-sacred ideology problem reemerged when he convened the Ansari Commission in 1983. Although the commission's mandate to determine an Islamic consultative system of government predetermined its results, its members viewed their deliberations as one step in General Zia ul Haq's promised transition to civilian rule. The commission was "to provide the foundations of a political structure which is in consonance with the injunctions of the Quran and the Sunnah, Islamic values and traditions, requirements of the modern age, and the conditions obtaining in the country ... as would facilitate a definite progress in the direction of evolution of an Islamic democratic system in the country."[9] It was instructed to organize its discussions primarily around constitutional debates undertaken by the committees of ulema from 1949 to 1953. The fundamental nature of the proposed governance shifts, and their proposed application without public consultation or consent, seemed to bother only Justice Muhammad Gul, whose dissent declared the scope of the commission's deliberations beyond the boundaries allowed in *Nusrat Bhutto's case*, but who nevertheless accepted the promised transitional role of its recommendations. The commission therefore provided an institutional springboard from which General Zia was able to incorporate the Objectives Resolution as operative section 2-A of the revived constitution, an action later covered by the eighth amendment. Justice Hamoodur Rahman's hypothetical was thus made concrete by executive fiat rather than popular vote. The Objectives Resolution now resembles a constitutional preamble but offers scant direction for the state.

to reexamine the political *cum* ideological structure of the state. Kelsen's statement in "The Function of a Constitution," in Richard Tur and Willliam Twining, eds., *Essays on Kelsen* (Oxford: Clarendon Press, 1986), pp. 109–19.

9 *Report on Form of Governance*, Commission chaired by Muhammad Zafar Ahmad Ansari, 4 August 1983.

The Resolution's new constitutional role and the higher profile of Shariah law and the Federal Shariat Court has painted the structure of justice in a new and controversial color. The Shariat Court has assumed some powers originally vested in the high courts; for example, under the criminal provisions of the Hudood ordinances it acts as a court of appeal whose decisions are binding on all lower courts. Moreover, Shariat Court justices hold office at the discretion of the President rather than under the constitutionally fixed contract provisions that apply to civil court judges.

Perhaps most important, new Islamic laws oblige the courts to intercede in the economic and political arrangement of the state. The Federal Shariat Court was already in the business of checking the conformity of the civil laws to the Quran and Sunnah, although mechanisms to correct non-compliance are contested and incomplete. In some instances the court has issued judgments that contradict government policy; for example, it has ruled *riba* (interest) to be un-Islamic, despite former Prime Minister Nawaz Sharif's adherence to the practice.[10] The Shariah bench of the Supreme Court is required to review legislative compliance with the broad and vague provisions of the Objectives Resolution. In other words, the courts must undertake Islamization without benefit of legislative opinion, even while an elected parliament is in office. This problem has been highlighted in the 1991 Shariah Bill requirement that the judiciary act as final authority in interpreting Shariah law. Not only does this potentially diminish the scope of fundamental rights protections, but in effect, it gives to court rulings the force of law in arenas where parliament has not legislated and can thus place the courts at odds with the legislature. Moreover, the final version of the Shariah bill passed by the National Assembly in 1991 can be interpreted to limit the scope of fundamental rights protections in statute law. The concept of separate powers, historically dear to the superior courts, was thus undermined by the eighth amendment.

As a result, the courts now pursue an unsought, state-directed activism.[11] The difficulties in this mandate became clear once civilian govern-

[10] See *Dr. Mahmood-ur-Rahman Faisal and others v. Secretary, Ministry of Law, Justice and Parliamentary Affairs, Government of Pakistan*, PLD 1992 FSC 1, in which it was averred, in reference to *Bachal Memon's case*, that the Federal Shariat Court could strike down a law as repugnant to Islamic injunctions "whether promulgated before, during or after imposition of Martial Law as provided by Art. 270-A [the eighth amendment]." See *Mst. Sakina Bibi v. Federation of Pakistan*, *PLJ* 1992 Lahore 285, which argues that the function of Article 2-A "is quite different and distinct from those entrusted to Federal Shariat Court and Council of Islamic Ideology," and that the High Court can grant relief under Article 2-A.

[11] In the Supreme Court's judgment concerning the dissolution of Benazir Bhutto's government, Justice Sajjad Ali Shah suggested that there was now a "general trend which encourages superior Courts in the advanced countries of the world to indulge in judicial

ment was restored. Using the doctrinal preparation and experience of Indian class action cases, Justice Haleem's court entertained a suit on behalf of bonded laborers in 1989 to extend civil rights protections in the economic sphere.[12] One month later, however, its Shariah bench upheld a Federal Shariah Court ruling that found that the 1972 and 1977 land reform laws did not conform to Islamic injunctions.[13] The bonded laborer judgment sought to identify methods for pursuing rights protections in the context of a progressive state structure; in the land tenure judgment, however, the court required the government to overturn competently passed laws consistent with the policy principles it supported in the class action suit. Constitutional fundamental rights and judicial interpretations of Islamic codes clashed here: the court established a social contract between labor and the state in the bonded labor decision that it destroyed in its land tenure decision.

In the economic policy cases and the *Eighth Amendment case* the courts only discussed the validity of constitutional review, but future discussions about the separation of powers will inevitably determine the substance of state policy. The Supreme Court required the federal government to reformulate the land tenure laws by March 1990; disregarding the deadline, the government instead instructed provincial governments to implement the 1972 and 1977 laws, calling into question federal policy to follow judicial decisions.[14] While the court acts as guarantor for elected government, to violate its judgment in the sensitive arena of Islamic obligation is to reignite a state ideology dispute in a form that secular government is unlikely to win. Potential legal and political crises intersect again on the fields of ideology and constitutional structure.

If the judiciary has not fully confronted the issue of basic structure, the question of ideology has nonetheless returned firmly to constitutional consideration. Structure and ideology are two sides of the same issue. By default as much as design, the court has imputed a principle of basic

activism in order to do effective justice liberally." *Khwaja Ahmed Tariq Rahim v. Federation of Pakistan*, PLD 1992 Supreme Court 646.

12 *In the Matter of Enforcement of Fundamental Rights Re: Bonded Labour in the Brick Kiln Industry* (original jurisdiction), 1988 PSC 1171.

13 *Hafiz Muhammad Ameen, Etc. v. Islamic Republic of Pakistan and others* (PLD 1981 Federal Shariat Court 23) contested the immunity of Martial Law Regulation No. 115; *Haji Nizar Khan v. Additional District Judge, Lyallpur and others* (PLD 1976 Lahore 930) questioned the ways civil courts should apply Muslim law; Supreme Court (Shariat Bench) Shariat Appeals Nos. 1, 3, 4, 8, 9, 10 of 1981, 21 of 1984 and 1 of 1987 (*Qazal Bash Waqf v. Chief Land Commissioner, Punjab, Lahore and others*) declared this and other land reform laws did not conform to certain principles of Islamic law. *Ashfaq Ahmad v. Government of Pakistan*, PLD 1992 FSC 286 argued that the Federal Shariat Court "cannot enact a new statute, but can merely give its opinion to the Government."

14 "Provincial governments asked to ensure land reform," *Dawn* 6 April 1990, p. 5.

structure to its judgments, even if it will not recognize it as such. It has also brought to the fore serious conflicts between secular constitutionalism and state ideology. Indeed, Justice Muhammad Gul highlighted prospective tensions between the rules of secular and sacred law in 1975 in his separate note to the judgment against NAP: "In a secular State, the legislature is supreme, and laws are made in accordance with the will of the majority, free from any outside curbs ... This brings into bold relief the distinction between a secular State and an ideological State. According to this concept, the supreme authority vests with the Holy Qur'an." Moreover, as Justice Afzal Zullah noted in a contemporaneous case, "the 'residuary' law in Pakistan *vis-à-vis* the written Constitution and written law, is Islamic law, justice and equity."[15] In the ambit of the revived and amended 1973 Constitution, these problems are difficult to resolve.

Could the courts confront issues of basic structure directly? India's courts and politics offer little guidance. Unlike the Indian dialogue between legislative and judicial powers, the Pakistani experience has combined overwhelming executive power, uncertain constitutional resiliance and a cautious but consistent judicial quest for jurisdiction and justiciability. Despite lengthy debates about its constituent and legislative powers, parliament has rarely acted in either capacity to check the executive – in part, because its sovereignty is itself questionable. Constitutions more often have been vehicles to legalize the exercise of power than they have to legitimize its sources. The procedural definition of valid rather than legitimate law primly articulated in *Ziaur Rahman's case* and *F.B. Ali's case* – law competently made, by whomever is deemed competent to do so – has remained the prevailing concept of law in order to distinguish it from imposed rule.

This emphasis on procedure has accompanied the judiciary's primary concern with ensuring the persistence of the Pakistani state, even while that state has restricted the courts. From the beginning, the judiciary has viewed the state from the standpoint of its theoretical and legal origins rather than its later incarnations. It has judged politics according to standards that have not accommodated movements for ethnic nationalism, provincial rights and popular political power – processes that are as much the results as the causes of constitutional arrangements and judicial interpretation. The courts have nonetheless realized that while the structure of the state has retained a certain coherence its legitimacy is fundamentally contestable, both in the terms in which the early courts judged political consensus and those that the polity uses to judge the state. The social contract envisioned by the early courts was born once, in 1973, but

15 *Haji Nizar Khan*, at 1011 (Gul opinion cited as well).

the pains accompanying its birth were more than matched by the violence done by its authors and later, its abrogators. Contractarianism and constitutionalism have suffered coordinate fates. Moreover, this history calls into question the judiciary's functions. How can courts decide justly without standards of political legitimacy, and how can constitutions and political rules be legitimate if their results are considered unjust by the citizenry? Who should determine the source of judicial standards? If the courts seek political distance, how can state institutions be instructed to change? Where, finally, does sovereignty lie?

The judiciary's functional answers have been embedded in normative language. The courts have shadowed the state, defining its possibilities by echoing its limits. Guide and arbiter when this process has occurred, the judiciary has encoded the path and pace of political transition, symbolizing both continuity and change, accompanying real transitions with visions of the ideal. Justices Munir, Hamoodur Rahman and Haleem, custodians of the most dramatic transitions, all made clear their preferences for moderation rather than revolution, restraint rather than unbridled enthusiasm, transition rather than transformation. Only Justice Munir formally proposed and selected a constitution, but others determined constitutionality and legality to conform to the government of the day. For the courts, the problem of transition retains an ontology and epistemology based on established legal structures; the courts have treated politics as a controllable arena – the fallacy of vice-regal administration – rather than an open-ended process with uncertain results.

These dilemmas of judgment reappear in judicial attempts to understand the strained relationships between polity and state, between law and politics, and between rights and policy. Policy principles are constitutional appendages rather than directives, and although they are normatively contested in society they are immune from contest in the courts. Without consensus about the goals of the state – that is, without agreement about the sources of state sovereignty and legitimacy – they have little meaning; only the Objectives Resolution makes any claim to moral or political authority. Law as an instrument of social change has been bridled by the court itself, unleashed only in controlled, required or (as in the case of the eighth amendment) desperate circumstances. Principles of basic structure have been used to interpret constitutional law only when its meaning and consequences are least questioned. The courts have therefore not confronted fundamental questions about the justice of the laws they interpret, the justness of their application or the meaning of fidelity to the law.

*The structure of democracy* Judgments in the Indian fundamental rights cases were thought to infringe on parliamentary sovereignty and thus on the practice of democracy. Like other constitutional democracies, India has long believed that popularly elected legislatures embody and guarantee freedom and that judicial review limits parliament and by extension, popular sovereignty. Similar assumptions have long been voiced in Pakistan, but are realized infrequently. Prolonged states of emergency in Pakistan have been the norm rather than the exception; anticipating martial law has become a consistent, self-imposed limit on popular politics. Constitutions have only occasionally been documents of popular political possibility; more frequently, they enshrine an inequitable status quo.

The judiciary has employed three principles of governance to limit executive powers while supporting its own. The courts have revered the doctrine of separate powers – which they invoke as if directive principle – not only for making their own powers concrete but also for providing a foundation for federalism. Federalism, in turn, is supposed to offer the provinces a constitutional handle for dealing with the center. Finally, the concept of judicial autonomy has become their distinguishing element for an enduring federal state. For the courts, all these principles are essential components of democracy (although they have understood democracy to mean many different things), and are judicial aspirations for the polity.

When the sources of democracy are uncertain, and limited in practice and concept by the state, judicial review cannot be assumed to be anti-democratic. Certainly, the effects of living courts are measured by more than the content of their rulings. By allowing some discussion of executive behavior, courts have functioned as intermediate political actors – neither representatives nor electors, but architects of a limited space for public voice. This has held true under two polar conditions: when government has overwhelmed civil society, the courts have opened the door for political debate; when government has been unable to confront the problems of civil society, the courts have helped to legitimize its actions for the civil society. Judicial review can be a precursor of democracy, providing its prerequisite, free expression; it can also be democracy's guarantor by preserving its normative possibility in the absence of substantive protections.

The concept of democracy in Pakistan, often more ideal than real, has idiosyncratically combined process and content. The accumulated experience of self-government has reinforced a feudal economic system and a restricted political system, and thus strengthened the interests of the few against those of the many. These interests have come to be considered as both entitlements and rights, complicating jurisprudence and altering the dimensions of political change. Civil society has been held hostage to the manipulation of state institutions by vice-regal, martial law and mixed civil–military governments alike. Elected governments have created obstacles to accountable rule, using purportedly democratic institutions for purposes that are not wholly democratic. Constitutionalism in Pakistan mixes vague republicanism to fortify the state and a political pluralism serving the interests of the strong. They in turn define the interests of the state and conditions of citizenship, giving instrumental and limited meaning to constitutional rights.

The judiciary has faced difficult jurisdictional problems as it has mediated conflicts among institutions that derive their authority from diverse and sometimes incompatible sources. Equally difficult, the courts have decided conflicts between citizens and the state when the government is not empowered by the citizenry, when neither rights nor obligations are clear or fully known and when punitive sanctions often precede reasoned government judgment and action. When courts have helped to create conditions for democracy by acting as bulwarks for the citizenry against the state, the idea of democracy has taken on an anti-state character – a form that the courts, themselves state institutions, find discomfitting. Judicial review therefore enforces a concept of constitutionality while simultaneously institutionalizing skepticism about the structure of the state. Using the language of constitutionalism, the judiciary has supported the state while offering solace, counsel and place to those who wish to change fundamentally its character. Judicial review buttresses the state's strengths while providing voice to challengers and echoes the state's weaknesses while attacking its power. The structure of the state and the structure of justice thus run parallel to each other.

## Courts and politics

The courts have given the polity a vocabulary with which to speak when political language has been neither accurate nor reliable. When concepts of rights, autonomy and sovereignty are unclear – when the polity has found its leaders incapable of articulating palatable and workable vision – the judiciary has, if only temporarily and expediently, helped to define a context for political debate. Civil law has not consistently dominated the state, but it has framed communication between citizens and the state when other means were unavailable. The grammar of law supplements and sometimes supplants the grammar of politics.

Persistently disavowing political issues by recourse to the doctrine of separate powers, the judiciary has consistently defined the range and scope of politics by the way it interprets its jurisdiction. Form and content converge: acknowledging that juridical questions have political causes and consequences, the courts have also come to admit that their construction of power helps to define the state and its politics. The courts have struggled to define mechanisms through which the state can arbitrate its conflicts and in so doing, brace the foundations of the polity. These are problems of generation and regeneration: locating the sources of political community and their appropriate institutional expressions; reconciling competing versions of history and nationalism; creating and sustaining habits of politics appropriate to the enterprise of building a nation. In short, they are the challenges of constituting a state.

As avenues of last recourse for the citizenry and the state itself, the superior courts face these issues in their most delicate forms. The courts have often practiced constitutional law without benefit of a constitution, approximating its functions when no document existed and assuming its goals when the polity obscured them. When civil courts have validated military power they have often tried to elude military law to avoid inviting a permanent military state and equally important, to secure the civilian judiciary against martial law tribunals. Their actions lend to the concepts of justice and fairness a disembodied quality, for they leave open the question of whose law the law really is.

Citizens have believed, often with good reason, that courts are accessible and useful. Belief, however, sometimes overwhelms proof. As arenas for relatively open political debate, the courts are generally viewed as unsullied, apolitical institutions within a compromised, corrupt and highly politicized state. As institutions of judgment, however, they more often support than challenge state power. Those who approach the courts in political cases are keen to dissent, and their desire to be heard can override their faith in the results; the means are more important than the end, and in some ways, are the end. At the same time, the politically aggrieved have turned to the courts not only to provide relief against an unsympathetic state, but also to find a way to express alternative constitutions, polities and politics. The judiciary has often objected to specific limitations on individual action while confirming the environment in which they exist; the sum of judicial decisions helps to reinforce existing patterns of power.

For the courts, judicial review has often meant creating a constitution. Judgment sometimes includes an air of invention: the doctrine of separate powers when only an imposed executive ruled, the doctrines of popular and legislative sovereignty when no elected parliament lived, even the doctrine of judicial autonomy when the courts were allowed only on sufferance and only for the illusion of stability that they presented to outside powers. As non-representative institutions, the courts cannot create all the conditions needed to maintain constitutional government, and they remain in the end creatures of existing constitutions. They have often translated this incapacity into a doctrine of self-restraint. The expression of justice has thus been a series of tentative steps circling those who exercise power, awaiting opportunities to criticize safely government's efforts to remake the state. The judiciary has given the state image, content and voice while providing a vocabulary for dissent.

Language can both obscure and illuminate, however, and the judiciary's discourse has done both in Pakistan. Courts consistently repeat their primary duty to protect the constitution, but political circumstances, inherited worldviews and procedural assumptions have combined to make this charge imagined as much as real. Since *Tamizuddin Khan's case*, Pakistan's judiciary has guarded legalistic visions of democratic constitutionalism while the state creates and recreates an instrumental political community. No matter how elusive the concepts of nationhood, statehood and political community, the state has functioned with remarkable resiliance. The fact that Pakistan has prevailed over its governments attests to the misconceived equations of power and authority with which its political and military leaders have approached the polity. But survival has its price. The long effort to define the state through executive power, limited legislative authority and dependent citizen rights is now realized in the weaknesses of the contemporary state; in the process, civil society has been forced to accommodate the state's inroads into its rights, culture and identities.

However, ratios of power and promise are not constant, and the judiciary has both reflected the evolution of state–civil society relationships and has helped to encourage such change. Chief Justice Nasim Hasan Shah, who was consistently optimistic about a transition to democracy from martial law long before it was evident, was able to capitalize on the polity's growing strength, however minute, when he revoked the dissolution of the National Assembly in 1993. His order to restore the Assembly surely demonstrated the Supreme Court's sense of its autonomy. Equally important, the court could depend on civil society to support its constitutional position. The durability of fundamental rights can be measured politically in the polity's impatience with the misappropriation of authority and, critically, its expectation that the court would necessarily rule to contain such abuse. In this sense, Pakistan and its courts have come a long way from the tentative rhetoric of the 1960s or the fearful judgments of the late 1970s.

To contain the state's coercive powers, the polity now relies upon constitutional structures that must be rewritten before the martial law state can be fully harnessed by civilian government. Critically, however, Pakistanis must be convinced, and must be able to persuade state institutions, that at least some problems of disintegration and atomism can indeed be solved through civil law. For the moment, neither constitutional revision nor political trust are common political traits. Governments in the post-Zia period, have found it useful to build on martial law practices and institutions rather than revoke them; this strategy, however, has allowed – or created – uncontrollable political forces that alter the federal state's relationships to local power holders in ways that are beyond the ken of the constitution. Perhaps most important, the character of civil law changes when the environment which supports it is more tolerant of martial law habits and political goals – a practiced praetorianism – than was the case when the state was born.

The judiciary is caught amid these quandaries. It judges the state, but is also a part of it; yet, its institutional definition assumes an adherence to a civil law whose own identity is changing. Courts must therefore discover methods with which to interpret political transitions without unduly determining their result. They must also find ways to enfranchise those whose political, economic and social exclusion has previously defined both the state and its opposition. In the absence of a representatively conceived constitution, the courts necessarily seek alternative ways to understand and enforce workable concepts of political legitimacy and order.

The dangers in this calculus also offer opportunities for the courts to think anew their roles as engines and carriages for political change. Even if the constitutional rules under which they operate lead to incremental and occasionally inconsistent judgments, the courts play a crucial part in giving meaning to the language of justice and constitutionalism. Prudence in the service of self-preservation may now require a new voice of assertion rather than self-restraint, providing conceptual content to the strategic choices that make the state governable, and helping to orchestrate understanding and consensus when other state institutions cannot. Construed optimistically, this contribution may help to define the principles and practice of democracy for the future Pakistan.

# Table of reported cases

| | |
|---|---|
| AIR | All India Reports |
| BLD | Bangladesh Law Documents |
| CLC | Civil Law Courts |
| DLR | Dacca Law Review |
| FC | Federal Court |
| FSC | Federal Shariat Court |
| PLD | All Pakistan Legal Decisions |
| Dacca | East Pakistan |
| Karachi | Sind Province |
| Lahore | Punjab Province |
| Peshawar | Northwest Frontier Province |
| Quetta | Baluchistan Province |
| SC | Supreme Court |
| W.P. | West Pakistan (under one unit) |
| PLJ | Pakistan Law Journal |
| PSC | Pakistan Supreme Court |

PAKISTAN

A.K. Fazlul Quader Chaudhry v. Shah Nawaz and 2 others
PLD 1966 Supreme Court 105

Abdul Aziz alias Labha and others v. The Province of West Pakistan
PLD 1958 Supreme Court (Pak.) 499

Abdul Ghaffar Lakhani v. Federal Government of Pakistan
PLD 1986 Karachi 525

Abdul Hafeez Pirzada v. Government of Sindh
Petition under Article 199 of 1973 Constitution

Abdul Hamid Khan v. The District Magistrate, Larkana and 2 others
PLD 1973 Karachi 344

Abdul Mujeeb Pirzada v. Federation of Islamic Republic of Pakistan and 87 others
PLD 1990 Karachi 9

Abdul Rauf Malik and another v. Government of Pakistan and another
PLD 1978 Lahore 410

Abdur Rahman Mobashir and 3 others v. Syed Amir Ali Shah Bokhari and 4 others
PLD 1978 Lahore 113

Abdus Sattar Khan Niazi v. The Crown
PLD 1954 Federal Court 187
Abul A'la Maudoodi, Misbahul Islam Faruqi, Umar Farooq v. the Government of West Pakistan and the Government of Pakistan, and Province of East Pakistan v. Tamizuddin Ahmad and the Government of Pakistan
PLD 1964 Supreme Court 673
Aftab Ahmad Khan Sherpao, President of Pakistan Peoples Party, N.W.F.P. v. The Governor, N.W.F.P.
PLD 1990 Peshawar 192
Aitzaz Ahsan and others v. Chief Election Commissioner and others
PLD 1989 Lahore 1
Aizaz Nazir v. Chairman, Summary Military Court, Sukkur and 2 others
PLD 1980 Karachi 444
Ali Asghar v. Chairman, Summary Military Court and 2 others
PLD 1978 Karachi 773
Anwar Ali v. CMLA and 3 others
PLD 1979 Karachi 804
Asad Ali and nine others v. Settlement and Claims Commission, Karachi and another
PLD 1974 Karachi 345
Asfandyar Wali v. The State
PLD 1978 Peshawar 38
Ashfaq Ahmad and others v. Government of Pakistan and others
PLD 1992 Federal Shariat Court 286
Asif Ali Zardari v. Special Judge (Suppression of Terrorist Activities) II, Karachi and 2 others
PLD 1992 Karachi 430
Asseff Ahmad Ali v. Muhammad Khan Junejo
PLD 1986 Lahore 310
B.Z. Kaikaus and 10 others v. President of Pakistan and 15 others
PLD 1980 Supreme Court 160
Begum Nazir Abdul Hamid v. Pakistan (Federal Government) through Secretary Interior
PLD 1974 Lahore 7
Begum Nusrat Bhutto v. The Chief of Army Staff and Federation of Pakistan
PLD 1977 Supreme Court 657
Begum Parveen Malik v. The State and 2 others
PLD 1977 Lahore 1017
Begum Shaheen Ramay v. The State and 2 others
PLD 1977 Lahore 1414
Benazir Bhutto v. Federation of Pakistan and another
PLD 1989 Supreme Court 66
Benazir Bhutto v. Federation of Pakistan and another
PLD 1988 Supreme Court 416
Brig. (Retd.) F.B. Ali and another v. The State
PLD 1975 Supreme Court 506
Ch. Zahur Ilahi MNA v. Mr. Zulfigar Ali Bhutto and 2 others and Mushtaq Raj v. Mr. Zulfigar Ali Bhutto and others
PLD 1975 Supreme Court 383

Ch. Zahur Ilahi v. Director, Anti-Corruption Unit and 2 others
PLD 1975 Lahore 532
Ch. Zahur Ilahi v. Secretary to Government of Pakistan, Ministry of Home and Kashmir Affairs
PLD 1975 Lahore 499
Ch. Zahur Ilahi, M.N.A. v. The State
PLD 1977 Supreme Court 273
Chander Ban v. Government of Sind and 2 others
PLD 1973 Karachi 241
Chowdhury Tanbir Ahmad Siddiky v. The Province of East Pakistan and another
PLD 1968 Supreme Court 185
Dr. Aijaz Hassan Quereshi v. The Government of the Punjab
PLD 1977 Lahore 1304
Dr. Mahmood-ur-Rahman Faisal and others v. Secretary, Ministry of Law, Justice and Parliamentary Affairs, Government of Pakistan, Islamabad
PLD 1992 Federal Shariat Court 1
Dosso and another v. the state and others
PLD 1957 (W.P.) Quetta 9
Ex-Major-General Akbar Khan and Faiz Ahmad Faiz v. The Crown
PLD 1954 Federal Court 87 (Appellate Jurisdiction)
F.B. Ali v. The State
PLD 1975 Lahore 999
Fakhre Alam v. The State and another
PLD 1973 Supreme Court 525
Fauji Foundation and another v. Shamimur Rehman
PLD 1983 Supreme Court 457
Fazlul Quader Chowdhry and others v. Mr. Muhammad Abdul Haque
PLD 1963 Supreme Court 486
Federation of Pakistan and another v. Malik Ghulam Mustafa Khar
PLD 1989 Supreme Court 26
Federation of Pakistan and another v. Haji Muhammad Saifullah Khan and others
1988 PSC 315
Federation of Pakistan and others v. Haji Muhammad Saifullah Khan and others
1988 PSC 338
Federation of Pakistan and others v. Ch. Manzur Elahi
PLD 1976 Supreme Court 430
Federation of Pakistan et al. v. Moulvi Tamizuddin Khan.
PLD 1955 FC 240
Federation of Pakistan v. Aitzaz Ahsan
1988 PSC 1283
Federation of Pakistan v. Muhammad Akram Shaikh and Haji Muhammad Saifullah v. Federation of Pakistan
PLD 1989 Supreme Court 690
Federation of Pakistan v. United Sugar Mills Ltd., Karachi
PLD 1977 Supreme Court 397
Fida Muhammad v. Province of NWFP through Home Secretary, Peshawar
PLD 1973 Peshawar 156

Ghulam Mujtaba Khan v. Martial Law Administrator, Zone "D," Quetta and 5 others
PLD 1978 Quetta 199
Government of East Pakistan v. Mrs. Rowshan Bijaya Shaukat Ali Khan
PLD 1966 Supreme Court 286
Government of the Punjab v. Dr. Ijaz Hasan Quereshi
PLD 1985 Supreme Court 28
Government of West Pakistan v. Begum Agha Abdul Karim Shorish Kashmiri
PLD 1969 Supreme Court 14
Government of West Pakistan v. Haider Bix Jatoi and another
PLD 1969 Supreme Court 210
Governor General's Reference No. 1 of 1955
PLD 1955 Federal Court 435
Gulab Din v. Major A.T. Shaukat
PLD 1961 (W.P.) Lahore 952
Gulzar Hassan and 8 others v. Islamic Republic of Pakistan
PLD 1975 Lahore 1219
Habibul Wahhab Elkeiri v. Kh. Abdul Wali Khan and 4 others
PLD 1978 Supreme Court 85
Haji Abdullah v. Presiding Officers, Summary Military Court No. 9, Karachi
PLD 1980 Karachi 498
Haji Muhammad Saifullah v. Federal Government
PLD 1992 Federal Shariat Court 376
Hakim Muhammad Anwar Babri v. Federation of Pakistan, through Secretary to the Government of Pakistan, Ministry of Foreign Affairs
PLD 1974 Lahore 33
Humayun Saifullah Khan v. Federation of Pakistan and 2 others
PLD 1990 Supreme Court 290
Husain Naqi v. The State and another
PLD 1979 Lahore 810
Imtiaz Bashir v. Special High Powered Committee and 4 others
PLD 1978 Quetta 131
In the Matter of Enforcement of Fundamental Rights Re: Bonded Labour in the Brick Kiln Industry
1988 PSC 1171
Indo-Pakistan Corporation Ltd., Lahore v. Government of Pakistan
PLD 1975 Lahore 1050
Iqbal Ahmad Khan, Advocate and 51 others v. The State and 2 others
PLD 1977 Lahore 1337
Islamic Republic of Paistan v. Abdul Wali Khan
PLD 1975 Supreme Court 463
Islamic Republic of Pakistan v. Mr. Abdul Wali Khan
Reference No. 1 of 1975
Jahandad and 6 others v. President's Special Military Court No. 88, Sector 1, Zone "B" c/o Home Secretary Government of N.W.F.P., Peshawar and 3 others
PLD 1990 Peshawar 63

Jehangir Iqbal Khan v. Federation of Pakistan and 3 others
PLD 1979 Peshawar 67
Jibendra Kishore Chowdhury v. Province of East Pakistan
PLD 1957 Supreme Court (Pak) 9
Kanayalal v. The State
PLD 1977 Karachi 675
Kh. Muhammad Safdar v. The State and another
PLD 1974 Lahore 200
Khan Ajun Khan v. The Government of West Pakistan and 8 others
PLD 1958 (W.P.) Peshawar 191
Khan Iftikhar Hussain Khan of Mamdot v. Province of the Punjab
PLD 1950 Federal Court 24
Khan Muhmammad Yusuf Khan Khattak v. S.M. Ayub and 2 others
PLD 1973 Supreme Court 160
Khudiadad v. Deputy MLA, Zone "D," Baluchistan and another
PLD 1978 Quetta 177
Khawaja Ahmad Tariq Rahim v. Federation of Pakistan
PLD 1992 Supreme Court 646
Khwaja Ahmad Tariq Rahim v. Federation of Pakistan and others
PLD 1990 Lahore 505
Khwaja Muhammad Sharif v. Federation of Pakistan through Secretary Cabinet Division, Government of Pakistan and 18 others
PLD 1988 Lahore 725
Liaqat Ali v. The Government of Sind
PLD 1973 Karachi 78
M. Inayat Khan v. M. Anwar and 2 others
PLD 1976 Supreme Court 354
M. Yamim Quereshi v. Islamic Republic of Pakistan and another
PLD 1980 Supreme Court 22
M.D. Tahir v. Federal Government and 12 others
1989 CLC Lahore 1369
Mahmud Ali Kasuri, Bar-at-Law v. Punjab Government through Secretary, Home Affairs
PLD 1977 Lahore 1400
Mahmud Ali Qasuri v. The State
PLD 1969 Supreme Court 485
Mairaj Muhammad Khan v. Government of West Pakistan and Superintendent of Jail, Karachi
PLD 1966 (W.P.) Karachi 282
Mairaj Muhammad Khan v. The State
PLD 1978 Karachi 308
Majibur Rahman and 3 others v. Federal Government of Pakistan and another
PLD 1985 Federal Shariat Court 8
Major General (Retd.) Mian Ghulam Jilani v. Federal Government
PLD 1975 Lahore 65
Major-General (Ret.) Nasirullah Khan Babar v. Chief of Army Staff and another
PLD 1979 Peshawar 23

Malik Feroz Khan Noon v. The State
PLD 1958 Supreme Court 333
Malik Ghulam Jilani v. Asst. Commission, Kohlu and another
PLD 1975 Karachi 728
Malik Ghulam Jilani v. Deputy Commissioner, Karachi et al.
PLD 1969 Karachi 253
Malik Ghulam Jilani v. the Government of West Pakistan
PLD 1967 Supreme Court 373
Malik Ghulam Jilani v. The Province of Punjab and others
PLD 1979 Lahore 564
Malik Ghulam Mustafa Khar and others v. Pakistan and others
PLD 1988 Lahore 49
Malik Hamid Sarfraz v. The Deputy Commissioner, Lahore
PLD 1966 (W.P.) Lahore 847
Malik Toti Khan etc. v. District Magistrate, Sibi and Ziarat
PLD 1957 (W.P.) Quetta 1
Manzoor Elahi v. The State
PLD 1959 Lahore 243
Master Abdul Rashid v. Sub-Martial Law Administrator, Sector 2, Rawalpindi and 3 others
PLD 1980 Lahore 356
Maulana Abdus Sattar Khan Niazi v. The State
PLD 1974 Lahore 324
Maulana Musahib Ali v. The State
PLD 1975 Karachi 909
Maulvi Tamizuddin Khan v. The Federation of Pakistan
PLD 1955 Sind 96
Mehboob Ali v. Deputy Commissioner and Tribunal and 3 others
PLD 1975 Karachi 391
Mian Ejaz Ahmad v. Government of Punjab through Secretary, Home Department and another
PLD 1974 Lahore (Note 69)
Mian Iftikhar-ud-Din and Arif Iftikhar v. Muhammad Sarfraz
PLD 1961 Lahore 842
Mian Iftikhar-ud-Din and Arif Iftikhar v. Muhammed Sarfraz and the Government of Pakistan, and vice versa
PLD 1961 Supreme Court 585
Mir Abdul Baqi Baluch v. Government of Pakistan
PLD 1968 Supreme Court 313
Mir Ahmad Nawaz Khan Bughti v. Superintendent, District Jail, Lyallpur
PLD 1966 Supreme Court 357
Mir Hassan and another v. The State
PLD 1969 Lahore 786
Mirza Jawad Beg v. The State
PLD 1975 Karachi 628
Mirza Khurshid Ahmad and another v. Government of Punjab
PLD 1992 Lahore 1

Miss Asma Jilani v. The Government of the Punjab and another and Mrs. Zarina Gauhar v. the Province of Sind and two others
PLD 1972 Supreme Court 139
Miss Benazir Bhutto v. Federation of Pakistan and another
PLD 1988 Supreme Court 416
Mohammed Ayub Khuhro v. Federation of Pakistan
PLD 1950 Sind 49
Mr. Abdul Hafez v. Government of East Pakistan and others
19 DLR (1967) 539
Mr. Zulfikar Bhutto v. The State
PLD 1978 Supreme Court 40
Mr. Zulfigar Ali Bhutto v. The State
PLD 1978 Supreme Court 125
Mrs. Habiba Jilani v. The Federation of Pakistan, through the Secretary, Interior Ministry
PLD 1974 Lahore 153
Mrs. Zarina Gauhar v. Province of Sind and 3 others
PLD 1976 Karachi 1257
Mst. Rehmat Bibi v. S.H.O. Police Station Samanabad, Lahore
PLJ 1992 Lahore 193
Mst. Sakina Bibi v. Federation of Pakistan
PLJ 1992 Lahore 285
Mst. Zohra Naqi v. Asghar Khan, D.S.P. and others
PLD 1979 Lahore 587
Muhammad Abdul Haque v. Fazlul Quader Chowdhury et al.
PLD 1963 Dacca 669
Muhammad Afzal Bangash v. The Crown
PLD 1955 Peshawar 35 (Judicial Commissioner's Court)
Muhammad Afzal v. The Commissioner, Lahore Division and The Estate Officer, Lahore Improvement Trust
PLD 1963 Supreme Court 401
Muhammad Akbar v. Dr. Khan Sahib, Chief Minister of West Pakistan
PLD 1957 (W.P.) Karachi 387
Muhammad Akhtar Rana v. Special Tribunal, Punjab
PLD 1977 Lahore 957
Muhammad Akram Sheikh, Advocate v. Federation of Pakistan and others
PLD 1989 Supreme Court 229
Muhammad Anwar Durrani v. Province of Baluchistan through Chief Secretary and 10 others
PLD 1989 Quetta 25
Muhammad Aslam Saleemi, Advocate v. The Pakistan Television Corporation and another
PLD 1977 Lahore 852
Muhammad Ayub Khuhro v. Pakistan, through the Ministry of Interior
PLD 1960 Supreme Court 237
Muhammad Bachal Memon v. Government of Sind
PLD 1987 Karachi 296

Muhammad Din and others v. The State
PLD 1977 Supreme Court 52
Muhammad Ismail v. Summary Military Court, Mirpurkhas and another
PLD 1980 Karachi 47
Muhammad Nazir alias Pappu v. The State
PLD 1992 Lahore 258
Muhammad Nazir Khan v. Dr. Mubashar Hasan and another
PLD 1974 Lahore 49
Muhammad Rafiq Mir, Publisher "Musawat" v. Punjab Government
NLR 1988 Civil 614
Muhammad Sharif v. Federation of Pakistan
PLD 1988 Lahore 725
Muhammad Siddiq Khan v. District Magistrate
PLD 1992 Lahore 140
Muhammad Umar Khan v. The Crown
PLD 1953 Lahore 528
Mujeeb-ur-Rehman and 3 others v. Federal Government of Pakistan
PLD 1984 Federal Shariat Court 136
Mumtaz Ali Bhutto and another v. The Deputy Martial Law Administrator, Sector 1, Karachi and 2 others
PLD 1979 Karachi 307
Muzaffar Qadir v. The District Magistrate, Lahore
PLD 1975 Lahore 1198
Nasir Ahmad and another v. The State
PLJ 1992 Cr.C (Lahore) 427
National Industrial Cooperative Credit Corporation Ltd. v. Province of Punjab/ Government of Punjab
PLD 1992 Lahore 462
Nawab Begum v. Home Secretary, Government of Punjab, Lahore
PLD 1974 Lahore 344
Nazar Muhammad Khan v. Pakistan and 2 others
PLD 1986 Karachi 516
Nazeer Ahmed v. Lt. Col. Abbas Ali Khan, President, Special Military Court No. 10 and 2 others
PLD 1978 Karachi 777
Niaz Ahmed Khan v. Province of Sind and others
PLD 1977 Karachi 604
Nisar alias Nisari and another v. Government of Pakistan and 2 others
PLD 1984 Supreme Court 373 (Shariat Bench)
Pakistan v. Ali Ahmed Shah
PLD 1955 Federal Court 522
Province of Baluchistan (through Home Secretary) v. Sher Mohammad Marri
PLD 1975 Lahore 1372
Province of East Pakistan et al. v. Sirajul Huq Patwari and others
PLD 1966 Supreme Court 854
Province of East Pakistan v. Md. Mehdi Ali Khan and 7 others
PLD 1959 Supreme Court 387

Province of East Pakistan v. Md. Mehdi Ali Khan Panni
PLD 1959 Supreme Court (Pak) 387
Province of Punjab through Its Home Secretary and 3 others v. Gulzar Hassan, Advocate and 3 others
PLD 1978 Lahore 1298
Province of the Punjab and others v. Syed Myhammad Akram Shah
PLD 1984 Supreme Court 409
Punjab Province v. Malik Khizar Hayat Khan Tiwana
PLD 1956 Federal Court 200 (Appellate jurisdiction)
Rana Muhammad Ashraf v. District Magistrate, Rawalpindi
PLD 1977 Lahore 1006
Reference by His Excellency the Governor-General
PLD 1955 Federal Court 435 (Advisory Jurisdiction), Special Reference No. 1 of 1955
Reference by the President of Pakistan under Article 162 of the constitution of Islamic Republic of Pakistan
PLD 1957 Supreme Court 219 (Advisory Jurisdiction)
Reference of the Speaker of Balochistan Assembly Under Article 63(2), Constitution of Pakistan
PLD 1992 Journal 125
Reference No. 1 of 1988, made by the President of Pakistan under Article 186 of the Constitution of the Islamic Republic of Pakistan
PLD 1989 Supreme Court 75
Rustam Ali v. MLA, Zone "C" and 3 others
PLD 1978 Karachi 736
Saeed Ahmad Malik v. Federation of Pakistan
PLD 1978 Lahore 1218
Saifullah Saif v. Federation of Pakistan and 3 others
PLD 1977 Lahore 1174
Saiyyid Abul A'la Maudoodi, et al. v. The Government of West Pakistan and The Government of Pakistan and The Province of East Pakistan v. Tamizuddin Ahmad and The Government of Pakistan
PLD 1964 Supreme Court 673
Saleh Muhammad v. Presiding Officers, Summary Military Court, Karachi and 2 others
PLD 1980 Karachi 26
Sangbad Ltd. and Khandker Nurul Haque v. Deputy Commissioner, Dacca, Province of East Pakistan, Additional Deputy Commission
19 DLR (1967) 581
Sarfaraz Ali v. The Crown
1951 Federal Court 78
Satar Gul and another v. Martial Law Administrator, Zone "B," N.W.F.P., Peshawar, and 2 others
PLD 1979 Peshawar 119
Sh. Karamat Ali v. The State
PLD 1976 Supreme Court 476
Sh. Rahmat Ullah v. Government of Pakistan
PLD 1975 Lahore 1513

Shamimur Rehman v. Government of Pakistan and others
PLD 1980 Karachi 345
Sharaf Faridi and 3 others v. Federation of the Islamic Republic of Pakistan and another
PLD 1989 Karachi 404
Sheikh Muhammad Afzal Khan v. The Province of West Pakistan
PLD 1958 (W.P.) Peshawar 54
Sher Ali and others v. Sheikh Zahoor Ahmed
PLD 1977 Supreme Court 545
Sherajul Haque Patwari v. Sub-divisional Officer, Chandpur
PLD 1966 Dacca 331
Sir Edward Snelson v. the Judges of the High Court of West Pakistan, Lahore and the Central Government of Pakistan
PLD 1961 Supreme Court 237
Special Reference Under Article 187 of the Interim Constitution of the Islamic Republic of Pakistan by President Zulfikar Ali Bhutto
PLD 1973 Supreme Court 563
State v. Abdul Wali Khan and others
Before the Special Court Set Up under Section 4 of the Criminal Law Amendment (Special Court) Ordinance, 1975 (XXIX of 1975) by Notification No. F.44 (1)\76-A, Dated 20–2–1976
State v. Abdul Wali Khan and others
Special Court (Central Prison) Hyderabad
PLD 1977 Journal 315
State v. Dosso and another
PLD 1958 Supreme Court 533
State v. Habib Jalib
PLD 1967 Lahore 1297
State v. Syed Qaim Ali Shah
PLJ 1992 Supreme Court 625
State v. Sir Edward Snelson
PLD 1961 (W.P.) Lahore 78
State v. Yusaf Lodhi
PLD 1973 Peshawar 25
State v. Zia-ur-Rahman and others
PLD 1973 Supreme Court 49
State v. Zulfigar Ali Bhutto
PLD 1978 Lahore 523
Syed Abual A'ala Maududi v. The State Bank of Pakistan and the Central Government of Pakistan
PLD 1969 Lahore 908
Syed Essa Noori v. Deputy Commissioner, Turbat and 2 others
PLD 1979 Quetta 189
Syed Sharifuddin Pirzada v. Federation of Pakistan and another
PLD 1973 Karachi 132
Syed Sibte Hasan v. The Crown
PLD 1954 Lahore 142
Tamizuddin Ahmed v. The Government of East Pakistan
PLD 1964 Dacca 795

Toffazal Hossain v. Government of East Pakistan and another
17 DLR (1965) 76
Toffazal Hossain and Motahar Hossain Siddiqui v. Province of East Pakistan and others
17 DLR (1965) 498
Toffazal Hossain and Motahar Hossain Siddique and Zahirul Islam v. Government of East Pakistan through Home Secretary
19 DLR (1967) 79
Usif Patel and 2 others v. The Crown
PLD 1955 Federal Court 387 (Appellate Jurisdiction)
Yaqoob Ali v. Presiding Officer, Summary Military Court, Karachi
PLD 1985 Karachi 243
Zafar Iqbal v. Province of Sind and 2 others
PLD 1973 Karachi 316
Zewar Khan v. Superintendant, Land Customs, Torkham and 2 others
PLD 1969 Peshawar 252
Zia-ur-Rahman v. The State
PLD 1972 Lahore 382
Zulfikar Ali Bhutto and 3 others v. The State
PLD 1979 Supreme Court 38
Zulfikar Ali Bhutto v. The State
PLD 1979 Supreme Court 741
Zulfikar Ali Bhutto v. The State
PLD 1979 Supreme Court 53
Zulfikar Ali Bhutto v. The State
PLD 1978 Supreme Court 40

## BANGLADESH

Anwar Hossain Chowdhury v. Bangladesh
1989 BLD (Spl) 1

## INDIA

His Holiness Kesavananda Bharati Sripadagalvaru v. State of Kerala and another
AIR 1973 Supreme Court 1561
I.C. Golak Nath v. Punjab
AIR 1967 Supreme Court 1463
Minerva Mills Limited v. Union
AIR 1980 Supreme Court 1789

# Bibliography


NEWSPAPERS AND MAGAZINES

*Civil and Military Gazette* (Lahore) [*CMG*]
*Dawn* (Karachi)
*Forum* (Dacca)
*Friday Times* (Lahore)
*Frontier Post* (Peshawar and Lahore)
*Herald* (Karachi)
*Holiday* (Dacca)
*Khyber Mail* (Peshawar)
*Muslim* (Islamabad)
*Nation* (Lahore)
*Newsline* (Karachi)
*Pakistan Observer* (Dacca)
*Pakistan Times* (Lahore)
*Today* (Karachi)
*Viewpoint* (Lahore)

GOVERNMENT DOCUMENTS AND LAWS

Awan, Malik Muhammad Rashied, ed. *The Constitution of Pakistan 1973 (Incorporating all Amendments up to Date)*. National Law Reporter, Lahore: Lahore Law Times Publications, n.d.

Awan, Muhammad Akbar and Malik Muhammad Rashied Awan. *First Information Reports*. Lahore: Lahore Law Times Publications, 1987

Bajwa, Zafar Iqbal. *The Pakistan Penal Code (XLV of 1860)*. Lahore: Civil and Criminal Law Publications, 1983

Baloch, Shah Ahmad. *Hadood & Tazir with Rules and Ordinances*. Lahore: Civil and Criminal Law Publications, n.d.

Constitution of the Islamic Republic of Pakistan 1956. Lahore: Pak Book Depot, 1957

Constitution of the Islamic Republic of Pakistan 1973. Lahore: Kausar Brothers, 1981

Ghafoor, Raja Anwar. *Manual of Waqf Laws*. Lahore: Kausar Brothers, 1983

Government of Afghanistan. *White Book: Pakistan's Subversive Activities Against the Afghan Revolution*. DRA Ministry of Foreign Affairs, Information and Press Department, Kabul, 1984

Government of Great Britain. *Report by the Select Committee of the House of Lords appointed to Join with a Committee of the House of Commons to Consider the Future Government of India and, in particular, to Examine and Report upon the Proposals Contained in Command Paper 4628*. Joint Committee on Indian Constitutional Reform, Session 1933–34, London, 1934

Government of Pakistan. *Comparative Statement of the Constitution as it Stood Before the 20th March 1985 and as it Stands After That Date*. Ministry of Justice and Parliamentary Affairs, 1985

*Constitutional Documents (Pakistan)*. Volume IV–B: Orders and Proclamations. Volume V: Constitution 1962 and President's Orders. Ministry of Law and Parliamentary Affairs, Law Division, Karachi, 1964

*Martial Law Regulations, Orders and Instructions by the Chief Martial Law Administrator and All the Zonal Martial Law Administrators*. Lahore: Law Publishing Company, 1983, 4th edition

*Report on Form of Governance* (Ansari Commission). Islamabad, 1983

*Report on General Elections Pakistan 1970–71*, Vol. I. Islamabad: 1972 Election Commission

*The Gazette of Pakistan, Report on the Constitution Committee*. Islamabad, 31 December 1971

*The Qanun-E-Shahadat Order 1984*. Lahore: Kausar Brothers

*White Paper on Baluchistan*. Rawalpindi, 19 October 1974

*White Paper on the Crisis in East Pakistan*. Rawalpindi, 5 August 1971

*White Paper on the Performance of the Bhutto Regime*. Vols. I–IV, Islamabad, 1979

Government of Sind. *Sind Local Government Ordinance 1979*. Karachi: Karachi Law Publishers, 1981

Government of the United States. *Country Development Strategy Statement FY1988 – FY1993*. Washington, DC: Agency for International Development, 11 April 1987

*Hadood and Tazir Laws with Rules and Ordinances*. Lahore: Civil and Criminal Law Publication, 1985

*Interim Constitution of the Islamic Republic of Pakistan as Amended by Post Constitution P.O. No. 1 of 1972*, May 1972. Karachi: Pakistan Publishing House

Janjua, Zia-ul-Islam. *The Copyright Laws*. Lahore: Lahore Government Law Times Publications, 1983

Khan, Asmat Kamal. *Provisional Constitutional Order 1981*. Lahore: Civil and Criminal Law Publication, 1983

Khan, Javed Iqbal. *The Evidence Act (1 of 1872)*. Lahore: Mansoor Book House, n.d.

Khan, M. Kazim. *The Civil Courts Ordinance*. Lahore: Civil and Criminal Publication, 1983

Khan, Makhdoom Ali, ed. *The Constitution of the Islamic Republic of Pakistan (as amended up to December 1988)*. Karachi: Pakistan Law House, 1986, 1988

Mahmood, Shaukat. *Law of Bail*. Lahore: Legal Research Centre, 1975

*Constitution of the Islamic Republic of Pakistan 1973*. Lahore: Legal Research Center, 1973

*Major Acts*. Lahore: Lahore Law Times Publications

Mian, Mushtaq Ahmad and Zafar, Sh. Muhammad. *The Muslim Law*. Lahore: Kausar Brothers, 1982

National Assembly of Pakistan. *Constitution-Making in Pakistan*. Islamabad, 1975

*Constitution-Making Debates, 1973*

Rehman, K.S.A. *The Defence of Pakistan Ordinance, 1971, With Rules 1971*. Lahore: Khyber Law Publishers, n.d.

*Report of the Court of Inquiry Constituted under Punjab Act II of 1954 to Enquire into the Punjab Disturbance of 1953*. Lahore: Government Printing, Punjab, 1954

Sharif, Kh. Muhammad. *The Press and Publications Ordinance 1963*. Lahore: Mansoor Book House, n.d.

Supreme Court of Pakistan. *Pleadings and orders in Supreme Court in Government's Reference on Dissolution of NAP*. Islamabad: Directorate of Research, Reference and Publications, Ministry of Information and Broadcasting, 1975

Judgement on Dissolution of NAP. Rawalpindi, 30 October 1975

Supreme Court Rules 1980. Karachi: KLR Publication, 1980

### BOOKS AND ARTICLES

Abbott, Freeland. *Islam and Pakistan*. Ithaca: Cornell University Press, 1968

Ahamad, Emajuddin. *Society and Politics in Bangladesh*. Dhaka: Academic Publishers, 1989

Ahmad, Akhtaruddin. *Nationalism or Islam*. New York: Vantage Press, 1982

Ahmad, Iftikhar. *Pakistan General Elections 1970*. Lahore: South Asian Institute, Punjab University, 1976

Ahmad, Khurshid. *Proportional Representation and the Revival of Democratic Process in Pakistan*. Islamabad: Institute of Policy Studies, 1983

Ahmad, Masud. *Pakistan: A Study of its Constitutional History*. Lahore: Research Society of Pakistan, May 1978

Ahmad, Mushtaq. *Pakistan at the Crossroads*. Karachi: Royal Book Company, 1985

*Politics of Crisis*. Karachi: Royal Book Company, 1987

Ahmad, Sayed Riaz. *Maulana Maududi and the Islamic State*. Lahore: People's Publishing House, 1976

Ahmad, Syed Nur. *From Martial Law to Martial Law: Politics in the Punjab 1919–1958*. Edited Craig Baxter. Translated Mahmud Ali. Lahore: Vanguard Books Ltd., 1985

Ahmed, Akbar S. *Pakistan Society: Islam, Ethnicity and Leadership in South Asia*. Karachi: Oxford University Press, 1986

*Pukhtun Economy and Society: Traditional Structure and Economic Development in a Tribal Society*. London: Routledge and Kegan Paul, 1980

Ahmed, Amin. *Judicial Review of Administrative Actions in Pakistan*. Kamini Kumar Datta Memorial Law Lectures, Dacca: University of Dacca, 1969

Ahmed, Feroz, ed. *Focus on Baluchistan and Pushtoon Question*. Lahore: People's Publishing House, 1975

Ahmed, Ishtiaq. *The Concept of an Islamic State: An Analysis of the Ideological Controversy in Pakistan*. London: Frances Pinter, 1987

Ahmed, Moudud. *Bangladesh: Constitutional Quest for Autonomy 1950–1971*. Dacca: University Press Ltd., 1979

*Bangladesh: Era of Sheikh Mujibur Rahman*. Dhaka: University Press Ltd., 1984

Ahmed, Sufia. *Muslim Community in Bengal 1884–1912*. Distributed by Oxford University Press, Dacca, 1974

Ahmed, Viqar and Rashid Amjad. *The Management of Pakistan's Economy 1947–1982*. Karachi: Oxford University Press, 1984

Akhlaque Husain, Justice Syed. "Writ Jurisdiction of Superior Courts in Pakistan." PLD 1958 Journal 1–10

Alavi, Hamza. "The Army and Bureaucracy in Pakistan." *International Socialist Journal*, 3, No. 14 (March–April 1966): 149–81

"The Crisis of Nationalities and the State in Pakistan." *Journal of Contemporary Asia*, 1, no. 3 (1971): 42–66

"The State in Postcolonial Societies: Pakistan and Bangladesh." In Kathleen Gough and Hari P. Sharma, eds. *Imperialism and Revolution in South Asia*. New York: Monthly Review Press, 1973

Alavi, Hamza and Thedor Shanin, eds. *Introduction to the Sociology of 'Developing Societies'*. New York: Monthly Review Press, 1982

Albright, David E. "Research Note: a comparative conceptualization of civil–military relations." *World Politics*, 32, No. 4 (July 1980): 553–76

Ali, Chaudhri Muhammad. *The Emergence of Pakistan*. New York: Columbia University Press, 1967

*The Task Before Us: Selected Speeches and Writings*. Edited by Salahuddin Khan. Lahore: Research Society of Pakistan, University of the Punjab, 1974

Ali, Imran. *The Punjab Under Imperialism 1885–1947*. Princeton: Princeton University Press, 1988

Ali, Karamat, ed. *Pakistan: The Political Economy of Rural Development*. 2nd edition. Lahore: Vanguard Books, Ltd., 1986

Ali, Mehrunnisa. "Federalism and Regionalism in Pakistan." *Pakistan Study Centre Research Series*, vol. I. Karachi: Pakistan Study Centre, University of Karachi, 1985

Ali, Tariq. *Can Pakistan Survive? The Death of a State*. Harmondsworth: Penguin Books, 1983

Amnesty International. *Islamic Republic of Pakistan: An Amnesty International Report*. London, 1977

*Pakistan: Special Military Courts, Unfair Trials and the Death Penalty*. London, 1987

*The Trial and Treatment of Political Prisoners Convicted by Special Military Courts in Pakistan*. London, 1985

Anderson, Benedict. *Imagined Communities: Reflections on the Origin and Spread of Nationalism*. London: Verso, 1983

Anderson, J.N.D. and Norman J. Coulson. *Islamic Law in Contemporary Cultural Change*. Edited by M. Farani. Lahore: Lahore Law Times Publications, n.d.

Anwar, Muhammad Rafi. *Presidential Government in Pakistan*. Lahore: Caravan Book House, 1967

Atiyah, P.S. and R.S. Summers, *Form and Substance in Anglo-American Law: A Comparative Study of Legal Reasoning, Legal Theory, and Legal Institutions*. Oxford: Clarendon Press, 1987

Austin, Granville. *The Indian Constitution: Cornerstone of a Nation*. Oxford: Clarendon Press, 1966

Awan, A.B. *Baluchistan: Historical and Political Processes*. London: New Century Publishers, 1985

Ayoob, Mohammed. "Pakistan's New Political Structure: Change and Continuity." *International Studies*, 12, No. 2 (April–June 1973): 183–206

"Pakistan's Political Development 1947 to 1970: Bird's Eye View." *Economic and Political Weekly*, 4, No. 3–4–5 (January Annual Number 1971): 199–204

Azfar, Kamal. *Pakistan: Political and Constitutional Dilemmas*. Karachi: Pakistan Law House, 1987

Aziz, K.K. *Party Politics in Pakistan 1947–1958*. Islamabad: National Commission on Historical and Cultural Research, 1976

Aziz, K.K. ed. *The All India Muslim Conference 1928–1935*. Karachi: National Publishing House Ltd., 1972

Aziz, Sartaj, ed. *Different Views on the Eighth Amendment*. Islamabad, 1989

Bahadur, Kalim. *The Jama'at-i-Islami of Pakistan: Political Thought and Political Action*. Lahore: Progressive Books, 1983

*Bangladesh Documents*. Lahore: Vanguard Books, Ltd., n.d.

Baxi, Upendra. *Courage, Craft and Contention: The Indian Supreme Court in the Eighties*. Bombay: N.M. Tripathi Private Limited, 1985

*The Indian Supreme Court and Politics*. Lucknow: Eastern Book Company, 1980

*Towards a Sociology of Indian Law*. New Delhi: Satvahan Publications, 1986

Baxter, Craig, ed. *Zia's Pakistan: Politics and Stability in a Frontline State*. Lahore: Vanguard Books, Ltd., 1985

Bell, John. "The Judge as Bureaucrat." In John Eekelaar and John Bell, eds. *Oxford Essays in Jurisprudence*. Third series. Oxford: Clarendon Press, 1987

*Policy Arguments in Judicial Decisions*. Oxford: Clarendon Press, 1983

Berry, Willard. *Aspects of the Frontier Crimes Regulation in Pakistan*. Monograph and Occasional Papers Series, Number 3. Durham: Duke University Commonwealth Studies Center, 1966

Bhattacharjee, G.P. *Renaissance and Freedom Movement in Bangladesh*. Calcutta: Minerva Associates, 1973

Bhuiyan, Md. Abdul Wadud. *Emergence of Bangladesh and Role of Awami League*. New Delhi, Vikas Publishing House Pvt. Ltd., 1982

Bhutto, Benazir. *Daughter of Destiny: An Autobiography*. New York: Simon and Schuster, 1989

*The Gathering Storm*. New Delhi: Vikas Publishing House Pvt. Ltd., 1983

Bhutto, Mumtaz. *Confederation*. Private publication. January 1984

Bhutto, Zulfikar Ali. *If I am Assassinated*. New Delhi: Vikas Publishing House, 1979

*Political Situation in Pakistan*. Lahore: Pakistan People's Party, Political Series No. 1, 2nd edition, 1969

*The Great Tragedy*. Pakistan People's Party. Karachi: Vision Publications Ltd., September 1971

*The Quest for Peace*. Karachi: The Pakistan Institute of International Affairs, 1966

*The Third World: New Directions*. London: Quartet Books, 1977

*Speeches and Statements*. Karachi: Department of Films and Publications, Government of Pakistan, 1972

Binder, Leonard. "Problems of Islamic Political Thought in the Light of Recent Developments in Pakistan." *Journal of Politics*, 20, No. 4 (November 1958): 655–75

*Religion and Politics in Pakistan*. Berkeley and Los Angeles: University of California Press, 1963

Bose, Sarat Chandra. "A Constitution of Myths and Denials." *Indian Law Review* (January 1950). Reprinted in Commemoration Volume, Calcutta: Sarat Bosc Academy, 1982

Braibanti, Ralph. "Pakistan: Constitutional Issues in 1964." *Asian Survey*, 5, No. 2 (February 1965): 79–87

"Public Bureaucracy and Judiciary in Pakistan." In Joseph LaPalombara, ed. *Bureaucracy and Political Development*. Princeton: Princeton University Press, 1963

Brohi, A.K. *An Adventure in Self Expression*. 2nd edition. Karachi: Din Muhammadi Press, 1955

*Fundamental Law of Pakistan*. Karachi: Din Muhammadi Press, 1958

Brookfield, F.M. "The Courts, Kelsen, and the Rhodesian Revolution." *University of Toronto Law Journal*, 19 (1969): 326–52

Burki, Shahid Javed. "Ayub's Fall: A Socio-Economic Explanation." *Asian Survey*, 12, No. 3 (March 1972): 201–12

*Pakistan Under Bhutto 1971–1977*. 2nd edition. London: Macmillan Press, 1988

Burnes, James. *A Visit to the Court of Sinde*. Karachi: Oxford University Press, 1974

Callard, Keith B. *Pakistan: A Political Study*. London: George Allen and Unwin, 1957

*Political Forces in Pakistan 1947–1959*. New York: Institute of Pacific Relations, 1959

Chaudhri, Mohammed Ahsen. *Pakistan and the Great Powers*. Karachi: Council for Pakistan Studies, 1970

Chaudhri, Nazir Hussain. *Chief Justice Muhammad Munir: His Life, Writings and Judgments*. Lahore: Research Society of Pakistan, University of the Punjab, 1973

Chisti, Faiz Ali. *Betrayals of Another Kind: Islam, Democracy and the Army in Pakistan*. Rawalpindi: PCL Publishing House, 1989

Choudhury, G.W. *Constitutional Development in Pakistan*. 1st edition: London, New York & Toronto: Longmans, Green and Co., 1959. 2nd edition: Vancouver: University of British Columbia, 1969

ed. *Documents and Speeches on the Constitution of Pakistan*. Dacca: Green Book House, 1967

*Pakistan's Relations with India 1947–1966*. New York: Praeger, 1968

Chowdhury, Hamidul Huq. *Memoirs*. Dhaka: Associated Printers Ltd., 1989

Chowdhury, Najma. *The Legislative Process in Bangladesh: Politics and Function of the East Bengal Legislature 1947–1958*. Dacca: University of Dacca, 1980

Citizens for Democracy. *Democracy and Constitution (Forty-second Amendment Bill)*. Bombay, 1976

Cohen, Stephen P. *The Pakistan Army*. New Delhi: Himalayan Books, 1984

Hussain, Asaf. "Ethnicity, National Identity and Praetorianism: The Case of Pakistan." *Asian Survey*, 16, No. 10 (October 1976): 918–30

Hussain, Mushahid. *Pakistan's Politics: The Zia Years*. Lahore: Progressive Publishers, 1990

Hussain, Shaukat. "Advisory Jurisdiction of the Superior Courts." PLD 1986 Journal 138–45

"Federalism and Provincial Autonomy." PLD 1984 Journal 108–13

"Fundamental Rights as Granted by Islam and Guaranteed by the Constitution of Pakistan 1973 – A Comparative Study." PLD 1984 Journal 156–63

Ikramullah, Shaista Suhrawardy. *Huseyn Shaheed Suhrawardy: A Biography*. Karachi: Oxford University Press, 1991

Inayatullah, ed. *District Administration in West Pakistan: Its Problems and Challenges*. Peshawar: Pakistan Academy for Rural Development, 1964

Independent Planning Commission of Pakistan. *Federal and Sovereign: A Policy Framework for the Economic Development of Pakistan*. Draft Report. Lahore: August 1985

Indian Round Table Conference. *The Question of Constituting Sind as a Separate Province*. Karachi: Indus Publications, 1979

Iqbal, Afzal. *Islamisation of Pakistan*. Delhi: Idarah-i-Adabiyat-i-Delhi, 1984

Ishaque, Khalid M. *Constitutional Limitations: An essay on limits on exercise of political power*. Karachi: Pakistan Publishing House, 1972

Iyer, T.K.K. "Constitutional Law in Pakistan: Kelsen in the Courts." *American Journal of Comparative Law*, 21 (1973): 759–71

Jafri, Rais Ahmad. *Ayub: Soldier and Statesman*. Lahore: Mohammad Ali Academy, 1966

Jahan, Rounaq. *Bangladesh Politics: Problems and Issues*. Dhaka: University Press Ltd., 1980

*Pakistan: Failure in National Integration*. New York: Columbia University Press, 1972

Jahangir, Asma and Hina Jilani. *The Hudood Ordinances: A Divine Sanction?* Lahore: Rhotas Books, 1990

Jalal, Ayesha. *The Sole Spokesman: Jinnah, the Muslim League and the demand for Pakistan*. Cambridge: Cambridge University Press, 1985

*The State of Martial Rule: The Origins of Pakistan's Political Economy of Defence*. Cambridge: Cambridge University Press, 1990

Jeffrey, Robin, ed. *People, Princes and Paramount Power: Society and politics in the Indian princely states*. Delhi: Oxford University Press, 1978

Jennings, Ivor. *Constitutional Problems in Pakistan*. Cambridge: Cambridge University Press, 1957

Jung, Nawab Nazir Yar. *The Pakistan Issue*. Delhi: Anmol Publications, 1985

Kabir, Muhammad Ghulam. *Minority Politics in Bangladesh*. New Delhi: Vikas Publishing House, 1980

Kagzi, Mangal Chandra Jain. *The June Emergency and Constitutional Amendments [The Amended Constitution]*. New Delhi: Metropolitan Book Co. Pvt. Ltd., 1977

Kamal, K.L. *Pakistan: The Garrison State*. New Delhi: Intellectual Publishing House, 1982

Kamenka, Eugene. "The Concept of a Political Revolution." In Carl J. Friedrich, ed. *Revolution*. Nomos VIII. New York: Atherton Press, 1966

Kardar, Abdul Hafiz. *Pakistan's Soldiers of Fortune*. Lahore: Ferozsons, 1988

Kardar, Shahid. *Political Economy of Pakistan*. Lahore: Progressive Publishers, 1987

Karim, Fazal. *Jurisdiction and Judicial Review*. Lahore: Law Publishing Company, 1983

Kaushik, Surendra Nath. *Pakistan Under Bhutto's Leadership*. New Delhi: Uppal Publishing House, 1985

Kayani, M.R. *A Judge May Laugh and Even Cry*. Lahore: Pakistan Writers Co-operative Society, 1970

*Half Truths*. Lahore: Pakistan Writers Cooperative Society, 1966

Kazi, Mushtak Ali. *Journey Through Judiciary*. Karachi: Royal Book Company, 1990

Kelsen, Hans. *General Theory of Law and the State*. Translated by Anders Wedberg. New York: Russell and Russell, 1961

*Pure Theory of Law*. Translated from second German edition by Max Knight. Berkeley: University of California Press, 1967

"Professor Stone and the Pure Theory of Law." *Stanford Law Review*, 17 (July 1965): 1129–57

"The Function of a Constitution." Translated by Iain Steward. In Richard Tur and William Twining, eds., *Essays on Kelsen*. Oxford: Clarendon Press, 1986

Kennedy, Charles H. *Bureaucracy in Pakistan*. Karachi: Oxford University Press, 1987

Khaliq, Mian Abdul. *Digested Cases on Construction of Law (1900–1969)*. Lahore: Lahore Law Times Publications, 1969

Khan, Abdul Ghaffar. *Badshah Khan Visits India*. New Delhi: Ghaffar Khan Sarhad Gandhi Sakgirah Samiti, 1968

Khan, D. Shah. "Military and Politics in Pakistan." *Defence Journal*, 4, No. 11 (1978): 20–37

Khan, Fazal Muqeem. *Pakistan's Crisis in Leadership*. Islamabad: National Book Foundation, 1973

Khan, Liaqat Ali. *Pakistan: The Heart of Asia*. Cambridge: Harvard University Press, 1951

Khan, Mahmood Hasan. *Underdevelopment and Agrarian Structure in Pakistan*. Lahore: Vanguard Books, Ltd., 1986

Khan, Mohammad Asghar Khan. *Generals in Politics: Pakistan 1958–1982*. Delhi: Vikas Publishing House, 1983

Khan, Mohammad Asghar Khan. ed. *The Pakistan Experience: State and religion*. Lahore: Vanguard Books, Ltd., 1985

Khan, Mohammad Ayub. *Friends Not Masters: A political autobiography*. Karachi: Oxford University Press, 1967

Khan, Mohammad Najibullah. *Legislation in Conflict with Fundamental Law: A study of validity of laws in Pakistan*. Two volumes. Karachi: Indus Publications, 1971, 1973

Khan, Shafique Ali. *Separate Electorates as the Genesis of Pakistan*. Hyderabad: Markez-i-Shahoor-o-Adab, 1976

Khan, Tamizuddin. *The Test of Time: My life and days*. Dhaka: University Press Ltd., 1989

Khan, Wali. *Facts Are Facts: The untold story of India's partition*. Translated by Dr. Syeda Saiyidain Hameed. New Delhi: Vikas Publishing House, 1987

Khan, Zillur R. and Rahman, A.T.R. *Provincial Autonomy and Constitution Making: The case of Bangladesh*. Dacca: Green Book House Ltd., 1973

Kheli, Shirin Tahir. "The Military in Contemporary Pakistan." *Armed Forces and Society*, 6, No. 4 (Summer 1980): 639–53

Khuhro, Hameeda. *The Making of Modern Sind: British policy and social change in the nineteenth century*. Karachi: Indus Publications, 1978

Khuhro, Mohammad Ayub. *Sufferings of Sind*. Karachi: October 1983, 2nd edition

Kumar, Satish. "Pakistan Since the Emergence of Bangladesh." *South Asian Studies*, 9, Nos.1–2 (January–July 1974): 78–93

Lakhi, M.V. "Constitutional Developments in Pakistan: The first phase 1947–56." *South Asian Studies*, 5, No. 1 (January 1970): 1–14

LaPorte, Robert Jr. "Succession in Pakistan: Continuity and change in a garrison state." *Asian Survey*, 9, No. 11 (November 1969): 842–61

Laski, Harold J. *The Foundations of Sovereignty and Other Essays*. Freeport: Books for Libraries Press, Inc., 1968 (originally published by Harcourt, Brace and Company, 1921)

*A Grammar of Politics*. 2nd edition. New Haven: Yale University Press, 1931

Lasser, William. *The Limits of Judicial Power: The Supreme Court in American Politics*. Chapel Hill: University of North Carolina, 1988

Lev, D.S. "Judicial Authority and the Struggle for an Indonesian Rechtsstaat." *Law and Society Review*, 13 (1978): 37–71

Lindholm, Charles. *Generosity and Jealousy: The Swat Pukhtun of Northern Pakistan*. New York: Columbia University Press, 1982

Lodhi, Maleeha. "Pakistan in Crisis." *Journal of Commonwealth and Comparative Politics*, 16 (1978): 60–78

MacDermott. "Law and Order in Times of Emergency." *Juridical Review*, 17 N.S. (1972): 1–21

MacDonald, Duncan B. *Development of Muslim Theology, Jurisprudence and Constitutional Theory*. New York: Charles Scribner's and Sons, 1903

McWhinney, Edward. *Constitution-making: Principles, Process, Practice*. Toronto: University of Toronto Press, 1981

*Supreme Courts and Judicial Law-Making: Constitutional Tribunals and Constitutional Review*. Dordrecht: Martinus Nijhoff Publishers, 1986

Mahmood, Dilawar. *Preventive Detention*. Lahore: Kausar Brothers, 1988

Mahmood, Safdar. *A Political Study of Pakistan*. Lahore: Sang-E-Meel Publications, 1987

*Pakistan Divided*. Lahore: Ferozsons Ltd., 1984

*The Deliberate Debacle*. Lahore: Sh. Muhammad Ashraf, 1976

Mahmud-un-Nasir, Syed. *Constitutional History of Pakistan*. Lahore: Mansoor Book House, 1984

Malik, Abdullah, ed. *Mian Iftikhar-ud-Din: Selected Speeches and Statements*. Lahore: Nigarishat, 1976

Maniruzzaman, Talukdar. "Crises in Political Development and Collapse of the Ayub Regime." *The Journal of Developing Areas*, 5 (January 1971): 221–38

"Group Interest in Pakistan Politics 1947–1958." *Pacific Affairs*, 39 (1966): 83–97

*Military Withdrawal From Politics: A Comparative Study*. Dhaka: University Press Ltd., 1988

"National Integration and Political Development in Pakistan." *Asian Survey*, 7, No. 12 (December 1967): 876–85

Mannon, M.A. "The Doctrine of Civil or State Necessity." PLD 1979 Journal 22–28

*The Superior Courts of Pakistan: The development of their powers and jurisdiction*. Lahore: Zafar Law Associates, 1973

Marasinghe, M L. and Conklin, William E., eds. *Essays on Third World Perspectives in Jurisprudence*. Singapore: Malayan Law Journal Pte., Ltd., 1984

Marri, Mir Khuda Bakhsh. *A Judge May Speak*. Lahore: Ferozsons (Pvt.) Ltd., 1990

Marshall, Charles Burton. "Reflections on a Revolution in Pakistan." *Foreign Affairs*, 37 (January 1959): 247–56

Mathews, K.K. *Three Lectures*. Lucknow: Eastern Book Company, 1983

Menon, V.P. *Montague-Chelmsford Reforms*. Bombay: Bharatiya Vidya Bhavan, 1965

Morris-Jones, W.H. "Creeping Authoritarianism: India, 1975–6." *Government and Opposition*, 12, No. 1 (1977): 20–41

"Pakistan Post-Mortem and the Roots of Bangladesh." The Political Quarterly, 43, No. 2 (April–June 1972): 187–200

Mumtaz, Khawar and Farida Shaheed. *Women of Pakistan: Two Steps Forward, One Step Back?* Lahore: Vanguard Books, Ltd., 1987

Munir, Muhammad. *From Jinnah to Zia*. Lahore: Vanguard Books, Ltd., 1986

Munir, Muhammad. ed. *Constitution of the Islamic Republic of Pakistan, Being a Commentary on the Constitution of Pakistan, 1962*. Lahore: All Pakistan Legal Decisions, 1965

*Constitution of the Islamic Republic of Pakistan, Being a Commentary on the Constitution of Pakistan, 1973*. Lahore: Law Publishing Company, 1975

Musa, General Mohammad. *Jawan to General: Recollections of a Pakistani Soldier*. Karachi: East and West Publishing Co., 1984

Naseem, S.M. *Underdevelopment, Poverty and Inequality in Pakistan*. Lahore: Vanguard Books, Ltd., 1986

Nettl, J.P. "The State as a Conceptual Variable." *World Politics*, 20, No. 4 (1968): 559–92

Newberg, Paula R. "Dateline Islamabad: Bhutto's Back." *Foreign Policy* No. 95, Summer 1994: 161–74.

"Pakistan at the Edge of Democracy." *World Policy Journal*, 6, No. 3 (Summer 1989): 563–87

"Pakistan's Troubled Landscape." *World Policy Journal*, 4, No. 2 (Spring 1987): 313–32

*Zia's Law: Human Rights under Military Rule in Pakistan*. New York: Lawyers Committee for Human Rights, 1985

Newman, K.J. *Essays on the Constitution of Pakistan*. Dacca: Pakistan Co-operative Book Society Ltd., 1956. Reprinted in Lahore by Falcon Printing Press, 1980

"Pakistan's Preventive Autocracy and its Causes." *Pacific Affairs*, 32, No. 1 (March 1959): 18–33

Niazi, Kausar. *Last Days of Premier Bhutto*. Lahore: Jang Publishers, 1991

Niazi, Zamir. *Press in Chains*. Karachi: Karachi Press Club, 1986

Noman, Omar. *The Political Economy of Pakistan 1947–85*. London: KPI Ltd., 1988

Nyrop, Richard F., ed. *Pakistan: A Country Study*. United States Government Foreign Area Studies (American University), 1984

Page, David. *Prelude to Partition: The Indian Muslims and the Imperial System of Control 1920–1932*. Delhi: Oxford University Press, 1982

Pakistan Economist Research Unit. *General Elections 1970: An Analysis of Socio-economic Trends in Pakistan*. 1973

Patel, Rashida. *Islamisation of Laws in Pakistan?* Karachi: Faiza Publishers, 1986

*Women and Law in Pakistan*. Karachi: Faiza Publishers, 1979

Pennock, J. Roland. "Federal and Unitary Government: Disharmony and Frustration." *Behavioral Science*, 4 (1959): 147–57

Petren, Gustaf, et al. *Pakistan: Human Rights After Martial Law*. Geneva: International Commission of Jurists, 1987

Pirzada, Syed Sharifuddin, ed. *Foundations of Pakistan: All-India Muslim League Documents: 1906–1947*. Vol. II (1924–47). Karachi: National Publishing House Ltd., 1970

*Fundamental Rights and Constitutional Remedies in Pakistan*. Lahore: All Pakistan Legal Decisions, 1966

*The Pakistan Resolution and the Historic Lahore Session*. Karachi: Din Muhammadi Press, 1968

Ponomarev, Yuri. *The Muslim League of Pakistan 1947–1977*. Lahore: People's Publishing House, 1986

Potter, David C. *India's Political Administrators 1919–1983*. Oxford: Clarendon Press, 1986

Prasad, Airudh. *Centre–State Relations in India: Constitutional Provisions, Judicial Review, Recent Trends*. New Delhi: Deep & Deep Publications, 1985

Qureshi, Saleem Ahmed. "An Analysis of Contemporary Pakistan Politics: Bhutto Versus the Military." *Asian Survey*, 19, No. 9 (September 1979): 910–21

Rahim, Enayatur. *Provincial Autonomy in Bengal (1937–1943)*. Dhaka: University Press Ltd. (Institute of Bangladesh Studies), 1981

Rahman, I.A. *Pakistan Under Siege*. Lahore: Rhotas Books, 1990

Rao, B. Shiva, ed. *The Framing of India's Constitution: Selected Documents*. Vol. II. Bombay: N.M. Tripathi Private Ltd., 1967

Rashid, Akhtar. *Elections '77 and Aftermath: A Political Appraisal*. Islamabad: PRAAS Publishers, August 1981

Rashiduzzaman, M. "The National Assembly of Pakistan under the 1962 Constitution." *Pacific Affairs*, 42, No. 4 (Winter 1969–70): 481–93

Raz, Joseph. "Government by Consent." In J. Roland Pennock and John W. Chapman, eds. *Authority Revisited*. Nomos XXIX. New York: New York University Press, 1987

*The Authority of Law: Essays on Law and Morality*. Oxford: Clarendon Press, 1979

*The Concept of a Legal System: An Introduction to the Theory of Legal Systems*. Oxford: Clarendon Press, 1980

Richter, William L. "Persistent Praetorianism: Pakistan's Third Military Regime." *Strategic Digest*, 9, No. 5 (May 1979): 277–93

Rizvi, Gowher. "Riding the Tiger: Institutionalizing the Military Regimes in Pakistan and Bangladesh." In Christopher Clapham and George Philip, eds. *The Political Dilemmas of Military Regimes*. London: Croom Helm, 1985

Rizvi, Hasan-Askari. *The Military and Politics in Pakistan 1947–86*. Lahore: Progressive Publishers, 1986

Robb, P.G. *The Government of India and Reform: Policies Towards Politics and the Constitution 1916–1921*. Oxford: Oxford University Press, 1976

Roy, Jayanta Kumar. *Democracy and Nationalism on Trial: A Study of East Pakistan*. Simla: Indian Institute of Advanced Study, 1968

Rudolph, Lloyd I. and Susanne Hoeber Rudolph. *In Pursuit of Lakshmi: The Political Economy of the Indian State*. Chicago: University of Chicago Press, 1987

Sayeed, Khalid Bin. "Collapse of Parliamentary Democracy in Pakistan." *Middle East Journal*, 13, No. 4 (Autumn 1959): 389–406

"Pakistan's Basic Democracies." *Middle East Journal*, 15, No. 3 (Summer 1961): 249–63

"Pakistan's Constitutional Autocracy." *Pacific Affairs*, 36, No. 4 (Winter 1963–64): 365–77

*Pakistan: The Formative Phase 1957–1948*. 2nd edition. London: Oxford University Press, 1968

*Politics in Pakistan: The Nature and Direction of Change*. New York: Praeger Publishers, 1980

Schacht, Joseph. *An Introduction to Islamic Law*. Oxford: Clarendon Press, 1950

Schofield, Victoria. *Bhutto: Trial and Execution*. London: Cassell, 1979

Schuler, Edgar A. and Kathryn R. *Public Opinion and Constitution Making in Pakistan 1958–1962*. Michigan State University Press, no location, 1967

Sen, Rangalal. *Political Elites in Bangladesh*. Dhaka: University Press Ltd., 1986

Shah, Nasim Hasan. *Articles and Speeches on Constitution, Law and Pakistan Affairs*. Lahore: Wajidalis, 1986

Shahi, Agha. *Pakistan's Security and Foreign Policy*. Edited by Hamid H. Kizilbash. Lahore: Progressive Publishers, 1988

Shaikh, Farzana. *Community and Consensus in Islam: Muslim Representation in Colonial India, 1860–1947*. Cambridge: Cambridge University Press, 1989

Sharan, P. *Government and Politics of Pakistan*. New Delhi: Metropolitan, 1983

Sherwani, Latif Ahmed. "The Constitutional Experiment in Pakistan." *Asian Survey*, 2, No. 6 (August 1962): 9–14

*The Pakistan Resolution*, Karachi: Quaid-i-Azam Academy, 1986

*Pakistan in the Making: Documents and Readings*. Karachi: Quaid-i-Azam Academy, 1987

Shetreet, Simon, ed. *The Role of Courts in Society*. Dordrecht: Martinus Nijhoff, 1988

Shils, Edward. *Tradition*. Chicago: University of Chicago Press, 1981

Sind Baloch Pushtoon Front: *A Confederal Constitution for Pakistan: An Outline*. August 1985

Spain, James W. *The Pathan Borderland*. The Hague, Mouton and Co., 1963

*The Way of the Pathans*. 2nd edition. Karachi: Oxford University Press, 1962, 1972

Spangenberg, Bradford. *British Bureaucracy in India: Status, Policy and the I.C.S. in the Late 19th Century*. Delhi: Manohar Books, 1976

Stavsky, Mark M. "The Doctrine of State Necesssity in Pakistan." *Cornell International Law Journal*, 16 (1983): 341–94

Strong, C.F. *Modern Political Constitutions: An Introduction to the Comparative Study of their History and Existing Forms*. Edited with a new introduction by M.G. Clarke, London: Sidgwick & Jackson, 1972 (1st edition, 1930)

Sugarman, David: *Legality, Ideology and the State*. New York: Academic Press, 1983

Suhrawardy, Huseyn Shaheed. "Political Stability and Democracy in Pakistan." *Foreign Affairs*, 35, No. 3 (April 1957): 422–31

Syed, Anwar Hussain. *Pakistan: Islam, Politics and National Solidarity*. Lahore: Vanguard Books, Ltd., 1984

"Zulfikar Ali Bhutto and the Dismemberment of Pakistan in 1971." Draft discussion paper, 1988

"Factional Conflict in the Punjab Muslim League 1947–1956: An Interpretation." Draft manuscript, 1988

Syed, Ziaullah and Samuel Baid, eds. *Pakistan: An End Without a Beginning*. New Delhi: Lancer International, 1985

Tahir-Kheli, Shirin. "The Military in Contemporary Pakistan." *Armed Forces and Society*, 6, No. 4 (Summer 1980): 639–53

Talbot, Ian. *Provincial Politics and the Pakistan Movement: The Growth of the Muslim League in North-West and North-East India 1937–47*. Karachi: Oxford University Press, 1988

Talukdar, Mohammad H.R., ed. *Memoirs of Huseyn Shaheed Suhrawardy with a Brief Account of his Life and Work*. Dhaka: University Press Limited, 1987

Tendulkar, D.G. *Abdul Ghaffar Khan: Faith is a Battle*. Bombay: Gandhi Peace Foundation, Popular Prakashan, 1967

Tiruchelvam, Neelan and Radhika Coomaraswamy. *The Role of the Judiciary in Plural Societies*. New York: St. Martin's Press, 1987

Tur, Richard and William Twining, eds. *Essays on Kelsen*. Oxford: Clarendon Press, 1986

Venkataramani, M.S. *The American Role in Pakistan 1947–1958*. Lahore: Vanguard Books, Ltd., 1984

Waseem, Mohammad. *Pakistan Under Martial Law 1977–1985*. Lahore: Vanguard Books, Ltd., 1987

Watt, E.D. *Authority*. New York: St. Martin's Press, 1982

Weber, Max. *Economy and Society*. Edited by Guenther Roth and Claus Wittich. Berkeley and Los Angeles: University of California Press, 1978

Weinbaum, M.G. "The March 1977 Elections in Pakistan: Where Everyone Lost." *Asian Survey*, 17, No. 7 (July 1977): 599–618

Wheeler, Richard. "Pakistan: New Constitution, Old Issues." *Asian Survey*, 3, No. 2 (February 1963): 107–15

Wilcox, Wayne A. Pakistan: *The Consolidation of a Nation*. New York: Columbia University Press, 1963

"The Pakistan Coup d'Etat of 1958." *Pacific Affairs*, 38, No. 2 (Summer 1965): 142–63

"Political Change in Pakistan: Structures, Functions, Constraints, and Goals." *Pacific Affairs*, 41, No. 3 (February 1968): 341–54

"Pakistan in 1969: Once Again at the Starting Point." *Asian Survey*, 10, No. 2 (February 1970): 73–81

Williams, Glanville. "The Defence of Necessity." *Current Legal Problems* (1953): 216–35

*Salmond on Jurisprudence*. 11th edition. London: Sweet and Maxwell, Ltd., 1957

Williams, L.F. Rushbrook. *The State of Pakistan*. London: Faber and Faber, 1962

Wilson, James Q. "The Rise of the Bureaucratic State." *Public Interest* 41 (Fall 1975): 77–103

Wolf-Phillips, Leslie. "Constitutional Legitimacy: A Study of the Doctrine of Necessity." *Third World Quarterly*, 1, No. 4 (October 1979): 97–133

*Constitutional Legitimacy: A Study of the Doctrine of Necessity*. London: Third World Foundation Monograph 6, n.d.

Wolpert, Stanley. *Jinnah of Pakistan*. New York: Oxford University Press, 1984

Zafar Law Associates. *Judge-made Laws: Precedent and List of Overruled Cases From January 1909–October 1974*. Lahore, no pub., no date

Zafar, S.M. *Through the Crisis*. Lahore: Book Centre, 1970

"Constitutional Crisis in Pakistan and Solution Thereof." PLD 1986 Journal 240–45

Zingel, Wolfgang and Lallemant, Stephanie Zingel Ave, eds. *Pakistan in the 80's: Ideology, Regionalism, Economy, Foreign Policy*. Lahore: Vanguard Books, Ltd., 1985

eds. *Pakistan in the 80's: Law and Constitution*. Lahore: Vanguard Books, Ltd., 1985

Ziring, Lawrence. "Militarism in Pakistan: The Yahya Khan Interregnum." *Asian Affairs*, 1, No. 6 (July–August 1974): 402–20

"Pakistan: The Vision and the Reality." *Asian Affairs*, 4, No. 6 (1977): 385–407

Ziring, Lawrence, Ralph Braibanti, W. Howard Wriggins, eds. *Pakistan: The Long View*. Durham: Duke University Press, 1977

Zuberi, Masarrat Husain. *Voyage Through History*. Two volumes. Karachi: Hamdard Foundation Press, 1984,

# Index

# Cambridge South Asian Studies

These monographs are published by the Syndics of Cambridge University Press in association with the Cambridge University Centre for South Asian Studies. The following books have been published in this series:

29 Ian Stone: *Canal Irrigation in British India: Perspectives on Technological Change in a Peasant Society*
30 Rosalind O'Hanlon: *Caste, Conflict and Ideology: Mahatmas Jotirao Phute and Low Caste Protest in Nineteenth-Century Western India*
31 Ayesha Jalal: *The Sole Spokesman: Jinnah, The Muslim League and the Demand for Pakistan*
32 N. R. F. Charlesworth: *Peasant and Imperial Rule: Agriculture and Agrarian Society in the Bombay Presidency, 1850–1935*
33 Claude Markovits: *Indian Business and Nationalist Politics, 1931–39. The Indigenous Capitalist Class and the Rise of the Congress Party*
36 Sugata Bose: *Agrarian Bengal: Economy, Social Structure and Politics, 1919–1947*
37 Atul Kohli: *The State and Poverty in India: The Politics of Reform*
38 Franklin A. Presler: *Religion Under Bureaucracy: Policy and Administration for Hindu Temples in South India*
39 Nicholas B. Dirks: *The Hollow Crown: Ethnohistory of an Indian Kingdom*
40 Robert Wade: *Village Republics: Economic Conditions for Collective Action in South India*
41 Laurence W. Preston: *The Devs of Cincvad: A Lineage and State in Maharashtra*
42 Farzana Shaikh: *Community and Consensus in Islam: Muslims Representation in Colonial India, 1860–1947*
43 Susan Bayly: *Saints, Goddesses and Kings: Muslims and Christians in South Indian Society, 1700–1900*
44 Gyan Prakash: *Bonded Histories: Genealogies of Labour Servitude in Colonial India*
45 Sanjay Subrahmanyam: *The Political Economy of Commerce: Southern India, 1500–1650*

46 Ayesha Jalal: *The State of Martial Rule: The Origins of Pakistan's Political Economy of Defence*
47 Bruce Graham: *Hindu Nationalism and Indian Politics: The Origins and Development of the Bharatiya Jana Sangh*
48 Dilesh Jayanntha: *Electoral Allegiance in Sri Lanka*
49 Stephen P. Blake: *Shahjahanabad: The Sovereign City in Mughal India, 1639–1739*
50 Sarah F. D. Ansari: *Sufi Saints and State Power: The Pirs of Sind, 1843–1947*
51 Rajnarayan Chandavarkar: *The Origins of Industrial Capitalism in India: Business Strategies and the Working Classes in Bombay, 1900–1940*
52 Tapati Guha-Thakurta: *The Making of a New 'Indian' Art: Artists, Aesthetics and Nationalism in Bengal, 1850–1920*
53 John R. McLane: *Land and Local Kingship in Eighteenth-Century Bengal*
54 Ross Mallick: *Development Policy of a Communist Government: West Bengal since 1977*
55 Dilip M. Menon: *Caste, Nationalism and Communism in South India: Malabar, 1900–1948*
56 Milton Israel: *Communications and Power: Propaganda and the Press in the Indian Nationalist Struggle, 1920–1947*
57 Joya Chatterji: *Bengal Divided: Hindu Communalism and Partition, 1932–1947*
58 [illegible]